REUNION

Book 12a in the ELFQUEST Reader's Collection

WOLFRIDER BOOKS

**Poughkeepsie
New York**

REUNION

Reprinting **Elfquest: Shards**
comic book issue numbers 9 through 16

Story by
Wendy & Richard Pini

Art by
Brandon McKinney & Terry Beatty,
Justin Bloomer & Kathryn Bolinger

About the ELFQUEST Reader's Collection

The twenty year — and ongoing — saga that is Elfquest has been told in many different comic book titles. The Elfquest Reader's Collection is our attempt to collect all the core stories in book form, so that readers new and old can follow the entire tale from its beginnings on up to the most recent work.

As planned the Elfquest Reader's Collection series will include the following volumes:

#1 - Fire and Flight
#2 - The Forbidden Grove
#3 - Captives of Blue Mountain
#4 - Quest's End
     The story of Cutter, chief of the Wolfriders, and his tribe as they confront the perils of their primitive world, encounter new races of elves, and embark on a grand and dangerous quest to unveil the secret of their past.

#5 - Siege at Blue Mountain
#6 - The Secret of Two-Edge
     The adventures of the Wolfriders some years after the end of the first quest, as they face the machinations of a villainess from their past and her enigmatic half-elf, half-troll son.

#7 - The Cry from Beyond
#8 - Kings of the Broken Wheel
     The Wolfriders face their most daunting challenge when one of their number kidnaps Cutter's mate and children into future time, to prevent the accident that first brought the elves to this world.

#8a - Dreamtime
     The visions of the Wolfriders as they slept for ten thousand years, waiting for the time when Cutter and his family can be united once more.

#9 - Rogue's Challenge
     Tales of the "bad guys" who have caused the Wolfriders so much trouble over the centuries.

#9a - Wolfrider!
     The tale of Cutter's sire Bearclaw, and how he brought two things to the Wolfriders — the enmity of humans and a monstrous tragedy, and a chief's son like no elf the tribe had ever known.

#10 - Shards
#11 - Legacy
#11a - Huntress
#12 - Ascent
#12a - Reunion
     Cutter and family are together again, but now a ruthless human warlord threatens the elves' very existence. The Wolfriders must become two tribes — one to fight a terrible war, the other to flee to ensure that the tribe continues. Volume #10 sets the stage; volumes #11 and #11a follow Cutter's daughter Ember as she leads the Wild Hunt elves into new lands; volumes #12 and #12a take Cutter and his warriors into the flames of battle.

#13 - the Rebels
#13a - Skyward Shadow
#14 - Jink!
#14a - Mindcoil
     In the far future of the World of Two Moons, human civilization has covered the planet — and the elves have disappeared. Where did they go? Volumes #13 and #13a follows a group of young adventurers as they seek the answer. Volumes #14 and #14a tell the story of a mysterious woman who is more than she seems — for she may be the last surviving descendant of the missing elves.

REUNION

Book 12a in the *ELFQUEST* Reader's Collection

Published by Warp Graphics, Inc.
under its Wolfrider Books imprint.

Entire contents
copyright © 1999
Warp Graphics, Inc.
All rights reserved worldwide.

Elfquest and the Warp Wolf logos are
registered trademarks, and all other
Elfquest characters, names, logos,
situations and all related indicia and their
distinctive likenesses are trademarks of
Warp Graphics, Inc.
43 Haight Avenue
Poughkeepsie, New York 12603

ISBN 0-936861-44-4
Printed in USA

www.elfquest.com

SHE HAS YET TO SEE HER NINETEENTH YEAR IN THE SHADOW OF THE DJUN'S CITADEL...
...YET SHUNA, THE MERCENARY'S DAUGHTER, HAS ALREADY IGNITED A TORCH TO DISPEL THAT DARKNESS...
...A FLAME THAT WILL NOT BE EASILY SNUFFED!
WHEEE-OUGH!
AAAGH!
< DIE, FOOT DOG! YOU'LL RULE OUR STREETS NO MORE!! >
TURNABOUT
PART 2

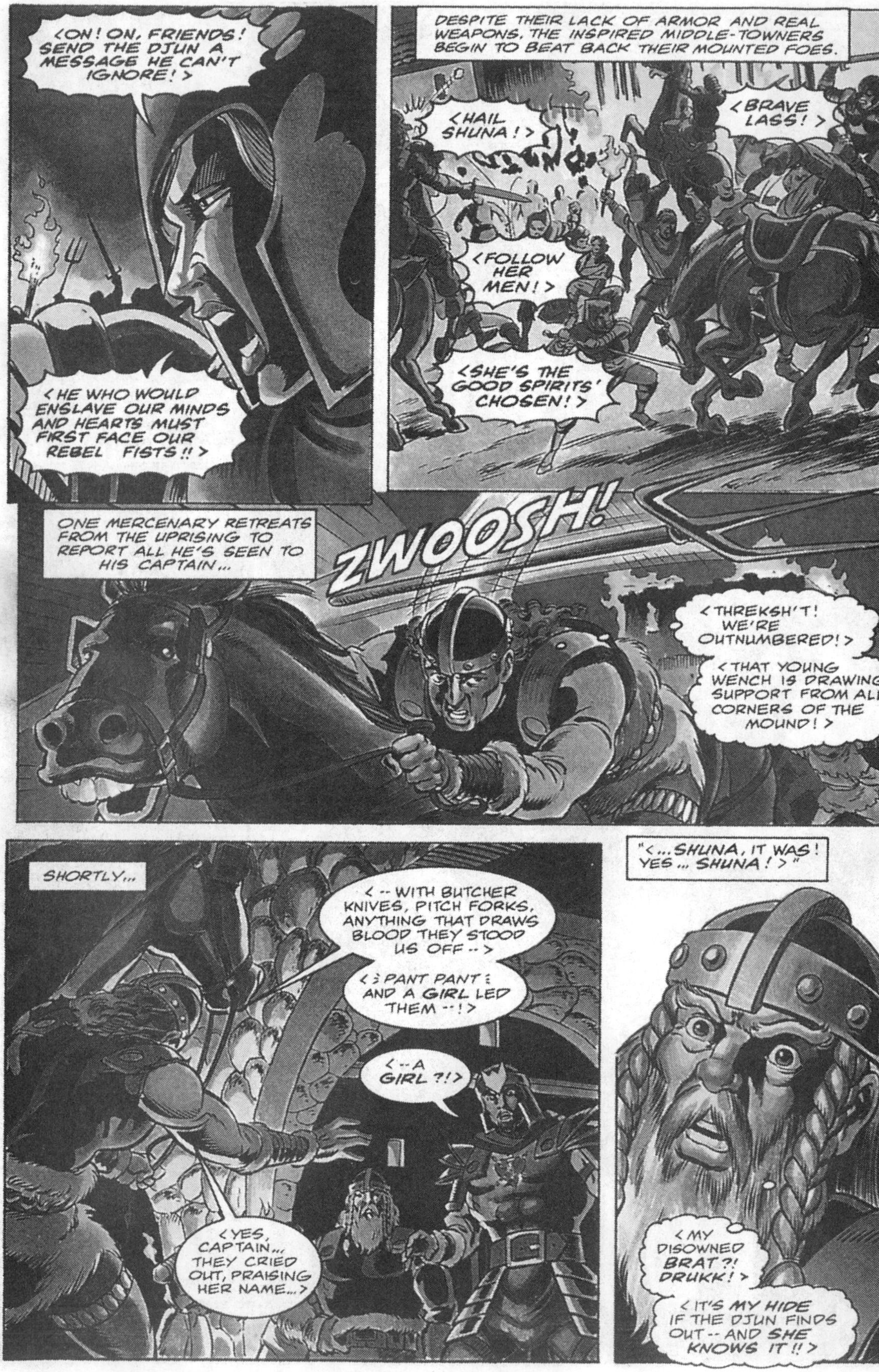

<ON! ON, FRIENDS! SEND THE DJUN A MESSAGE HE CAN'T IGNORE!>
<HE WHO WOULD ENSLAVE OUR MINDS AND HEARTS MUST FIRST FACE OUR REBEL FISTS!!>
DESPITE THEIR LACK OF ARMOR AND REAL WEAPONS, THE INSPIRED MIDDLE-TOWNERS BEGIN TO BEAT BACK THEIR MOUNTED FOES.
<HAIL SHUNA!>
<BRAVE LASS!>
<FOLLOW HER MEN!>
<SHE'S THE GOOD SPIRITS' CHOSEN!>
ONE MERCENARY RETREATS FROM THE UPRISING TO REPORT ALL HE'S SEEN TO HIS CAPTAIN...
ZWOOSH!
<THREKSH'T! WE'RE OUTNUMBERED!>
<THAT YOUNG WENCH IS DRAWING SUPPORT FROM ALL CORNERS OF THE MOUND!>
SHORTLY...
<--WITH BUTCHER KNIVES, PITCH FORKS, ANYTHING THAT DRAWS BLOOD THEY STOOD US OFF-->
<:PANT PANT: AND A GIRL LED THEM--!>
<--A GIRL?!>
<YES, CAPTAIN... THEY CRIED OUT, PRAISING HER NAME...>
"<...SHUNA, IT WAS! YES... SHUNA!>"
<MY DISOWNED BRAT?! DRUKK!>
<IT'S MY HIDE IF THE DJUN FINDS OUT--AND SHE KNOWS IT!!>

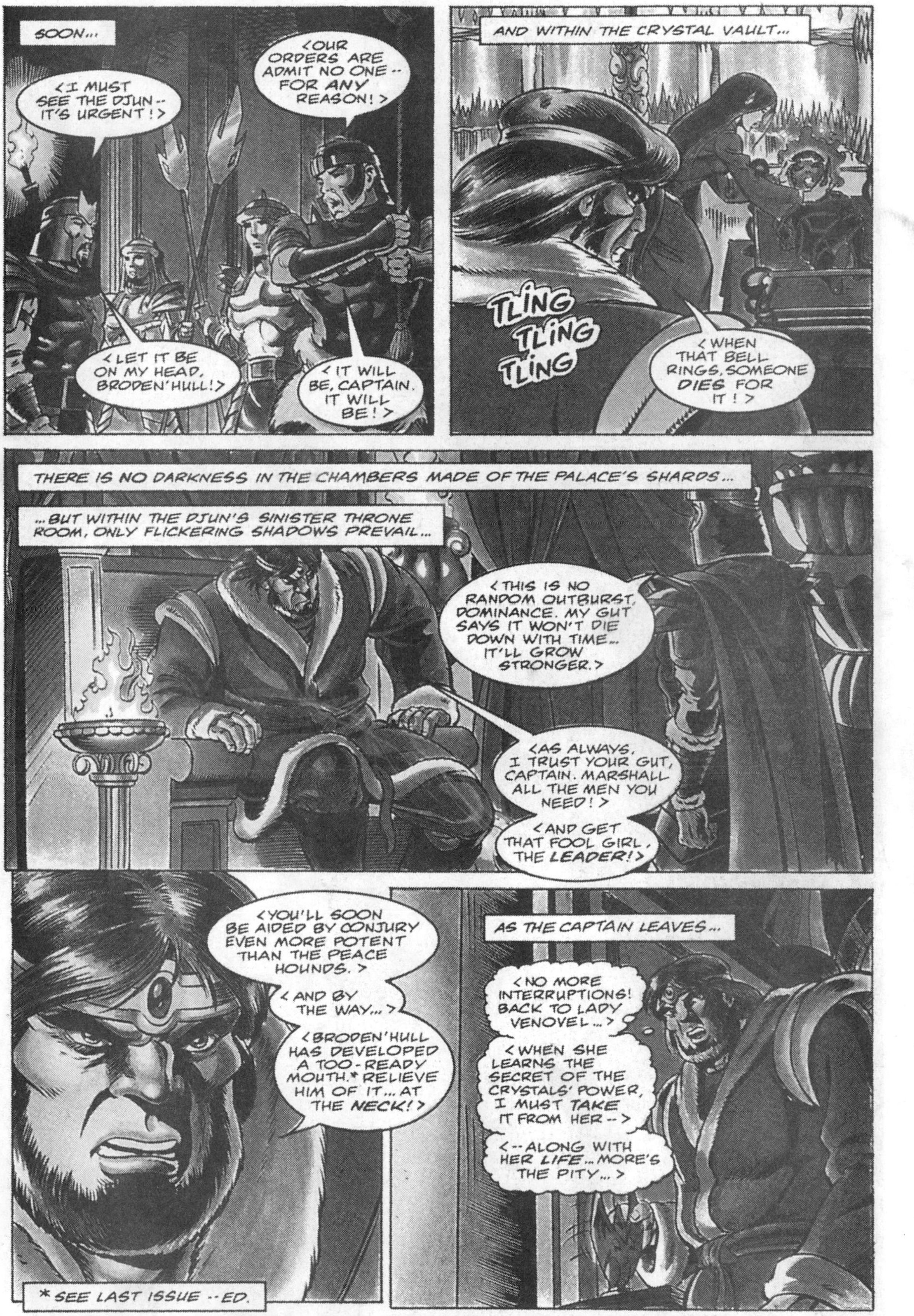
SOON...
<I MUST SEE THE DJUN -- IT'S URGENT!>
<OUR ORDERS ARE ADMIT NO ONE -- FOR ANY REASON!>
<LET IT BE ON MY HEAD, BRODEN'HULL!>
<IT WILL BE, CAPTAIN. IT WILL BE!>
AND WITHIN THE CRYSTAL VAULT...
TLING TLING TLING
<WHEN THAT BELL RINGS, SOMEONE DIES FOR IT!>
THERE IS NO DARKNESS IN THE CHAMBERS MADE OF THE PALACE'S SHARDS...
...BUT WITHIN THE DJUN'S SINISTER THRONE ROOM, ONLY FLICKERING SHADOWS PREVAIL...
<THIS IS NO RANDOM OUTBURST, DOMINANCE. MY GUT SAYS IT WON'T DIE DOWN WITH TIME... IT'LL GROW STRONGER.>
<AS ALWAYS, I TRUST YOUR GUT, CAPTAIN. MARSHALL ALL THE MEN YOU NEED!>
<AND GET THAT FOOL GIRL, THE LEADER!>
<YOU'LL SOON BE AIDED BY CONJURY EVEN MORE POTENT THAN THE PEACE HOUNDS.>
<AND BY THE WAY...>
<BRODEN'HULL HAS DEVELOPED A TOO-READY MOUTH.* RELIEVE HIM OF IT... AT THE NECK!>
* SEE LAST ISSUE --ED.
AS THE CAPTAIN LEAVES...
<NO MORE INTERRUPTIONS! BACK TO LADY VENOVEL...>
<WHEN SHE LEARNS THE SECRET OF THE CRYSTALS' POWER, I MUST TAKE IT FROM HER -->
<--ALONG WITH HER LIFE... MORE'S THE PITY...>

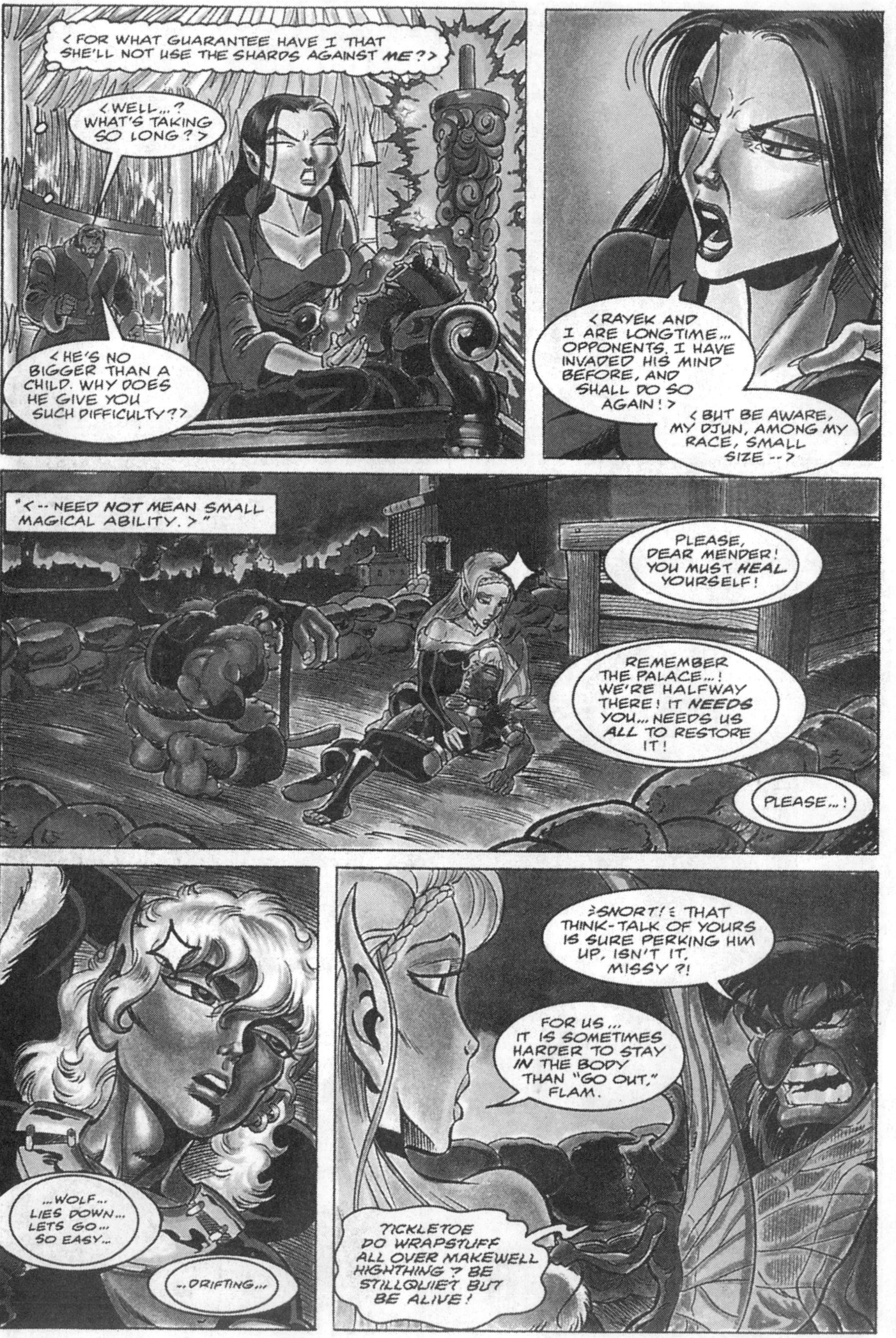
< FOR WHAT GUARANTEE HAVE I THAT SHE'LL NOT USE THE SHARDS AGAINST ME? >
< WELL...? WHAT'S TAKING SO LONG? >
< HE'S NO BIGGER THAN A CHILD. WHY DOES HE GIVE YOU SUCH DIFFICULTY?? >
< RAYEK AND I ARE LONGTIME... OPPONENTS. I HAVE INVADED HIS MIND BEFORE, AND SHALL DO SO AGAIN! >
< BUT BE AWARE, MY DJUN, AMONG MY RACE, SMALL SIZE -- >
"< -- NEED NOT MEAN SMALL MAGICAL ABILITY. >"
PLEASE, DEAR MENDER! YOU MUST HEAL YOURSELF!
REMEMBER THE PALACE...! WE'RE HALFWAY THERE! IT NEEDS YOU... NEEDS US ALL TO RESTORE IT!
PLEASE...!
...WOLF... LIES DOWN... LETS GO... SO EASY...
...DRIFTING...
:SNORT!: THAT THINK-TALK OF YOURS IS SURE PERKING HIM UP, ISN'T IT, MISSY?!
FOR US... IT IS SOMETIMES HARDER TO STAY IN THE BODY THAN "GO OUT," FLAM.
PICKLETOE DO WRAPSTUFF ALL OVER MAKEWELL HIGHTHING? BE STILLQUIET BUT BE ALIVE!

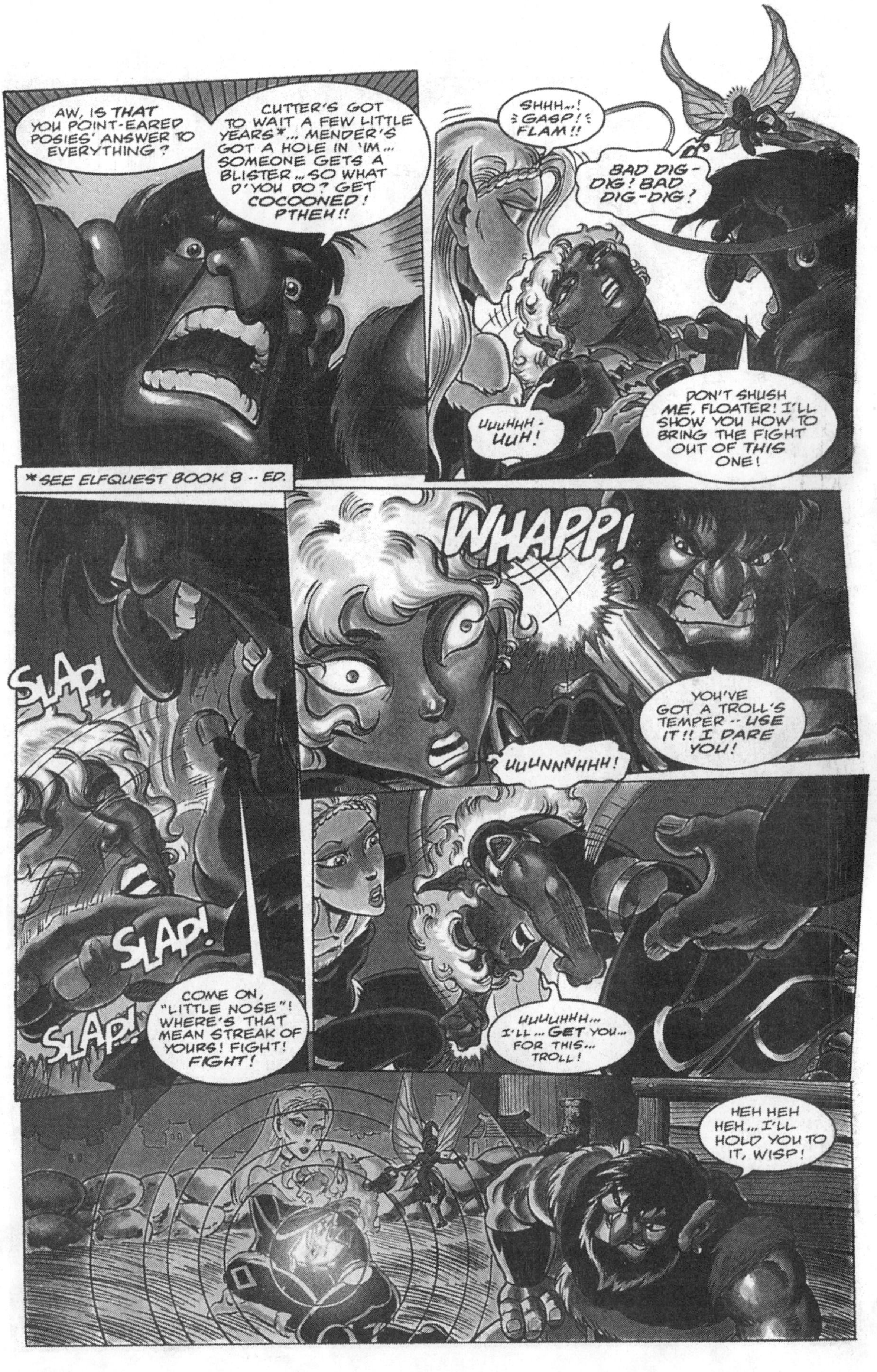
AW, IS THAT YOU POINT-EARED POSIES' ANSWER TO EVERYTHING?
CUTTER'S GOT TO WAIT A FEW LITTLE YEARS*... MENDER'S GOT A HOLE IN 'IM... SOMEONE GETS A BLISTER... SO WHAT D'YOU DO? GET COCOONED! PTHEH!!
SHHH..! GASP! FLAM!!
BAD DIG-DIG! BAD DIG-DIG!
UUUHHH-UUH!
DON'T SHUSH ME, FLOATER! I'LL SHOW YOU HOW TO BRING THE FIGHT OUT OF THIS ONE!
*SEE ELFQUEST BOOK 8 -- ED.
WHAPP!
YOU'VE GOT A TROLL'S TEMPER -- USE IT!! I DARE YOU!
UUUNNHHH!
SLAP!
SLAP!
SLAP!
COME ON, "LITTLE NOSE"! WHERE'S THAT MEAN STREAK OF YOURS! FIGHT! FIGHT!
UUUUHHH... I'LL... GET YOU... FOR THIS... TROLL!
HEH HEH HEH... I'LL HOLD YOU TO IT, WISP!

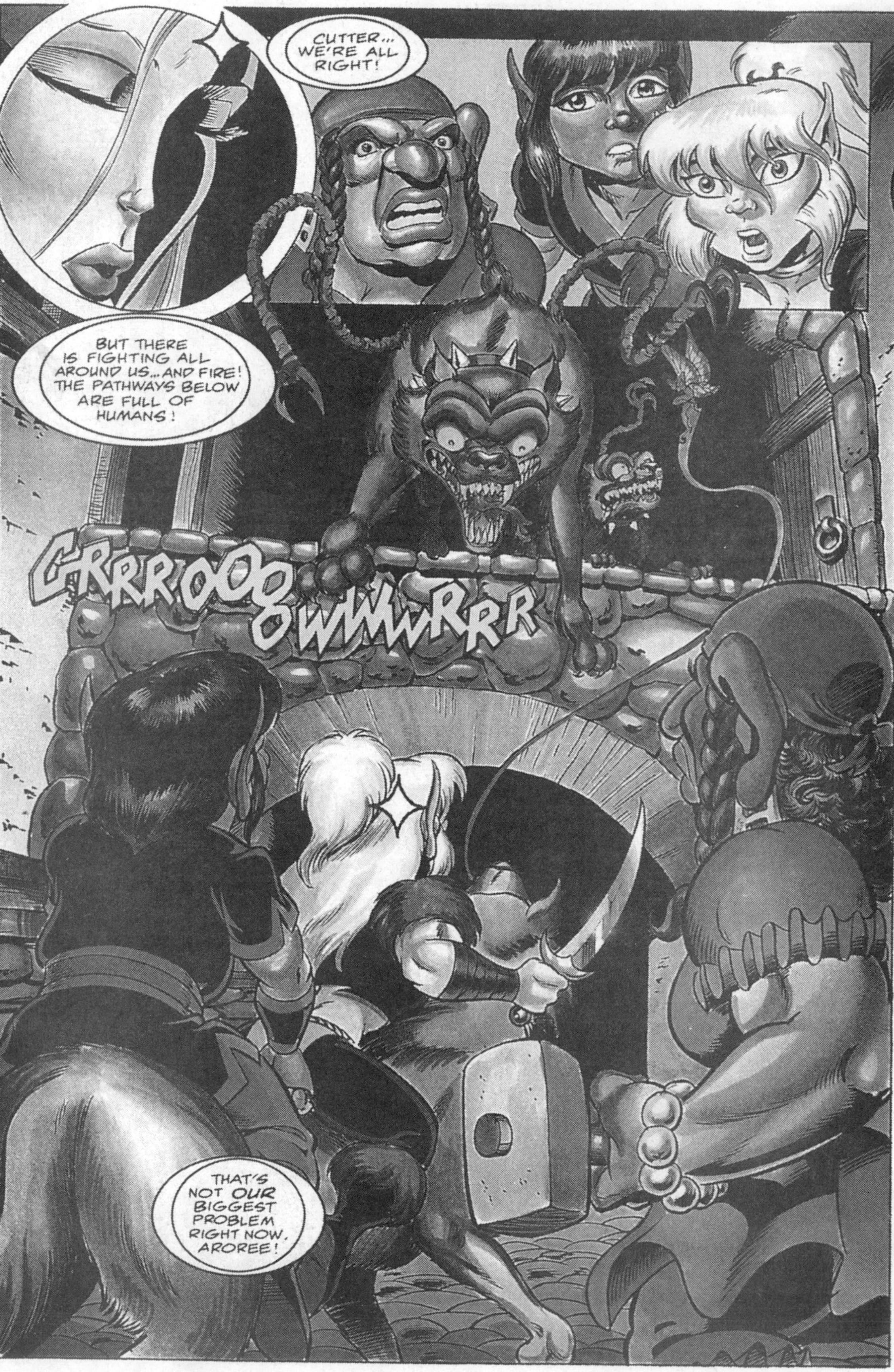
CUTTER... WE'RE ALL RIGHT!
BUT THERE IS FIGHTING ALL AROUND US...AND FIRE! THE PATHWAYS BELOW ARE FULL OF HUMANS!
GRRROOOOWWWWRRR
THAT'S NOT OUR BIGGEST PROBLEM RIGHT NOW, AROREE!

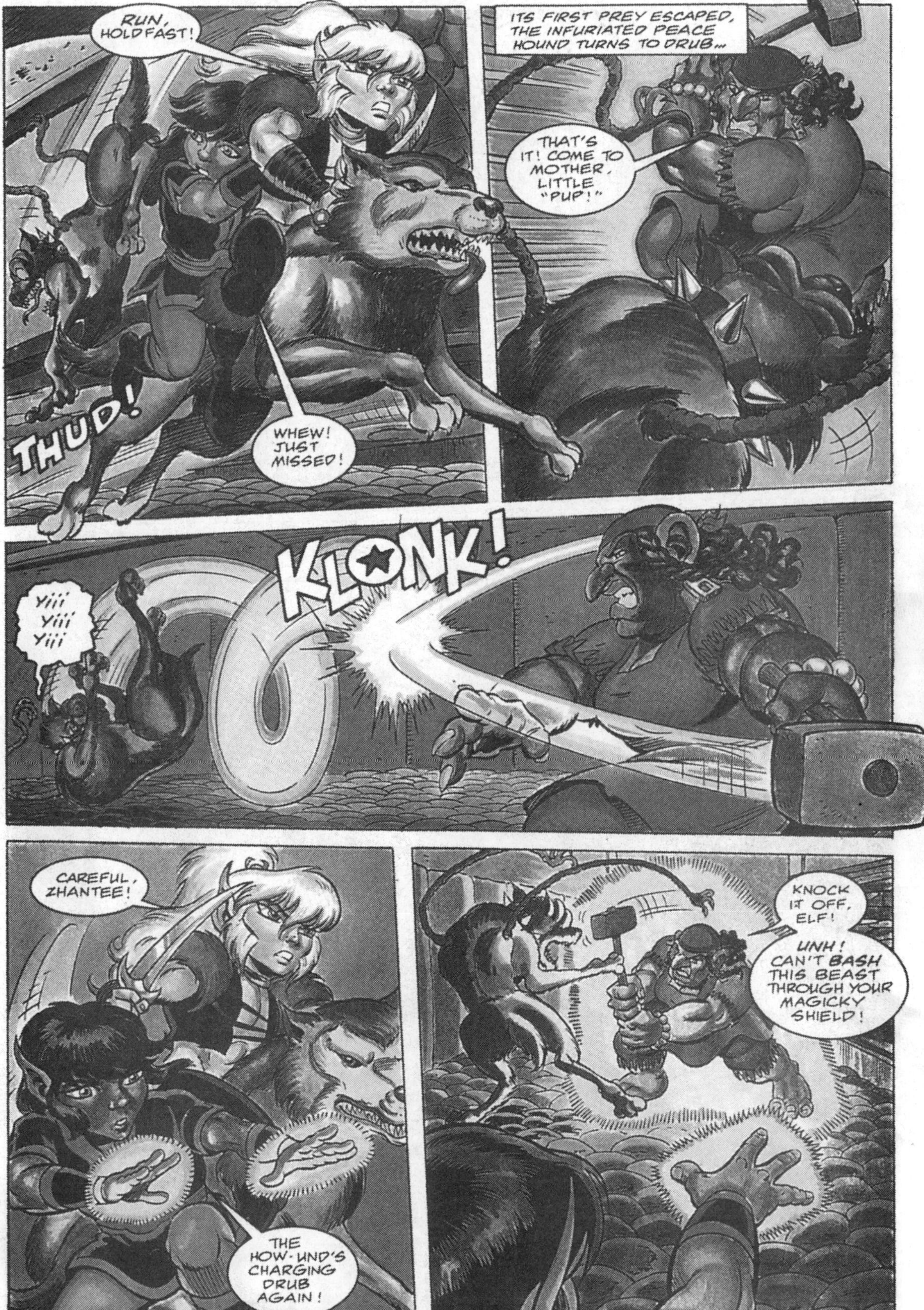
RUN, HOLDFAST!
THUD!
WHEW! JUST MISSED!
ITS FIRST PREY ESCAPED, THE INFURIATED PEACE HOUND TURNS TO DRUB...
THAT'S IT! COME TO MOTHER, LITTLE "PUP!"
KLONK!
Yiii Yiii Yiii
CAREFUL, ZHANTEE!
THE HOW-UND'S CHARGING DRUB AGAIN!
KNOCK IT OFF, ELF!
UNH! CAN'T BASH THIS BEAST THROUGH YOUR MAGICKY SHIELD!

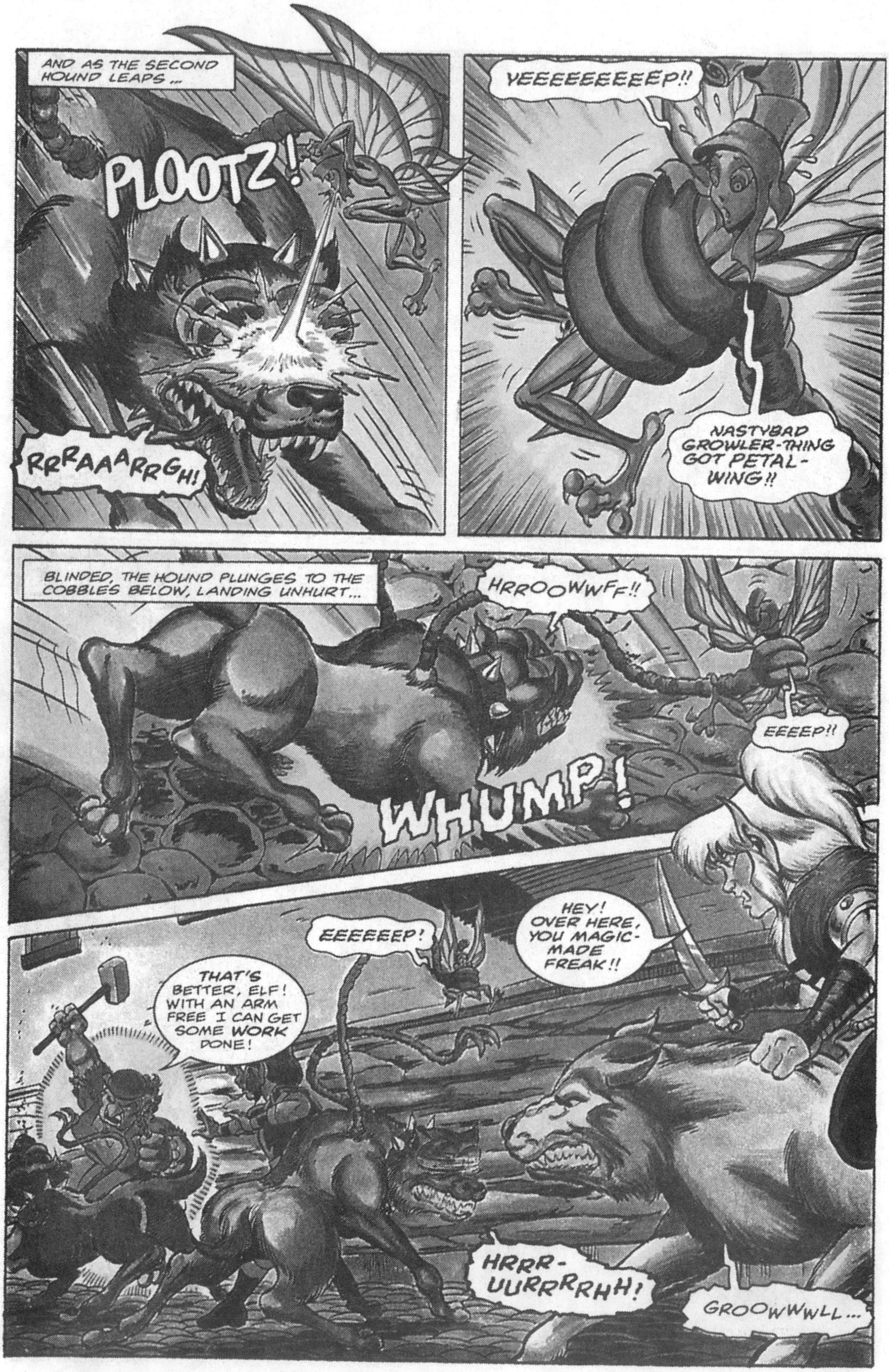
AND AS THE SECOND HOUND LEAPS ...
PLOOTZ!
RRRAAAARRGH!
YEEEEEEEEEEP!!
NASTYBAD GROWLER-THING GOT PETAL-WING!!
BLINDED, THE HOUND PLUNGES TO THE COBBLES BELOW, LANDING UNHURT...
HRROOWWFF!!
EEEEP!!
WHUMP!
EEEEEEP!
HEY! OVER HERE, YOU MAGIC-MADE FREAK!!
THAT'S BETTER, ELF! WITH AN ARM FREE I CAN GET SOME WORK DONE!
HRRR-UURRRRHH!
GROOWWWLL...

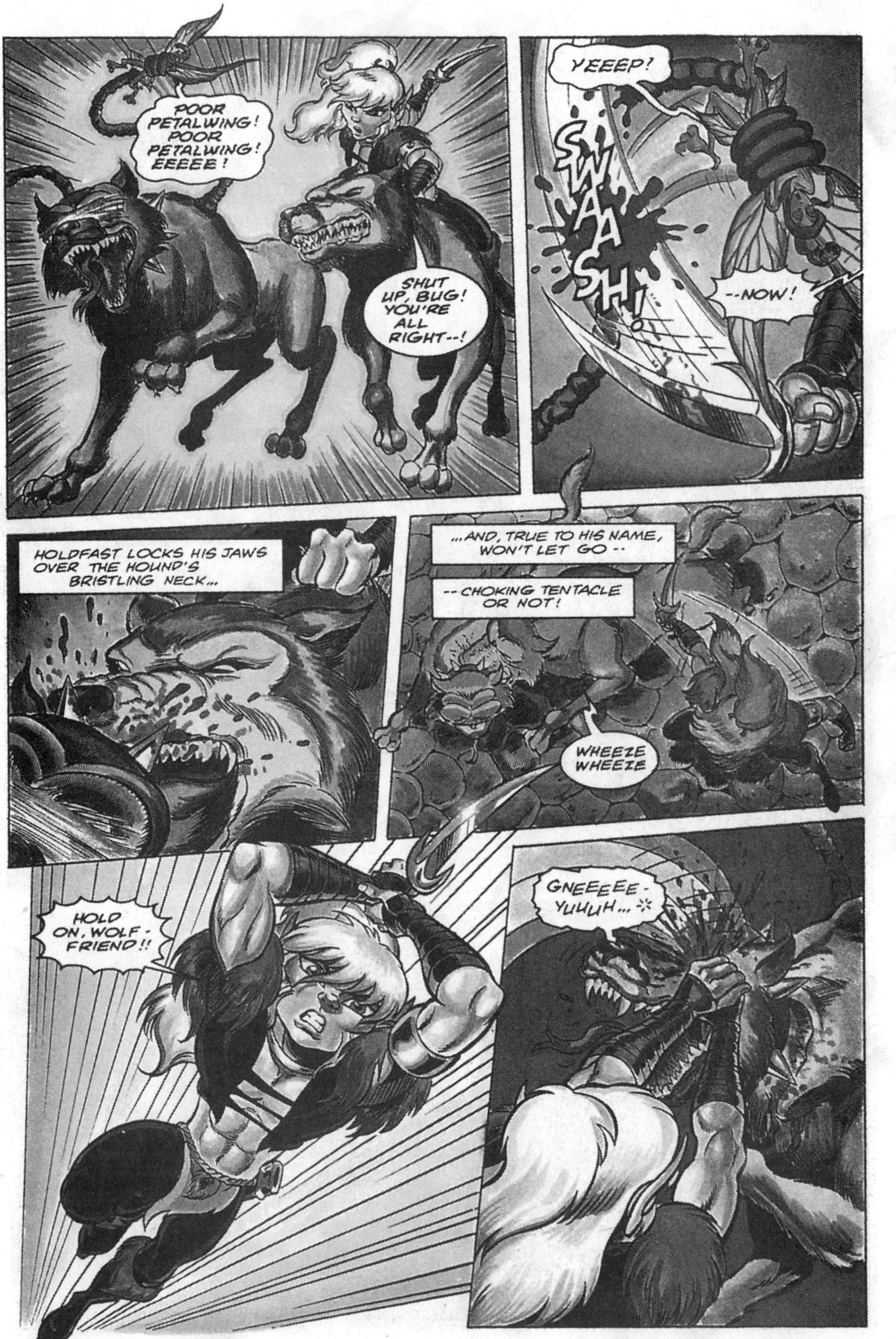
POOR PETALWING! POOR PETALWING! EEEEE!
SHUT UP, BUG! YOU'RE ALL RIGHT--!
YEEEP!
SWAASH!
--NOW!
HOLDFAST LOCKS HIS JAWS OVER THE HOUND'S BRISTLING NECK...
...AND, TRUE TO HIS NAME, WON'T LET GO --
--CHOKING TENTACLE OR NOT!
WHEEZE WHEEZE
HOLD ON, WOLF-FRIEND!!
GNEEEEEE-YUUUH...

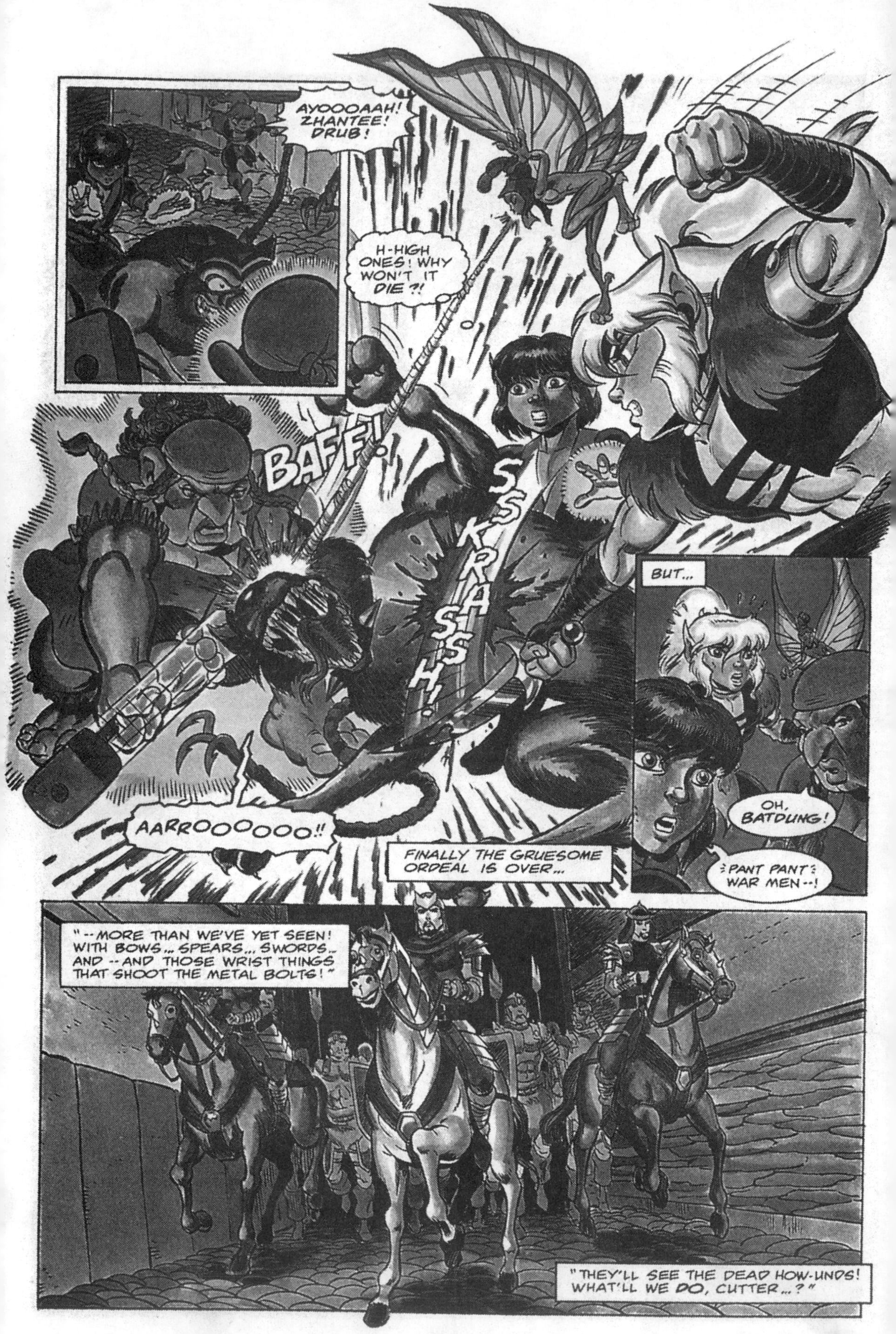
AYOOOAAH! ZHANTEE! DRUB!
H-HIGH ONES! WHY WON'T IT DIE ?!
BAFF!
SSKRASSH!
AARROOOOOOO!!
FINALLY THE GRUESOME ORDEAL IS OVER...
BUT...
OH, BATDUNG!
PANT PANT WAR MEN--!
"--MORE THAN WE'VE YET SEEN! WITH BOWS... SPEARS... SWORDS... AND--AND THOSE WRIST THINGS THAT SHOOT THE METAL BOLTS!"
"THEY'LL SEE THE DEAD HOW-UNDS! WHAT'LL WE DO, CUTTER...?"

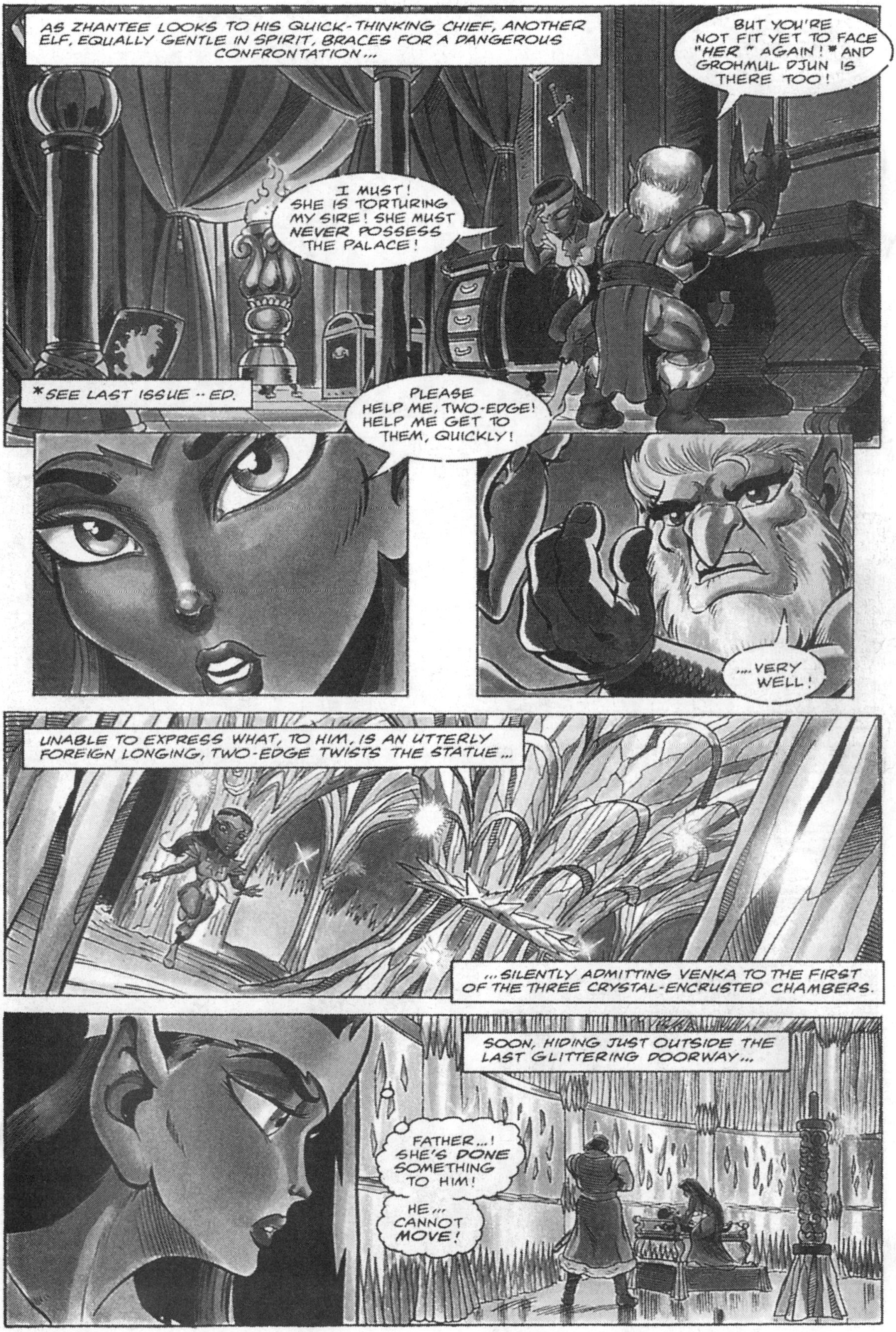
AS ZHANTEE LOOKS TO HIS QUICK-THINKING CHIEF, ANOTHER ELF, EQUALLY GENTLE IN SPIRIT, BRACES FOR A DANGEROUS CONFRONTATION...
BUT YOU'RE NOT FIT YET TO FACE "HER" AGAIN!* AND GROHMUL DJUN IS THERE TOO!
I MUST! SHE IS TORTURING MY SIRE! SHE MUST NEVER POSSESS THE PALACE!
*SEE LAST ISSUE -- ED.
PLEASE HELP ME, TWO-EDGE! HELP ME GET TO THEM, QUICKLY!
....VERY WELL!
UNABLE TO EXPRESS WHAT, TO HIM, IS AN UTTERLY FOREIGN LONGING, TWO-EDGE TWISTS THE STATUE...
...SILENTLY ADMITTING VENKA TO THE FIRST OF THE THREE CRYSTAL-ENCRUSTED CHAMBERS.
SOON, HIDING JUST OUTSIDE THE LAST GLITTERING DOORWAY...
FATHER...! SHE'S DONE SOMETHING TO HIM!
HE... CANNOT MOVE!

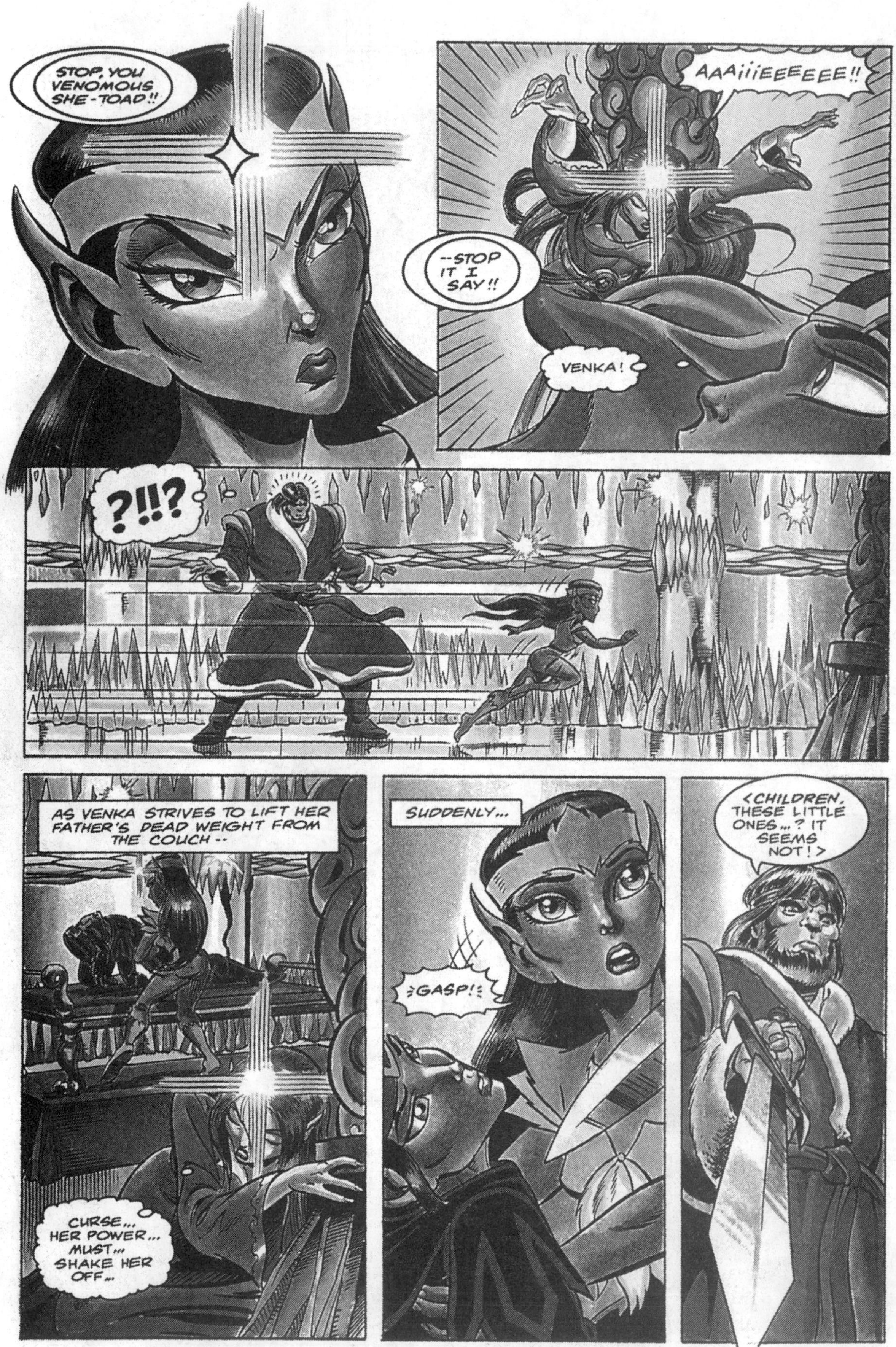
STOP, YOU VENOMOUS SHE-TOAD!!
AAAiiiiEEEEEEE!!
--STOP IT I SAY!!
VENKA!
?!!?
AS VENKA STRIVES TO LIFT HER FATHER'S DEAD WEIGHT FROM THE COUCH --
CURSE... HER POWER... MUST... SHAKE HER OFF...
SUDDENLY...
¡GASP!¡
<CHILDREN, THESE LITTLE ONES...? IT SEEMS NOT!>

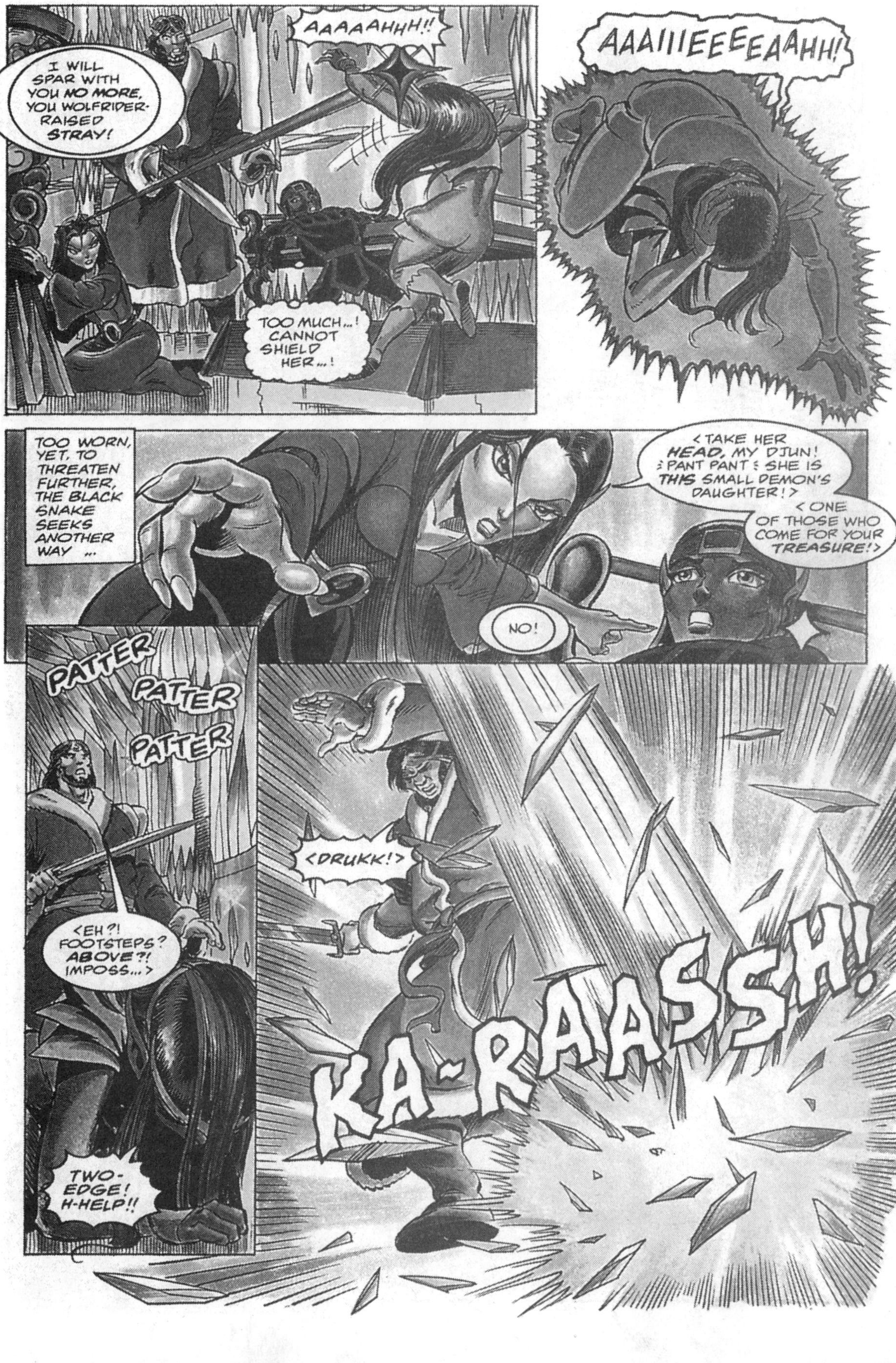

I WILL SPAR WITH YOU NO MORE, YOU WOLFRIDER-RAISED STRAY!
AAAAAHHH!!
TOO MUCH...! CANNOT SHIELD HER...!
AAAIIIIEEEEAAHH!
TOO WORN, YET, TO THREATEN FURTHER, THE BLACK SNAKE SEEKS ANOTHER WAY ...
<TAKE HER HEAD, MY DJUN! :PANT PANT: SHE IS THIS SMALL DEMON'S DAUGHTER!>
<ONE OF THOSE WHO COME FOR YOUR TREASURE!>
NO!
PATTER PATTER PATTER
<EH?! FOOTSTEPS? ABOVE?! IMPOSS...>
TWO-EDGE! H-HELP!!
<DRUKK!>
KA-RAASSH!

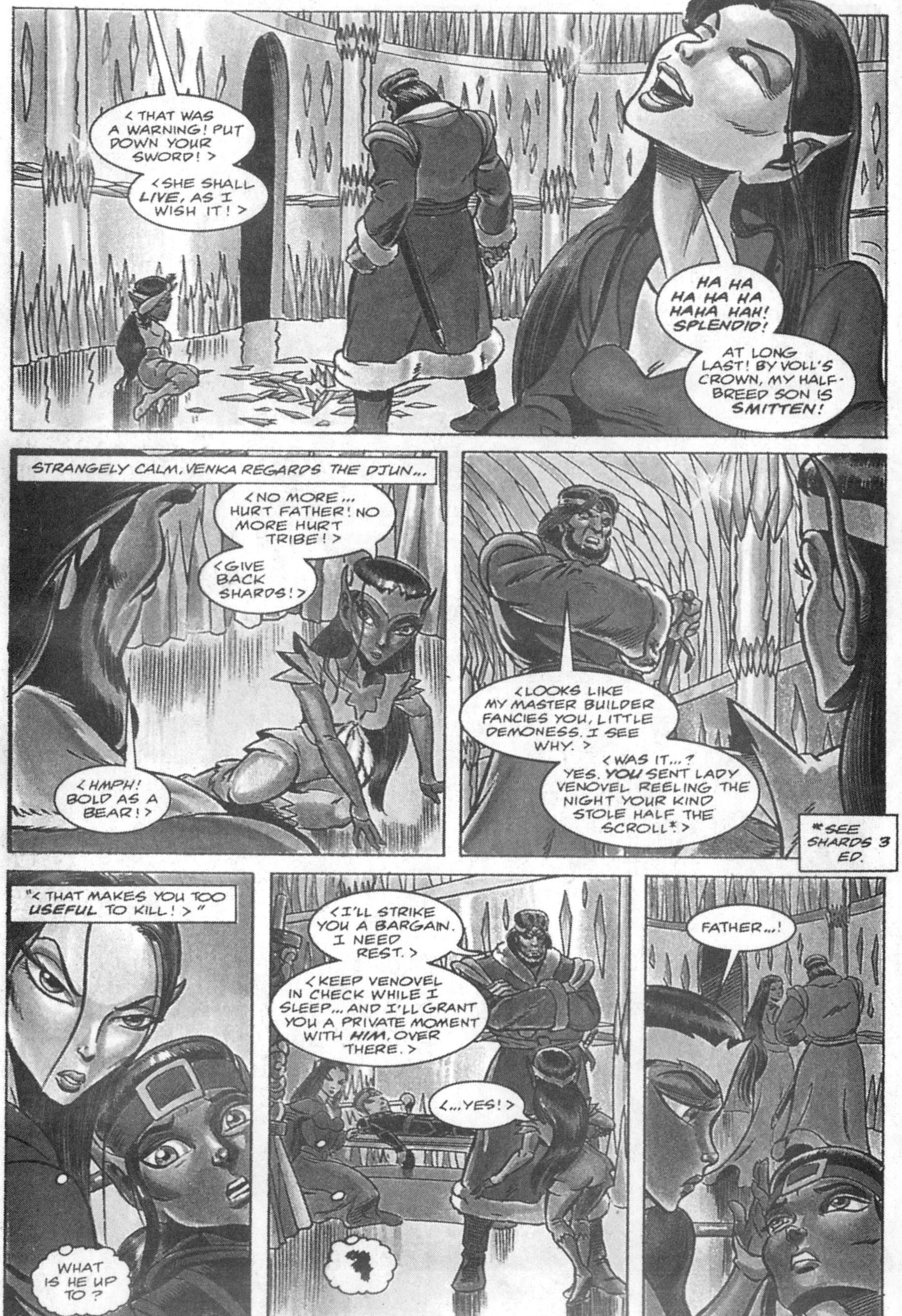
< THAT WAS A WARNING! PUT DOWN YOUR SWORD! >
< SHE SHALL LIVE, AS I WISH IT! >
HA HA HA HA HA HAHA HAH! SPLENDID!
AT LONG LAST! BY VOLL'S CROWN, MY HALF-BREED SON IS SMITTEN!
STRANGELY CALM, VENKA REGARDS THE DJUN...
< NO MORE... HURT FATHER! NO MORE HURT TRIBE! >
< GIVE BACK SHARDS! >
< HMPH! BOLD AS A BEAR! >
< LOOKS LIKE MY MASTER BUILDER FANCIES YOU, LITTLE DEMONESS. I SEE WHY. >
< WAS IT...? YES. YOU SENT LADY VENOVEL REELING THE NIGHT YOUR KIND STOLE HALF THE SCROLL*. >
*SEE SHARDS 3 ED.
"< THAT MAKES YOU TOO USEFUL TO KILL! >"
WHAT IS HE UP TO?
< I'LL STRIKE YOU A BARGAIN. I NEED REST. >
< KEEP VENOVEL IN CHECK WHILE I SLEEP... AND I'LL GRANT YOU A PRIVATE MOMENT WITH HIM, OVER THERE. >
< ...YES! >
FATHER...!

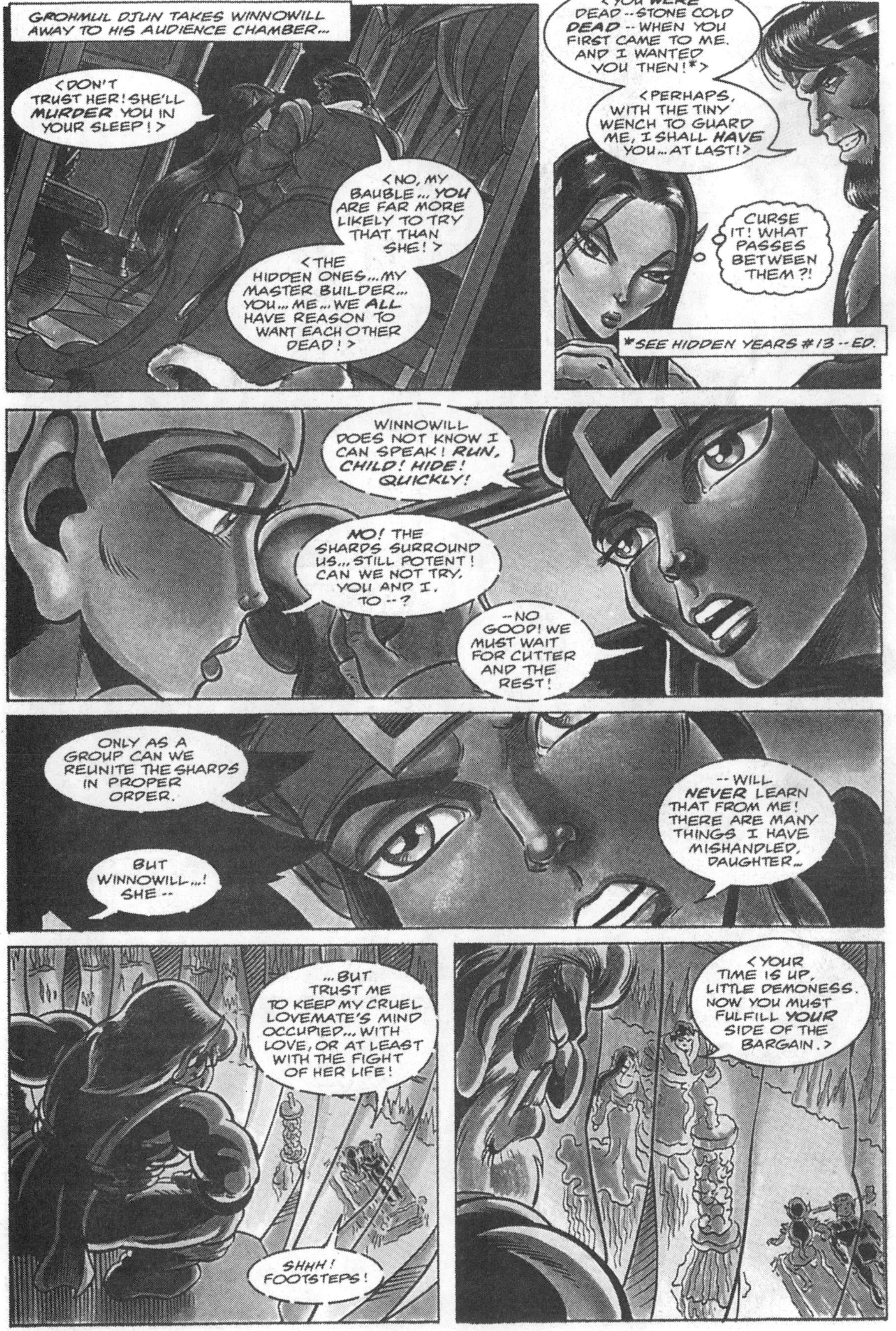
GROHMUL DJUN TAKES WINNOWILL AWAY TO HIS AUDIENCE CHAMBER...
<DON'T TRUST HER! SHE'LL MURDER YOU IN YOUR SLEEP!>
<NO, MY BAUBLE... YOU ARE FAR MORE LIKELY TO TRY THAT THAN SHE!>
<THE HIDDEN ONES... MY MASTER BUILDER... YOU... ME... WE ALL HAVE REASON TO WANT EACH OTHER DEAD!>
<YOU WERE DEAD -- STONE COLD DEAD -- WHEN YOU FIRST CAME TO ME. AND I WANTED YOU THEN!*>
<PERHAPS, WITH THE TINY WENCH TO GUARD ME, I SHALL HAVE YOU... AT LAST!>
CURSE IT! WHAT PASSES BETWEEN THEM?!
*SEE HIDDEN YEARS #13 -- ED.
WINNOWILL DOES NOT KNOW I CAN SPEAK! RUN, CHILD! HIDE! QUICKLY!
NO! THE SHARDS SURROUND US... STILL POTENT! CAN WE NOT TRY, YOU AND I, TO --?
--NO GOOD! WE MUST WAIT FOR CUTTER AND THE REST!
ONLY AS A GROUP CAN WE REUNITE THE SHARDS IN PROPER ORDER.
BUT WINNOWILL...! SHE --
--WILL NEVER LEARN THAT FROM ME! THERE ARE MANY THINGS I HAVE MISHANDLED, DAUGHTER...
...BUT TRUST ME TO KEEP MY CRUEL LOVEMATE'S MIND OCCUPIED... WITH LOVE, OR AT LEAST WITH THE FIGHT OF HER LIFE!
SHHH! FOOTSTEPS!
<YOUR TIME IS UP, LITTLE DEMONESS. NOW YOU MUST FULFILL YOUR SIDE OF THE BARGAIN.>

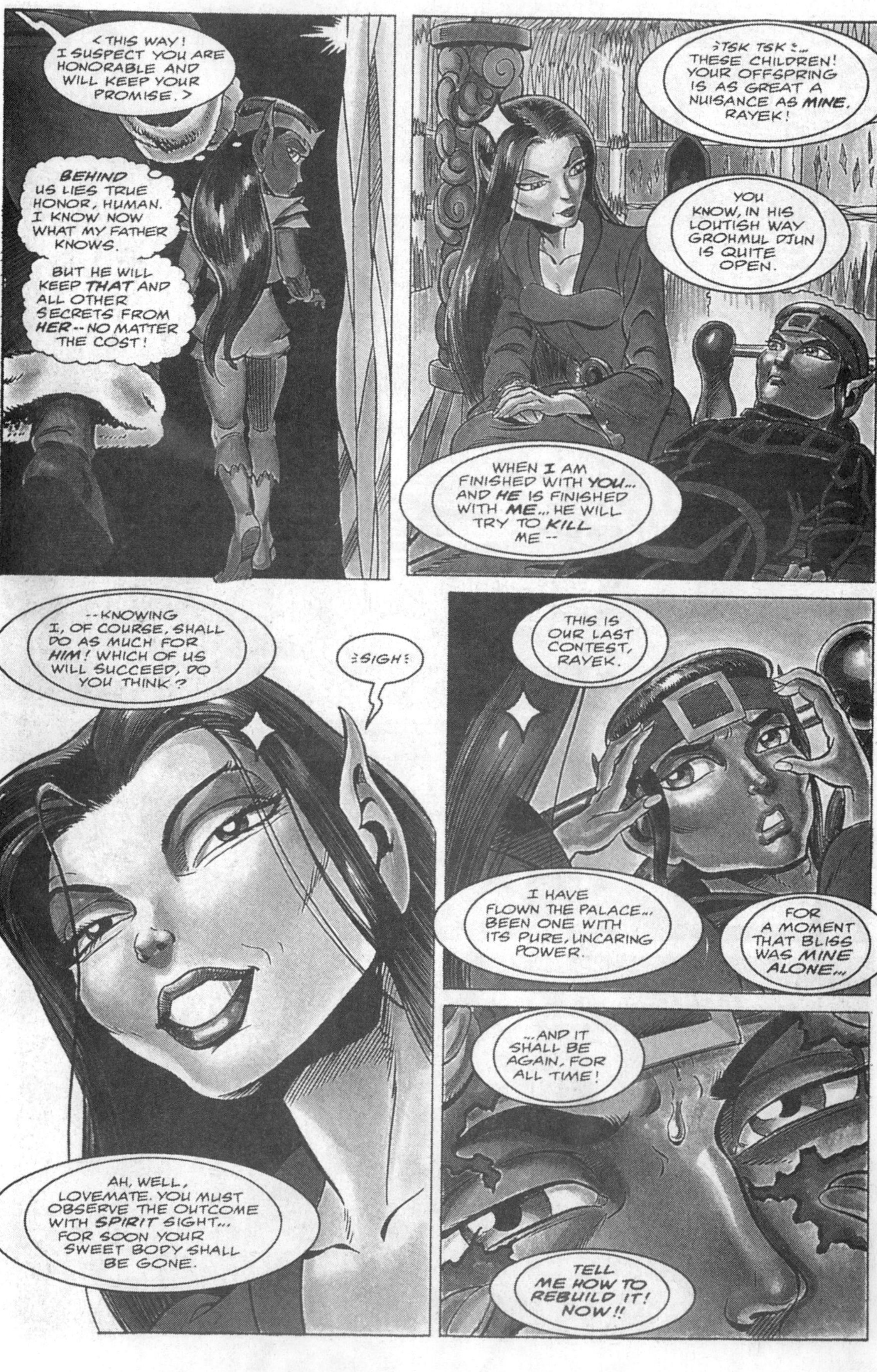

<THIS WAY! I SUSPECT YOU ARE HONORABLE AND WILL KEEP YOUR PROMISE.>
BEHIND US LIES TRUE HONOR, HUMAN. I KNOW NOW WHAT MY FATHER KNOWS.
BUT HE WILL KEEP THAT AND ALL OTHER SECRETS FROM HER--NO MATTER THE COST!
:TSK TSK:.. THESE CHILDREN! YOUR OFFSPRING IS AS GREAT A NUISANCE AS MINE, RAYEK!
YOU KNOW, IN HIS LOUTISH WAY GROHMUL DJUN IS QUITE OPEN.
WHEN I AM FINISHED WITH YOU... AND HE IS FINISHED WITH ME... HE WILL TRY TO KILL ME--
--KNOWING I, OF COURSE, SHALL DO AS MUCH FOR HIM! WHICH OF US WILL SUCCEED, DO YOU THINK?
:SIGH:
AH, WELL, LOVEMATE. YOU MUST OBSERVE THE OUTCOME WITH SPIRIT SIGHT... FOR SOON YOUR SWEET BODY SHALL BE GONE.
THIS IS OUR LAST CONTEST, RAYEK.
I HAVE FLOWN THE PALACE... BEEN ONE WITH ITS PURE, UNCARING POWER.
FOR A MOMENT THAT BLISS WAS MINE ALONE...
...AND IT SHALL BE AGAIN, FOR ALL TIME!
TELL ME HOW TO REBUILD IT! NOW!!

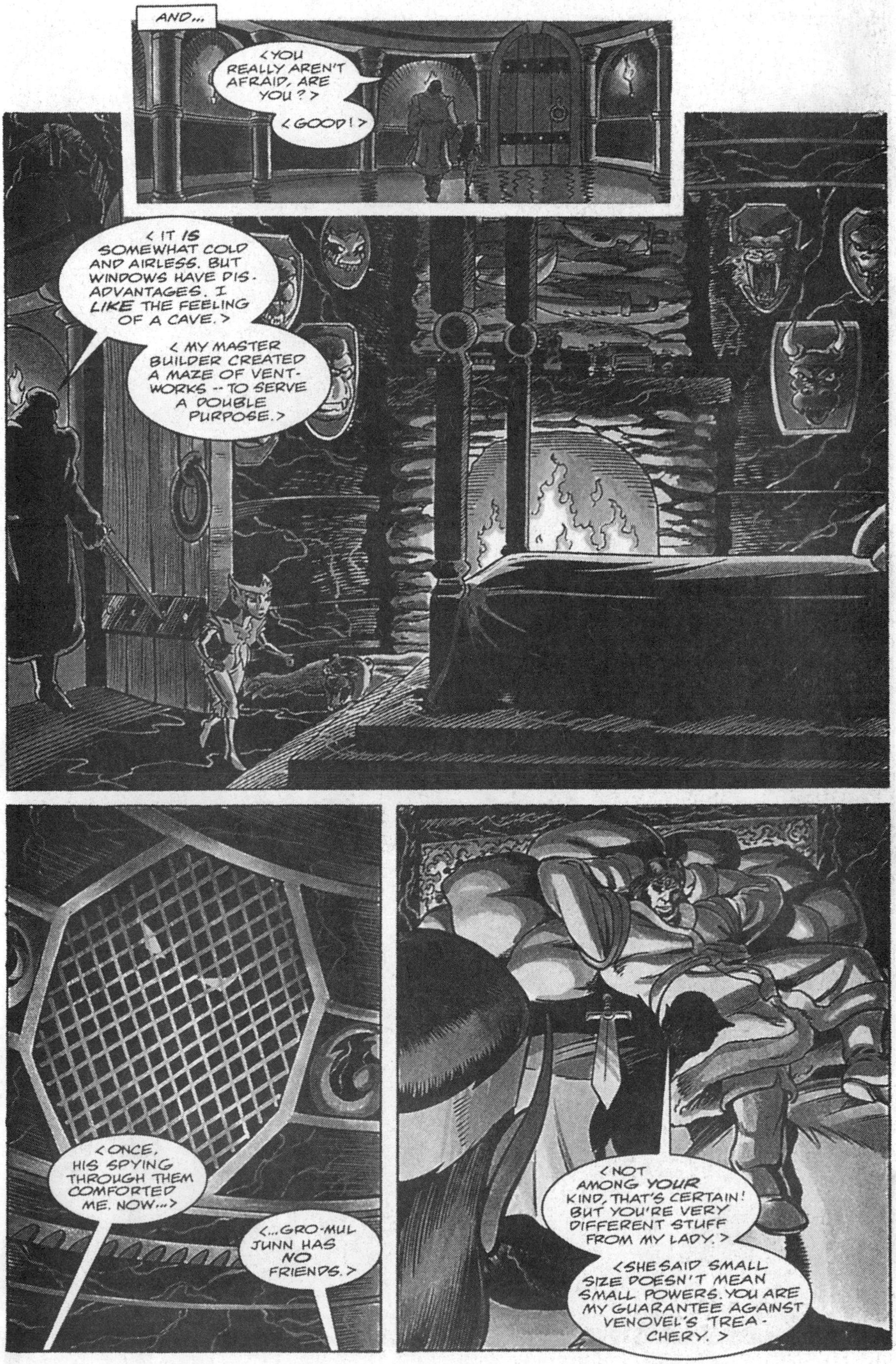
AND...
<YOU REALLY AREN'T AFRAID, ARE YOU?>
<GOOD!>
<IT IS SOMEWHAT COLD AND AIRLESS. BUT WINDOWS HAVE DIS-ADVANTAGES. I LIKE THE FEELING OF A CAVE.>
<MY MASTER BUILDER CREATED A MAZE OF VENT-WORKS -- TO SERVE A DOUBLE PURPOSE.>
<ONCE, HIS SPYING THROUGH THEM COMFORTED ME. NOW...>
<...GRO-MUL JUNN HAS NO FRIENDS.>
<NOT AMONG YOUR KIND, THAT'S CERTAIN! BUT YOU'RE VERY DIFFERENT STUFF FROM MY LADY.>
<SHE SAID SMALL SIZE DOESN'T MEAN SMALL POWERS. YOU ARE MY GUARANTEE AGAINST VENOVEL'S TREA-CHERY.>

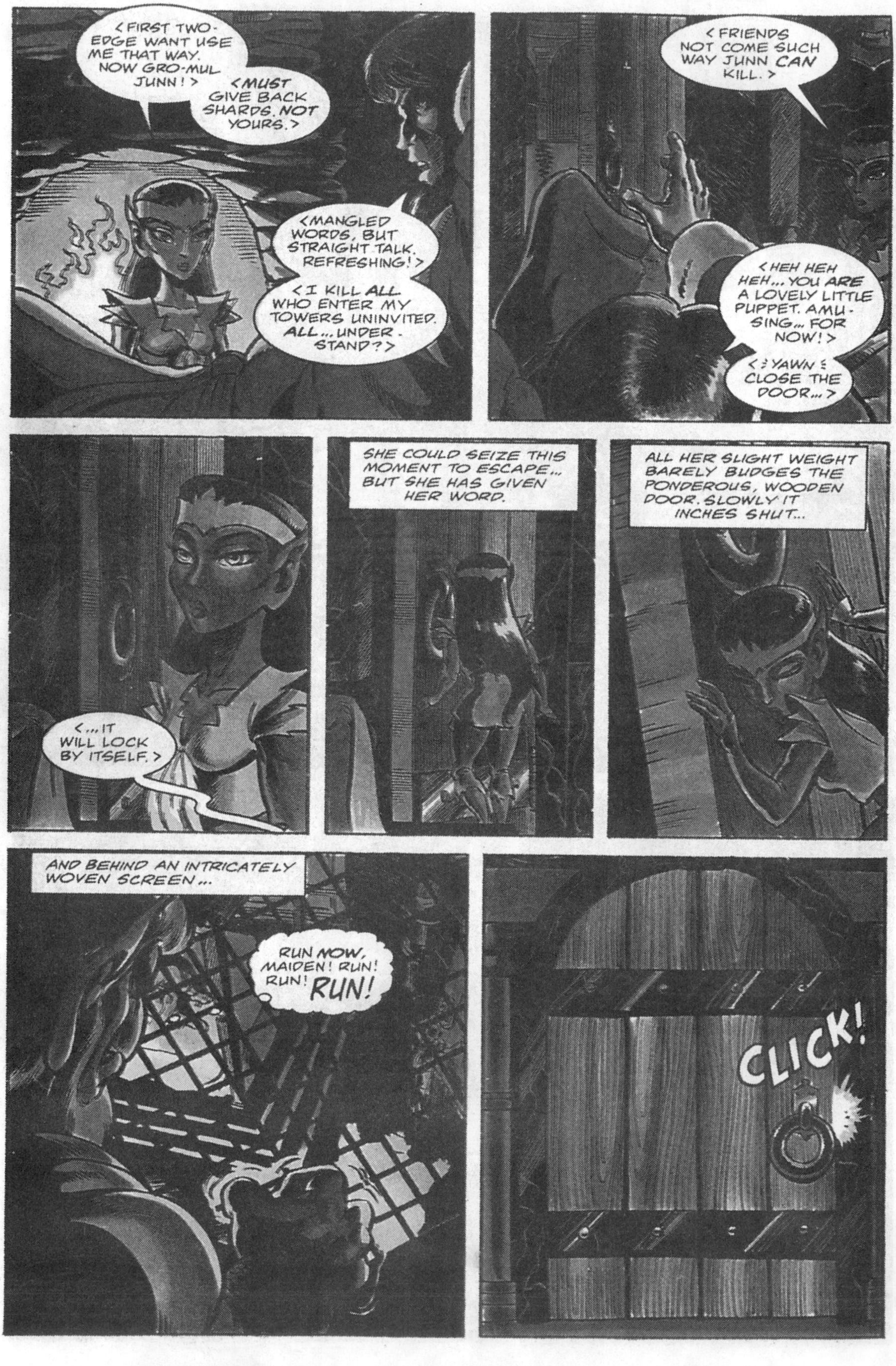
<FIRST TWO-EDGE WANT USE ME THAT WAY. NOW GRO-MUL JUNN!>
<MUST GIVE BACK SHARDS. NOT YOURS.>
<MANGLED WORDS, BUT STRAIGHT TALK. REFRESHING!>
<I KILL ALL WHO ENTER MY TOWERS UNINVITED. ALL... UNDER-STAND?>
<FRIENDS NOT COME SUCH WAY JUNN CAN KILL.>
<HEH HEH HEH... YOU ARE A LOVELY LITTLE PUPPET. AMU-SING... FOR NOW!>
<:YAWN: CLOSE THE DOOR...>
<...IT WILL LOCK BY ITSELF.>
SHE COULD SEIZE THIS MOMENT TO ESCAPE... BUT SHE HAS GIVEN HER WORD.
ALL HER SLIGHT WEIGHT BARELY BUDGES THE PONDEROUS, WOODEN DOOR. SLOWLY IT INCHES SHUT...
AND BEHIND AN INTRICATELY WOVEN SCREEN...
RUN NOW, MAIDEN! RUN! RUN! RUN!
CLICK!

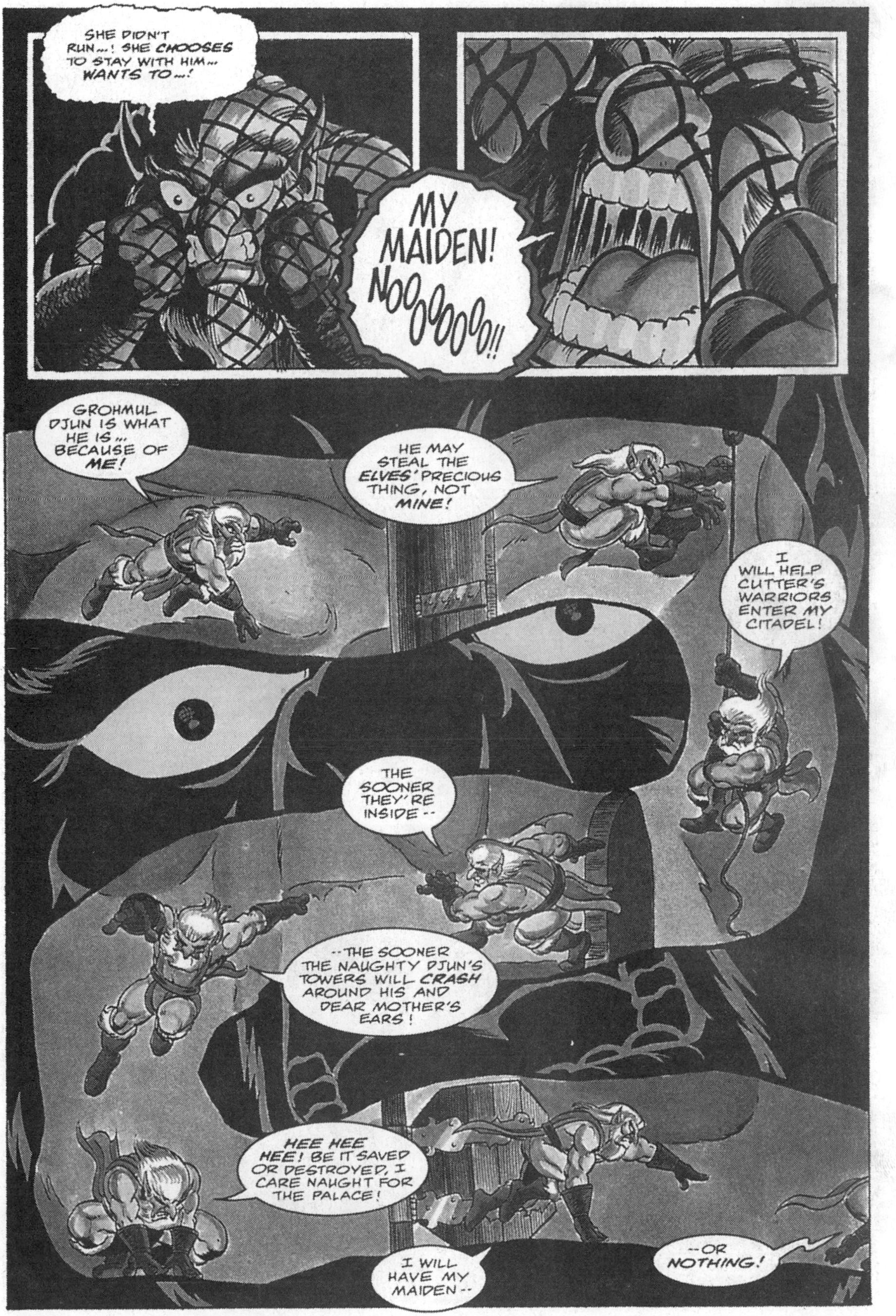

SHE DIDN'T RUN...! SHE CHOOSES TO STAY WITH HIM... WANTS TO...!
MY MAIDEN! NOOOOOOOO!!
GROHMUL DJUN IS WHAT HE IS... BECAUSE OF ME!
HE MAY STEAL THE ELVES' PRECIOUS THING, NOT MINE!
I WILL HELP CUTTER'S WARRIORS ENTER MY CITADEL!
THE SOONER THEY'RE INSIDE --
-- THE SOONER THE NAUGHTY DJUN'S TOWERS WILL CRASH AROUND HIS AND DEAR MOTHER'S EARS!
HEE HEE HEE! BE IT SAVED OR DESTROYED, I CARE NAUGHT FOR THE PALACE!
I WILL HAVE MY MAIDEN --
-- OR NOTHING!

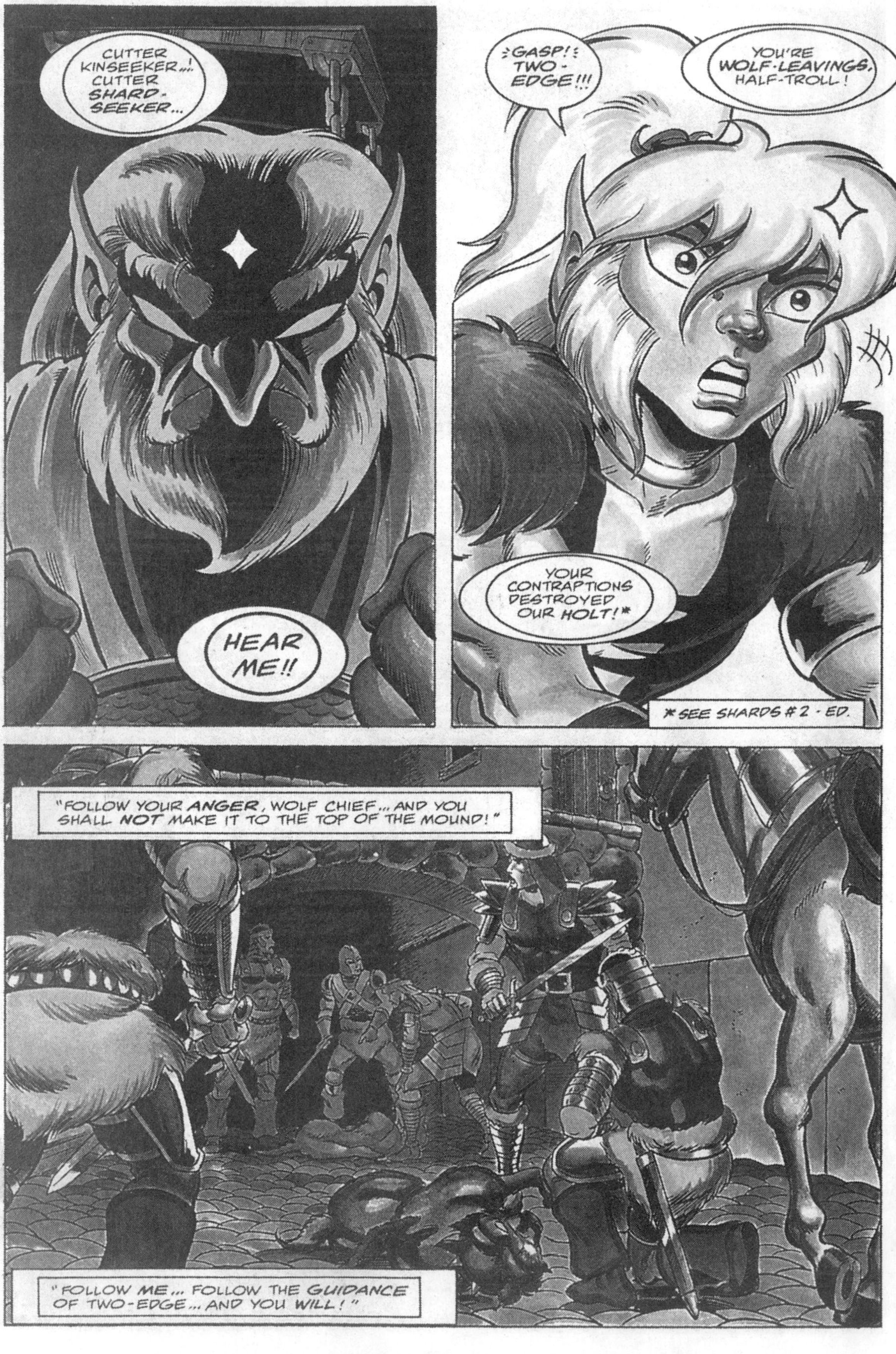
CUTTER KINSEEKER...! CUTTER SHARD-SEEKER...
HEAR ME!!
:GASP!: TWO-EDGE!!!
YOU'RE WOLF-LEAVINGS, HALF-TROLL!
YOUR CONTRAPTIONS DESTROYED OUR HOLT!*
*SEE SHARDS #2 - ED.
"FOLLOW YOUR ANGER, WOLF CHIEF... AND YOU SHALL NOT MAKE IT TO THE TOP OF THE MOUND!"
"FOLLOW ME... FOLLOW THE GUIDANCE OF TWO-EDGE... AND YOU WILL!"

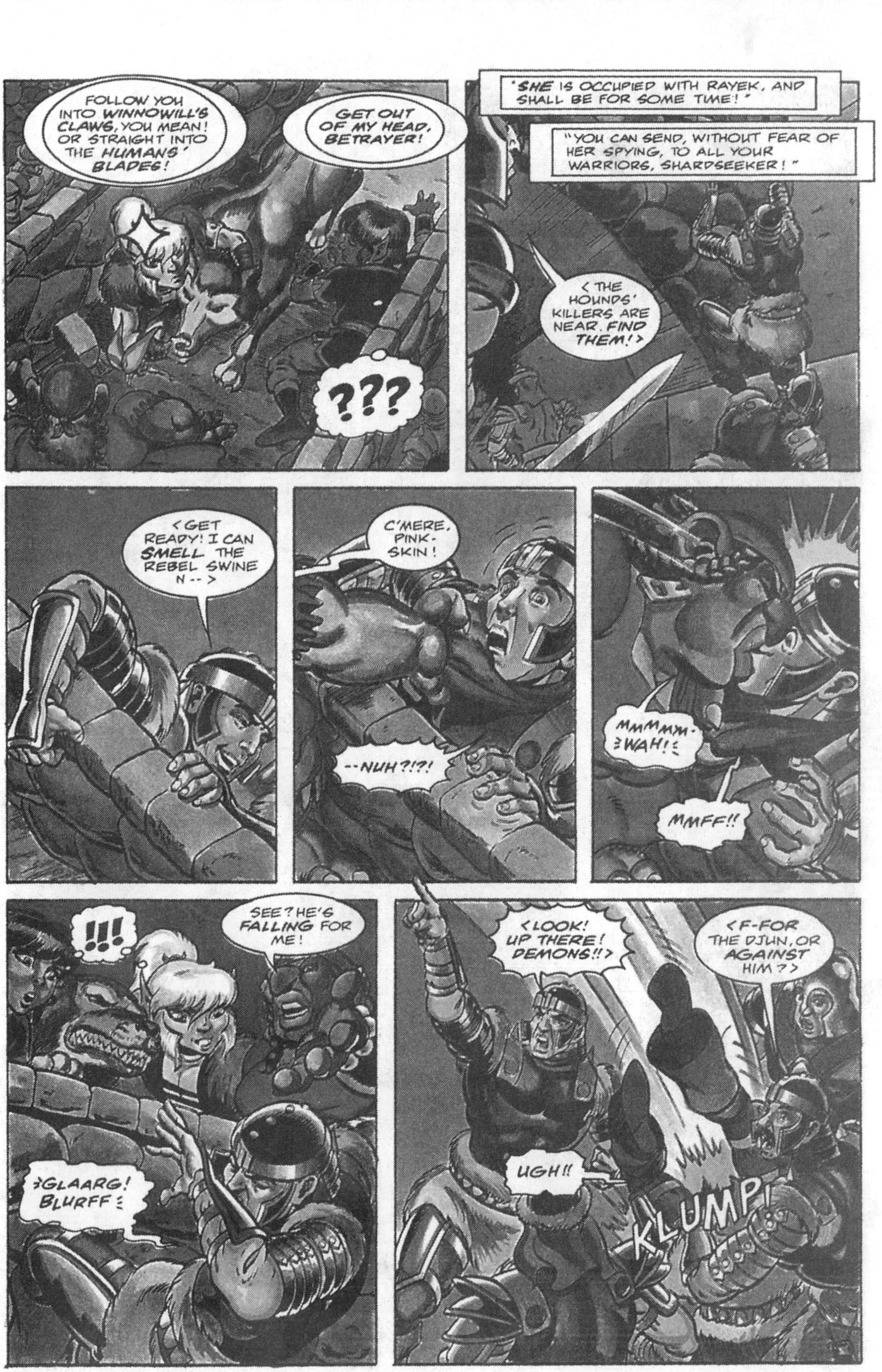

FOLLOW YOU INTO WINNOWILL'S CLAWS, YOU MEAN! OR STRAIGHT INTO THE HUMANS' BLADES!
GET OUT OF MY HEAD, BETRAYER!
???
"SHE IS OCCUPIED WITH RAYEK, AND SHALL BE FOR SOME TIME!"
"YOU CAN SEND, WITHOUT FEAR OF HER SPYING, TO ALL YOUR WARRIORS, SHARDSEEKER!"
< THE HOUNDS' KILLERS ARE NEAR. FIND THEM! >
< GET READY! I CAN SMELL THE REBEL SWINE N-- >
C'MERE, PINK-SKIN!
--NUH?!?!
MMMMM-WAH!
MMFF!!
!!!
SEE? HE'S FALLING FOR ME!
GLAARG! BLURFF
< LOOK! UP THERE! DEMONS!! >
< F-FOR THE DJUN, OR AGAINST HIM? >
UGH!!
KLUMP!

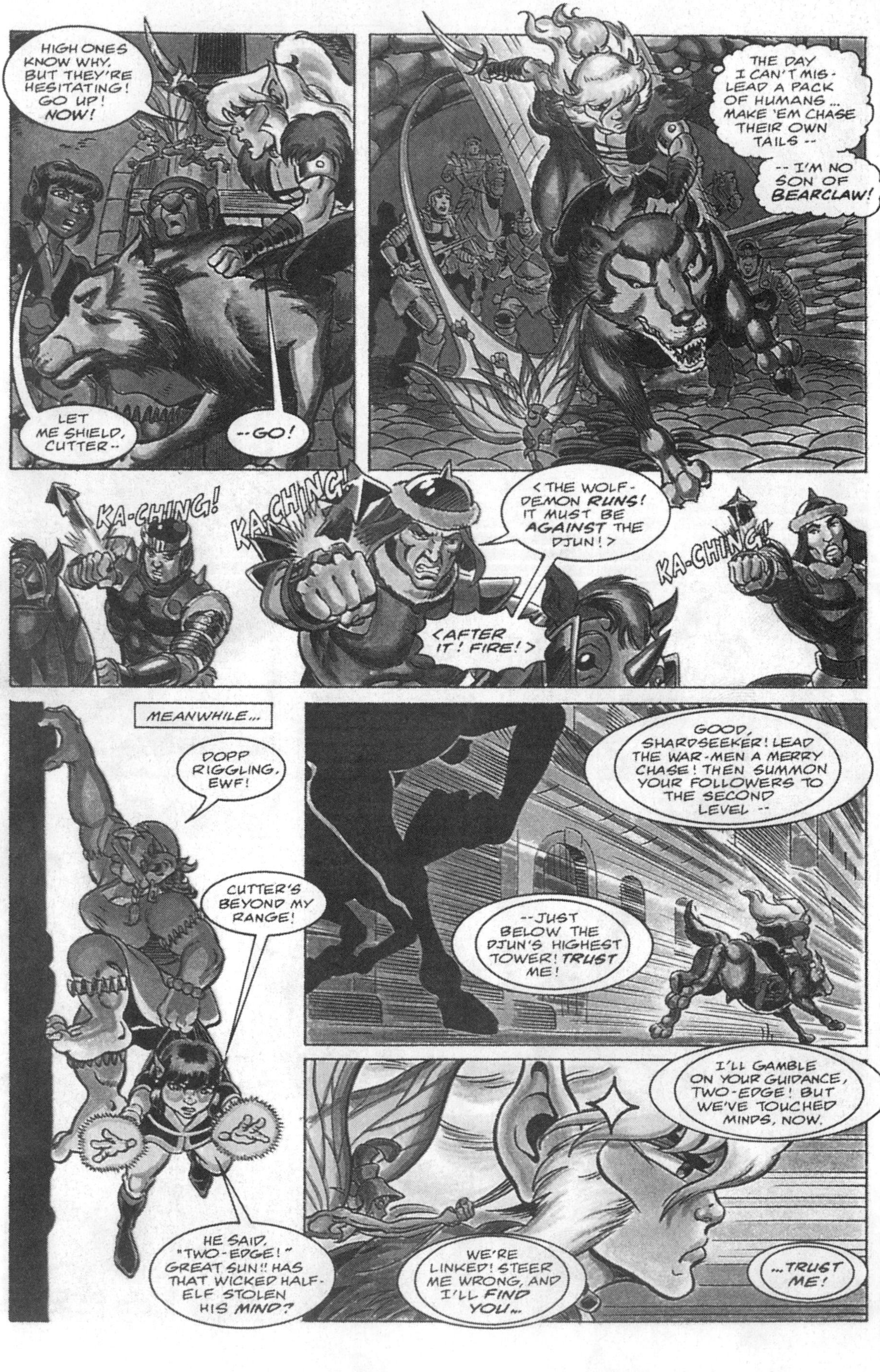
HIGH ONES KNOW WHY, BUT THEY'RE HESITATING! GO UP! NOW!
LET ME SHIELD, CUTTER--
--GO!
THE DAY I CAN'T MIS-LEAD A PACK OF HUMANS... MAKE 'EM CHASE THEIR OWN TAILS --
-- I'M NO SON OF BEARCLAW!
KA-CHING!
KA-CHING!
<THE WOLF-DEMON RUNS! IT MUST BE AGAINST THE DJUN!>
KA-CHING!
<AFTER IT! FIRE!>
MEANWHILE...
DOPP RIGGLING, EWF!
CUTTER'S BEYOND MY RANGE!
HE SAID, "TWO-EDGE!" GREAT SUN!! HAS THAT WICKED HALF-ELF STOLEN HIS MIND?
GOOD, SHARDSEEKER! LEAD THE WAR-MEN A MERRY CHASE! THEN SUMMON YOUR FOLLOWERS TO THE SECOND LEVEL --
--JUST BELOW THE DJUN'S HIGHEST TOWER! TRUST ME!
I'LL GAMBLE ON YOUR GUIDANCE, TWO-EDGE! BUT WE'VE TOUCHED MINDS, NOW.
WE'RE LINKED! STEER ME WRONG, AND I'LL FIND YOU...
...TRUST ME!

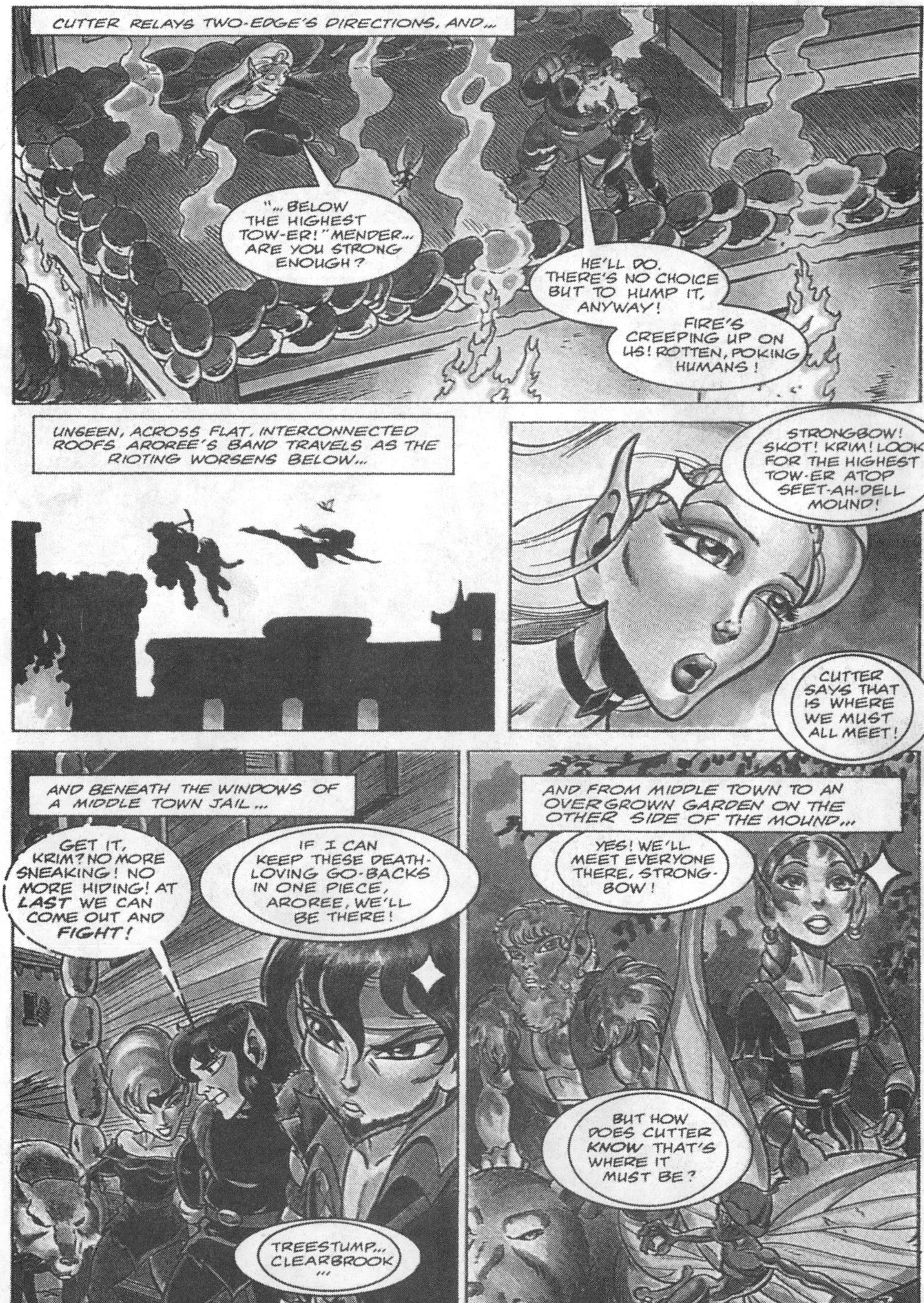

CUTTER RELAYS TWO-EDGE'S DIRECTIONS, AND...
"...BELOW THE HIGHEST TOW-ER!" MENDER... ARE YOU STRONG ENOUGH?
HE'LL DO. THERE'S NO CHOICE BUT TO HUMP IT, ANYWAY!
FIRE'S CREEPING UP ON US! ROTTEN, POKING HUMANS!
UNSEEN, ACROSS FLAT, INTERCONNECTED ROOFS AROREE'S BAND TRAVELS AS THE RIOTING WORSENS BELOW...
STRONGBOW! SKOT! KRIM! LOOK FOR THE HIGHEST TOW-ER ATOP SEET-AH-DELL MOUND!
CUTTER SAYS THAT IS WHERE WE MUST ALL MEET!
AND BENEATH THE WINDOWS OF A MIDDLE TOWN JAIL...
GET IT, KRIM? NO MORE SNEAKING! NO MORE HIDING! AT LAST WE CAN COME OUT AND FIGHT!
IF I CAN KEEP THESE DEATH-LOVING GO-BACKS IN ONE PIECE, AROREE, WE'LL BE THERE!
TREESTUMP... CLEARBROOK ...
AND FROM MIDDLE TOWN TO AN OVERGROWN GARDEN ON THE OTHER SIDE OF THE MOUND...
YES! WE'LL MEET EVERYONE THERE, STRONGBOW!
BUT HOW DOES CUTTER KNOW THAT'S WHERE IT MUST BE?
HOW INDEED?

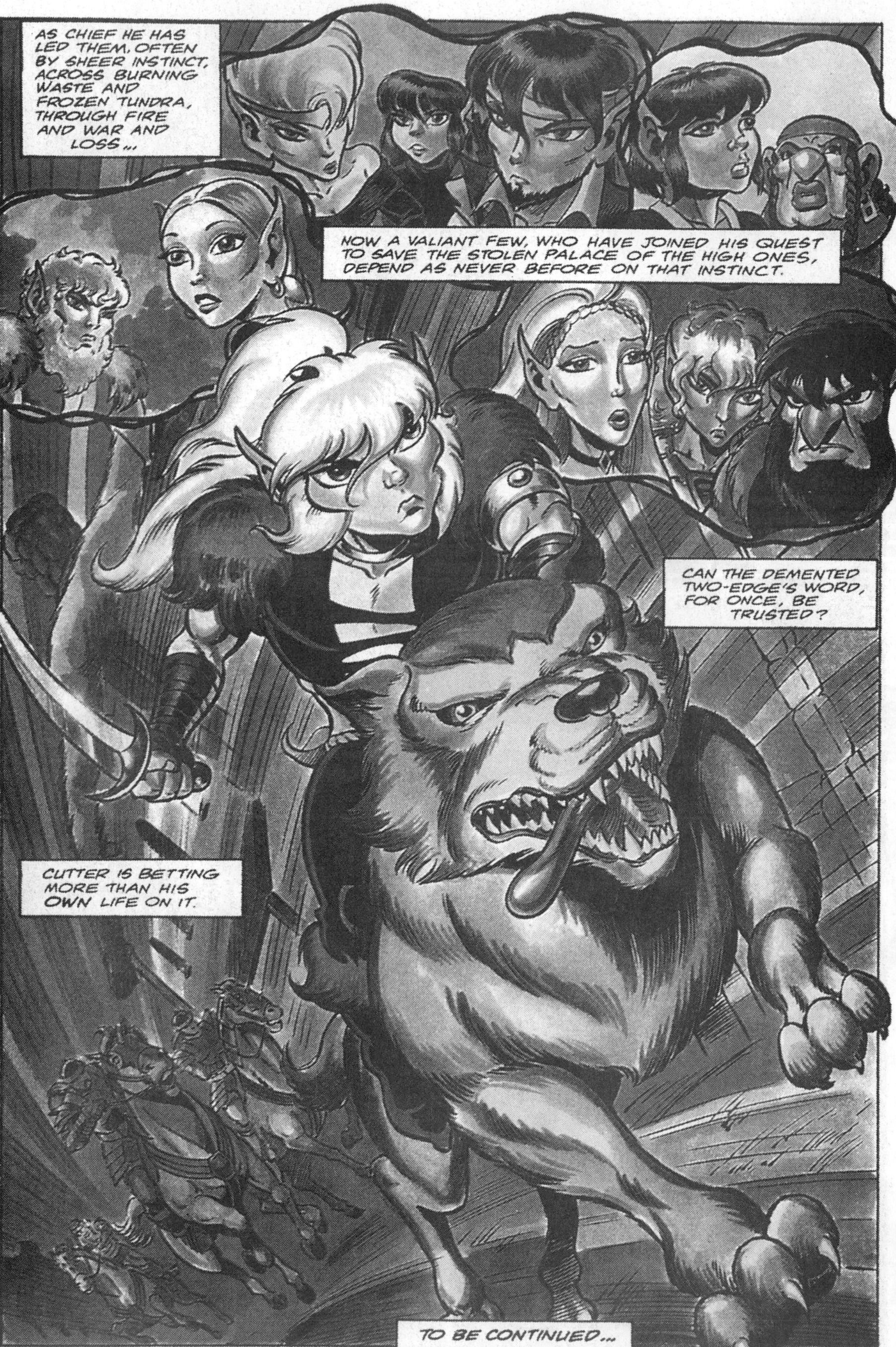
AS CHIEF HE HAS LED THEM, OFTEN BY SHEER INSTINCT, ACROSS BURNING WASTE AND FROZEN TUNDRA, THROUGH FIRE AND WAR AND LOSS...
NOW A VALIANT FEW, WHO HAVE JOINED HIS QUEST TO SAVE THE STOLEN PALACE OF THE HIGH ONES, DEPEND AS NEVER BEFORE ON THAT INSTINCT.
CAN THE DEMENTED TWO-EDGE'S WORD, FOR ONCE, BE TRUSTED?
CUTTER IS BETTING MORE THAN HIS OWN LIFE ON IT.
TO BE CONTINUED...

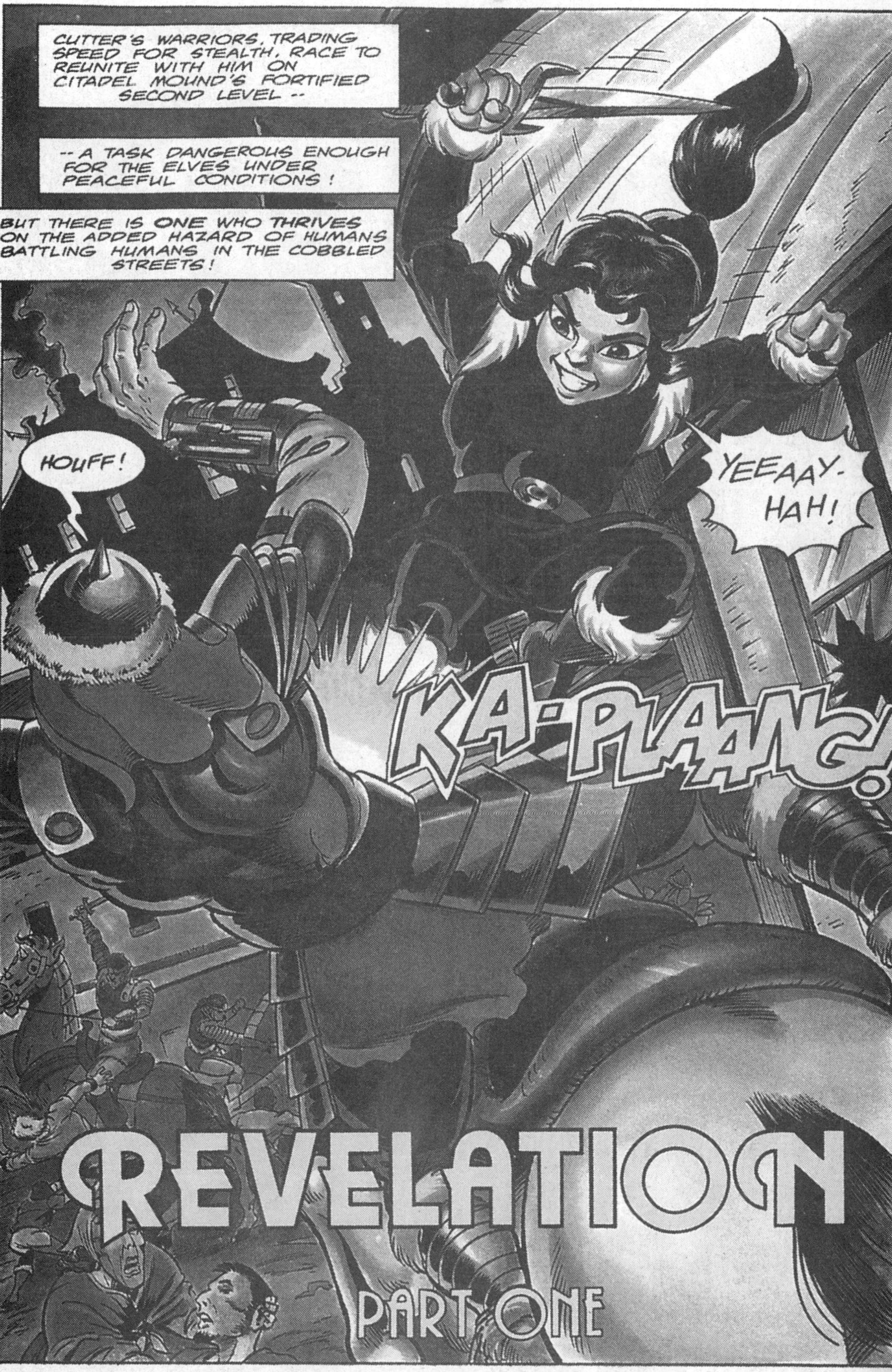
CUTTER'S WARRIORS, TRADING SPEED FOR STEALTH, RACE TO REUNITE WITH HIM ON CITADEL MOUND'S FORTIFIED SECOND LEVEL --
-- A TASK DANGEROUS ENOUGH FOR THE ELVES UNDER PEACEFUL CONDITIONS!
BUT THERE IS ONE WHO THRIVES ON THE ADDED HAZARD OF HUMANS BATTLING HUMANS IN THE COBBLED STREETS!
HOUFF!
YEEAAY-HAH!
KA-PLAANG!
REVELATION
PART ONE

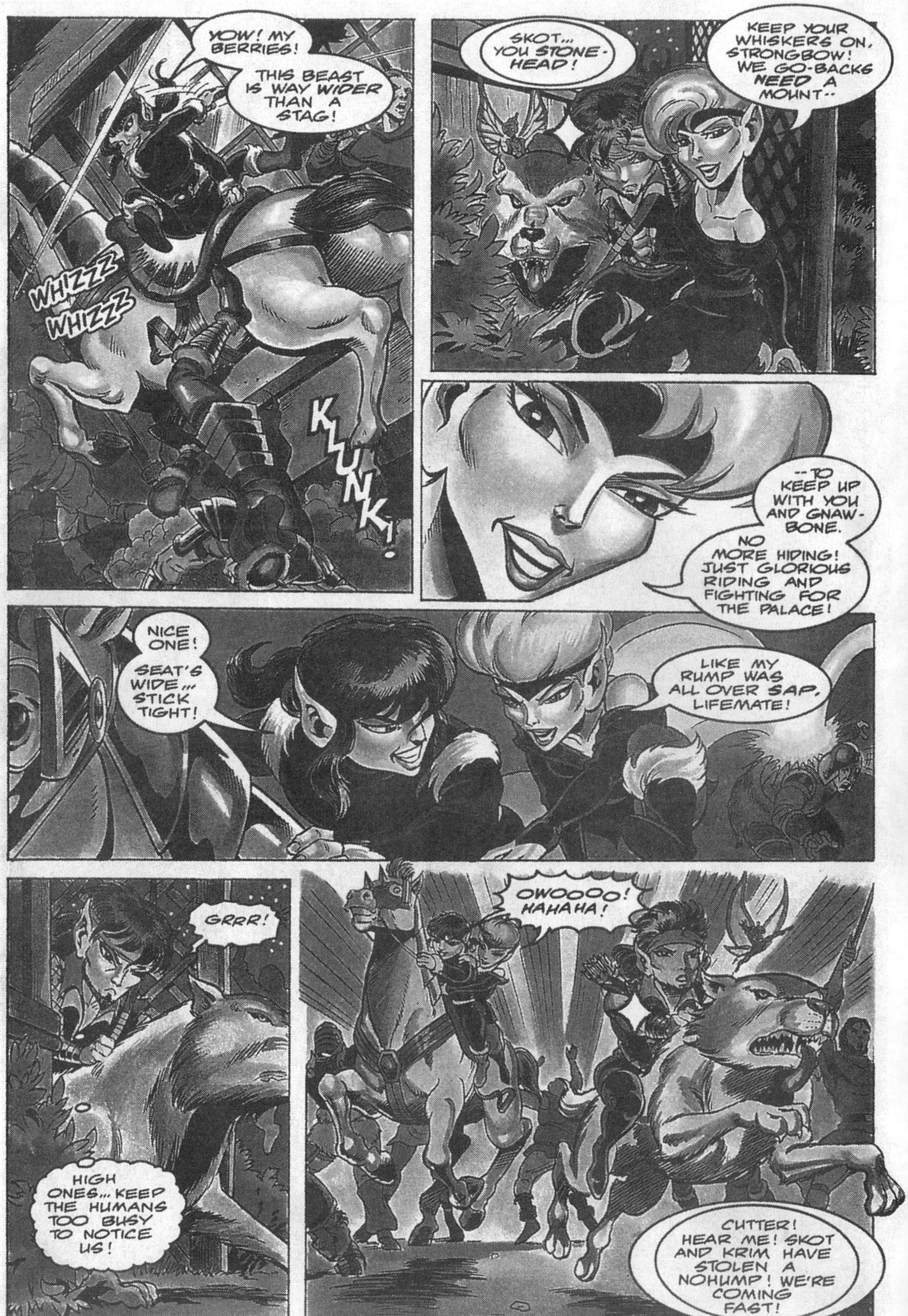
YOW! MY BERRIES!
THIS BEAST IS WAY WIDER THAN A STAG!
WHIZZZ
WHIZZZ
KLUNK!
SKOT... YOU STONE-HEAD!
KEEP YOUR WHISKERS ON, STRONGBOW! WE GO-BACKS NEED A MOUNT--
--TO KEEP UP WITH YOU AND GNAW-BONE.
NO MORE HIDING! JUST GLORIOUS RIDING AND FIGHTING FOR THE PALACE!
NICE ONE! SEAT'S WIDE... STICK TIGHT!
LIKE MY RUMP WAS ALL OVER SAP, LIFEMATE!
GRRR!
HIGH ONES... KEEP THE HUMANS TOO BUSY TO NOTICE US!
OWOOOO! HAHAHA!
CUTTER! HEAR ME! SKOT AND KRIM HAVE STOLEN A NOHUMP! WE'RE COMING FAST!

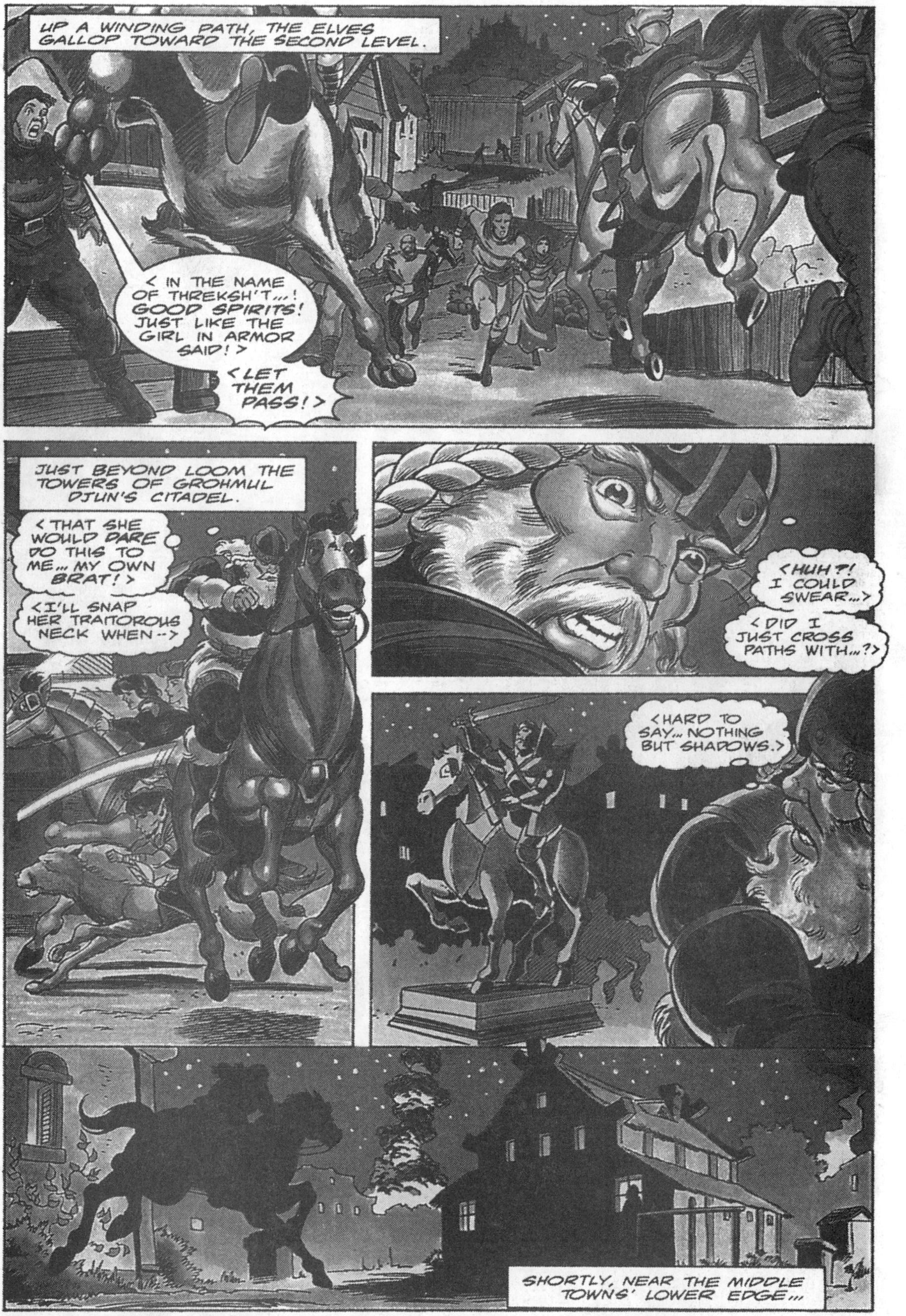
UP A WINDING PATH, THE ELVES GALLOP TOWARD THE SECOND LEVEL.
< IN THE NAME OF THREKSH'T...! GOOD SPIRITS! JUST LIKE THE GIRL IN ARMOR SAID! >
< LET THEM PASS! >
JUST BEYOND LOOM THE TOWERS OF GROHMUL DJUN'S CITADEL.
< THAT SHE WOULD DARE DO THIS TO ME... MY OWN BRAT! >
< I'LL SNAP HER TRAITOROUS NECK WHEN -- >
< HUH?! I COULD SWEAR... >
< DID I JUST CROSS PATHS WITH...? >
< HARD TO SAY... NOTHING BUT SHADOWS. >
SHORTLY, NEAR THE MIDDLE TOWNS' LOWER EDGE...

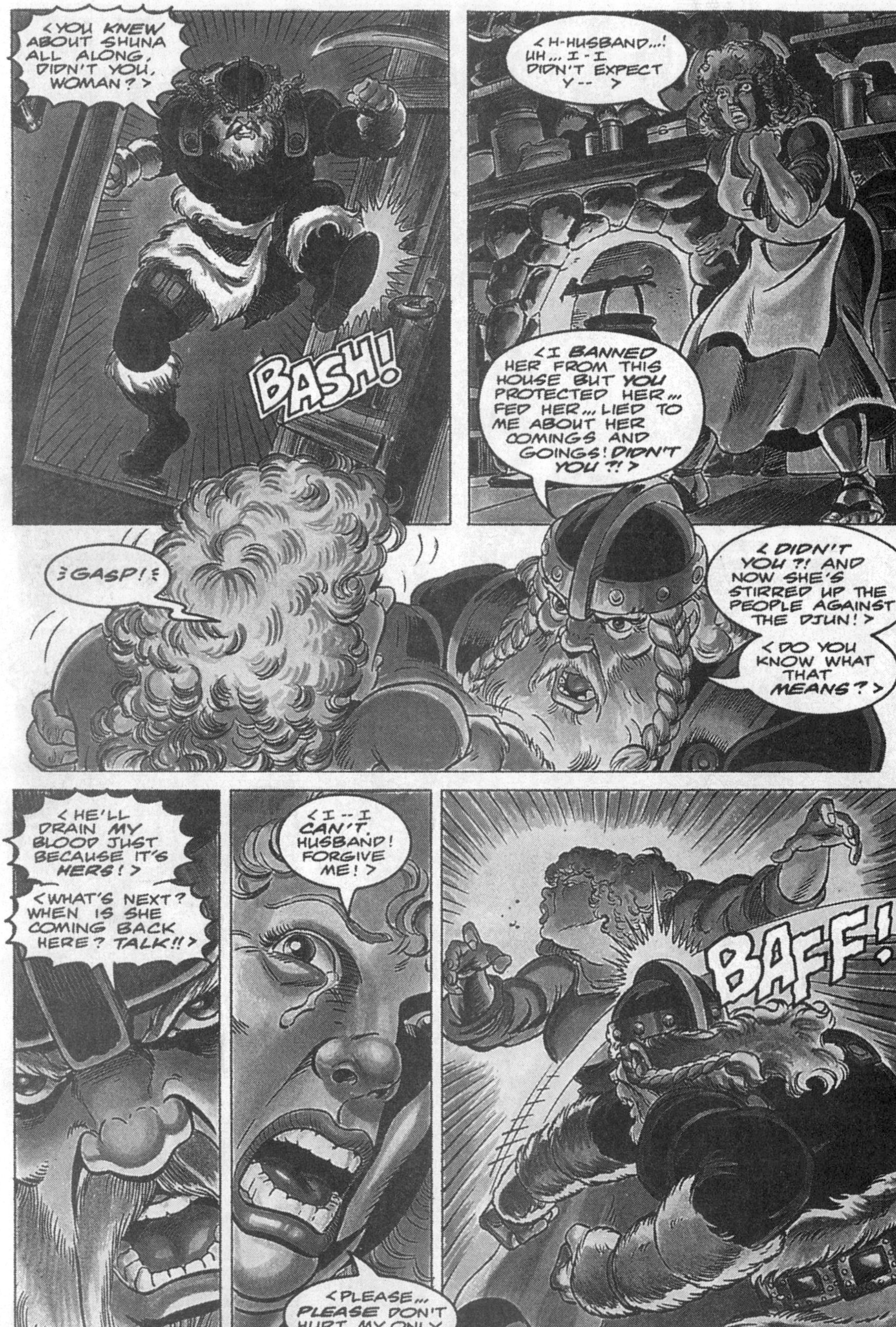
<YOU KNEW ABOUT SHUNA ALL ALONG, DIDN'T YOU, WOMAN?>
BASH!
<H-HUSBAND...! UH... I-I DIDN'T EXPECT Y-- >
<I BANNED HER FROM THIS HOUSE BUT YOU PROTECTED HER... FED HER... LIED TO ME ABOUT HER COMINGS AND GOINGS! DIDN'T YOU?!>
GASP!
<DIDN'T YOU?! AND NOW SHE'S STIRRED UP THE PEOPLE AGAINST THE DJUN!>
<DO YOU KNOW WHAT THAT MEANS?>
<HE'LL DRAIN MY BLOOD JUST BECAUSE IT'S HERS!>
<WHAT'S NEXT? WHEN IS SHE COMING BACK HERE? TALK!!>
<I--I CAN'T, HUSBAND! FORGIVE ME!>
<PLEASE... PLEASE DON'T HURT MY ONLY CHI--!>
BAFF!

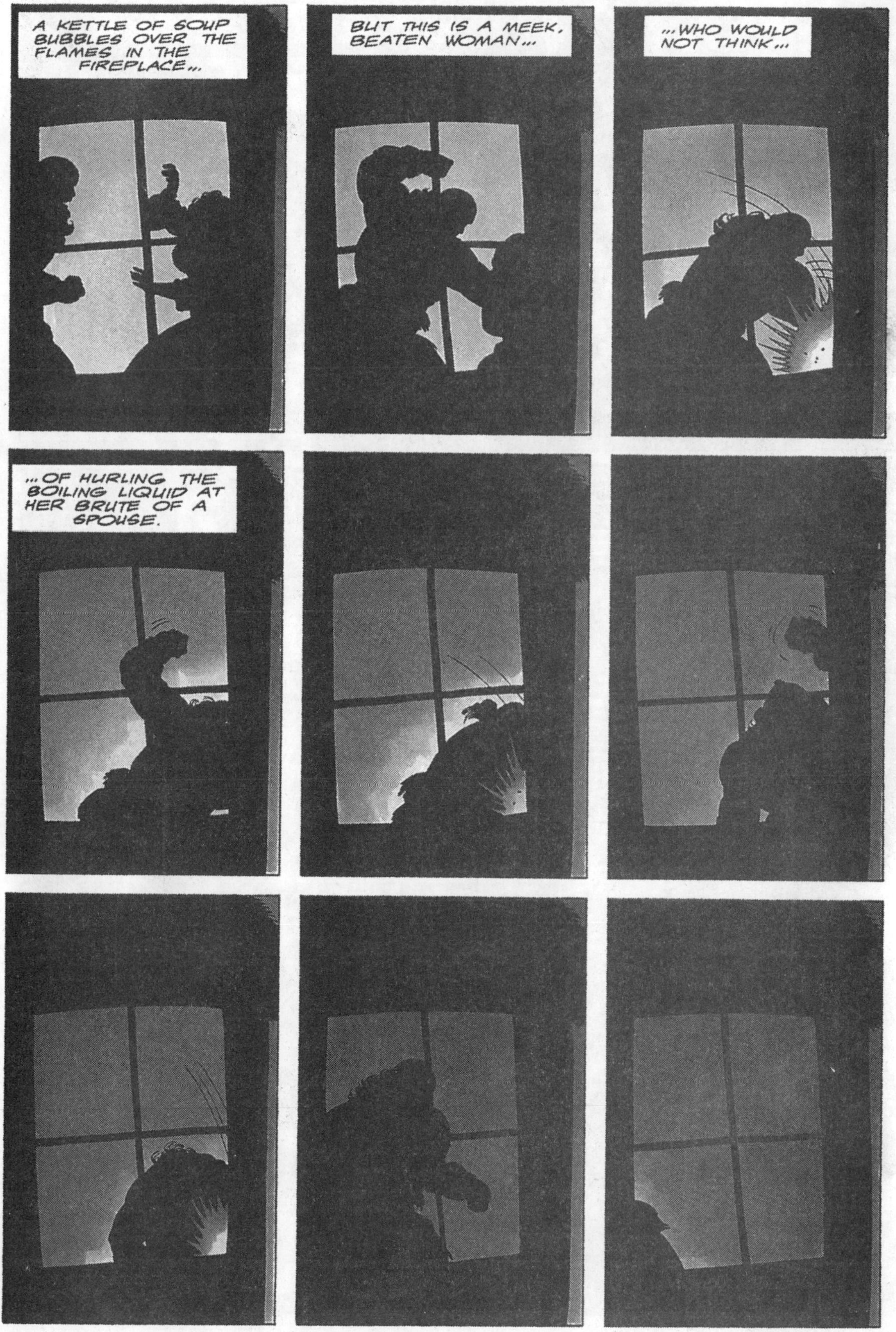
A KETTLE OF SOUP BUBBLES OVER THE FLAMES IN THE FIREPLACE...
BUT THIS IS A MEEK, BEATEN WOMAN...
...WHO WOULD NOT THINK...
...OF HURLING THE BOILING LIQUID AT HER BRUTE OF A SPOUSE.

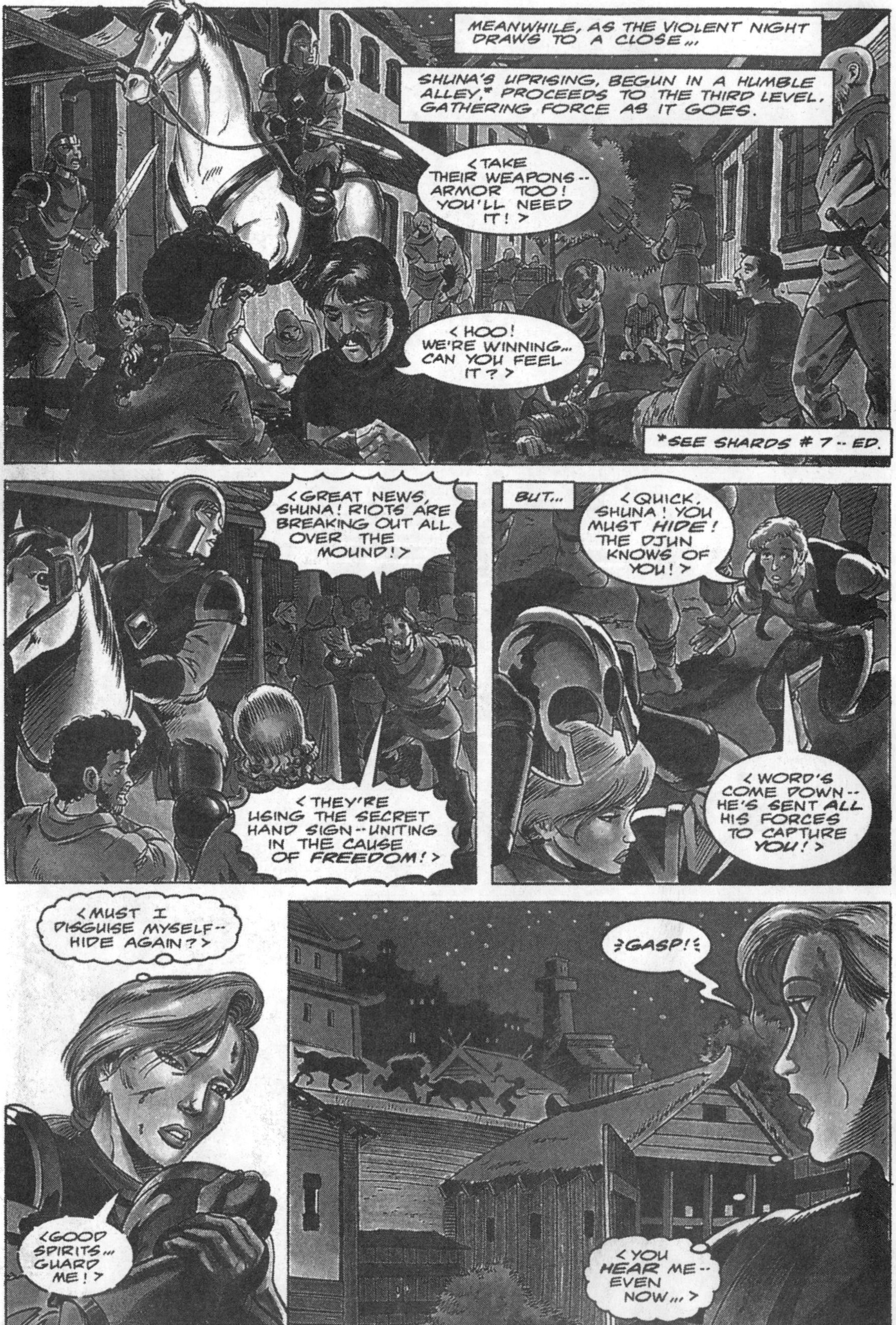
MEANWHILE, AS THE VIOLENT NIGHT DRAWS TO A CLOSE...
SHUNA'S UPRISING, BEGUN IN A HUMBLE ALLEY,* PROCEEDS TO THE THIRD LEVEL, GATHERING FORCE AS IT GOES.
<TAKE THEIR WEAPONS-- ARMOR TOO! YOU'LL NEED IT!>
<HOO! WE'RE WINNING... CAN YOU FEEL IT?>
*SEE SHARDS # 7 -- ED.
<GREAT NEWS, SHUNA! RIOTS ARE BREAKING OUT ALL OVER THE MOUND!>
<THEY'RE USING THE SECRET HAND SIGN--UNITING IN THE CAUSE OF FREEDOM!>
BUT...
<QUICK, SHUNA! YOU MUST HIDE! THE DJUN KNOWS OF YOU!>
<WORD'S COME DOWN-- HE'S SENT ALL HIS FORCES TO CAPTURE YOU!>
<MUST I DISGUISE MYSELF-- HIDE AGAIN?>
<GOOD SPIRITS... GUARD ME!>
GASP!
<YOU HEAR ME-- EVEN NOW...>

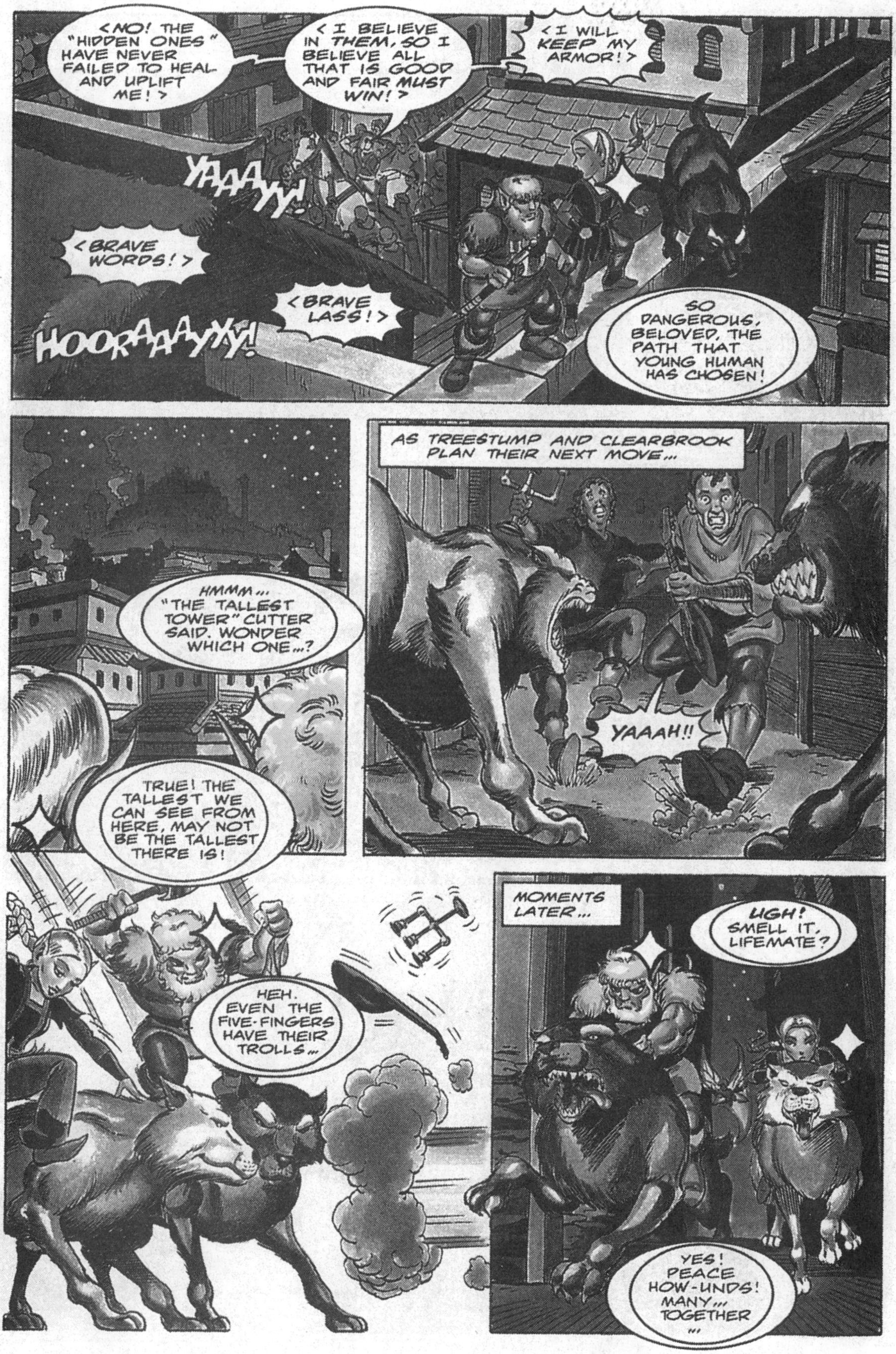

<NO! THE "HIDDEN ONES" HAVE NEVER FAILED TO HEAL AND UPLIFT ME!>
<I BELIEVE IN THEM, SO I BELIEVE ALL THAT IS GOOD AND FAIR MUST WIN!>
<I WILL KEEP MY ARMOR!>
YAAAYY!
<BRAVE WORDS!>
<BRAVE LASS!>
HOORAAAYYY!
SO DANGEROUS, BELOVED, THE PATH THAT YOUNG HUMAN HAS CHOSEN!
HMMM... "THE TALLEST TOWER" CUTTER SAID. WONDER WHICH ONE...?
TRUE! THE TALLEST WE CAN SEE FROM HERE, MAY NOT BE THE TALLEST THERE IS!
AS TREESTUMP AND CLEARBROOK PLAN THEIR NEXT MOVE...
YAAAH!!
HEH. EVEN THE FIVE-FINGERS HAVE THEIR TROLLS...
MOMENTS LATER...
UGH! SMELL IT, LIFEMATE?
YES! PEACE HOW-UNDS! MANY... TOGETHER ...

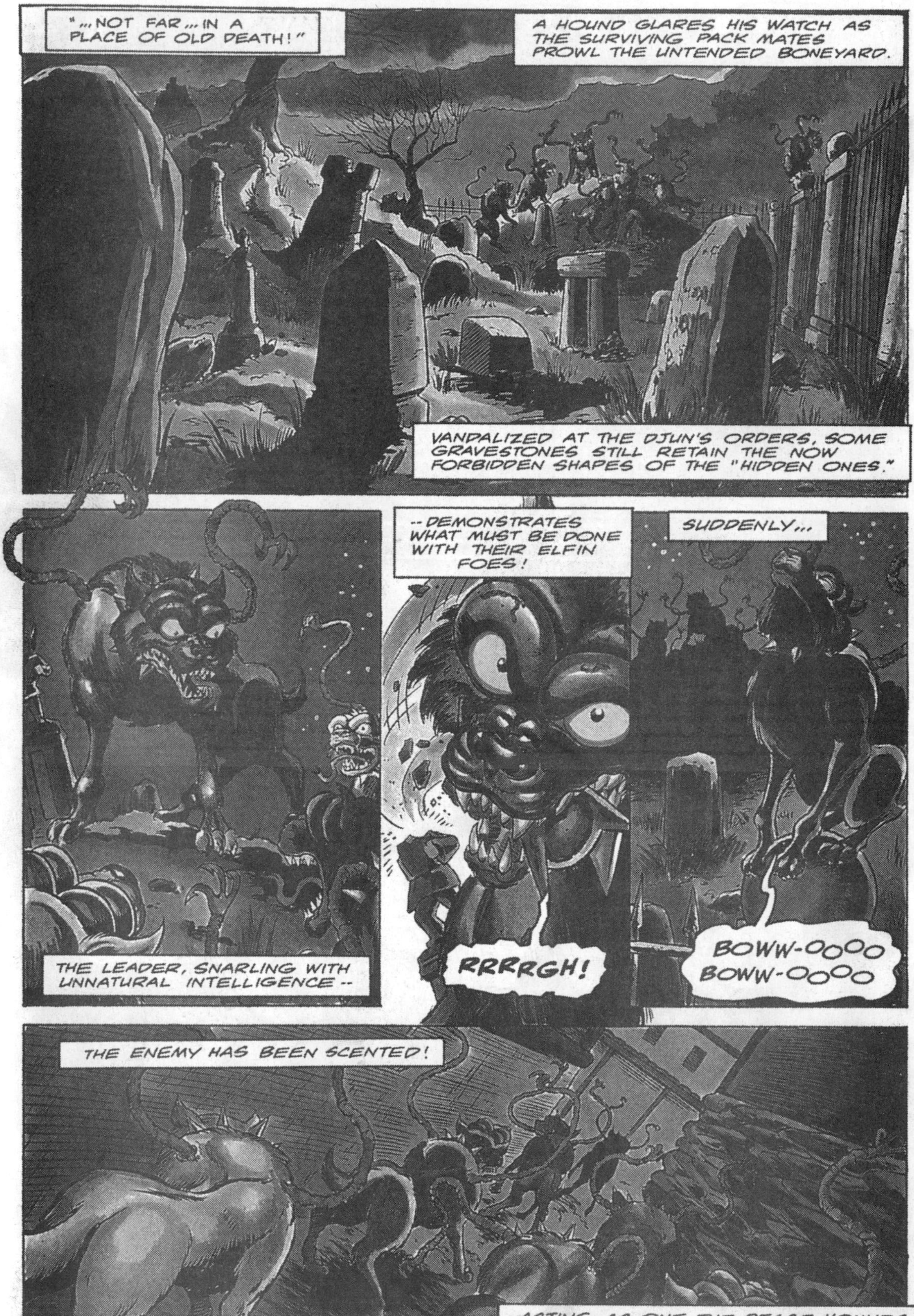
"...NOT FAR...IN A PLACE OF OLD DEATH!"
A HOUND GLARES HIS WATCH AS THE SURVIVING PACK MATES PROWL THE UNTENDED BONEYARD.
VANDALIZED AT THE DJUN'S ORDERS, SOME GRAVESTONES STILL RETAIN THE NOW FORBIDDEN SHAPES OF THE "HIDDEN ONES."
THE LEADER, SNARLING WITH UNNATURAL INTELLIGENCE --
--DEMONSTRATES WHAT MUST BE DONE WITH THEIR ELFIN FOES!
RRRRGH!
SUDDENLY...
BOWW-OOOO
BOWW-OOOO
THE ENEMY HAS BEEN SCENTED!
ACTING AS ONE, THE PEACE HOUNDS FOLLOW THE TWO ELDER WOLFRIDERS.

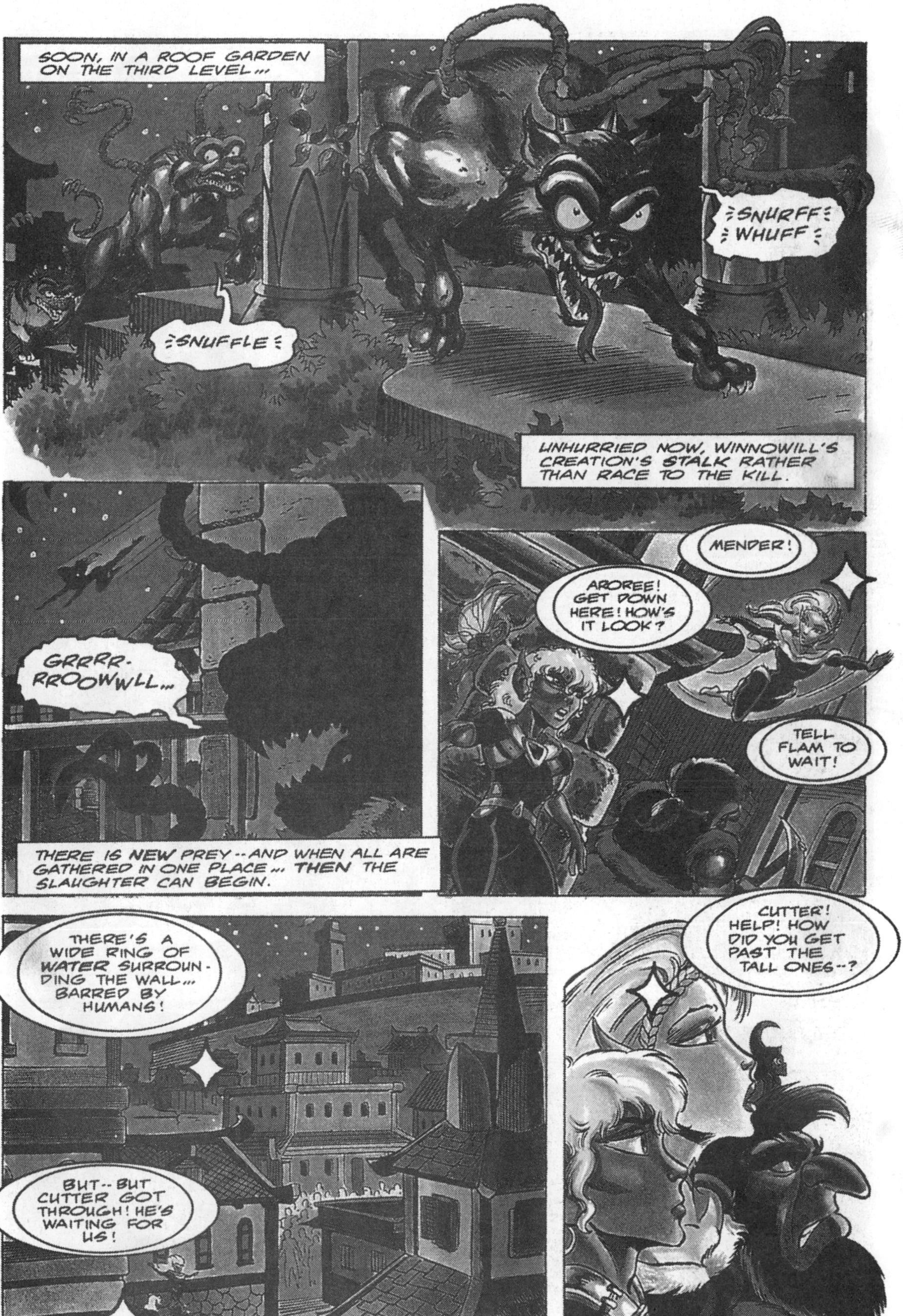
SOON, IN A ROOF GARDEN ON THE THIRD LEVEL...
SNUFFLE
SNURFF WHUFF
UNHURRIED NOW, WINNOWILL'S CREATION'S STALK RATHER THAN RACE TO THE KILL.
GRRRR-RROOWWLL...
THERE IS NEW PREY--AND WHEN ALL ARE GATHERED IN ONE PLACE... THEN THE SLAUGHTER CAN BEGIN.
MENDER!
AROREE! GET DOWN HERE! HOW'S IT LOOK?
TELL FLAM TO WAIT!
THERE'S A WIDE RING OF WATER SURROUNDING THE WALL... BARRED BY HUMANS!
BUT--BUT CUTTER GOT THROUGH! HE'S WAITING FOR US!
CUTTER! HELP! HOW DID YOU GET PAST THE TALL ONES--?

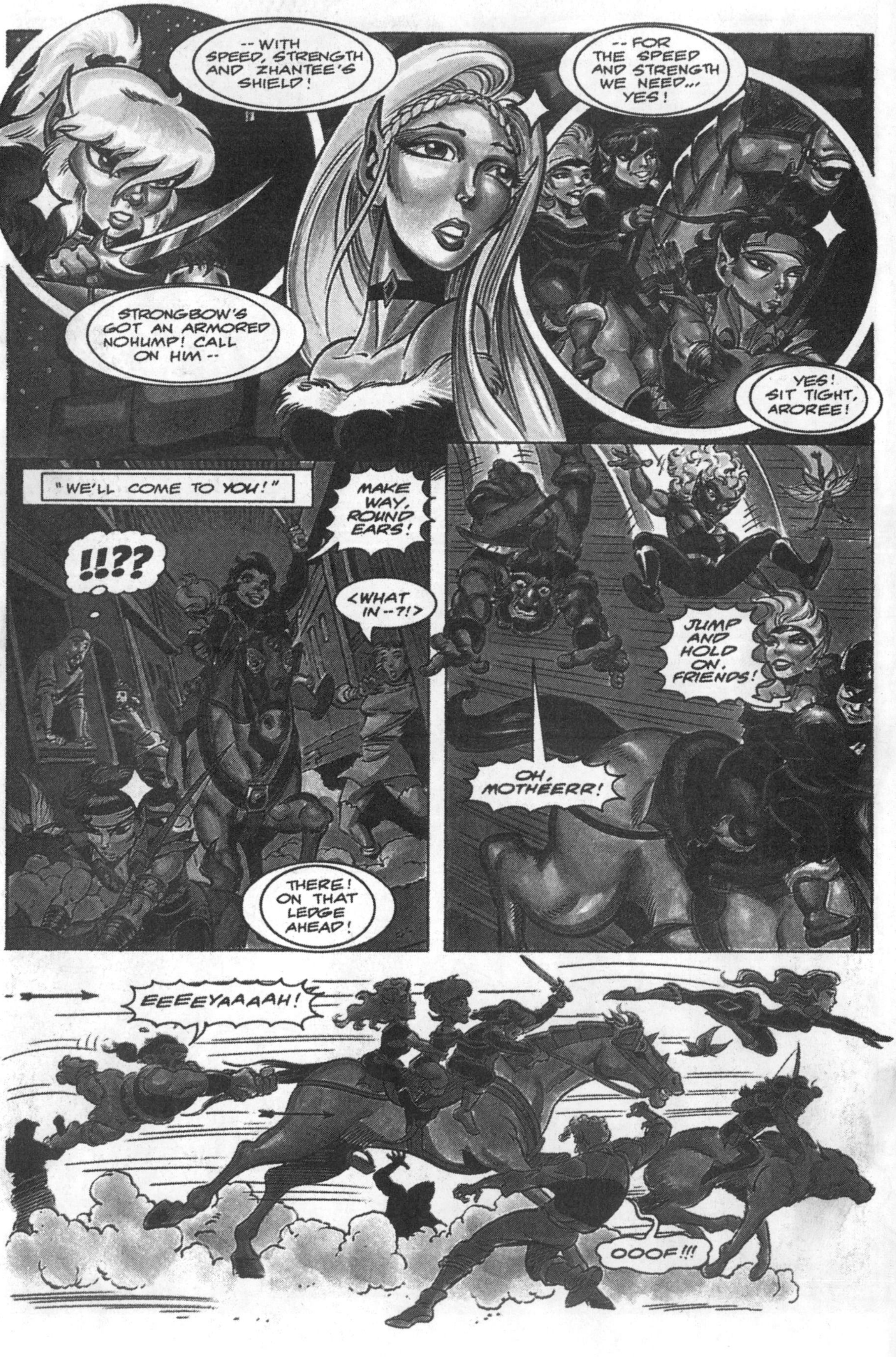
-- WITH SPEED, STRENGTH AND ZHANTEE'S SHIELD!
STRONGBOW'S GOT AN ARMORED NOHUMP! CALL ON HIM --
-- FOR THE SPEED AND STRENGTH WE NEED... YES!
YES! SIT TIGHT, AROREE!
"WE'LL COME TO YOU!"
MAKE WAY, ROUND EARS!
!!??
<WHAT IN --?!>
THERE! ON THAT LEDGE AHEAD!
JUMP AND HOLD ON, FRIENDS!
OH, MOTHEERR!
EEEEYAAAAH!
OOOF!!!

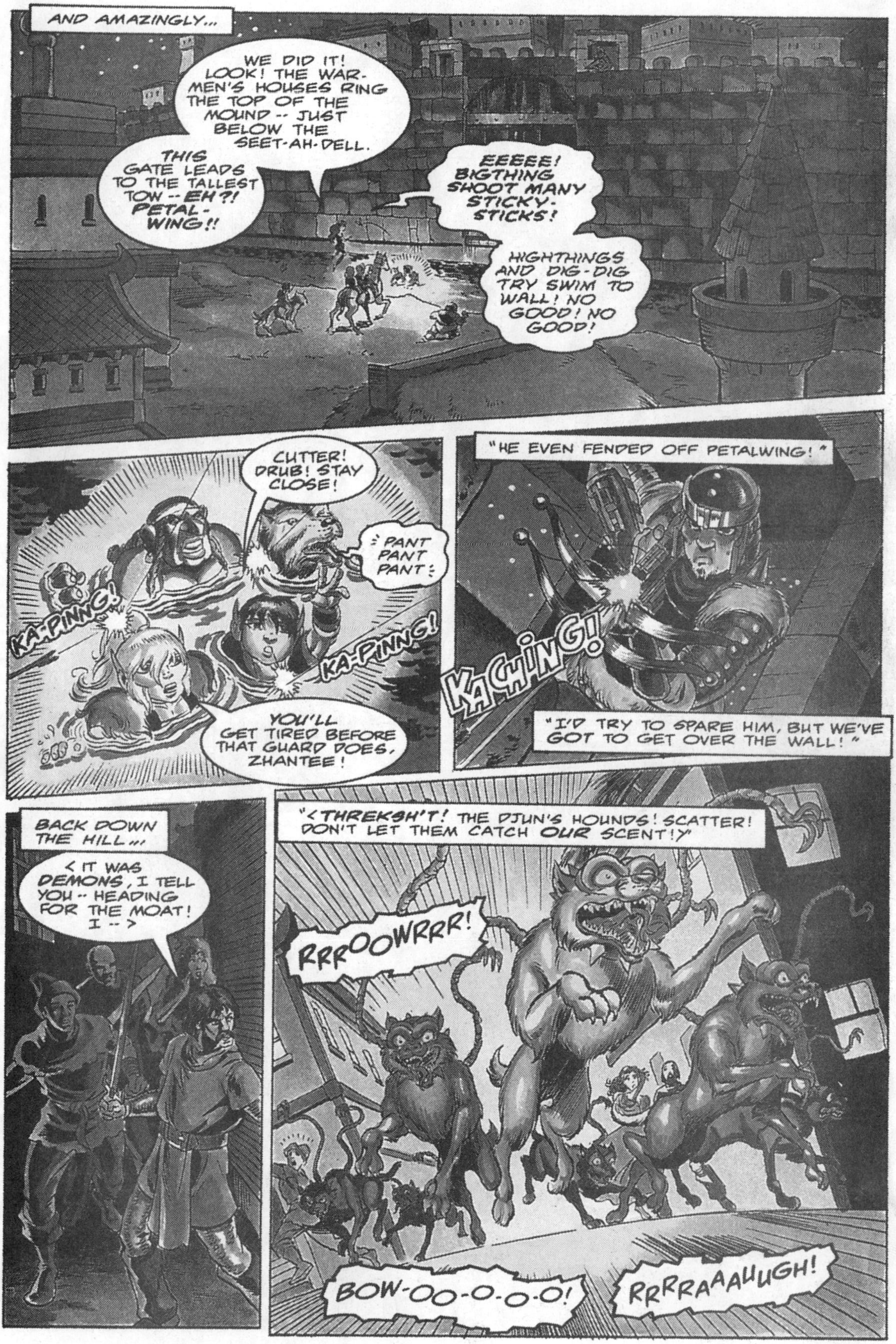
AND AMAZINGLY...
WE DID IT! LOOK! THE WAR-MEN'S HOUSES RING THE TOP OF THE MOUND -- JUST BELOW THE SEET-AH-DELL.
THIS GATE LEADS TO THE TALLEST TOW -- EH?! PETAL-WING!!
EEEEE! BIGTHING SHOOT MANY STICKY-STICKS!
HIGHTHINGS AND DIG-DIG TRY SWIM TO WALL! NO GOOD! NO GOOD!
CUTTER! DRUB! STAY CLOSE!
PANT PANT PANT
KA-PINNG!
KA-PINNG!
YOU'LL GET TIRED BEFORE THAT GUARD DOES, ZHANTEE!
"HE EVEN FENDED OFF PETALWING!"
KACHING!
"I'D TRY TO SPARE HIM, BUT WE'VE GOT TO GET OVER THE WALL!"
BACK DOWN THE HILL...
< IT WAS DEMONS, I TELL YOU -- HEADING FOR THE MOAT! I -- >
"<THREKSH'T! THE DJUN'S HOUNDS! SCATTER! DON'T LET THEM CATCH OUR SCENT!>"
RRROOWRRR!
BOW-OO-O-O-O!
RRRRAAAUUGH!

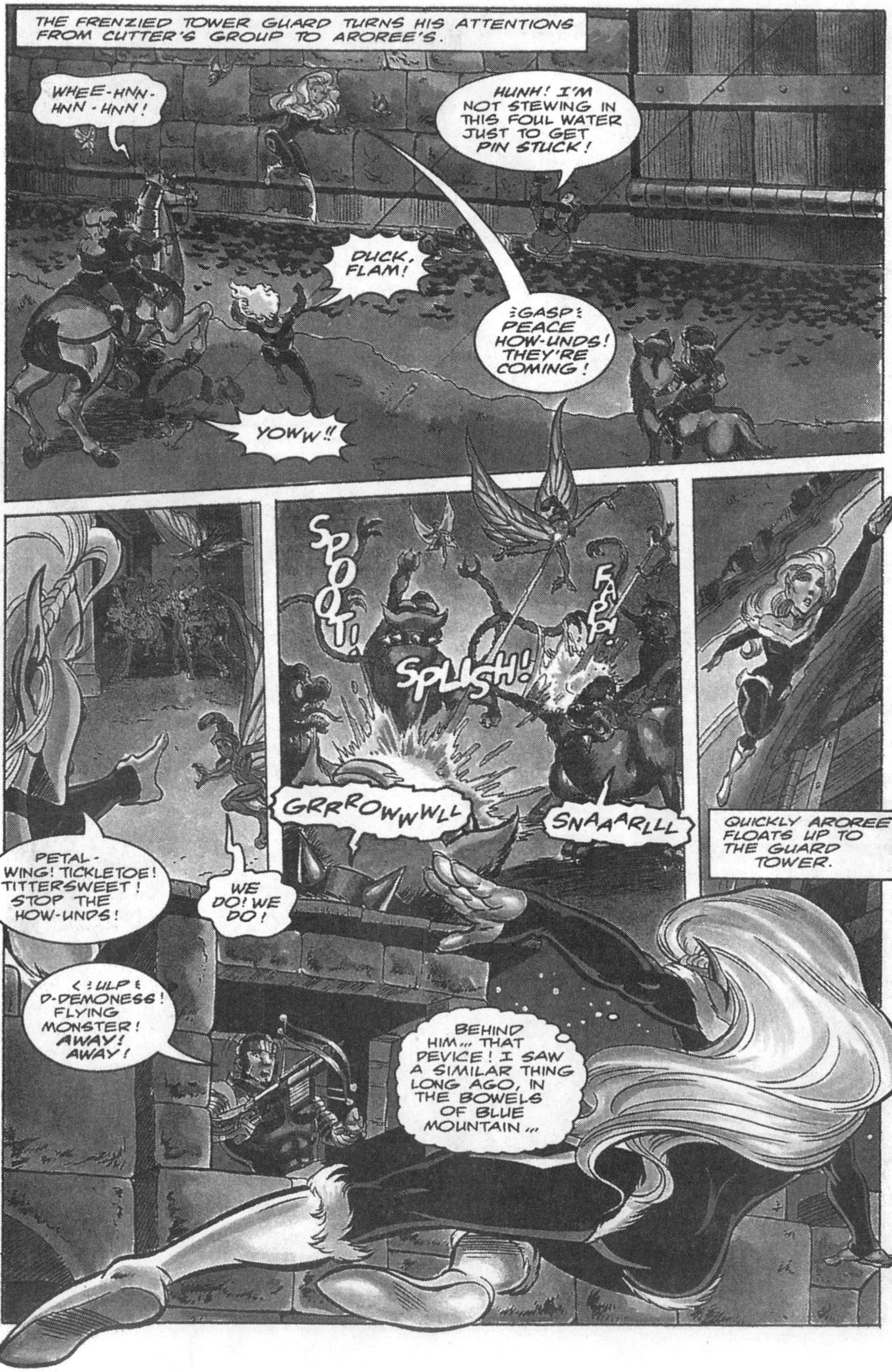

THE FRENZIED TOWER GUARD TURNS HIS ATTENTIONS FROM CUTTER'S GROUP TO AROREE'S.
WHEE-HNN-HNN-HNN!
HUNH! I'M NOT STEWING IN THIS FOUL WATER JUST TO GET PIN STUCK!
DUCK, FLAM!
:GASP: PEACE HOW-UNDS! THEY'RE COMING!
YOWW!!
SPOOT!
SPLISH!
FASH!
GRRROWWWLL
SNAAARLLL
QUICKLY AROREE FLOATS UP TO THE GUARD TOWER.
PETALWING! TICKLETOE! TITTERSWEET! STOP THE HOW-UNDS!
WE DO! WE DO!
:ULP: D-DEMONESS! FLYING MONSTER! AWAY! AWAY!
BEHIND HIM... THAT DEVICE! I SAW A SIMILAR THING LONG AGO, IN THE BOWELS OF BLUE MOUNTAIN...

...CREATED BY TWO-EDGE TO MIMIC THE MAGIC OF ROCK-SHAPERS!

SHIIINNG!

SHIIINNG!

CAREFUL, AROREE!

< I SAID STAY BACK! >

KA-CHING!

THE USUALLY MELANCHOLY GLIDER NOW SAILS INTO COMBAT --

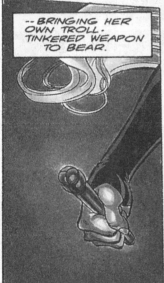

--BRINGING HER OWN TROLL-TINKERED WEAPON TO BEAR.

SNIK!

AAAAHH!

< I NO HURT TALL ONE! >

KLAK!

< NOOO! KEEP AWAY!! >

UNNOTICED, THE FALLING TORCH IGNITES THE BASE OF THE WOODEN DRAWBRIDGE!

SHH!

THAPP!

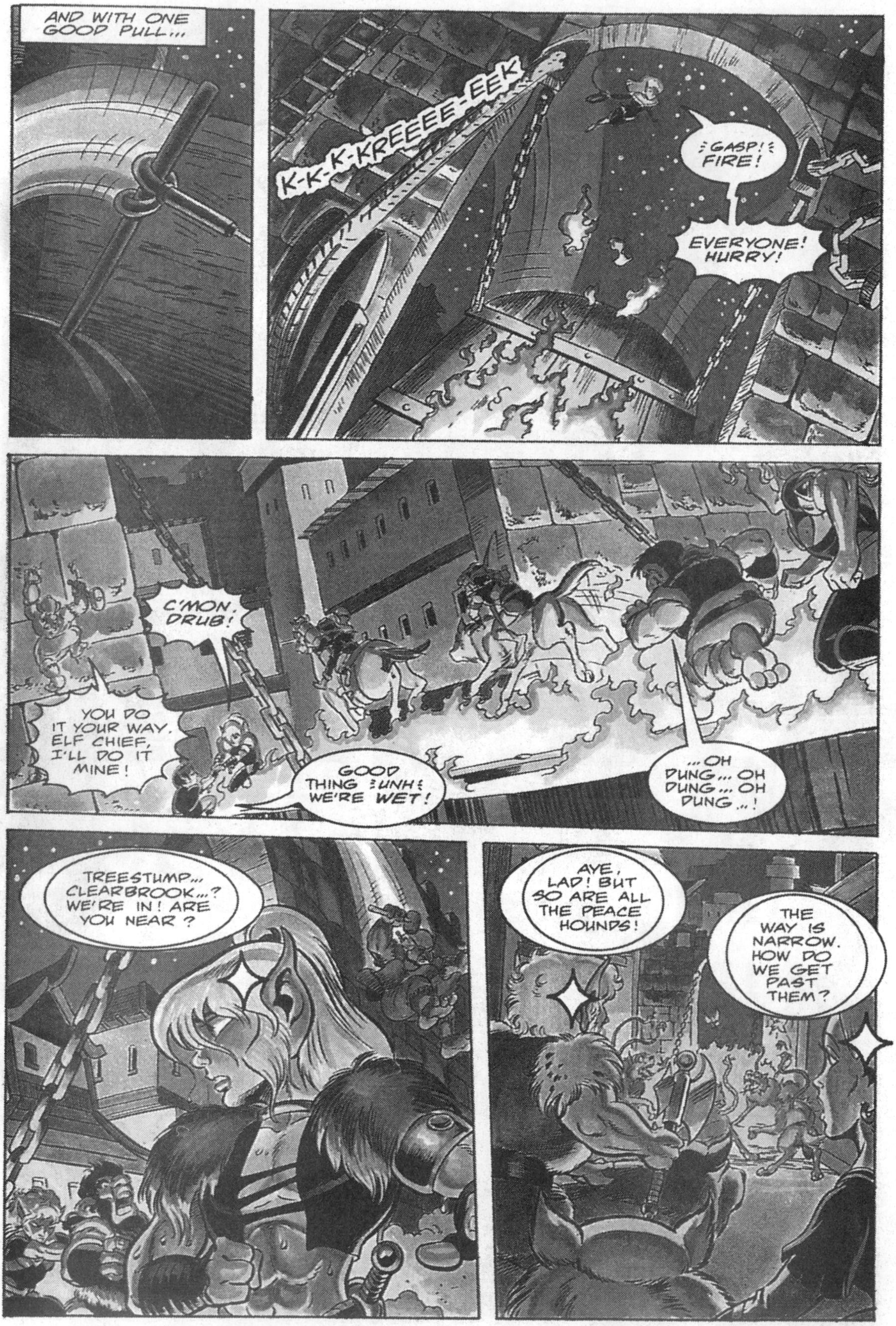
AND WITH ONE GOOD PULL...
K-K-K-KREEEEE-EEK
GASP! FIRE!
EVERYONE! HURRY!
C'MON, DRUB!
YOU DO IT YOUR WAY, ELF CHIEF, I'LL DO IT MINE!
GOOD THING UNH WE'RE WET!
...OH DUNG... OH DUNG... OH DUNG...!
TREESTUMP... CLEARBROOK...? WE'RE IN! ARE YOU NEAR?
AYE, LAD! BUT SO ARE ALL THE PEACE HOUNDS!
THE WAY IS NARROW. HOW DO WE GET PAST THEM?

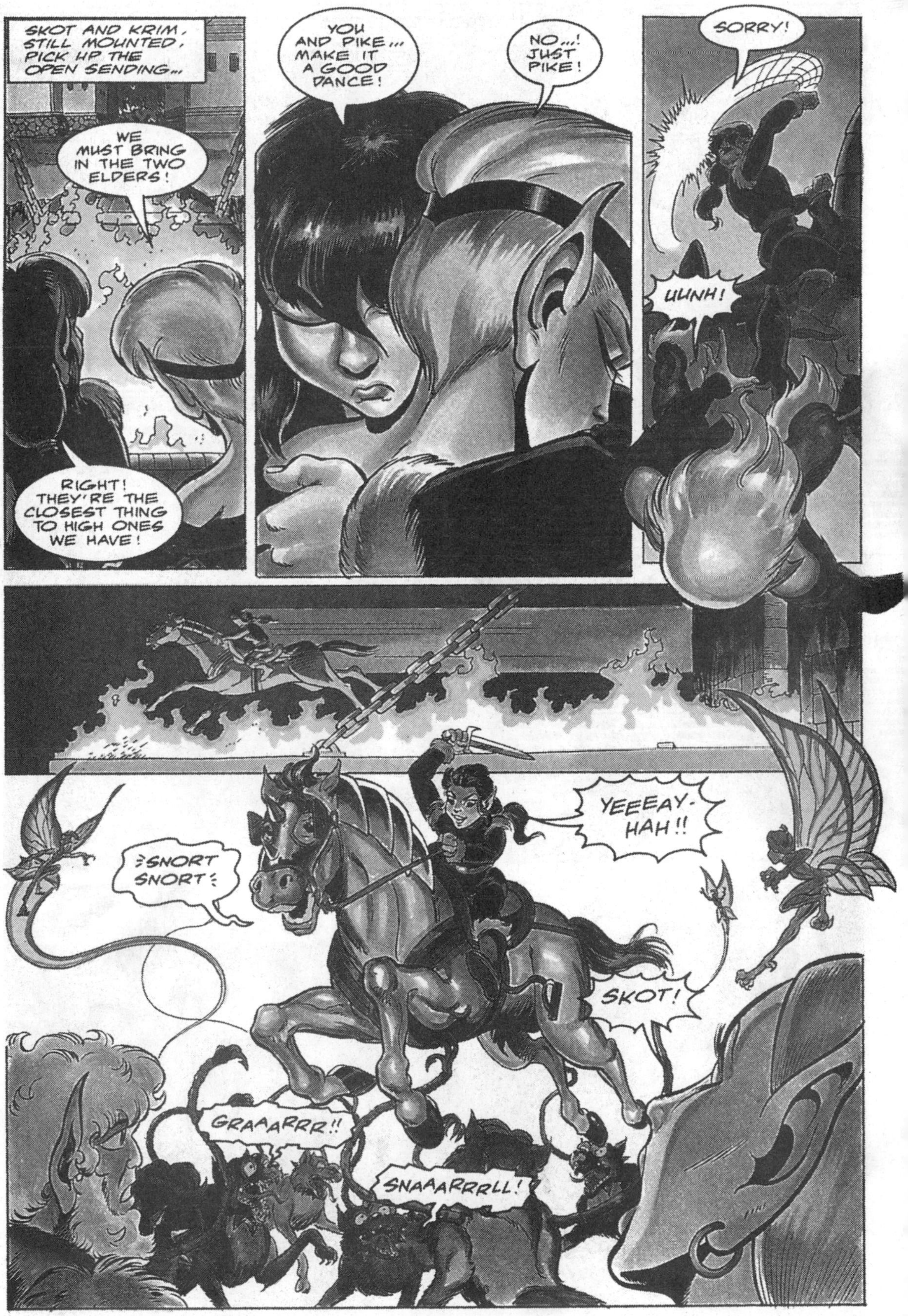
SKOT AND KRIM, STILL MOUNTED, PICK UP THE OPEN SENDING...
WE MUST BRING IN THE TWO ELDERS!
RIGHT! THEY'RE THE CLOSEST THING TO HIGH ONES WE HAVE!
YOU AND PIKE... MAKE IT A GOOD DANCE!
NO...! JUST PIKE!
SORRY!
UUNH!
YEEEAY-HAH!!
SNORT SNORT
SKOT!
GRAAARRR!!
SNAAARRRLL!

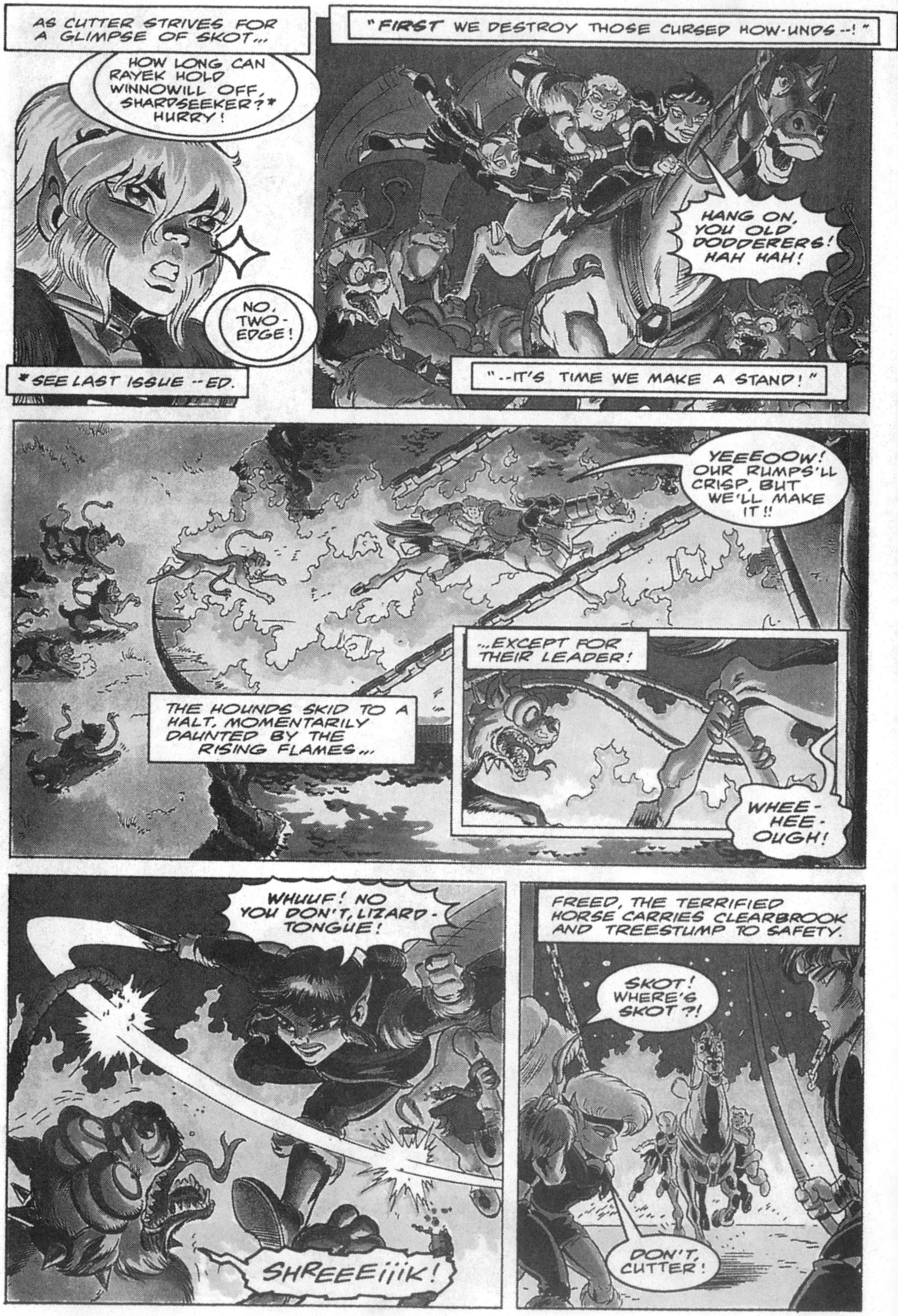

AS CUTTER STRIVES FOR A GLIMPSE OF SKOT...
HOW LONG CAN RAYEK HOLD WINNOWILL OFF, SHARDSEEKER?* HURRY!
NO, TWO-EDGE!
* SEE LAST ISSUE --ED.
"FIRST WE DESTROY THOSE CURSED HOW-UNDS--!"
HANG ON, YOU OLD DODDERERS! HAH HAH!
"--IT'S TIME WE MAKE A STAND!"
YEEEOOW! OUR RUMPS'LL CRISP, BUT WE'LL MAKE IT!!
THE HOUNDS SKID TO A HALT, MOMENTARILY DAUNTED BY THE RISING FLAMES...
...EXCEPT FOR THEIR LEADER!
WHEE-HEE-OUGH!
WHUUF! NO YOU DON'T, LIZARD-TONGUE!
SHREEEiiiK!
FREED, THE TERRIFIED HORSE CARRIES CLEARBROOK AND TREESTUMP TO SAFETY.
SKOT! WHERE'S SKOT?!
DON'T, CUTTER!

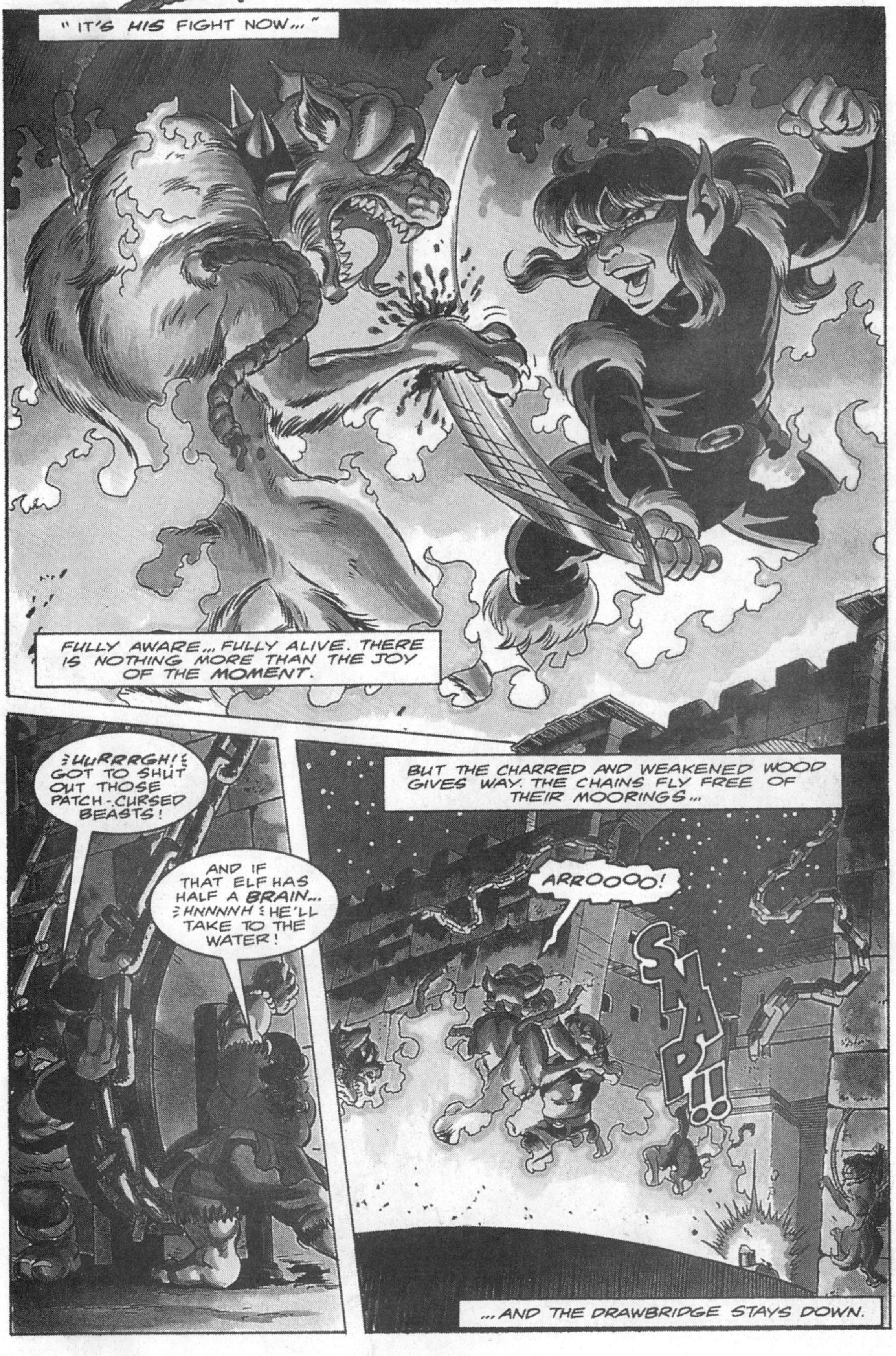
"IT'S HIS FIGHT NOW..."
FULLY AWARE... FULLY ALIVE. THERE IS NOTHING MORE THAN THE JOY OF THE MOMENT.
UURRRGH! GOT TO SHUT OUT THOSE PATCH-CURSED BEASTS!
AND IF THAT ELF HAS HALF A BRAIN... HNNNNH! HE'LL TAKE TO THE WATER!
BUT THE CHARRED AND WEAKENED WOOD GIVES WAY. THE CHAINS FLY FREE OF THEIR MOORINGS...
ARROOOO!
SNAP!!
...AND THE DRAWBRIDGE STAYS DOWN.

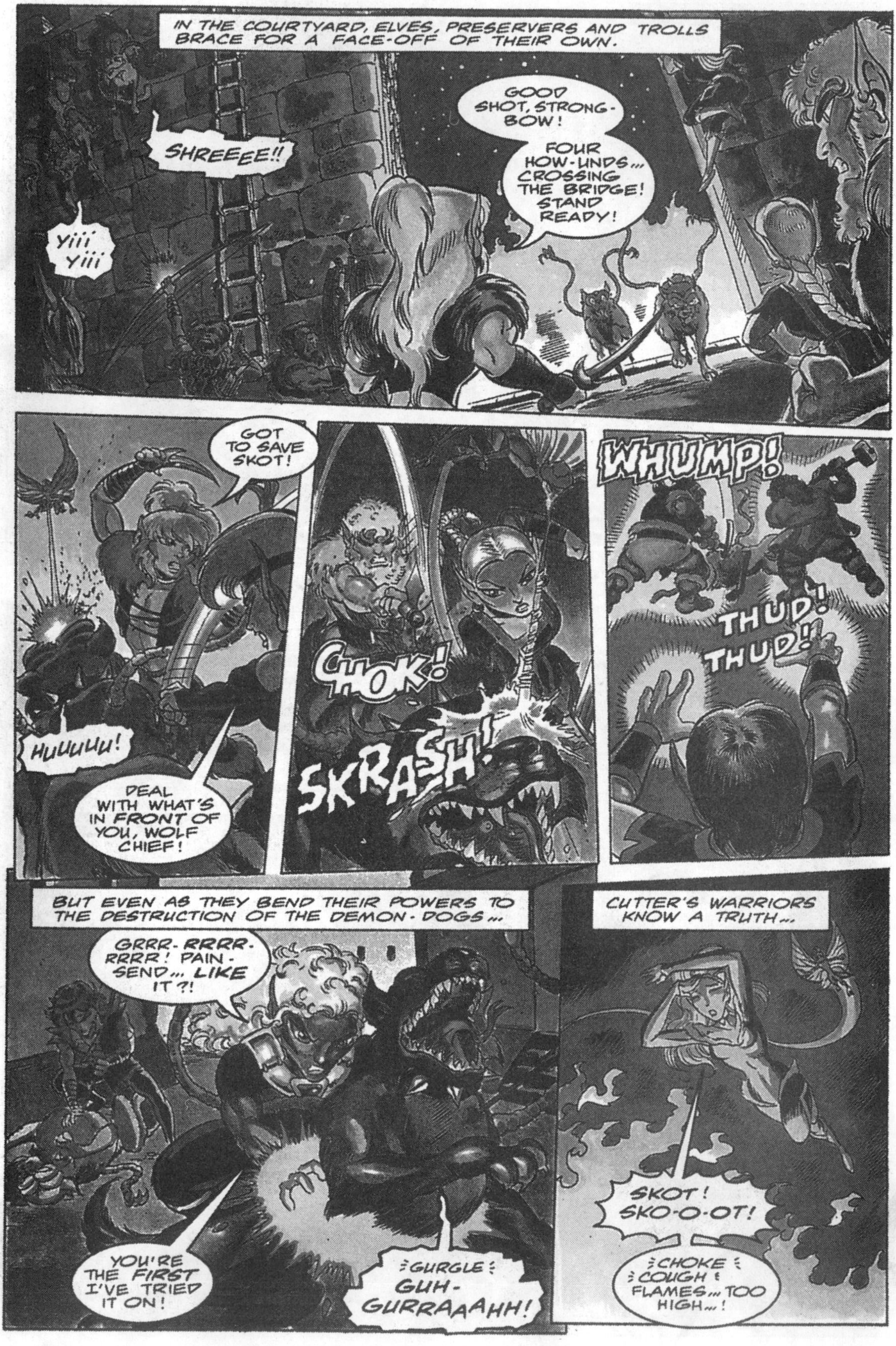
IN THE COURTYARD, ELVES, PRESERVERS AND TROLLS BRACE FOR A FACE-OFF OF THEIR OWN.
SHREEEEE!!
YIII YIII
GOOD SHOT, STRONG-BOW!
FOUR HOW-UNDS... CROSSING THE BRIDGE! STAND READY!
GOT TO SAVE SKOT!
HUUUUU!
DEAL WITH WHAT'S IN FRONT OF YOU, WOLF CHIEF!
CHOK!
SKRASH!
WHUMP!
THUD! THUD!!
BUT EVEN AS THEY BEND THEIR POWERS TO THE DESTRUCTION OF THE DEMON-DOGS...
GRRR-RRRR-RRRR! PAIN-SEND... LIKE IT?!
YOU'RE THE FIRST I'VE TRIED IT ON!
GURGLE GUH-GURRAAAHH!
CUTTER'S WARRIORS KNOW A TRUTH...
SKOT! SKO-O-OT!
CHOKE COUGH FLAMES... TOO HIGH...!

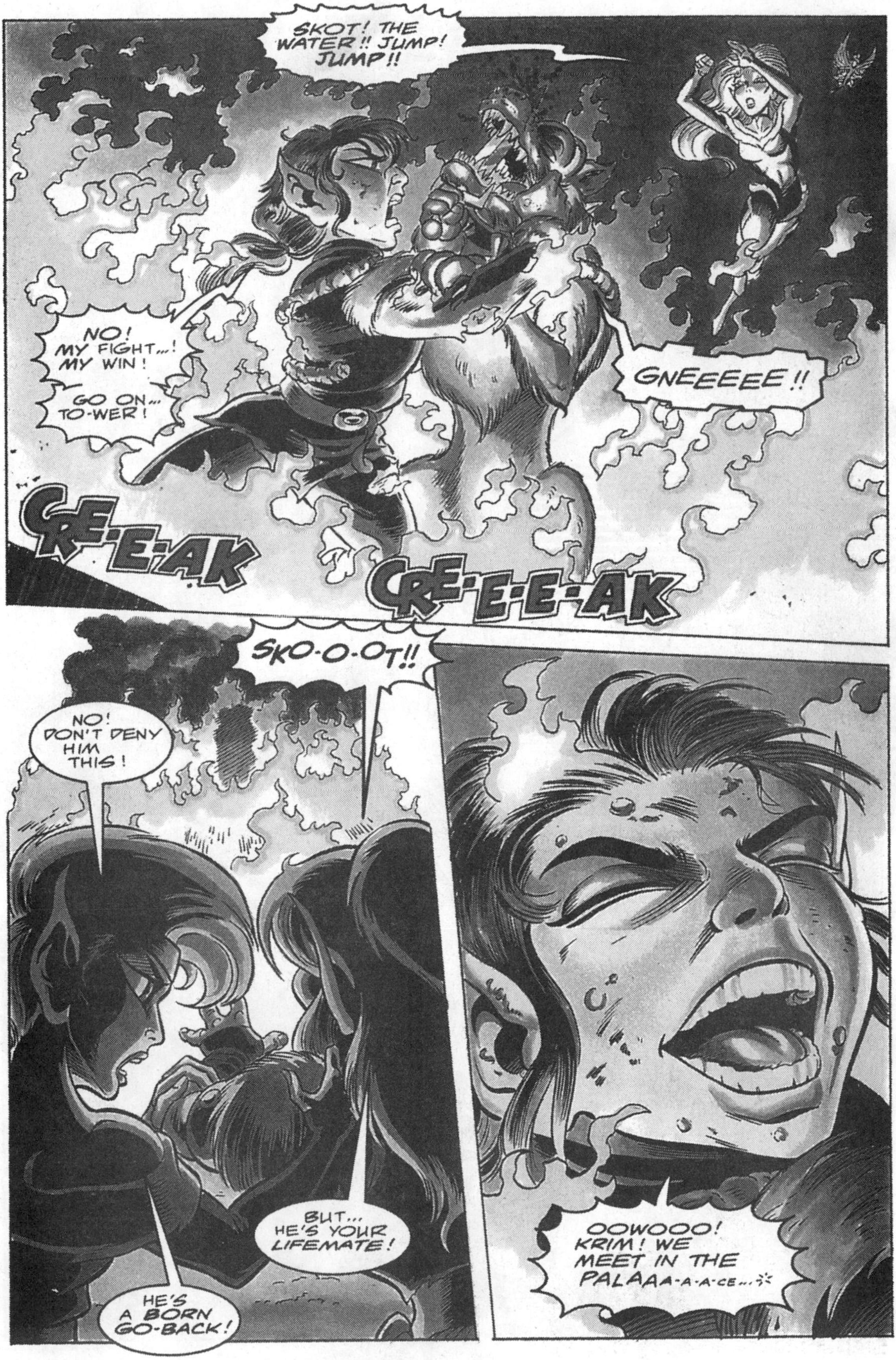
SKOT! THE WATER!! JUMP! JUMP!!
NO! MY FIGHT...! MY WIN!
GO ON... TO-WER!
GNEEEEEE!!
CRE-E-AK
CRE-E-E-AK
SKO-O-OT!!
NO! DON'T DENY HIM THIS!
BUT... HE'S YOUR LIFEMATE!
HE'S A BORN GO-BACK!
OOWOOO! KRIM! WE MEET IN THE PALAAA-A-A-CE...

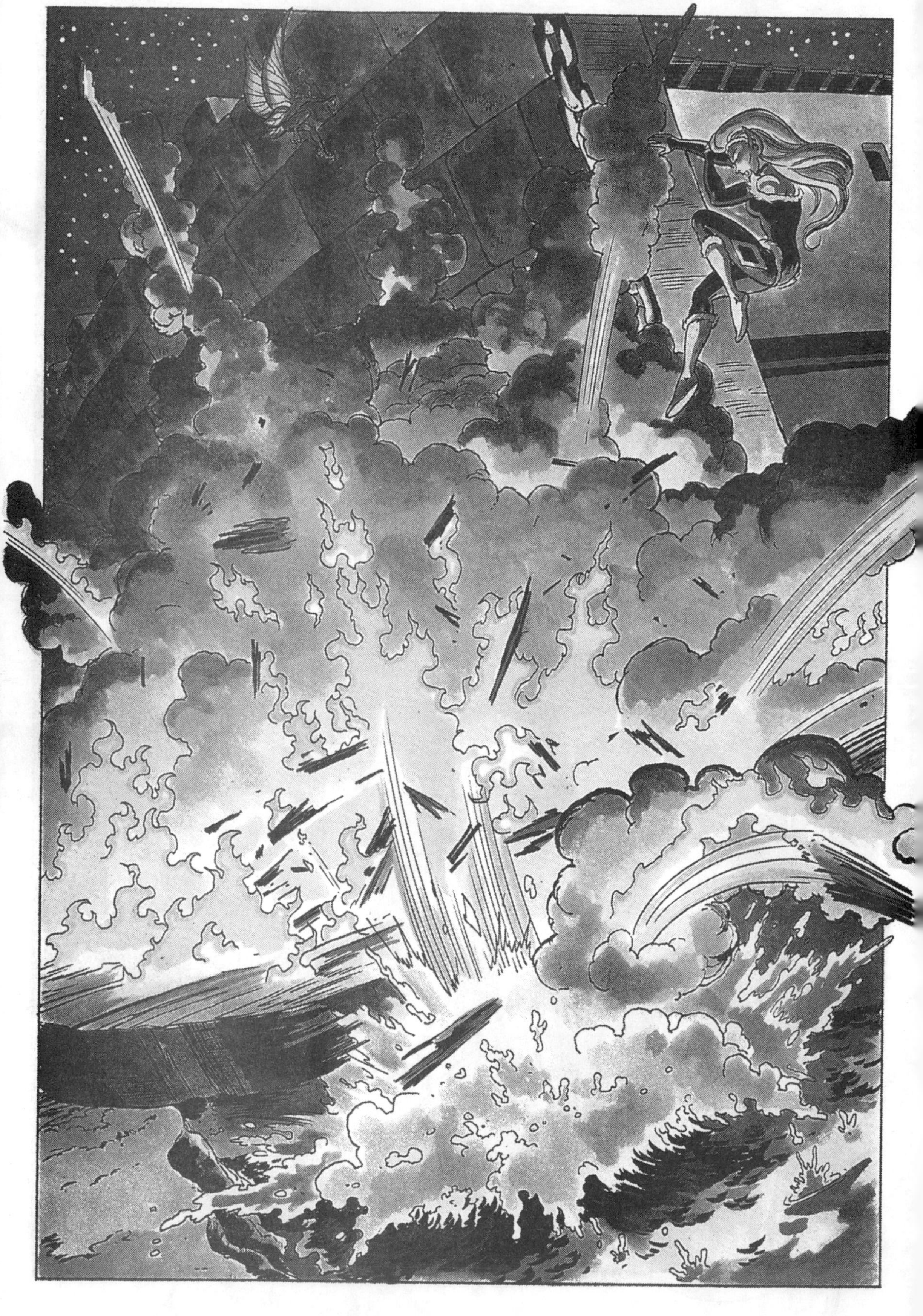

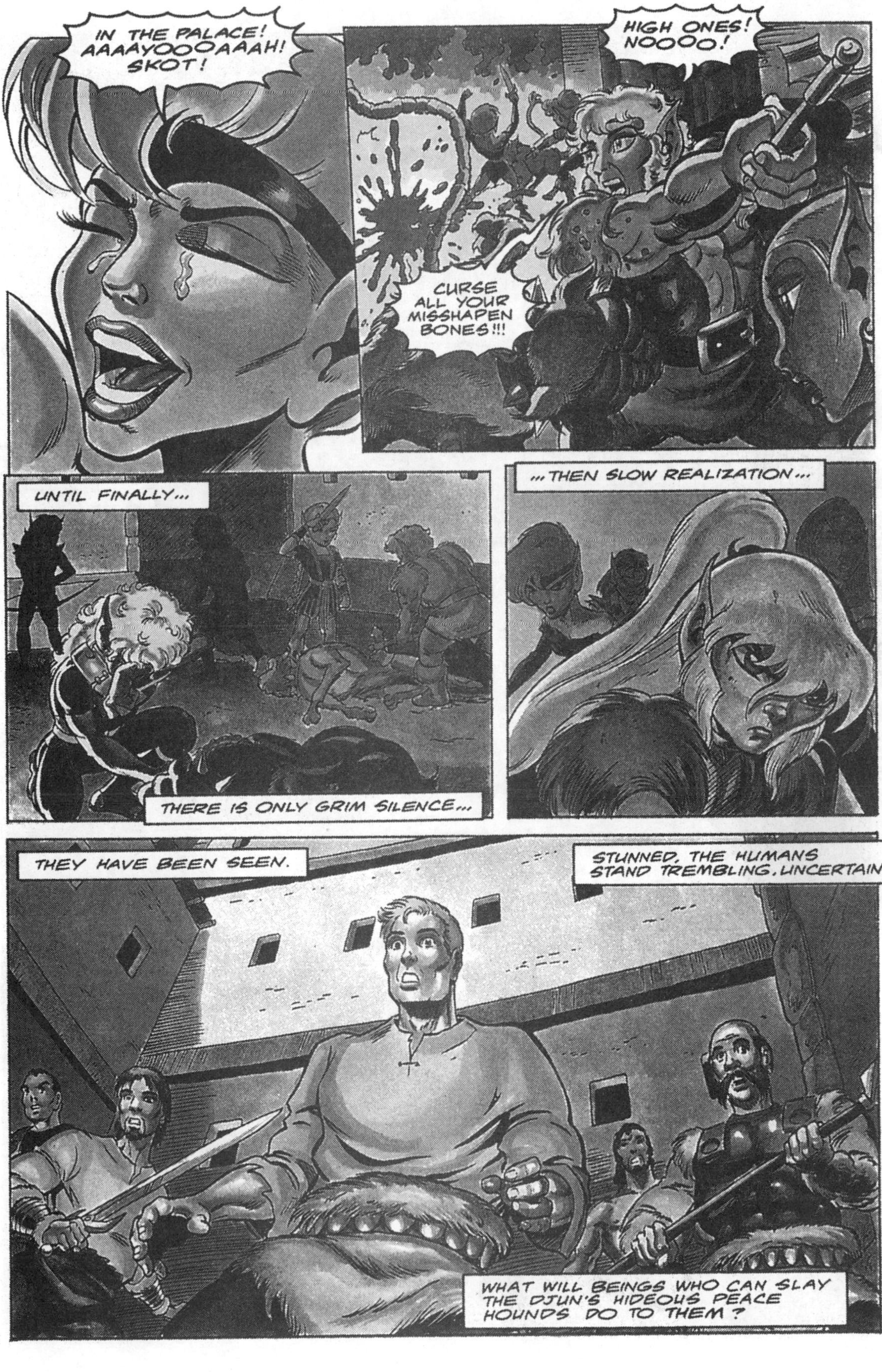
IN THE PALACE! AAAAYOOOAAAH! SKOT!
HIGH ONES! NOOOO!
CURSE ALL YOUR MISSHAPEN BONES!!!
UNTIL FINALLY...
THERE IS ONLY GRIM SILENCE...
...THEN SLOW REALIZATION...
THEY HAVE BEEN SEEN.
STUNNED, THE HUMANS STAND TREMBLING, UNCERTAIN.
WHAT WILL BEINGS WHO CAN SLAY THE DJUN'S HIDEOUS PEACE HOUNDS DO TO THEM?

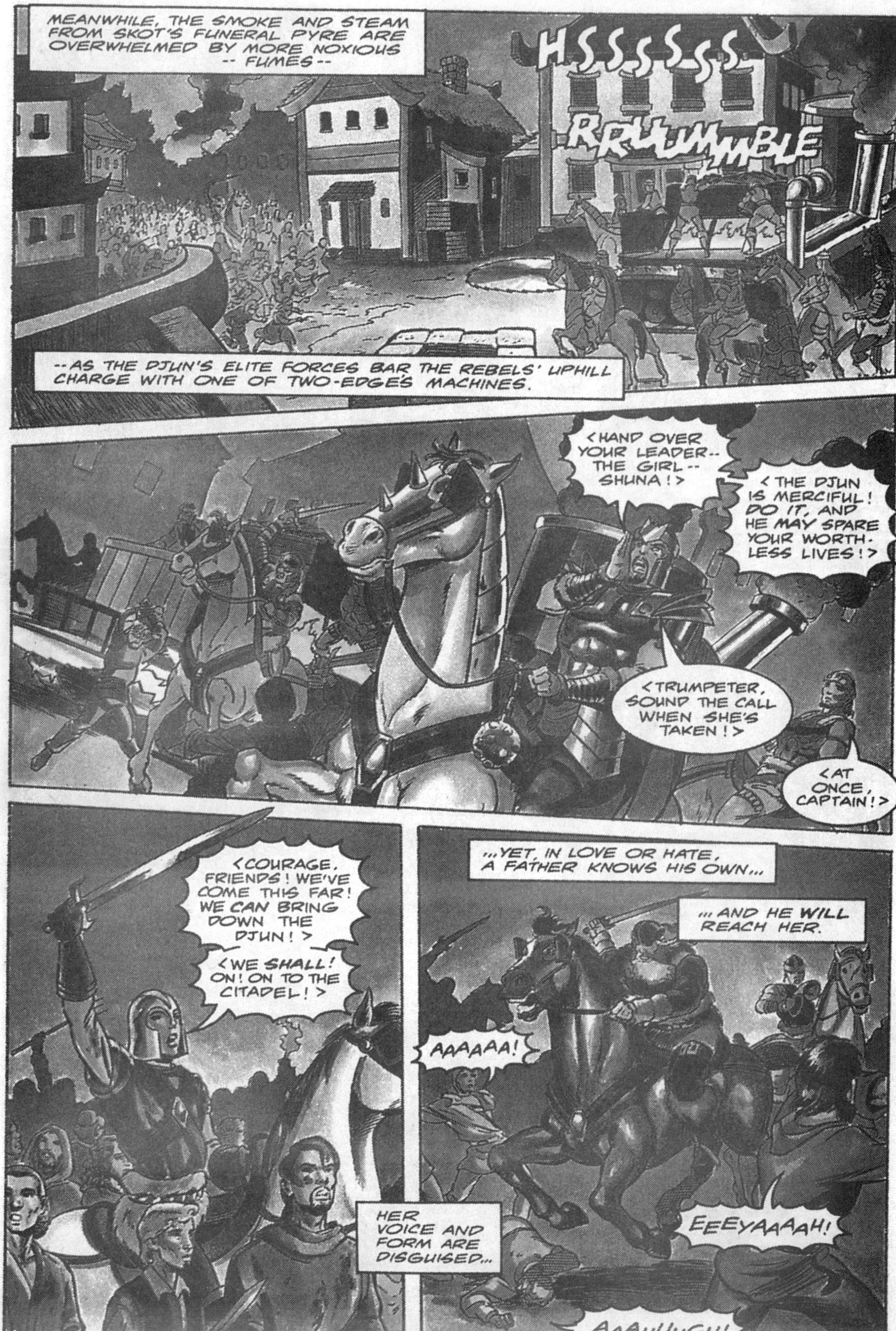
MEANWHILE, THE SMOKE AND STEAM FROM SKOT'S FUNERAL PYRE ARE OVERWHELMED BY MORE NOXIOUS -- FUMES --
HSSSSSS
RRUUMMBLE
-- AS THE DJUN'S ELITE FORCES BAR THE REBELS' UPHILL CHARGE WITH ONE OF TWO-EDGE'S MACHINES.
<HAND OVER YOUR LEADER -- THE GIRL -- SHUNA!>
<THE DJUN IS MERCIFUL! DO IT, AND HE MAY SPARE YOUR WORTHLESS LIVES!>
<TRUMPETER, SOUND THE CALL WHEN SHE'S TAKEN!>
<AT ONCE, CAPTAIN!>
<COURAGE, FRIENDS! WE'VE COME THIS FAR! WE CAN BRING DOWN THE DJUN!>
<WE SHALL! ON! ON TO THE CITADEL!>
HER VOICE AND FORM ARE DISGUISED...
...YET, IN LOVE OR HATE, A FATHER KNOWS HIS OWN...
...AND HE WILL REACH HER.
AAAAAA!
EEEYAAAAH!
AAAUUUGH!

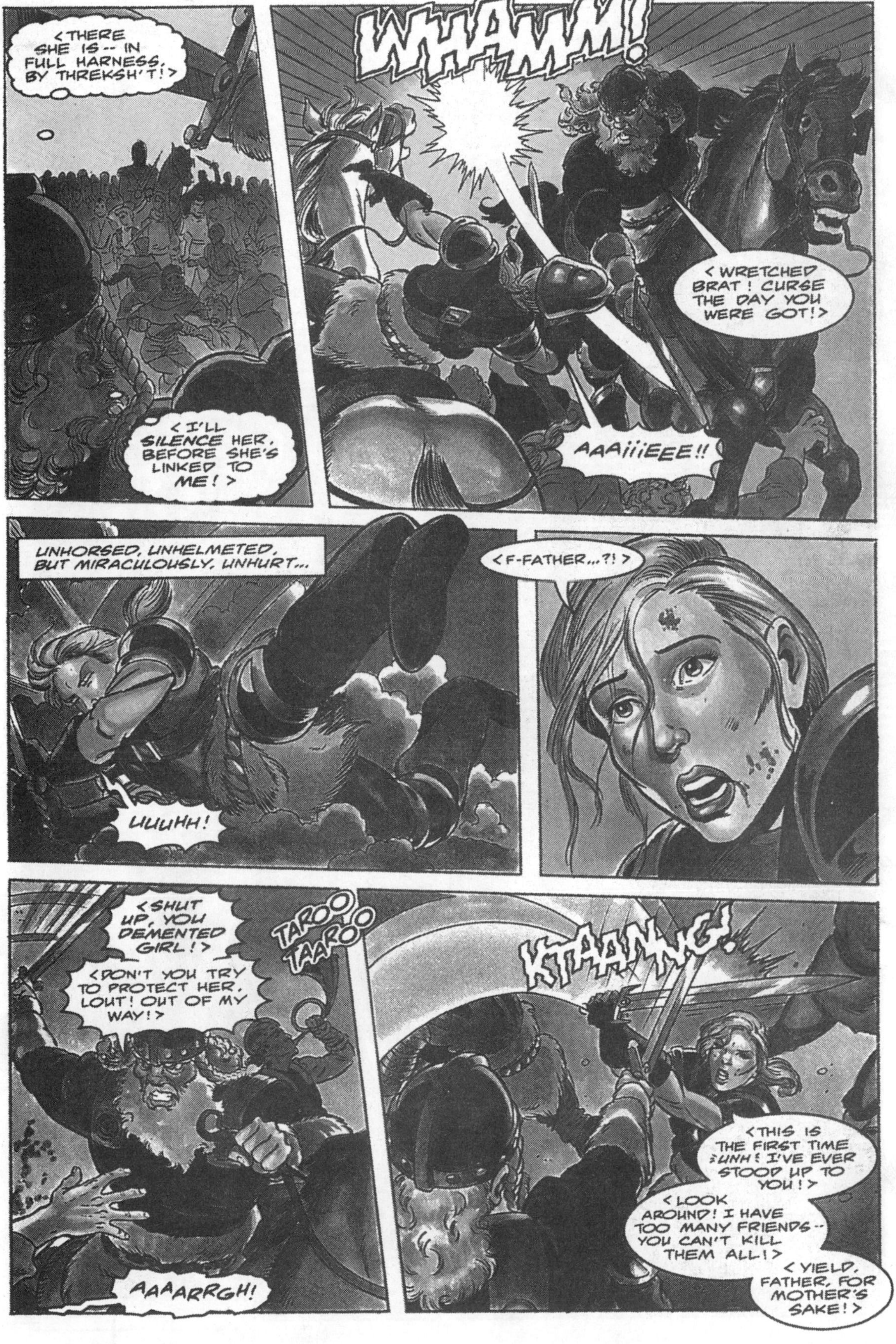
<THERE SHE IS -- IN FULL HARNESS, BY THREKSH'T!>
WHAMM!
<WRETCHED BRAT! CURSE THE DAY YOU WERE GOT!>
<I'LL SILENCE HER, BEFORE SHE'S LINKED TO ME!>
AAAiiiEEE!!
UNHORSED, UNHELMETED, BUT MIRACULOUSLY, UNHURT...
UUUHH!
<F-FATHER...?!>
<SHUT UP, YOU DEMENTED GIRL!>
<DON'T YOU TRY TO PROTECT HER, LOUT! OUT OF MY WAY!>
TAROO TAAROO
AAAARRGH!
KTAANNG!
<THIS IS THE FIRST TIME :UNH: I'VE EVER STOOD UP TO YOU!>
<LOOK AROUND! I HAVE TOO MANY FRIENDS -- YOU CAN'T KILL THEM ALL!>
<YIELD, FATHER, FOR MOTHER'S SAKE!>

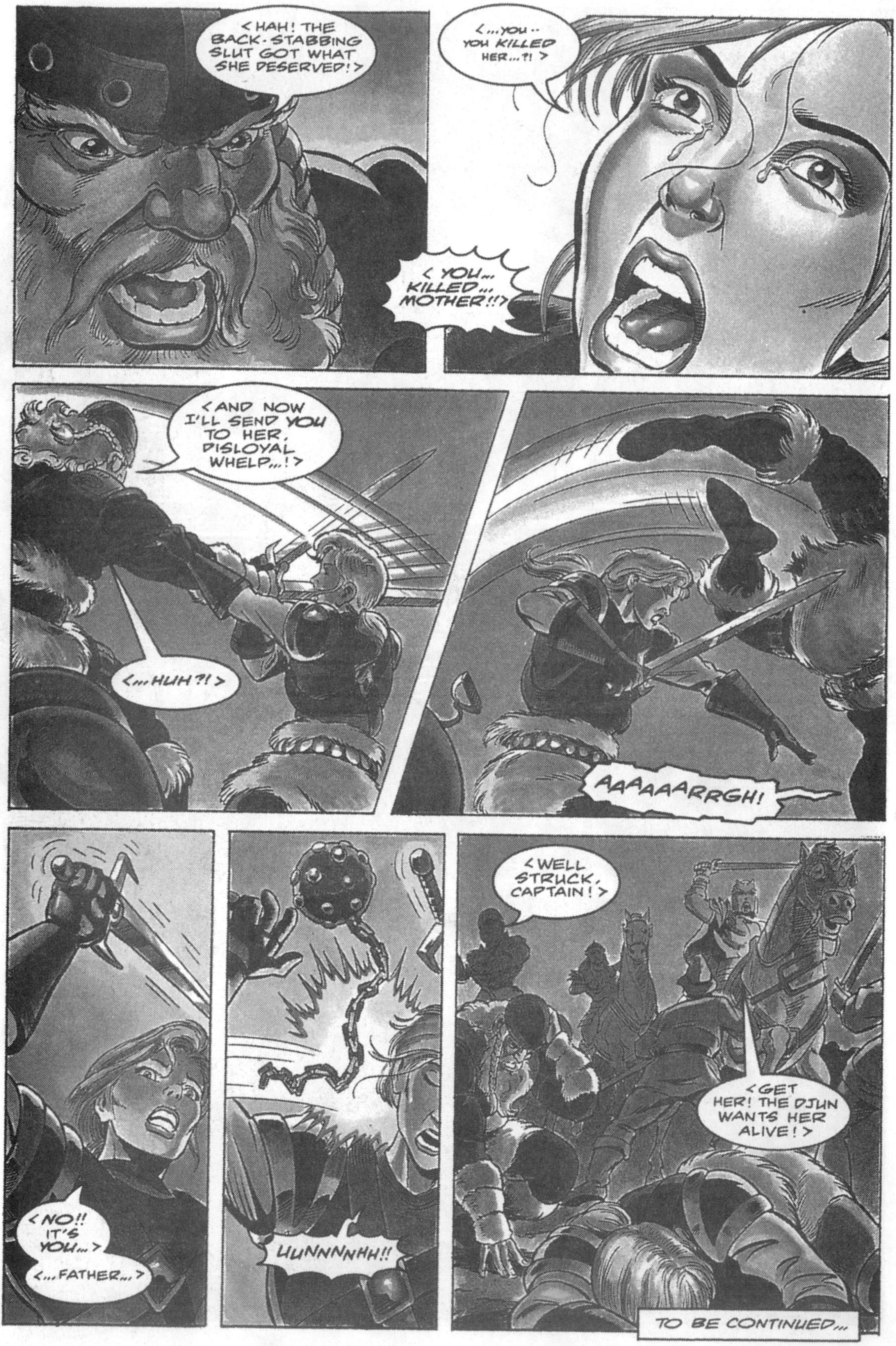
<HAH! THE BACK-STABBING SLUT GOT WHAT SHE DESERVED!>
<...YOU.. YOU KILLED HER...?!>
<YOU... KILLED... MOTHER!!>
<AND NOW I'LL SEND YOU TO HER, DISLOYAL WHELP...!>
<...HUH?!>
AAAAAARRGH!
<NO!! IT'S YOU...>
<...FATHER...>
UUNNNNHH!!
<WELL STRUCK, CAPTAIN!>
<GET HER! THE DJUN WANTS HER ALIVE!>
TO BE CONTINUED...

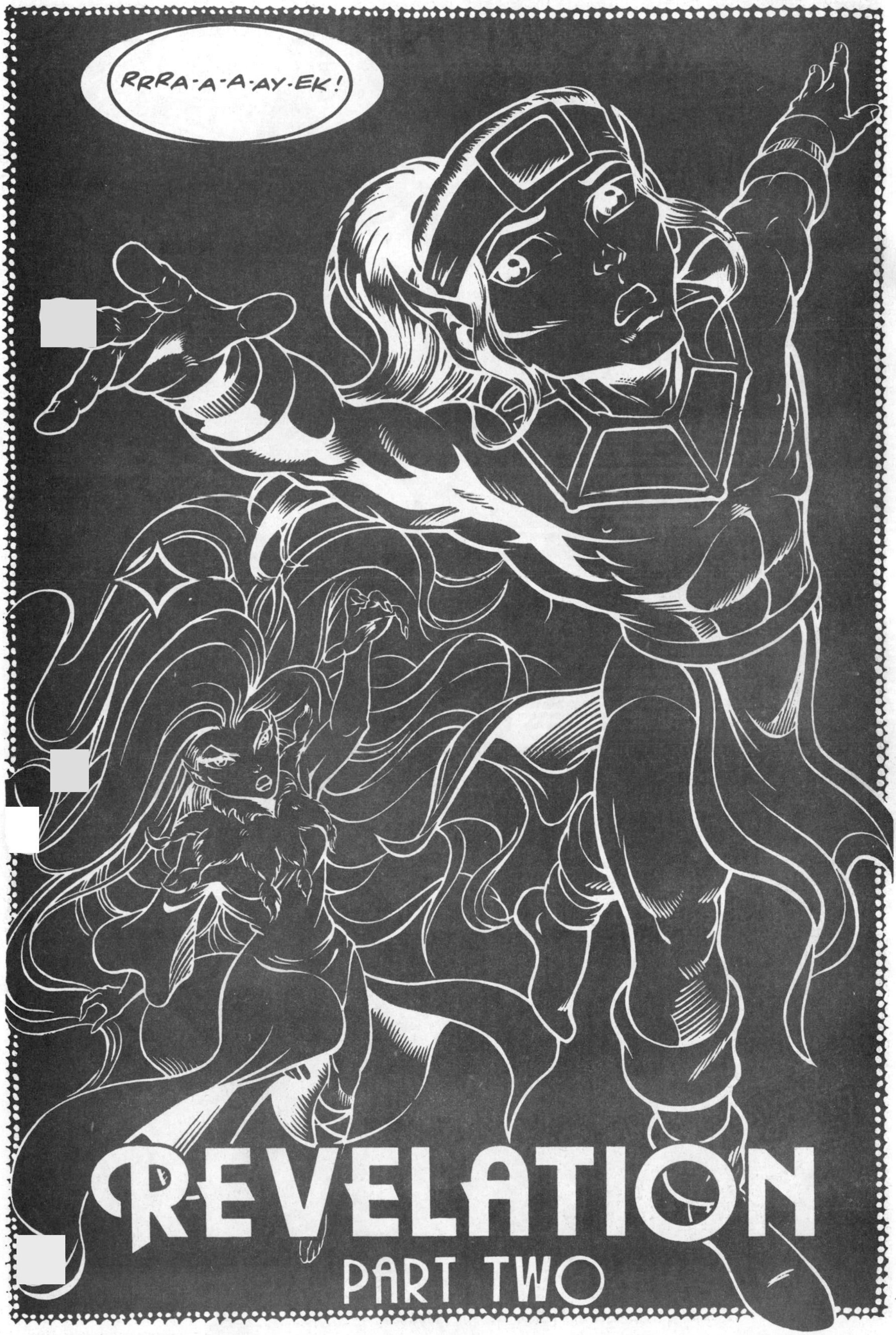
RRRA-A-A-AY-EK!
REVELATION
PART TWO

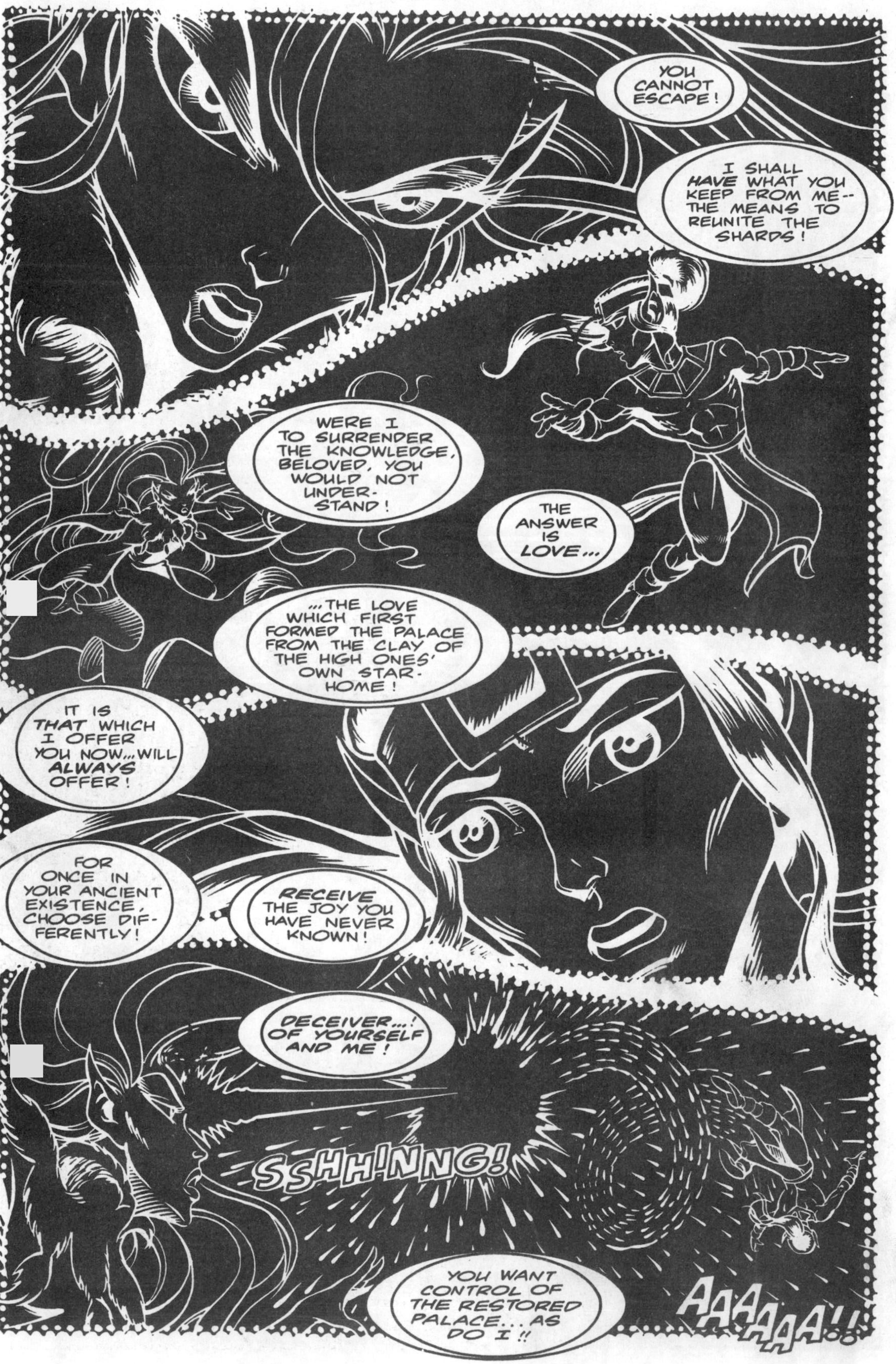
YOU CANNOT ESCAPE!
I SHALL HAVE WHAT YOU KEEP FROM ME-- THE MEANS TO REUNITE THE SHARDS!
WERE I TO SURRENDER THE KNOWLEDGE, BELOVED, YOU WOULD NOT UNDER-STAND!
THE ANSWER IS LOVE...
...THE LOVE WHICH FIRST FORMED THE PALACE FROM THE CLAY OF THE HIGH ONES' OWN STAR-HOME!
IT IS THAT WHICH I OFFER YOU NOW...WILL ALWAYS OFFER!
FOR ONCE IN YOUR ANCIENT EXISTENCE, CHOOSE DIF-FERENTLY!
RECEIVE THE JOY YOU HAVE NEVER KNOWN!
DECEIVER...! OF YOURSELF AND ME!
SSHHINNG!
YOU WANT CONTROL OF THE RESTORED PALACE...AS DO I!!
AAAAAAA!!

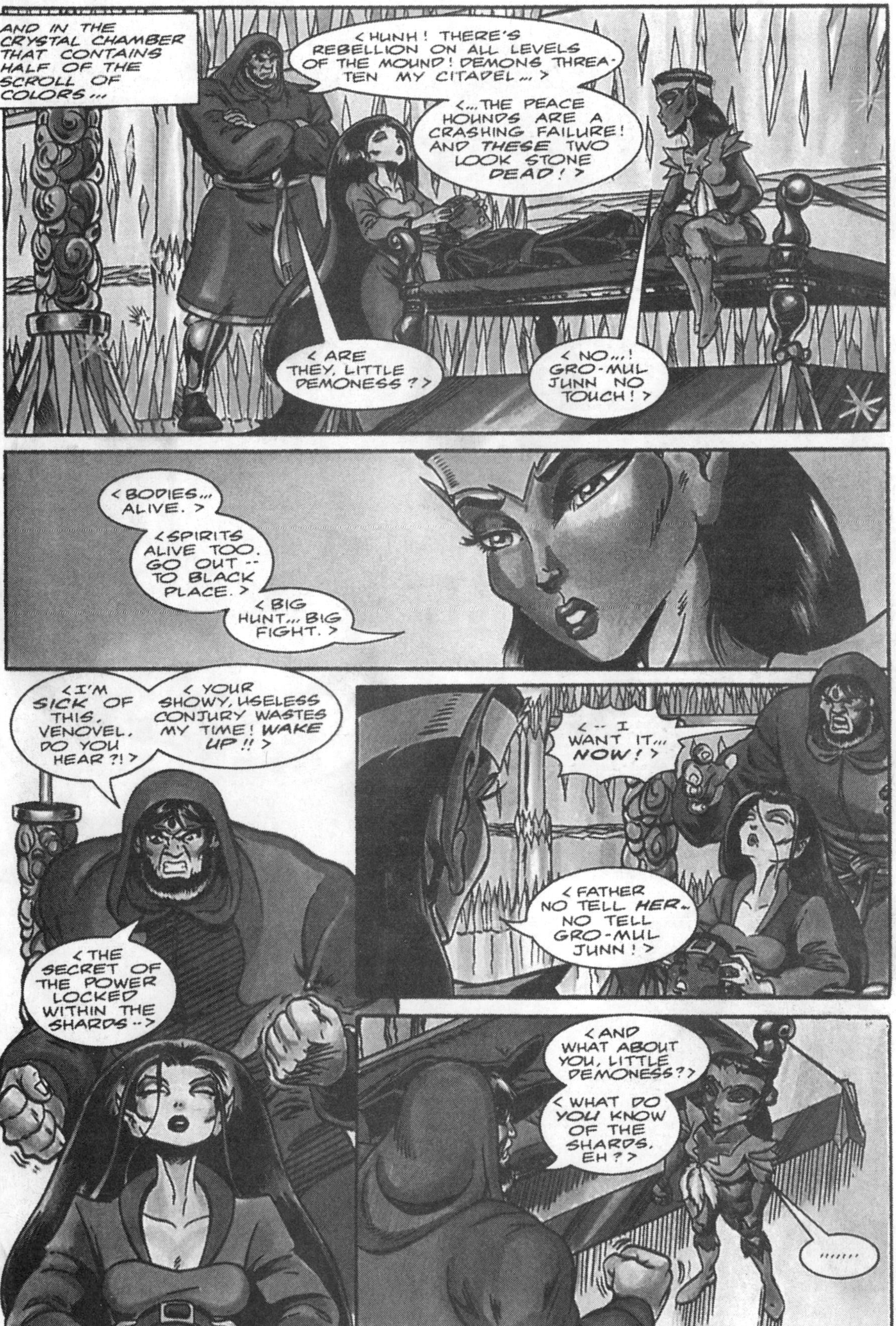
AND IN THE CRYSTAL CHAMBER THAT CONTAINS HALF OF THE SCROLL OF COLORS...
< HUNH! THERE'S REBELLION ON ALL LEVELS OF THE MOUND! DEMONS THREATEN MY CITADEL... >
< ...THE PEACE HOUNDS ARE A CRASHING FAILURE! AND THESE TWO LOOK STONE DEAD! >
< ARE THEY, LITTLE DEMONESS? >
< NO...! GRO-MUL JUNN NO TOUCH! >
< BODIES... ALIVE. >
< SPIRITS ALIVE TOO. GO OUT -- TO BLACK PLACE. >
< BIG HUNT... BIG FIGHT. >
< I'M SICK OF THIS, VENOVEL. DO YOU HEAR?! >
< YOUR SHOWY, USELESS CONJURY WASTES MY TIME! WAKE UP!! >
< THE SECRET OF THE POWER LOCKED WITHIN THE SHARDS -- >
< -- I WANT IT... NOW! >
< FATHER NO TELL HER... NO TELL GRO-MUL JUNN! >
< AND WHAT ABOUT YOU, LITTLE DEMONESS? >
< WHAT DO YOU KNOW OF THE SHARDS, EH? >
......

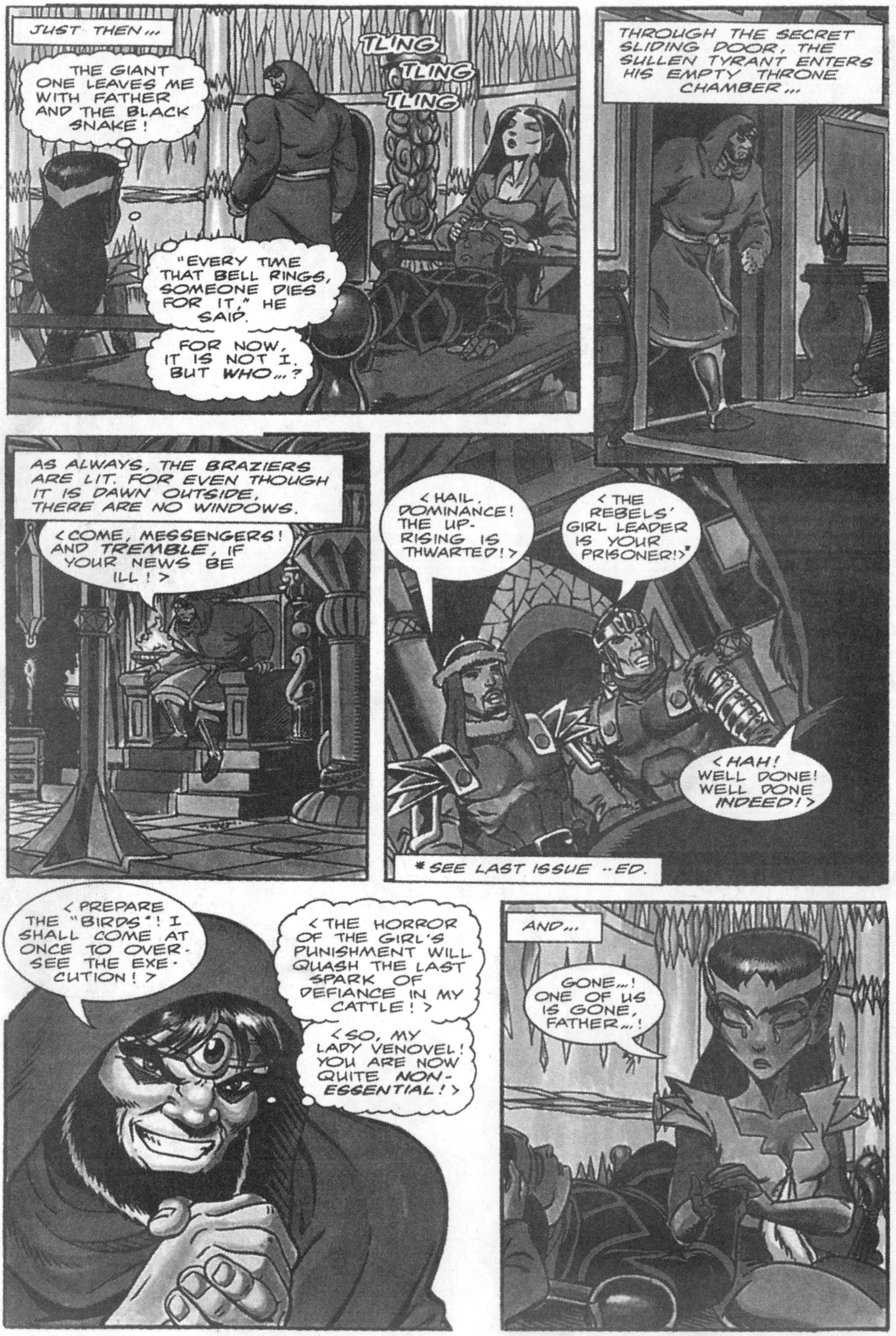
JUST THEN...
THE GIANT ONE LEAVES ME WITH FATHER AND THE BLACK SNAKE!
TLING
TLING
TLING
"EVERY TIME THAT BELL RINGS, SOMEONE DIES FOR IT," HE SAID.
FOR NOW, IT IS NOT I. BUT WHO...?
THROUGH THE SECRET SLIDING DOOR, THE SULLEN TYRANT ENTERS HIS EMPTY THRONE CHAMBER...
AS ALWAYS, THE BRAZIERS ARE LIT. FOR EVEN THOUGH IT IS DAWN OUTSIDE, THERE ARE NO WINDOWS.
<COME, MESSENGERS! AND TREMBLE, IF YOUR NEWS BE ILL!>
<HAIL, DOMINANCE! THE UP-RISING IS THWARTED!>
<THE REBELS' GIRL LEADER IS YOUR PRISONER!>*
<HAH! WELL DONE! WELL DONE INDEED!>
* SEE LAST ISSUE --ED.
<PREPARE THE "BIRDS"! I SHALL COME AT ONCE TO OVER-SEE THE EXE-CUTION!>
<THE HORROR OF THE GIRL'S PUNISHMENT WILL QUASH THE LAST SPARK OF DEFIANCE IN MY CATTLE!>
<SO, MY LADY VENOVEL! YOU ARE NOW QUITE NON-ESSENTIAL!>
AND...
GONE...! ONE OF US IS GONE, FATHER...!

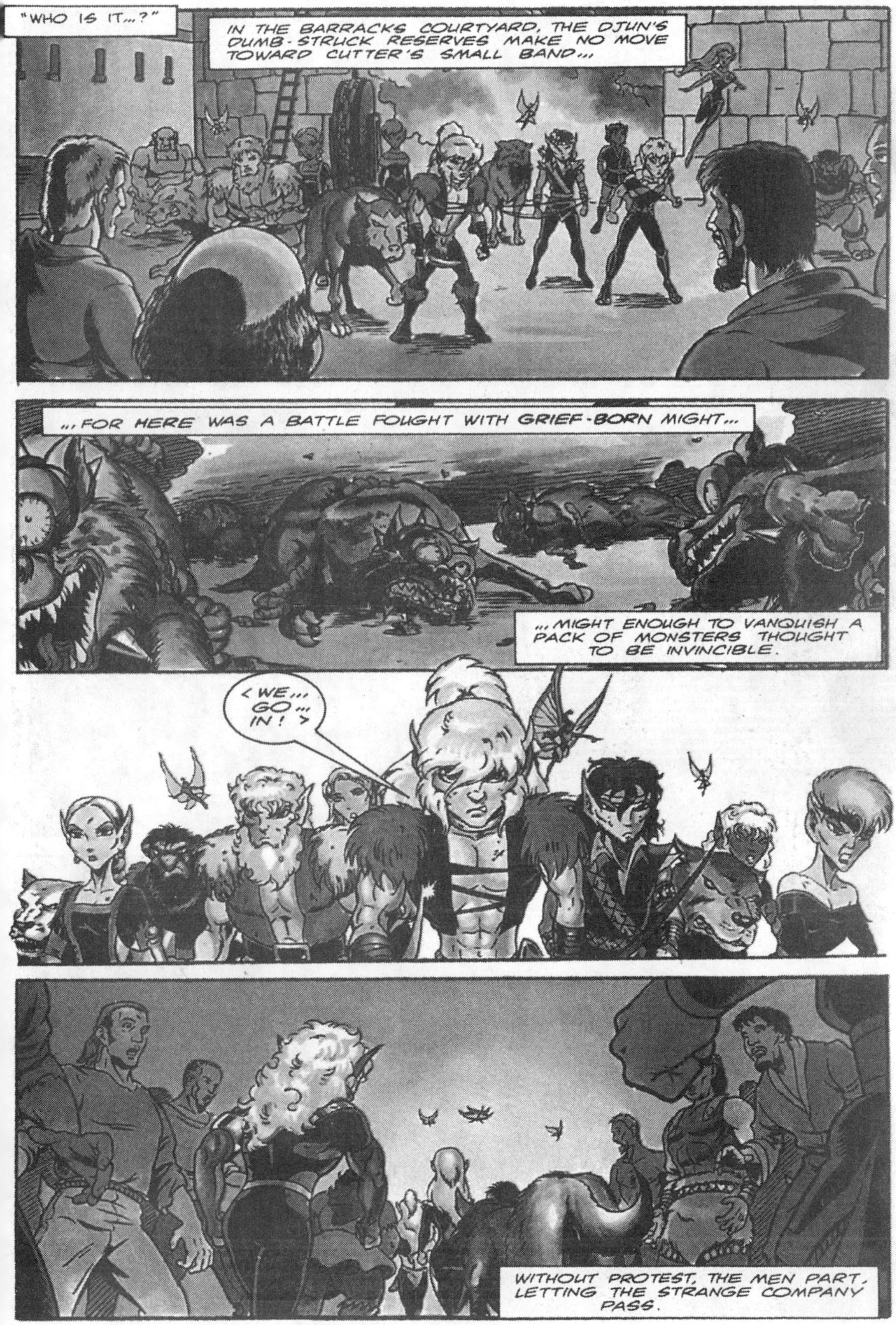
"WHO IS IT...?"
IN THE BARRACKS COURTYARD, THE DJUN'S DUMB-STRUCK RESERVES MAKE NO MOVE TOWARD CUTTER'S SMALL BAND...
...FOR HERE WAS A BATTLE FOUGHT WITH GRIEF-BORN MIGHT...
...MIGHT ENOUGH TO VANQUISH A PACK OF MONSTERS THOUGHT TO BE INVINCIBLE.
<WE... GO... IN!>
WITHOUT PROTEST, THE MEN PART, LETTING THE STRANGE COMPANY PASS.

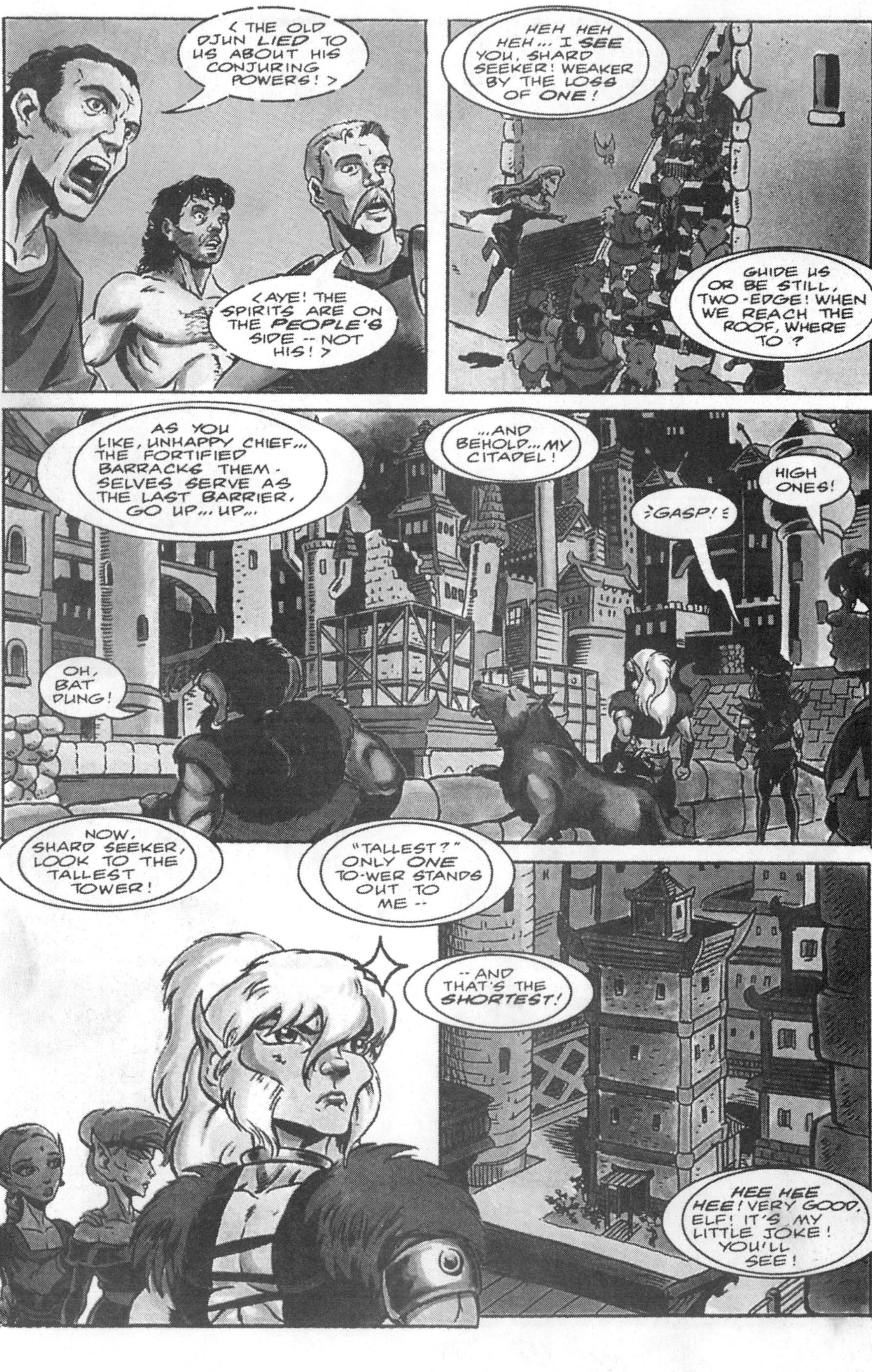
< THE OLD DJUN LIED TO US ABOUT HIS CONJURING POWERS! >
< AYE! THE SPIRITS ARE ON THE PEOPLE'S SIDE -- NOT HIS! >
HEH HEH HEH... I SEE YOU, SHARD SEEKER! WEAKER BY THE LOSS OF ONE!
GUIDE US OR BE STILL, TWO-EDGE! WHEN WE REACH THE ROOF, WHERE TO?
AS YOU LIKE, UNHAPPY CHIEF... THE FORTIFIED BARRACKS THEMSELVES SERVE AS THE LAST BARRIER. GO UP... UP...
...AND BEHOLD... MY CITADEL!
GASP!
HIGH ONES!
OH, BAT DUNG!
NOW, SHARD SEEKER, LOOK TO THE TALLEST TOWER!
"TALLEST?" ONLY ONE TO-WER STANDS OUT TO ME --
-- AND THAT'S THE SHORTEST!
HEE HEE HEE! VERY GOOD, ELF! IT'S MY LITTLE JOKE! YOU'LL SEE!

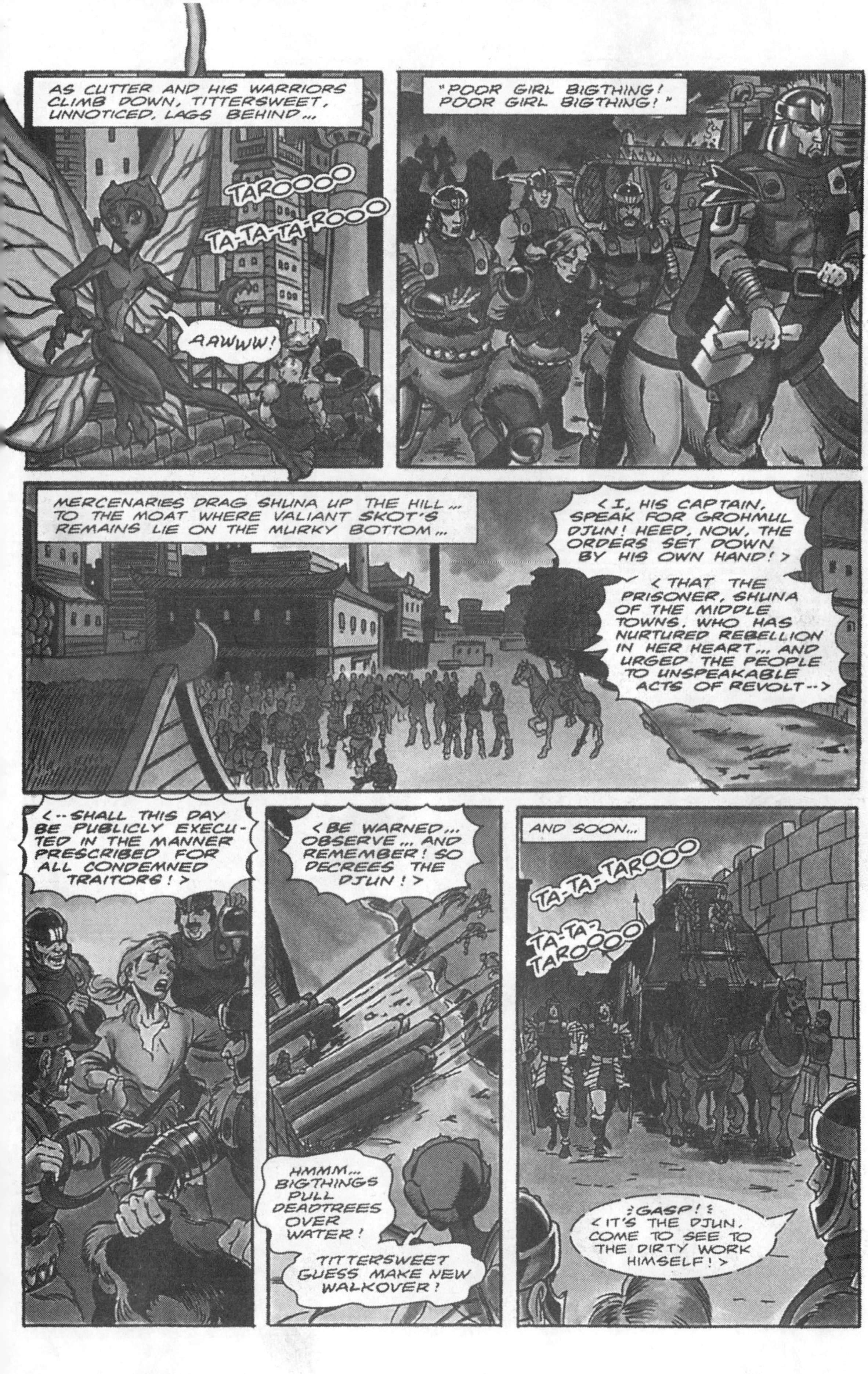

AS CUTTER AND HIS WARRIORS CLIMB DOWN, TITTERSWEET, UNNOTICED, LAGS BEHIND...
TAROOOOO
TA-TA-TA-ROOOO
AAWWW!
"POOR GIRL BIGTHING! POOR GIRL BIGTHING!"
MERCENARIES DRAG SHUNA UP THE HILL... TO THE MOAT WHERE VALIANT SKOT'S REMAINS LIE ON THE MURKY BOTTOM...
< I, HIS CAPTAIN, SPEAK FOR GROHMUL DJUN! HEED, NOW, THE ORDERS SET DOWN BY HIS OWN HAND! >
< THAT THE PRISONER, SHUNA OF THE MIDDLE TOWNS, WHO HAS NURTURED REBELLION IN HER HEART... AND URGED THE PEOPLE TO UNSPEAKABLE ACTS OF REVOLT-- >
< --SHALL THIS DAY BE PUBLICLY EXECUTED IN THE MANNER PRESCRIBED FOR ALL CONDEMNED TRAITORS! >
< BE WARNED... OBSERVE... AND REMEMBER! SO DECREES THE DJUN! >
HMMM... BIGTHINGS PULL DEADTREES OVER WATER!
TITTERSWEET GUESS MAKE NEW WALKOVER!
AND SOON...
TA-TA-TAROOO
TA-TA-TAROOOO
:GASP!:
< IT'S THE DJUN, COME TO SEE TO THE DIRTY WORK HIMSELF! >

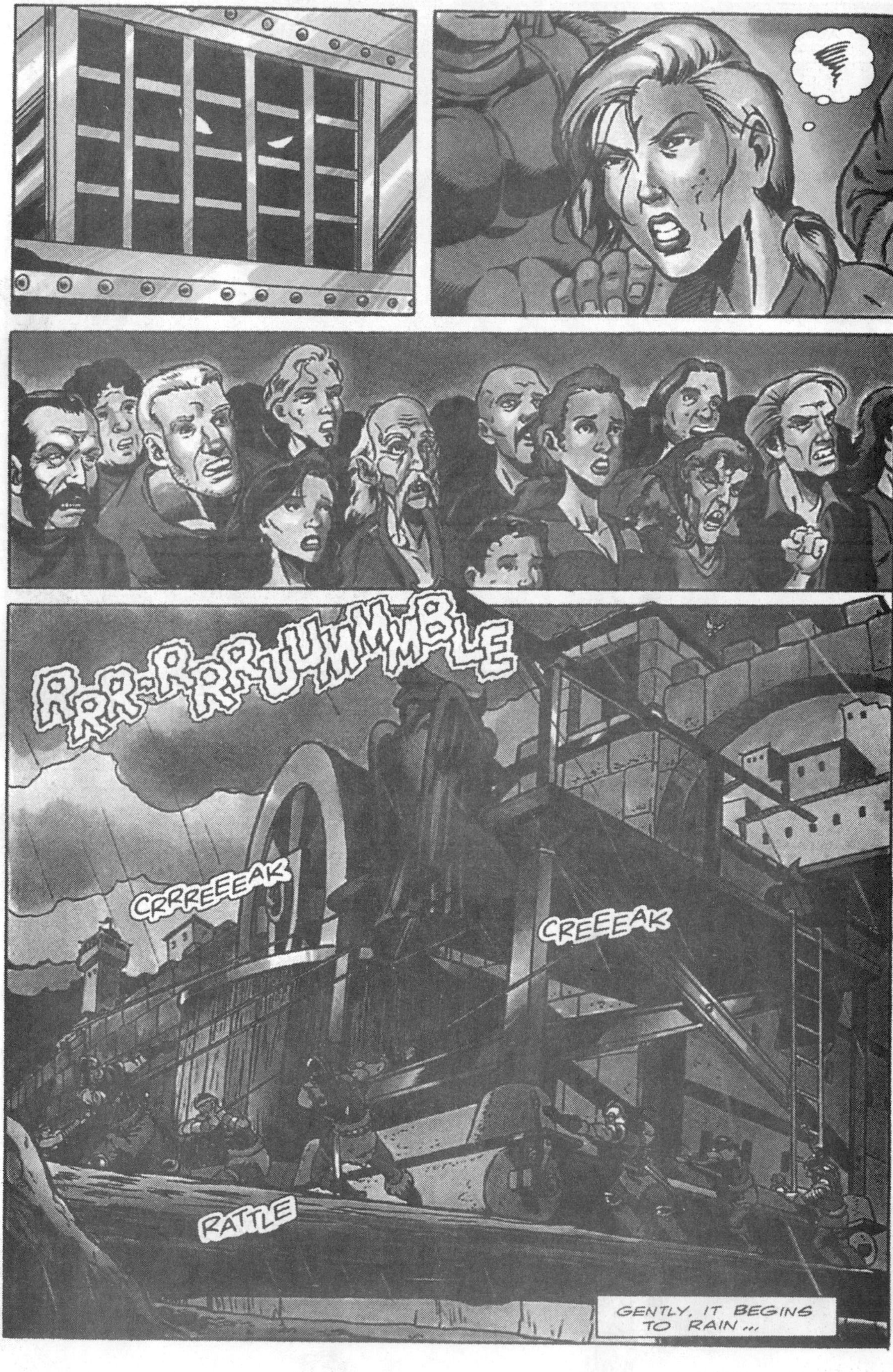
RRR-RRRUUMMMBLE
CRRREEEAK
CREEEAK
RATTLE
GENTLY, IT BEGINS TO RAIN...

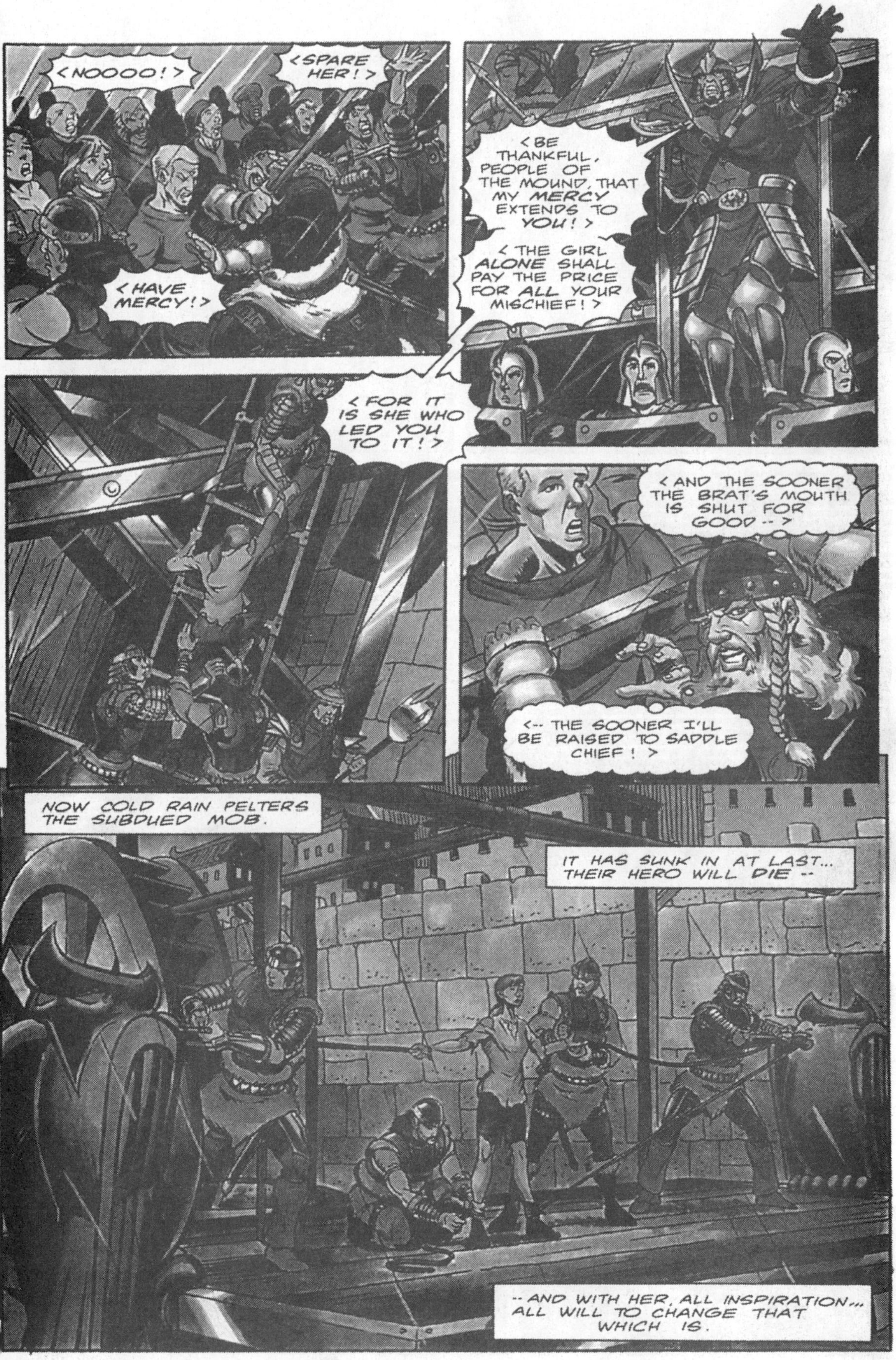
<NOOOO!>
<SPARE HER!>
<HAVE MERCY!>
<BE THANKFUL, PEOPLE OF THE MOUND, THAT MY MERCY EXTENDS TO YOU!>
<THE GIRL ALONE SHALL PAY THE PRICE FOR ALL YOUR MISCHIEF!>
<FOR IT IS SHE WHO LED YOU TO IT!>
<AND THE SOONER THE BRAT'S MOUTH IS SHUT FOR GOOD-->
<--THE SOONER I'LL BE RAISED TO SADDLE CHIEF!>
NOW COLD RAIN PELTERS THE SUBDUED MOB.
IT HAS SUNK IN AT LAST... THEIR HERO WILL DIE --
--AND WITH HER, ALL INSPIRATION... ALL WILL TO CHANGE THAT WHICH IS.

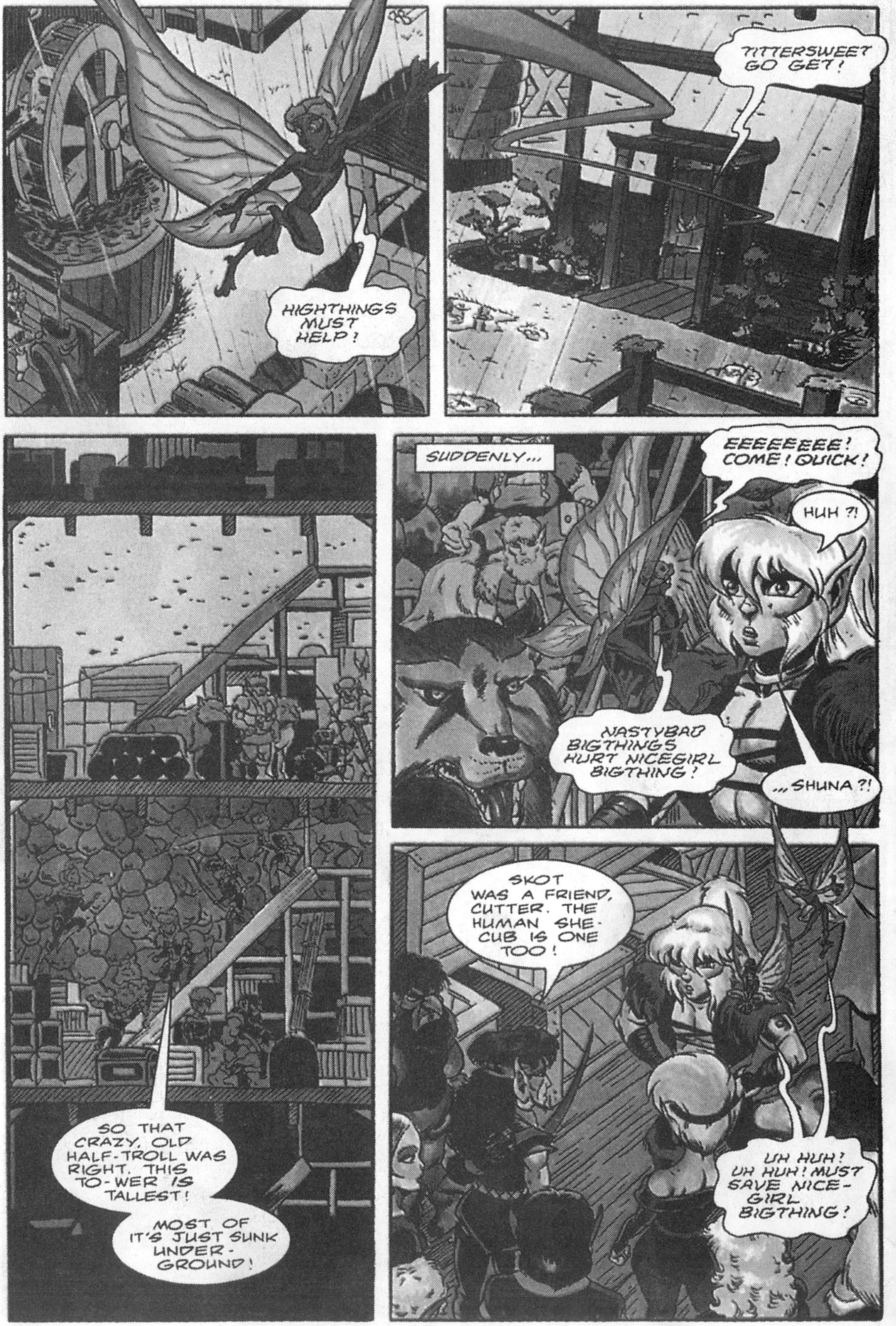
HIGHTHINGS MUST HELP!
?ITTERSWEET? GO GET!
SO THAT CRAZY, OLD HALF-TROLL WAS RIGHT. THIS TO-WER IS TALLEST!
MOST OF IT'S JUST SUNK UNDER-GROUND!
SUDDENLY...
EEEEEEEE! COME! QUICK!
HUH ?!
NASTYBAD BIGTHINGS HURT NICEGIRL BIGTHING!
... SHUNA ?!
SKOT WAS A FRIEND, CUTTER. THE HUMAN SHE-CUB IS ONE TOO!
UH HUH! UH HUH! MUST SAVE NICE-GIRL BIGTHING!

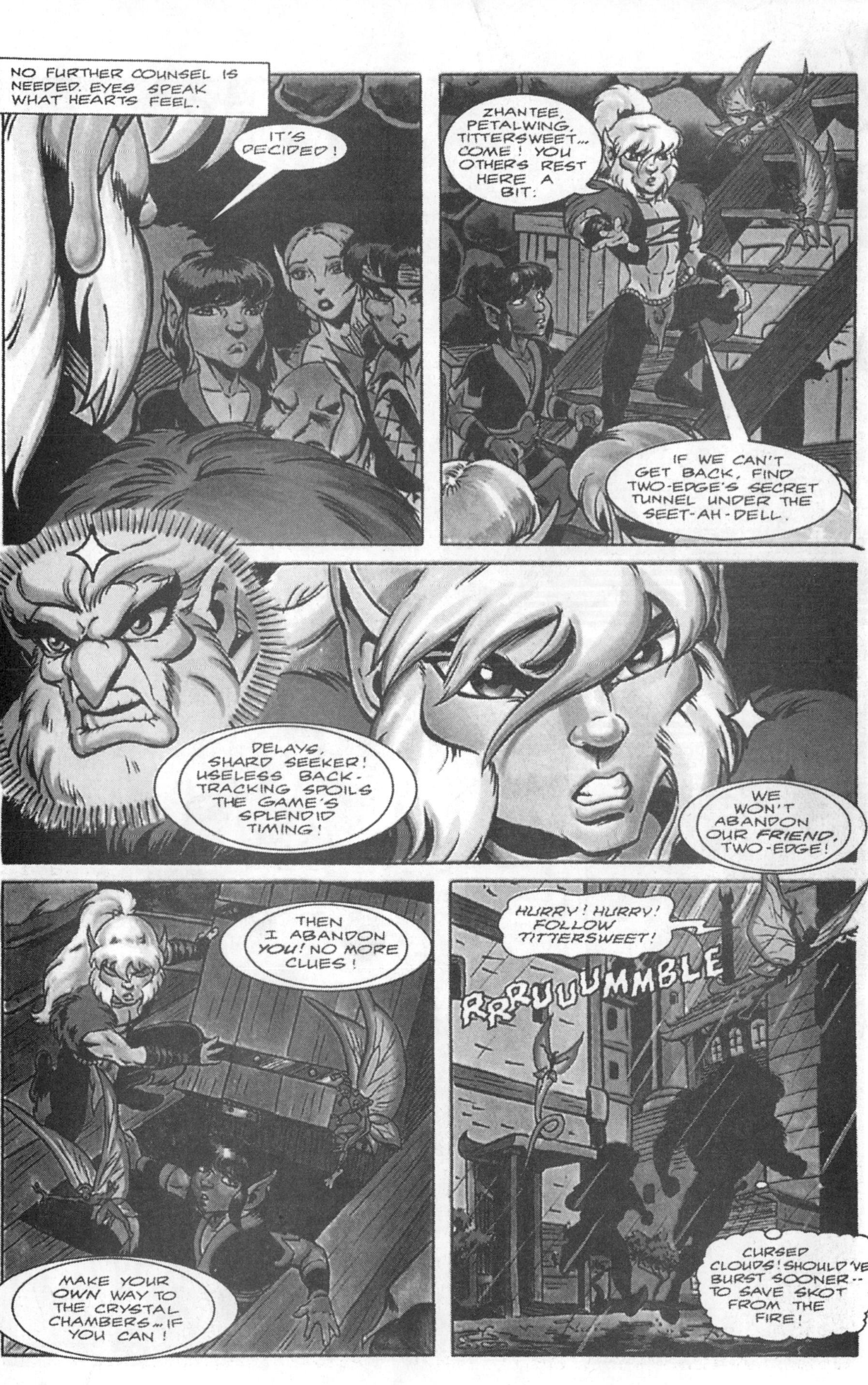

NO FURTHER COUNSEL IS NEEDED. EYES SPEAK WHAT HEARTS FEEL.
IT'S DECIDED!
ZHANTEE, PETALWING, TITTERSWEET... COME! YOU OTHERS REST HERE A BIT:
IF WE CAN'T GET BACK, FIND TWO-EDGE'S SECRET TUNNEL UNDER THE SEET-AH-DELL.
DELAYS, SHARD SEEKER! USELESS BACK-TRACKING SPOILS THE GAME'S SPLENDID TIMING!
WE WON'T ABANDON OUR FRIEND, TWO-EDGE!
THEN I ABANDON YOU! NO MORE CLUES!
MAKE YOUR OWN WAY TO THE CRYSTAL CHAMBERS... IF YOU CAN!
HURRY! HURRY! FOLLOW TITTERSWEET!
RRRUUUMMBLE
CURSED CLOUDS! SHOULD'VE BURST SOONER -- TO SAVE SKOT FROM THE FIRE!

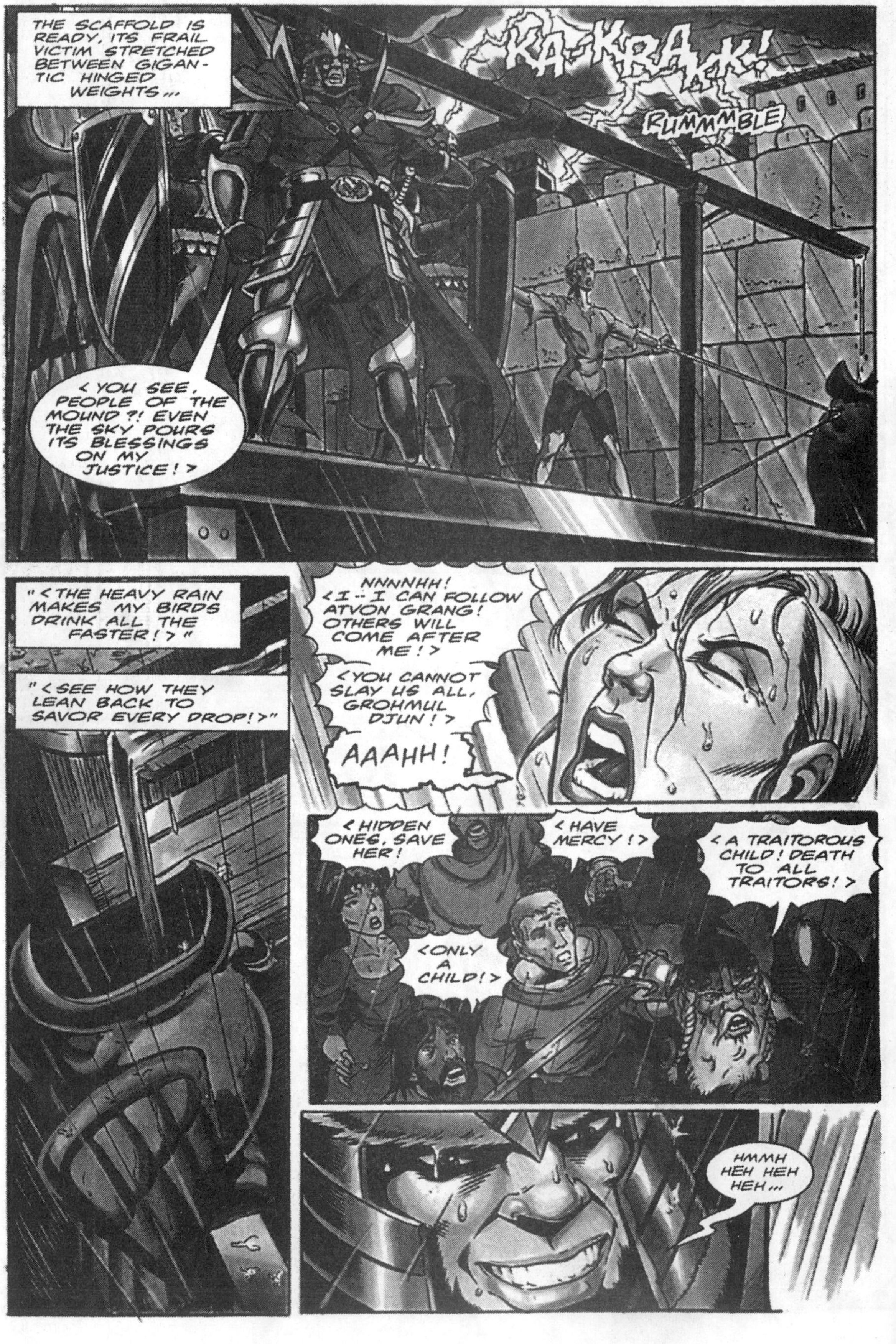
THE SCAFFOLD IS READY, ITS FRAIL VICTIM STRETCHED BETWEEN GIGANTIC HINGED WEIGHTS...
KA-KRAAKK!
RUMMMBLE
<YOU SEE, PEOPLE OF THE MOUND?! EVEN THE SKY POURS ITS BLESSINGS ON MY JUSTICE!>
"<THE HEAVY RAIN MAKES MY BIRDS DRINK ALL THE FASTER!>"
"<SEE HOW THEY LEAN BACK TO SAVOR EVERY DROP!>"
NNNNHH! <I-- I CAN FOLLOW ATVON GRANG! OTHERS WILL COME AFTER ME!>
<YOU CANNOT SLAY US ALL, GROHMUL DJUN!>
AAAHH!
<HIDDEN ONES, SAVE HER!
<HAVE MERCY!>
<A TRAITOROUS CHILD! DEATH TO ALL TRAITORS!>
<ONLY A CHILD!>
HMMH HEH HEH HEH...

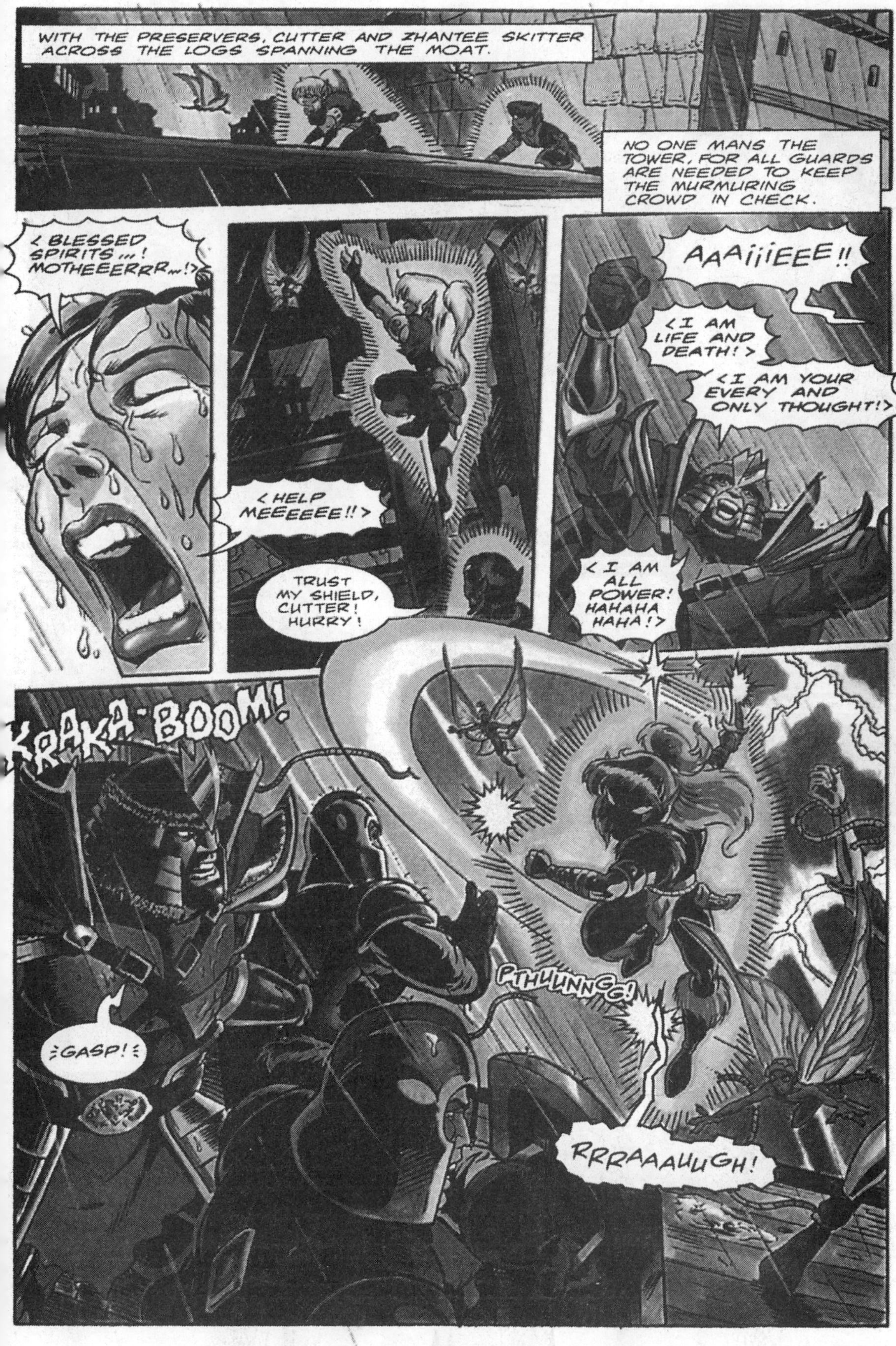
WITH THE PRESERVERS, CUTTER AND ZHANTEE SKITTER ACROSS THE LOGS SPANNING THE MOAT.
NO ONE MANS THE TOWER, FOR ALL GUARDS ARE NEEDED TO KEEP THE MURMURING CROWD IN CHECK.
< BLESSED SPIRITS...! MOTHEEERRR...! >
< HELP MEEEEEE!! >
TRUST MY SHIELD, CUTTER! HURRY!
AAAiiiEEE!!
< I AM LIFE AND DEATH! >
< I AM YOUR EVERY AND ONLY THOUGHT! >
< I AM ALL POWER! HAHAHA HAHA! >
KRAKA-BOOM!
PTHUUNNGG!
GASP!
RRRAAAUUGH!

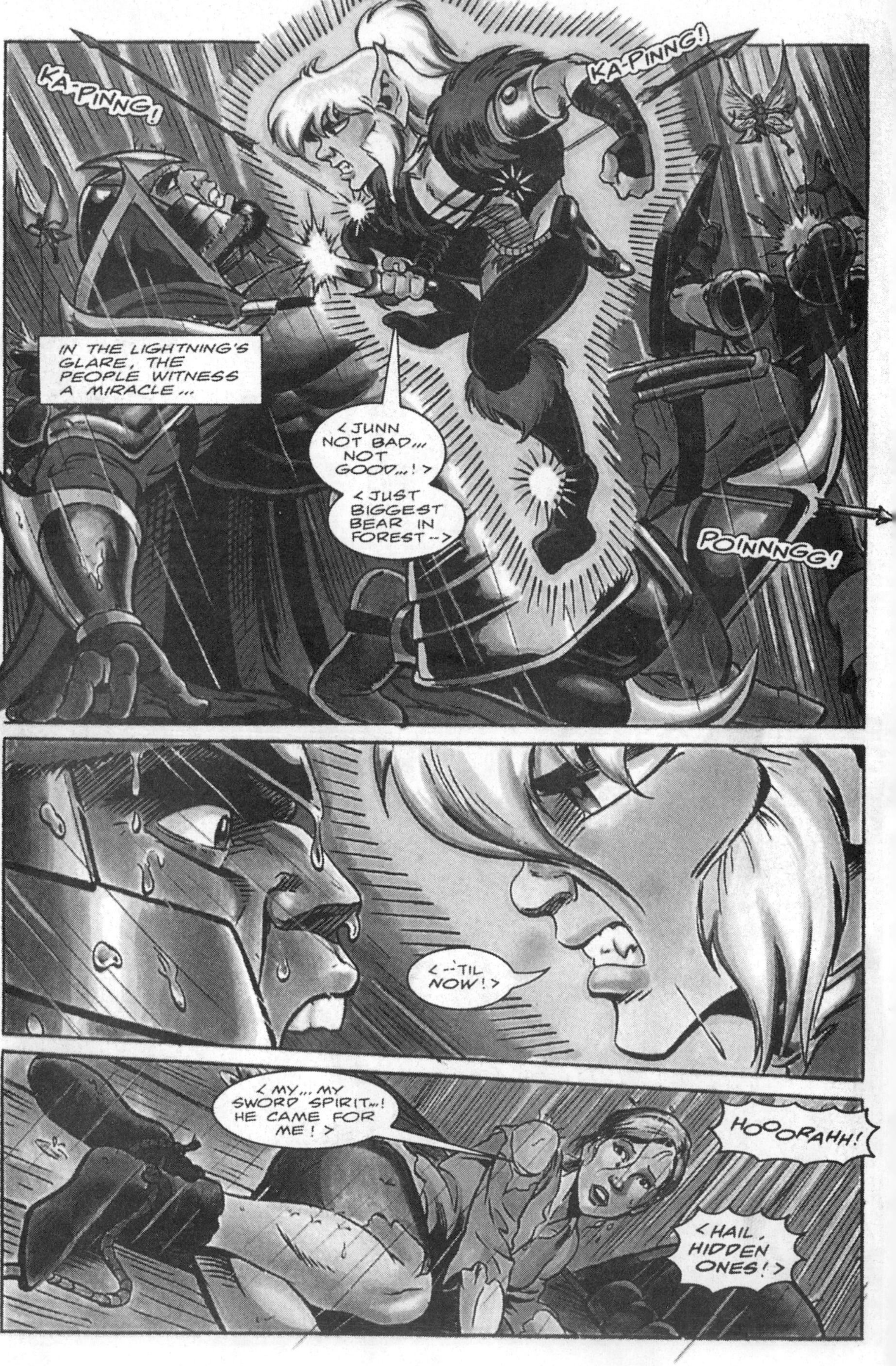
KA-PINNG!
KA-PINNG!
IN THE LIGHTNING'S GLARE, THE PEOPLE WITNESS A MIRACLE...
<JUNN NOT BAD... NOT GOOD...!>
<JUST BIGGEST BEAR IN FOREST-->
POINNNGG!
<--'TIL NOW!>
<MY... MY SWORD SPIRIT...! HE CAME FOR ME!>
HOOORAHH!
<HAIL, HIDDEN ONES!>

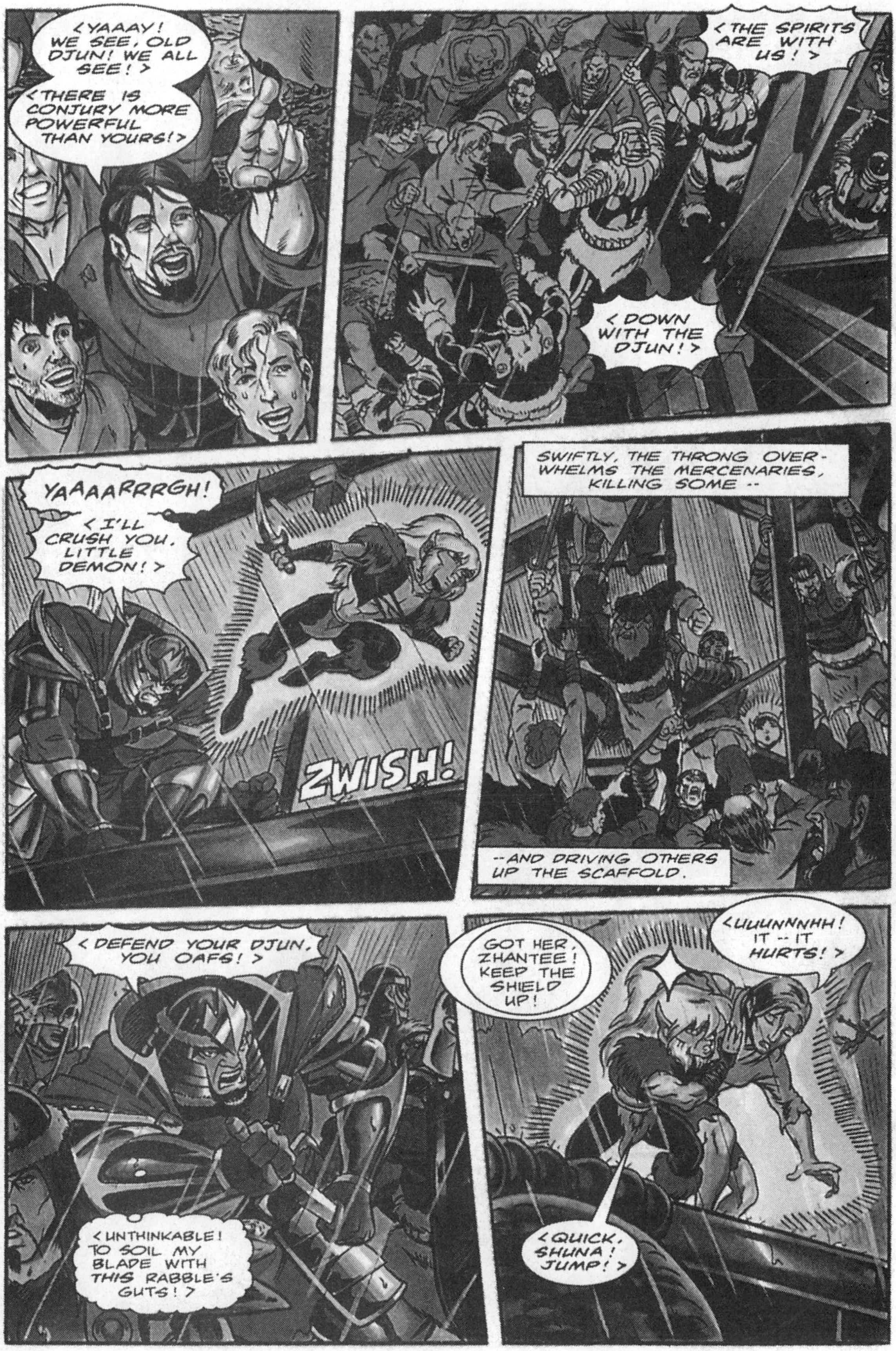
<YAAAAY! WE SEE, OLD DJUN! WE ALL SEE!>
<THERE IS CONJURY MORE POWERFUL THAN YOURS!>
<THE SPIRITS ARE WITH US!>
<DOWN WITH THE DJUN!>
YAAAARRRGH!
<I'LL CRUSH YOU, LITTLE DEMON!>
ZWISH!
SWIFTLY, THE THRONG OVER-WHELMS THE MERCENARIES, KILLING SOME --
--AND DRIVING OTHERS UP THE SCAFFOLD.
<DEFEND YOUR DJUN, YOU OAFS!>
<UNTHINKABLE! TO SOIL MY BLADE WITH THIS RABBLE'S GUTS!>
GOT HER, ZHANTEE! KEEP THE SHIELD UP!
<UUUUNNNHH! IT -- IT HURTS!>
<QUICK, SHUNA! JUMP!>

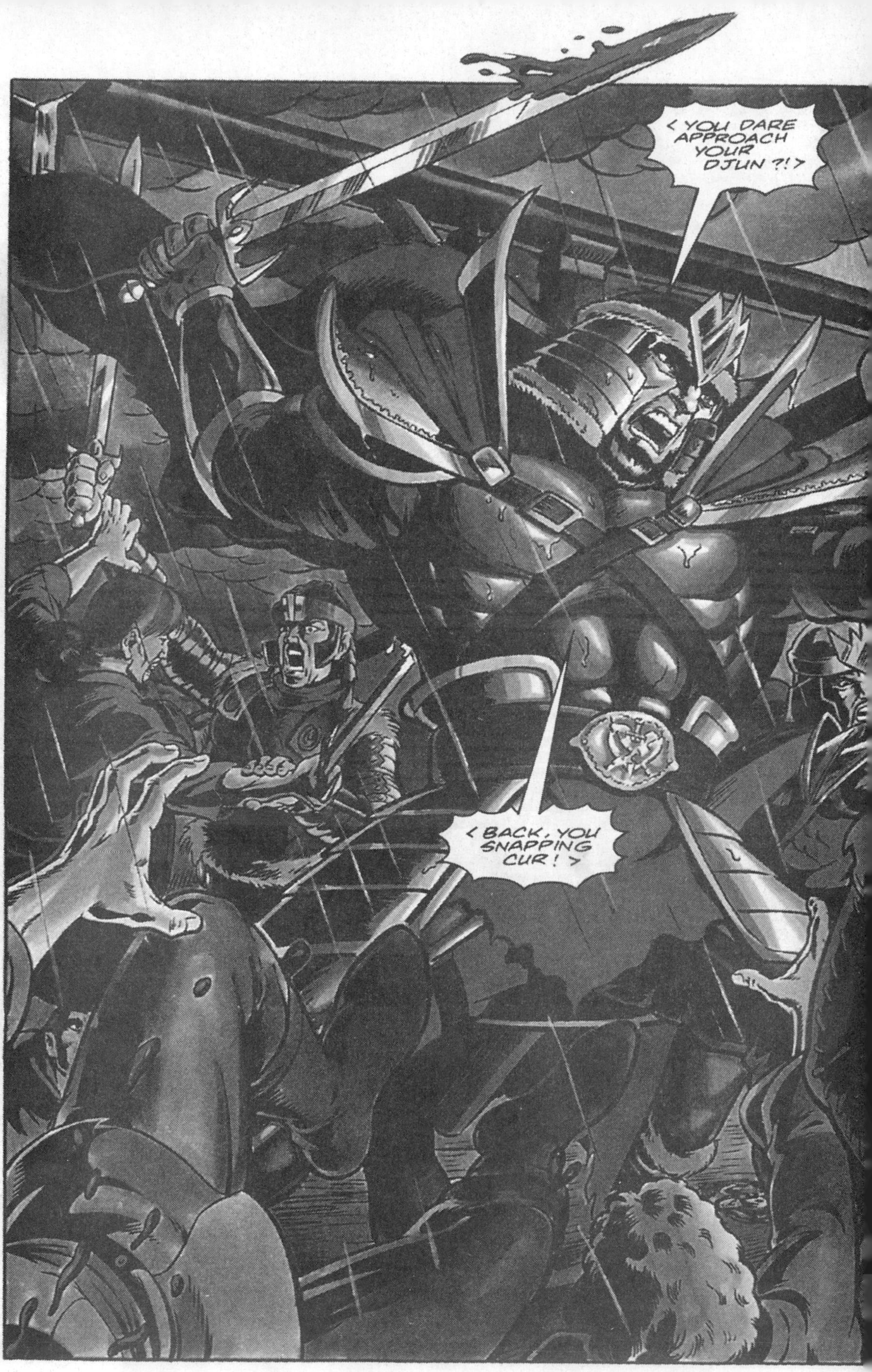

< YOU DARE APPROACH YOUR DJUN ?! >
< BACK, YOU SNAPPING CUR! >

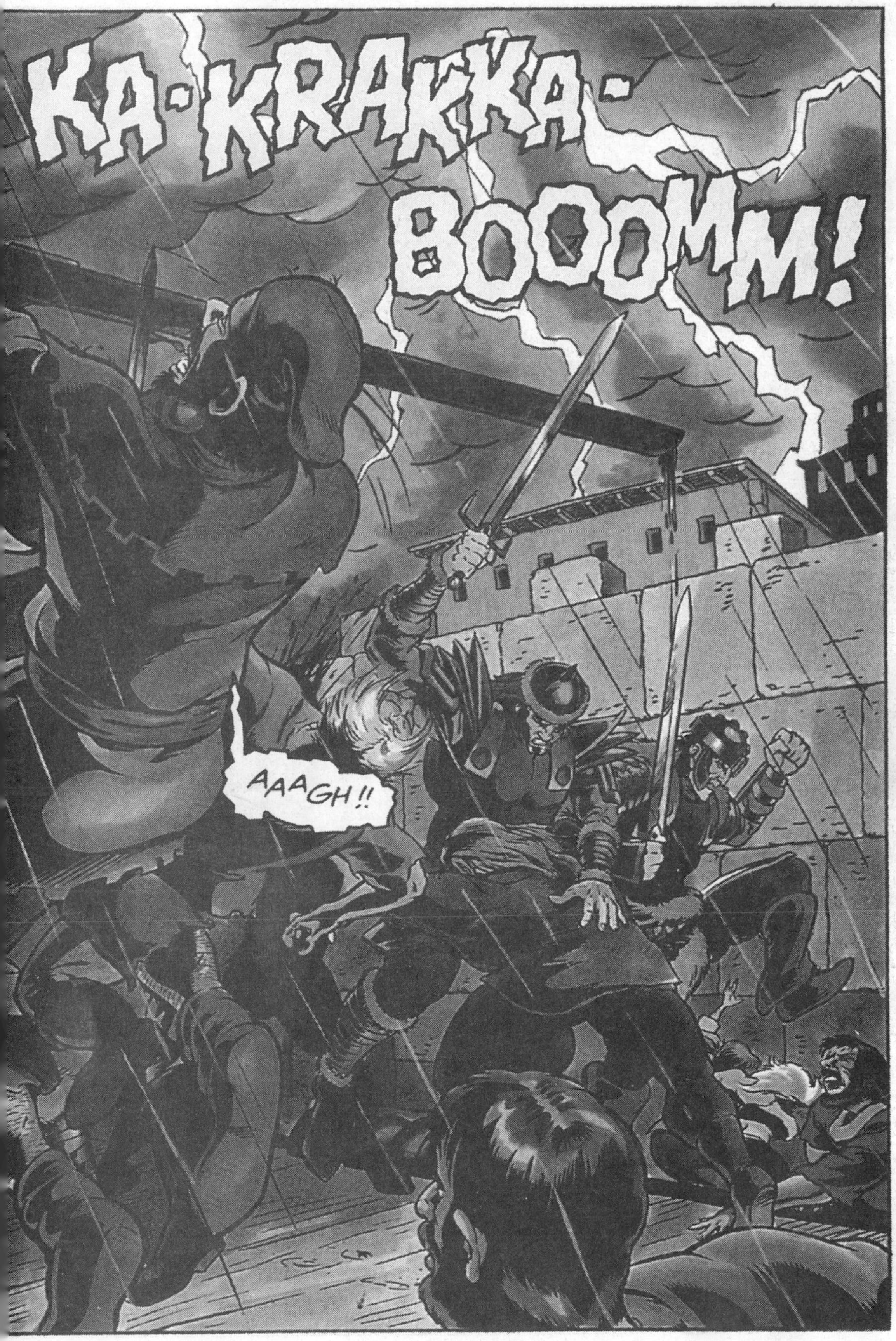
KA-KRAKKA-BOOOMM!
AAAGH!!

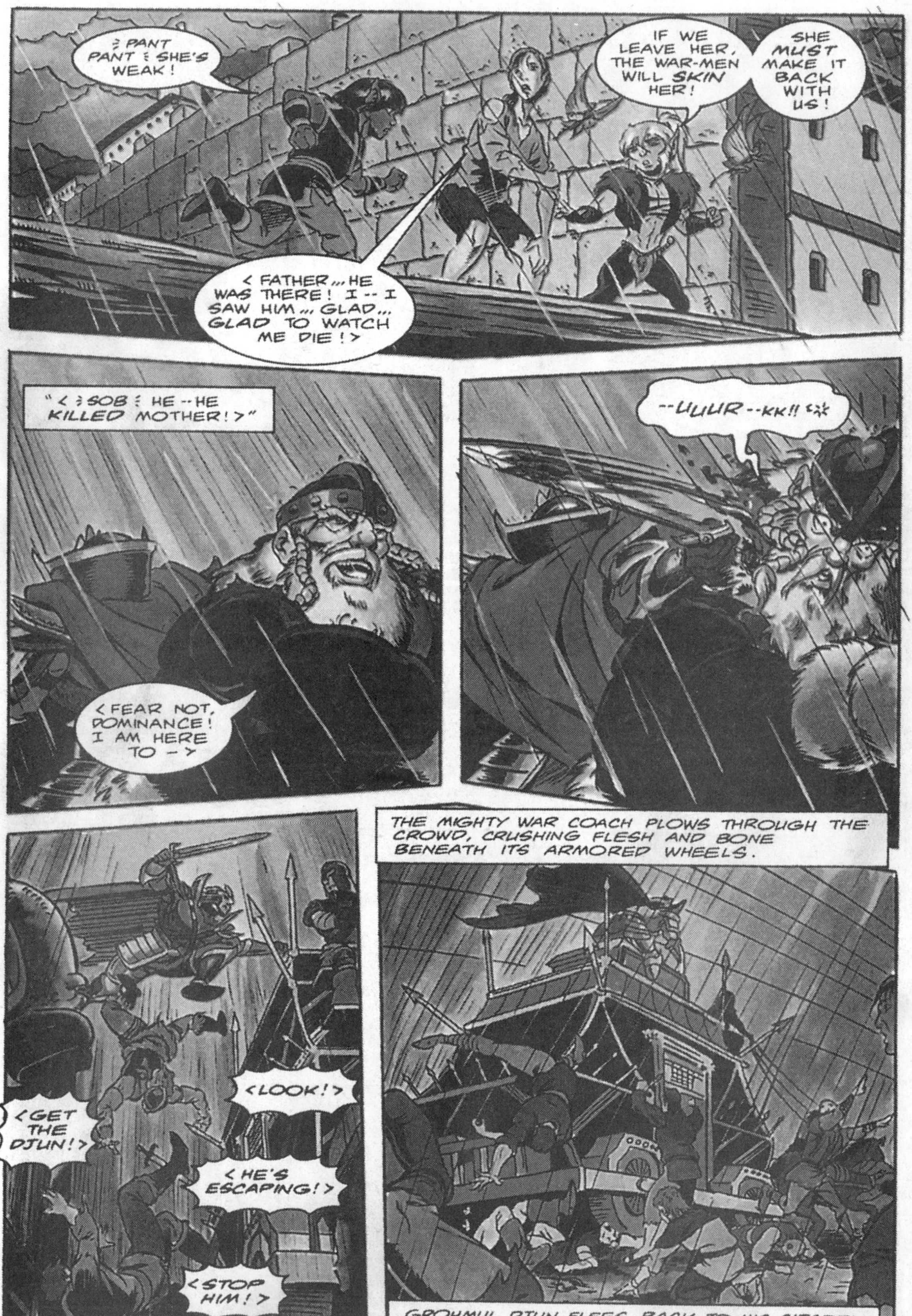

⁝ PANT PANT ⁝ SHE'S WEAK!
IF WE LEAVE HER, THE WAR-MEN WILL SKIN HER!
SHE MUST MAKE IT BACK WITH US!
< FATHER... HE WAS THERE! I -- I SAW HIM... GLAD... GLAD TO WATCH ME DIE! >
"< ⁝ SOB ⁝ HE -- HE KILLED MOTHER! >"
< FEAR NOT, DOMINANCE! I AM HERE TO -- >
-- UUUR -- KK!!
THE MIGHTY WAR COACH PLOWS THROUGH THE CROWD, CRUSHING FLESH AND BONE BENEATH ITS ARMORED WHEELS.
< LOOK! >
< GET THE DJUN! >
< HE'S ESCAPING! >
< STOP HIM! >
GROHMUL DJUN FLEES BACK TO HIS CITADEL, HIS ONE TRUE ACT OF JUSTICE... A MERE ACCIDENT.

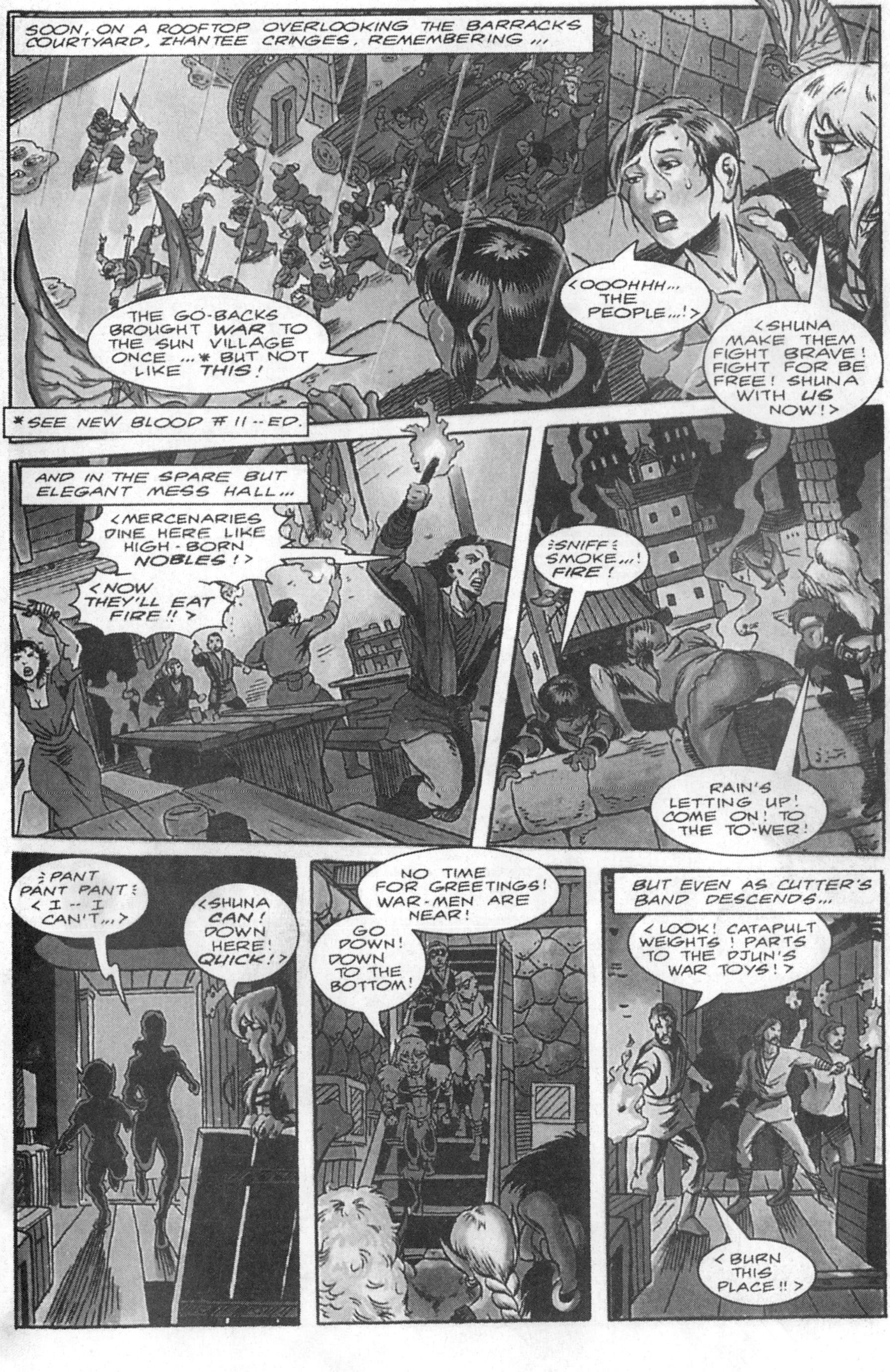
SOON, ON A ROOFTOP OVERLOOKING THE BARRACKS COURTYARD, ZHANTEE CRINGES, REMEMBERING ...
THE GO-BACKS BROUGHT WAR TO THE SUN VILLAGE ONCE ...* BUT NOT LIKE THIS!
<OOOHHH... THE PEOPLE...!>
<SHUNA MAKE THEM FIGHT BRAVE! FIGHT FOR BE FREE! SHUNA WITH US NOW!>
*SEE NEW BLOOD # 11 -- ED.
AND IN THE SPARE BUT ELEGANT MESS HALL...
<MERCENARIES DINE HERE LIKE HIGH-BORN NOBLES!>
<NOW THEY'LL EAT FIRE!!>
SNIFF SMOKE...! FIRE!
RAIN'S LETTING UP! COME ON! TO THE TO-WER!
PANT PANT PANT <I -- I CAN'T...>
<SHUNA CAN! DOWN HERE! QUICK!>
NO TIME FOR GREETINGS! WAR-MEN ARE NEAR!
GO DOWN! DOWN TO THE BOTTOM!
BUT EVEN AS CUTTER'S BAND DESCENDS...
<LOOK! CATAPULT WEIGHTS! PARTS TO THE DJUN'S WAR TOYS!>
<BURN THIS PLACE!!>

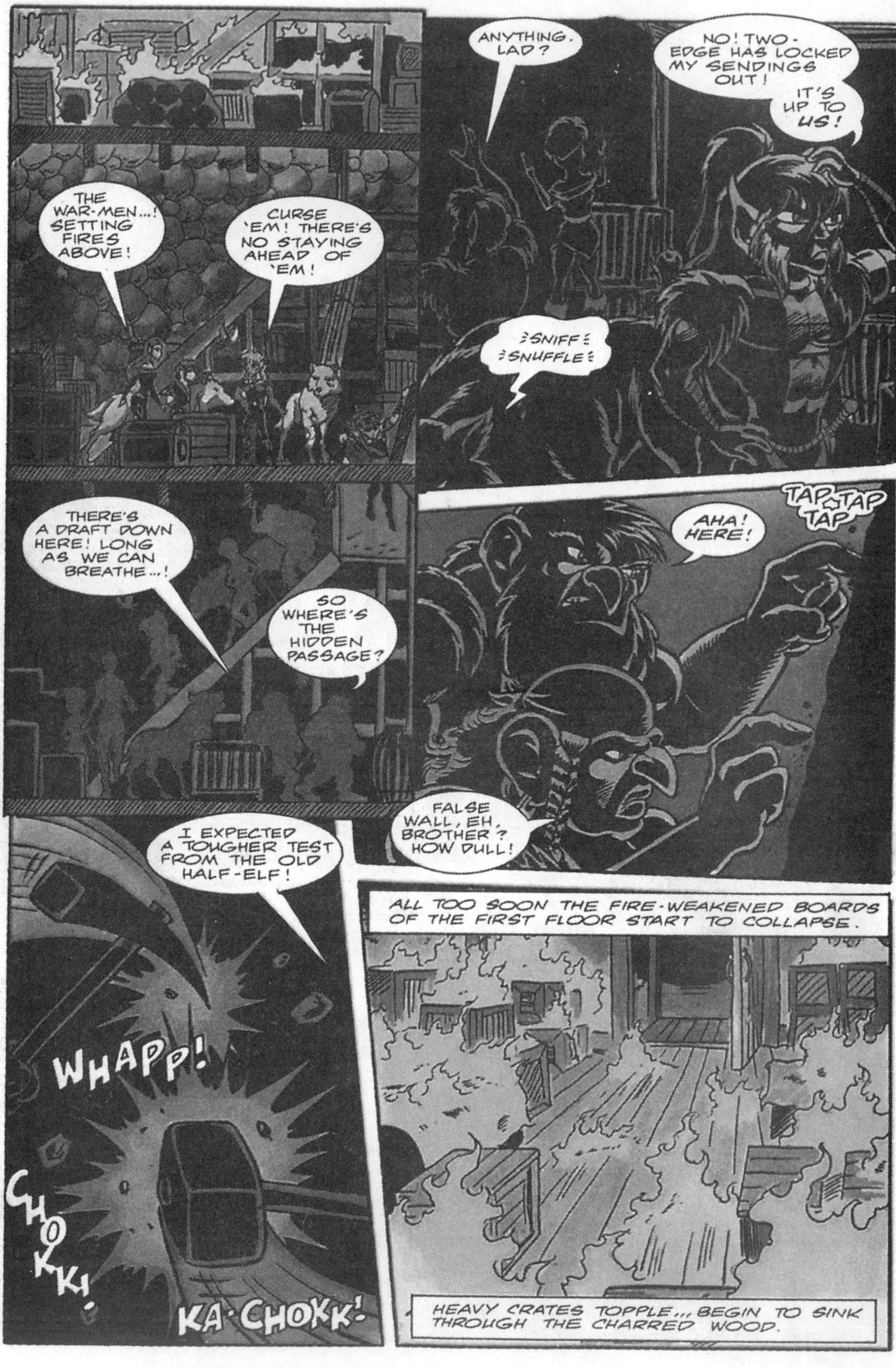
THE WAR-MEN...! SETTING FIRES ABOVE!
CURSE 'EM! THERE'S NO STAYING AHEAD OF 'EM!
ANYTHING, LAD?
NO! TWO-EDGE HAS LOCKED MY SENDINGS OUT!
IT'S UP TO US!
SNIFF SNUFFLE
THERE'S A DRAFT DOWN HERE! LONG AS WE CAN BREATHE...!
SO WHERE'S THE HIDDEN PASSAGE?
TAP TAP TAP
AHA! HERE!
FALSE WALL, EH, BROTHER? HOW DULL!
I EXPECTED A TOUGHER TEST FROM THE OLD HALF-ELF!
WHAPP!
CHOKK!
KA-CHOKK!
ALL TOO SOON THE FIRE-WEAKENED BOARDS OF THE FIRST FLOOR START TO COLLAPSE.
HEAVY CRATES TOPPLE... BEGIN TO SINK THROUGH THE CHARRED WOOD.

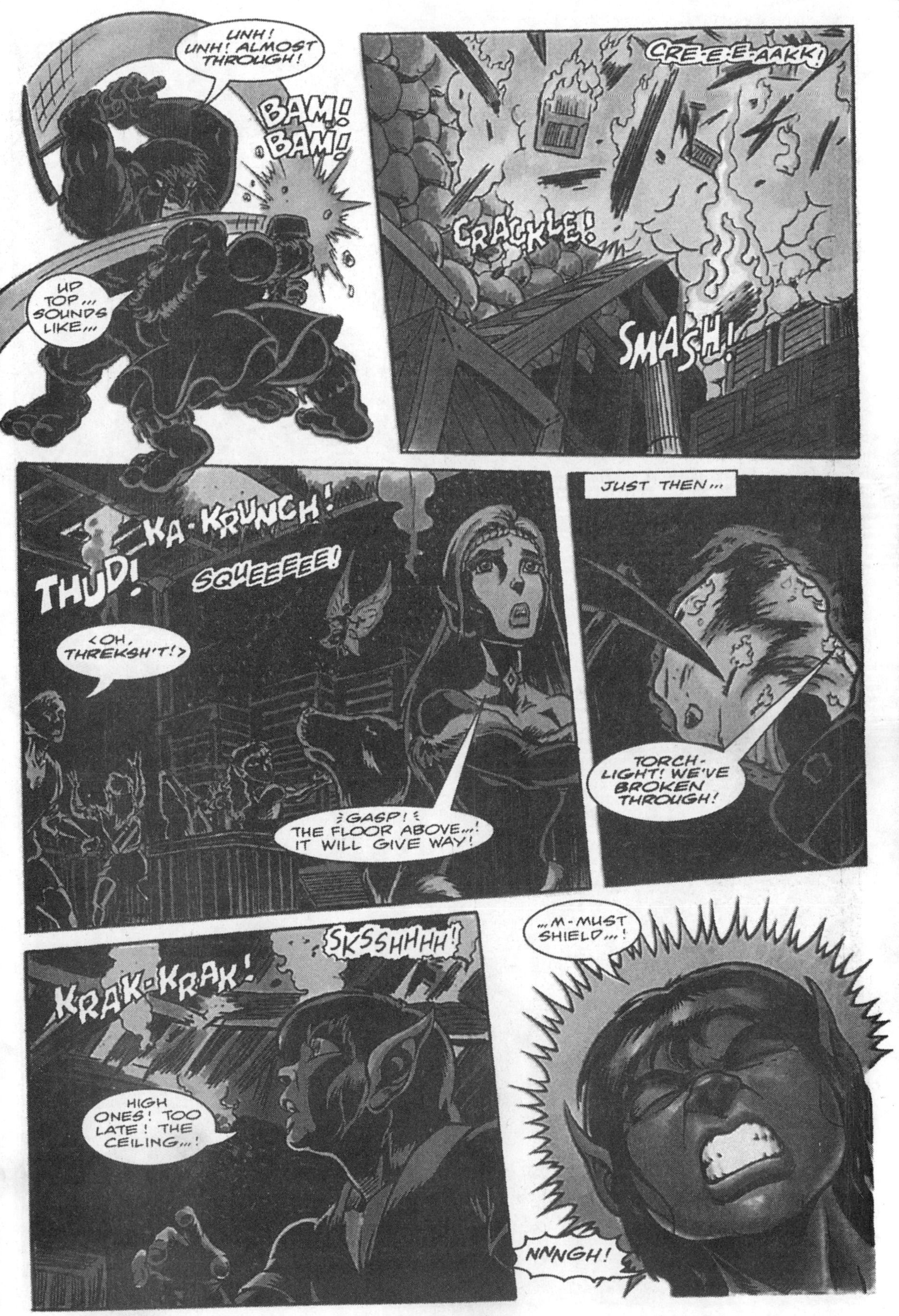

UNH! UNH! ALMOST THROUGH!
BAM! BAM!
UP TOP... SOUNDS LIKE...
CRE-E-E-AAKK!
CRACKLE!
SMASH!
KA-KRUNCH!
THUD!
SQUEEEEEE!
<OH, THREKSH'T!>
GASP! THE FLOOR ABOVE...! IT WILL GIVE WAY!
JUST THEN...
TORCH-LIGHT! WE'VE BROKEN THROUGH!
SKSSHHHH!
KRAK-KRAK!
HIGH ONES! TOO LATE! THE CEILING...!
...M-MUST SHIELD...!
NNNGH!

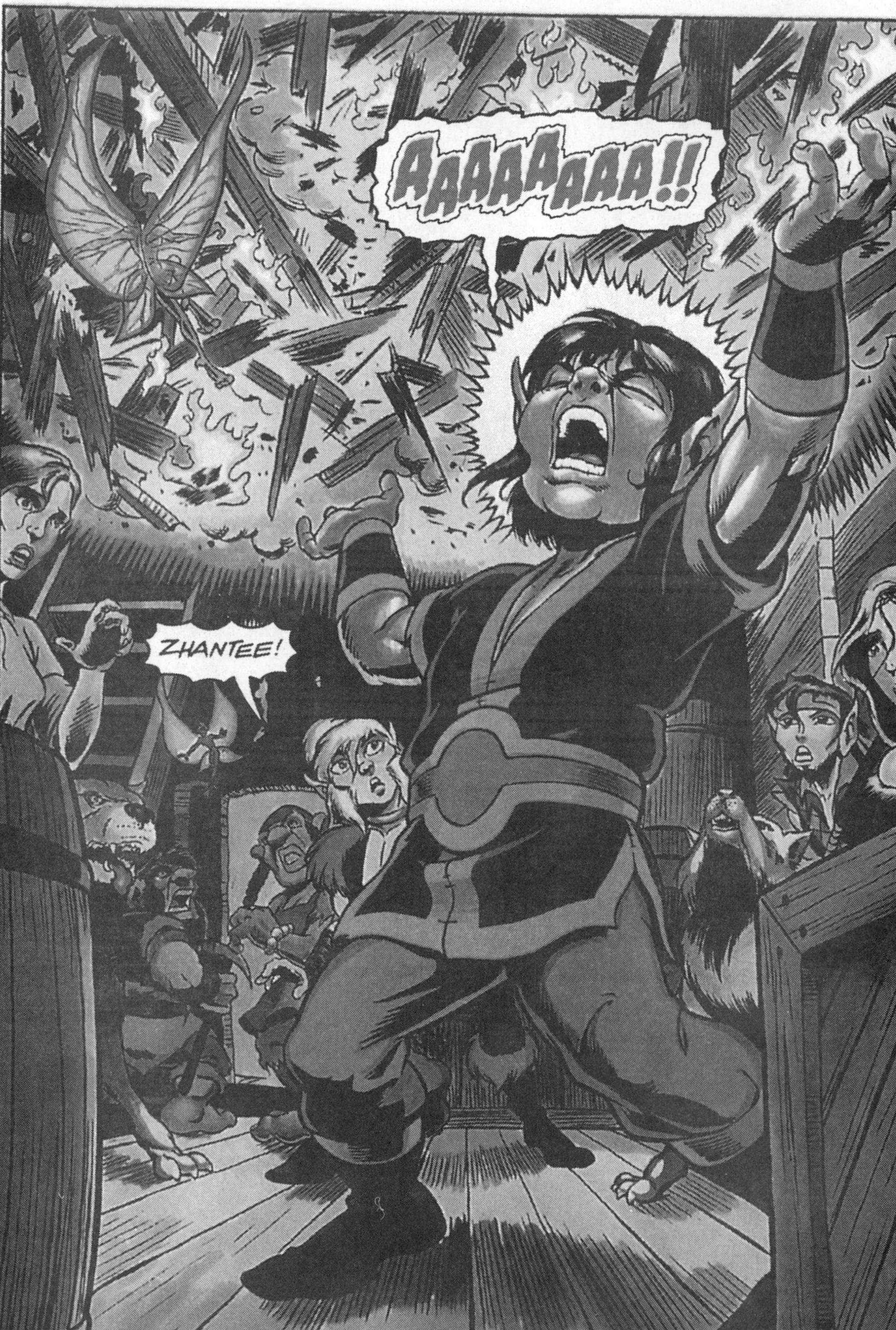
AAAAAAAA!!
ZHANTEE!

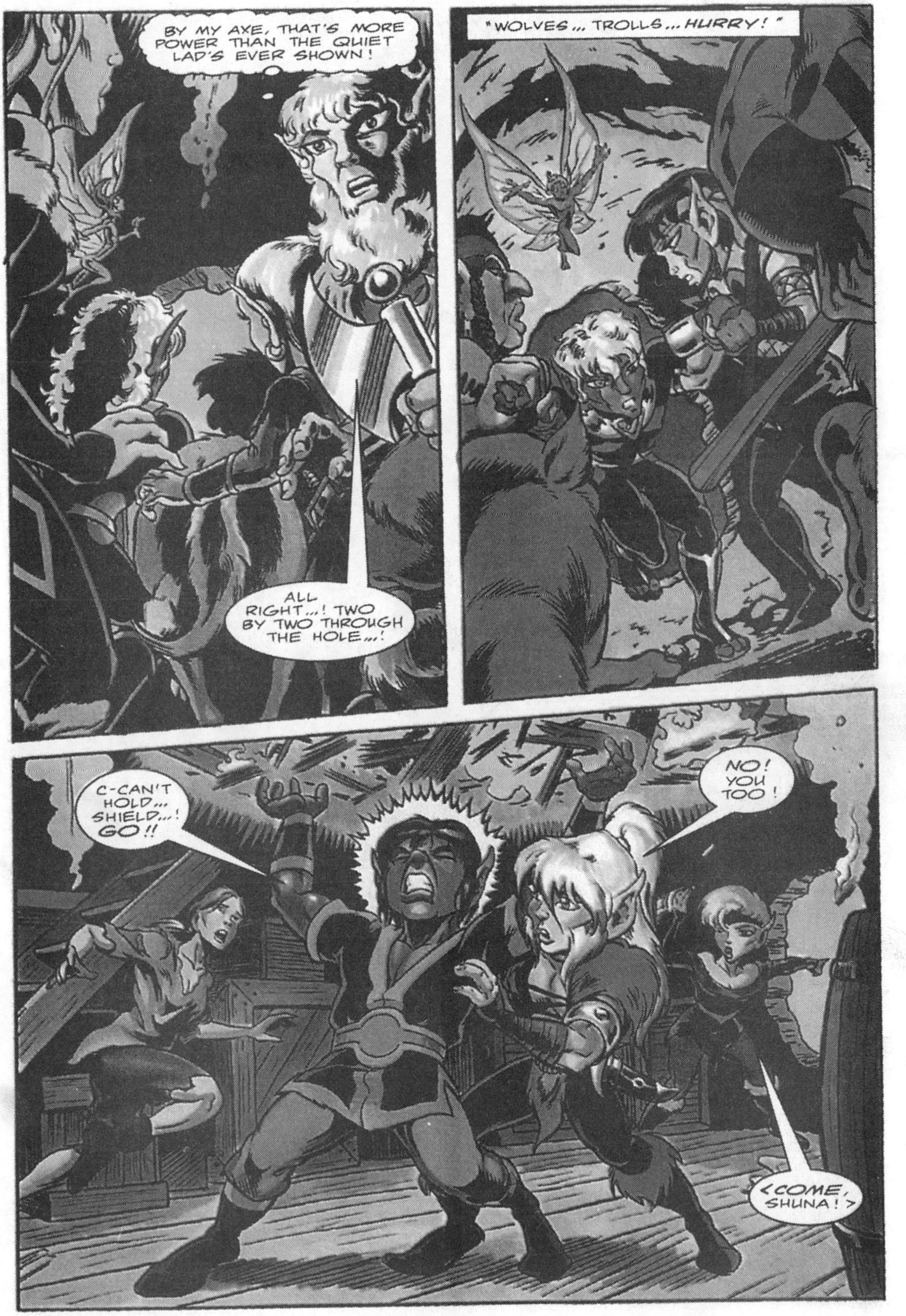
BY MY AXE, THAT'S MORE POWER THAN THE QUIET LAD'S EVER SHOWN!
ALL RIGHT...! TWO BY TWO THROUGH THE HOLE...!
"WOLVES... TROLLS... HURRY!"
C-CAN'T HOLD... SHIELD...! GO!!
NO! YOU TOO!
<COME, SHUNA!>

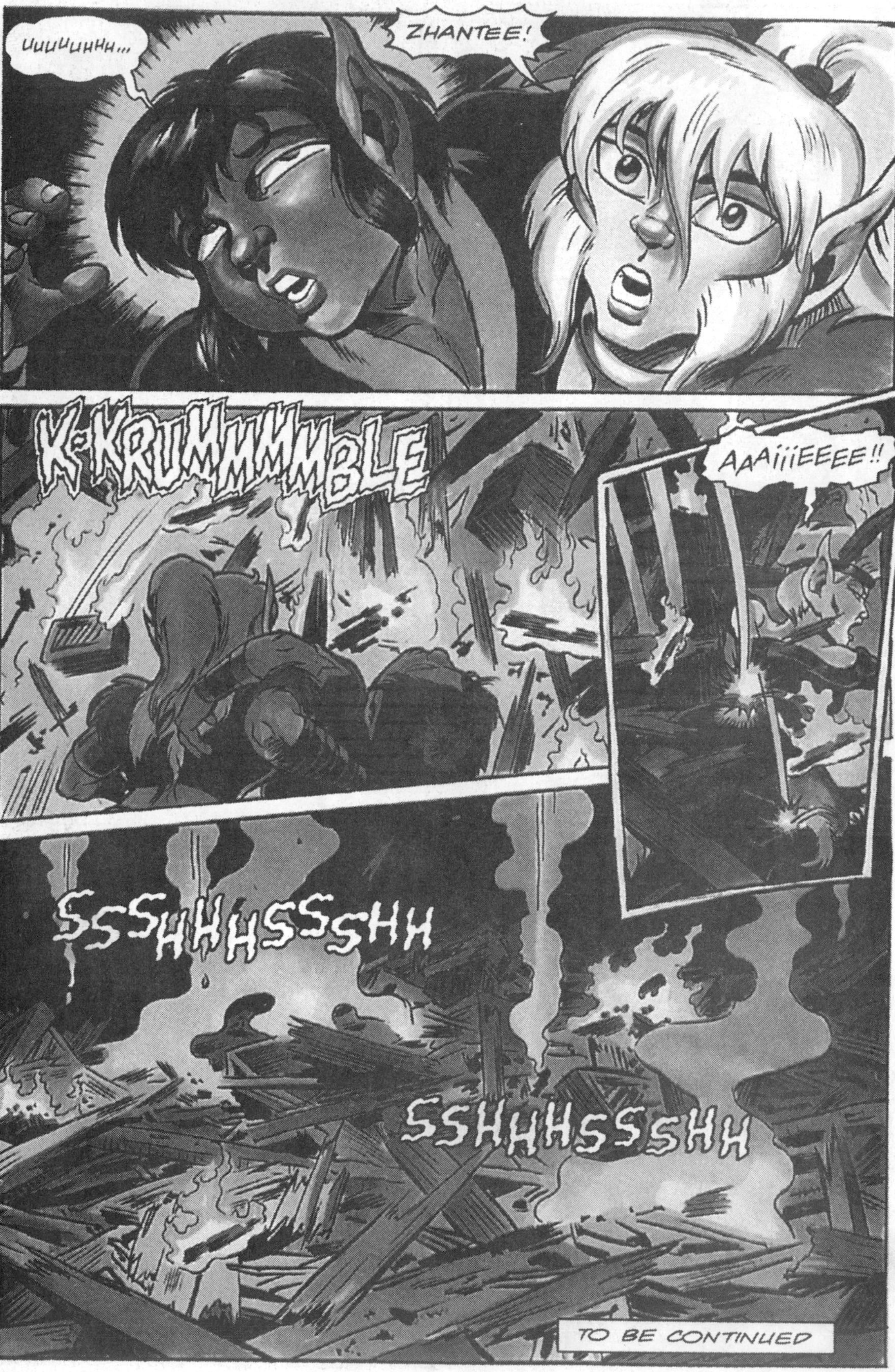

UUUUUHHH...
ZHANTEE!
K-KRUMMMMMBLE
AAAiiiiEEEEE!!
SSSHHHSSSSHH
SSHHHSSSSHH
TO BE CONTINUED

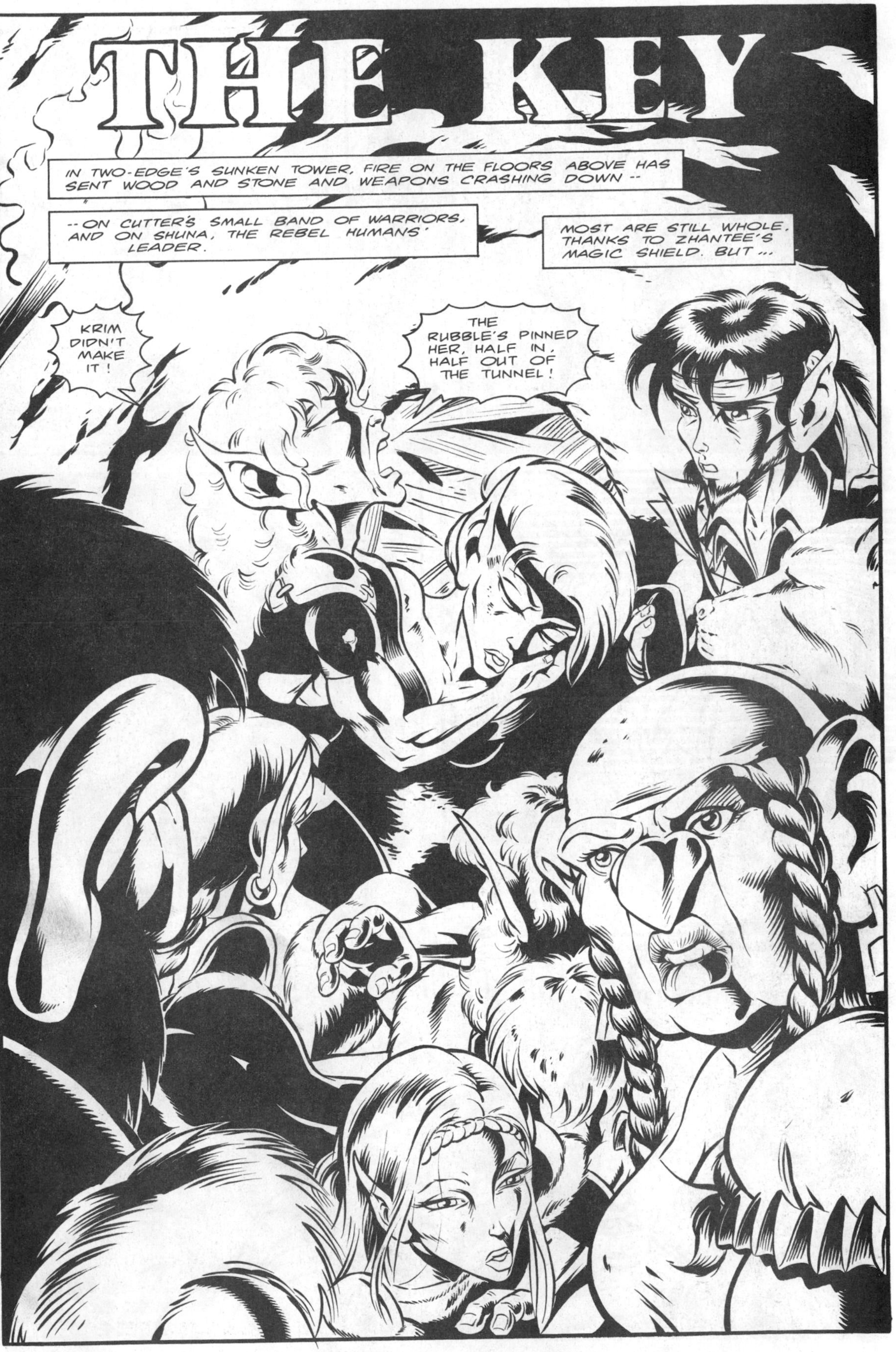
THE KEY
IN TWO-EDGE'S SUNKEN TOWER, FIRE ON THE FLOORS ABOVE HAS SENT WOOD AND STONE AND WEAPONS CRASHING DOWN --
--ON CUTTER'S SMALL BAND OF WARRIORS, AND ON SHUNA, THE REBEL HUMANS' LEADER.
MOST ARE STILL WHOLE, THANKS TO ZHANTEE'S MAGIC SHIELD. BUT ...
KRIM DIDN'T MAKE IT!
THE RUBBLE'S PINNED HER, HALF IN, HALF OUT OF THE TUNNEL!

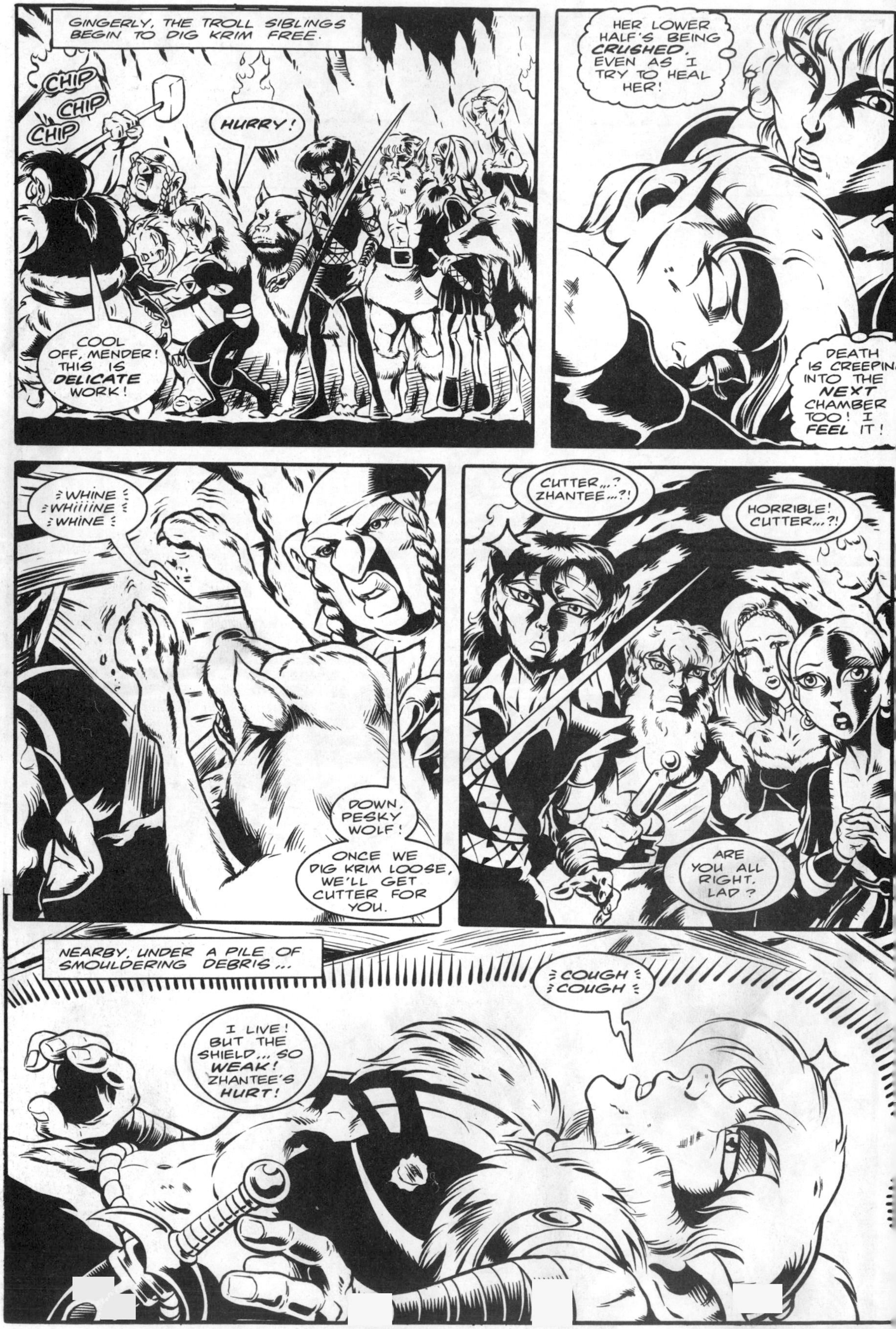
GINGERLY, THE TROLL SIBLINGS BEGIN TO DIG KRIM FREE.
CHIP CHIP CHIP
HURRY!
COOL OFF, MENDER! THIS IS DELICATE WORK!
HER LOWER HALF'S BEING CRUSHED. EVEN AS I TRY TO HEAL HER!
DEATH IS CREEPIN INTO THE NEXT CHAMBER TOO! I FEEL IT!
WHINE WHIIIINE WHINE
DOWN, PESKY WOLF!
ONCE WE DIG KRIM LOOSE, WE'LL GET CUTTER FOR YOU.
CUTTER...? ZHANTEE...?!
HORRIBLE! CUTTER...?!
ARE YOU ALL RIGHT, LAD?
NEARBY, UNDER A PILE OF SMOULDERING DEBRIS...
COUGH COUGH
I LIVE! BUT THE SHIELD... SO WEAK! ZHANTEE'S HURT!

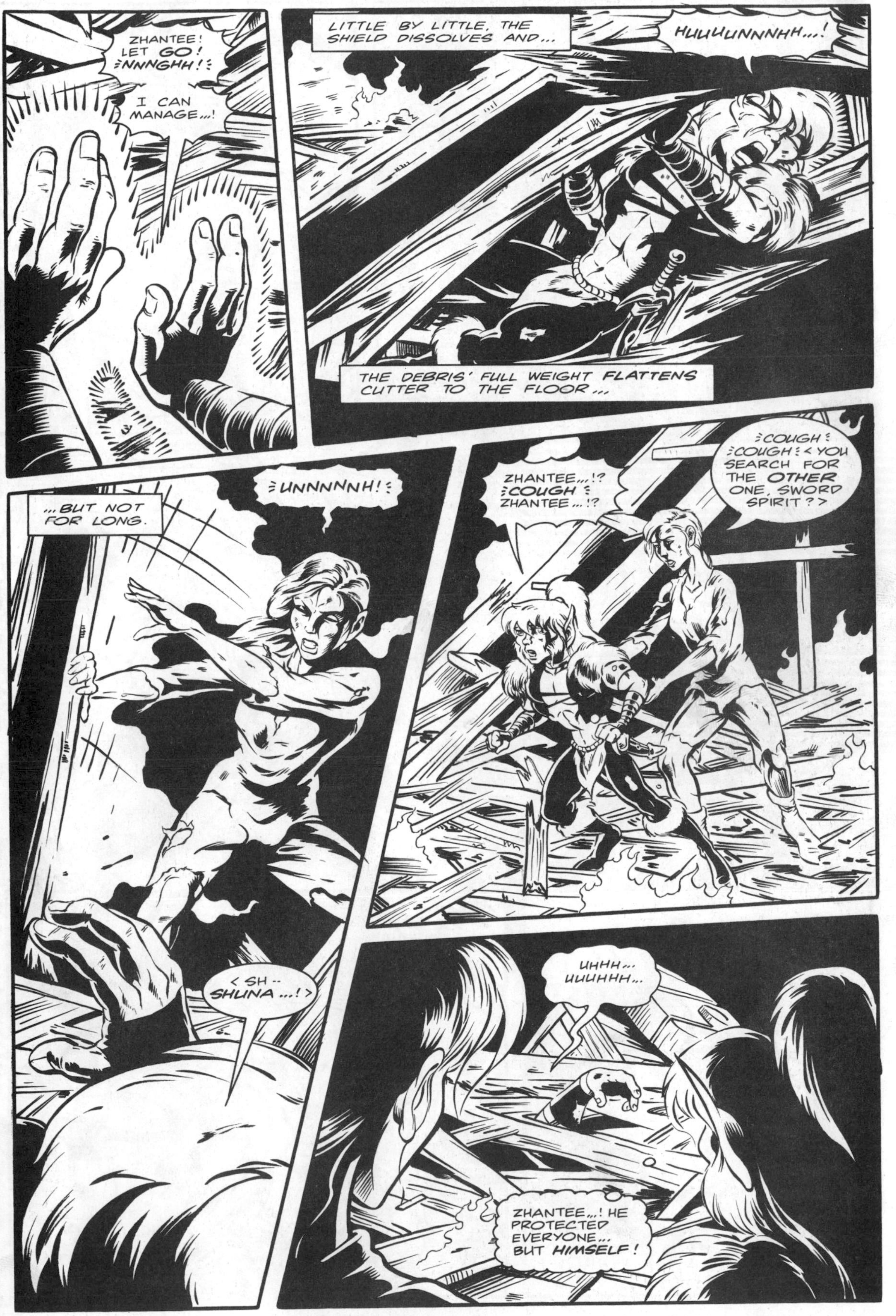
ZHANTEE! LET GO! NNNGHH!
I CAN MANAGE...!
LITTLE BY LITTLE, THE SHIELD DISSOLVES AND...
HUUUUNNNH...!
THE DEBRIS' FULL WEIGHT FLATTENS CUTTER TO THE FLOOR...
...BUT NOT FOR LONG.
UNNNNNH!
< SH-- SHUNA...! >
ZHANTEE...!? COUGH ZHANTEE...!?
COUGH COUGH < YOU SEARCH FOR THE OTHER ONE, SWORD SPIRIT? >
UHHH... UUUHHH...
ZHANTEE...! HE PROTECTED EVERYONE... BUT HIMSELF!

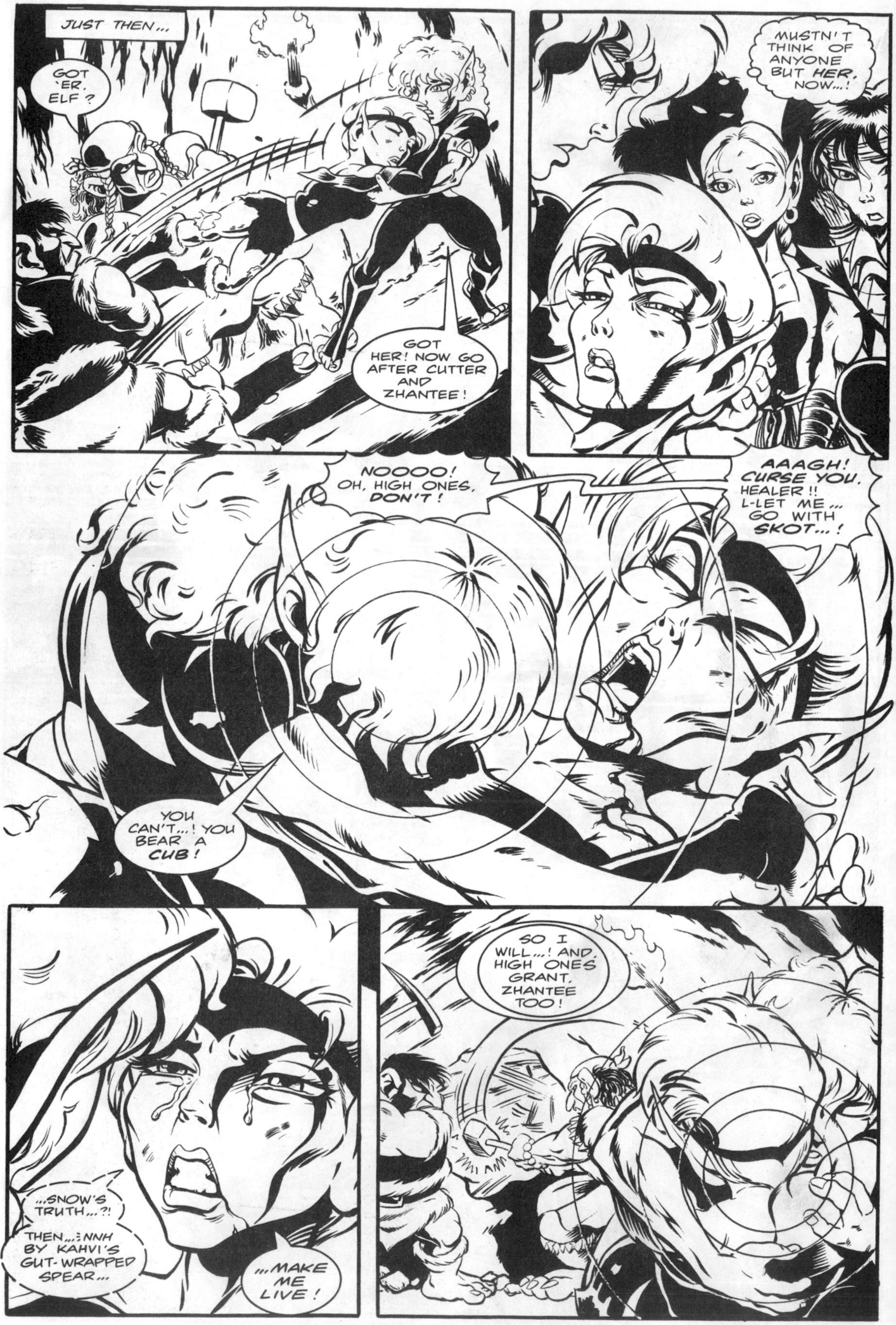
JUST THEN...
GOT 'ER, ELF?
GOT HER! NOW GO AFTER CUTTER AND ZHANTEE!
MUSTN'T THINK OF ANYONE BUT HER, NOW...!
NOOOO! OH, HIGH ONES, DON'T!
AAAGH! CURSE YOU, HEALER!! L-LET ME... GO WITH SKOT...!
YOU CAN'T...! YOU BEAR A CUB!
...SNOW'S TRUTH...?!
THEN... NNH BY KAHVI'S GUT-WRAPPED SPEAR...
...MAKE ME LIVE!
SO I WILL...! AND, HIGH ONES GRANT, ZHANTEE TOO!

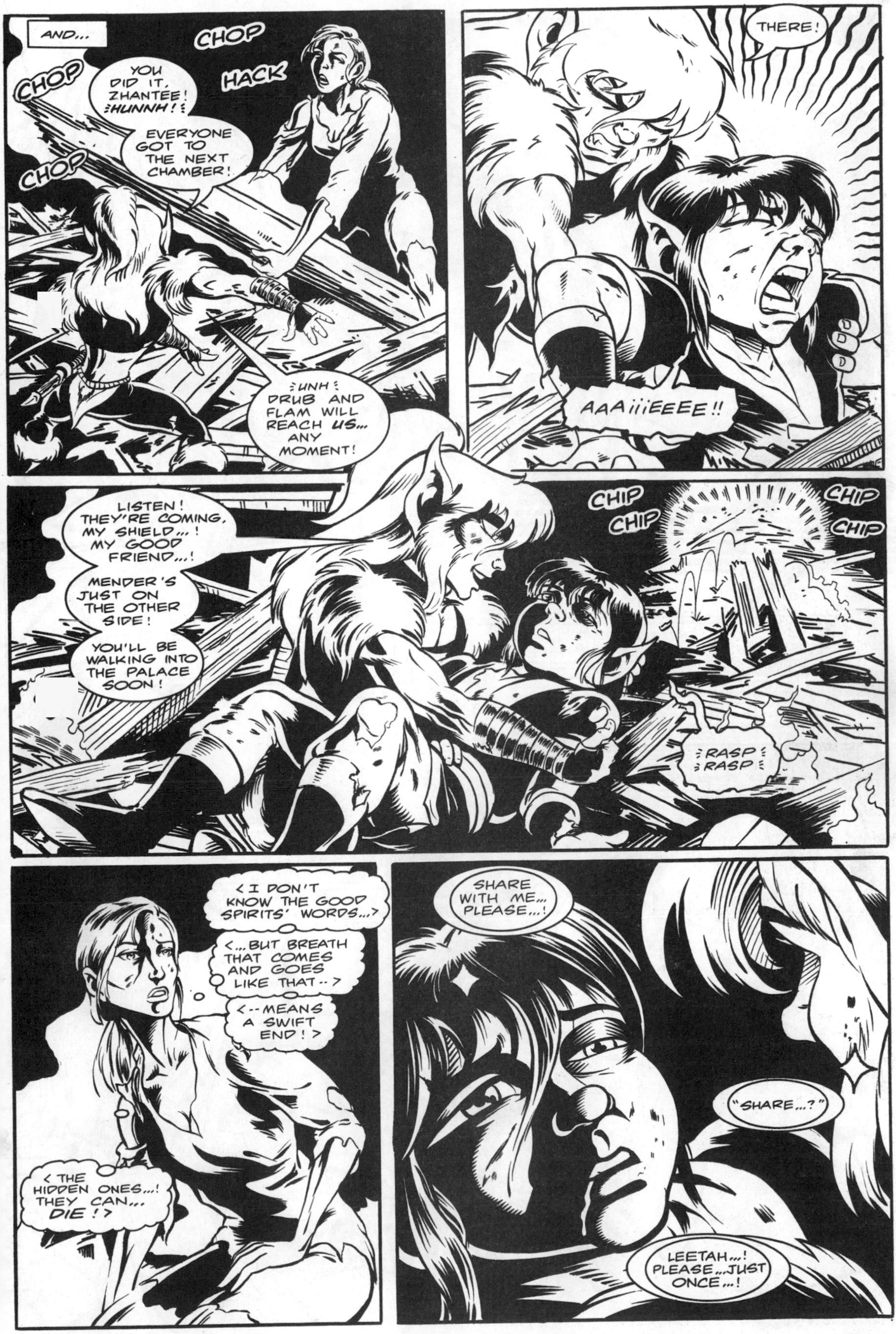

AND...
CHOP
CHOP
HACK
YOU DID IT, ZHANTEE! HUNNH!
EVERYONE GOT TO THE NEXT CHAMBER!
CHOP
UNH DRUB AND FLAM WILL REACH US... ANY MOMENT!
THERE!
AAAiiiEEEE!!
LISTEN! THEY'RE COMING, MY SHIELD...! MY GOOD FRIEND...!
MENDER'S JUST ON THE OTHER SIDE!
YOU'LL BE WALKING INTO THE PALACE SOON!
CHIP
CHIP
CHIP
CHIP
RASP RASP
< I DON'T KNOW THE GOOD SPIRITS' WORDS...>
<...BUT BREATH THAT COMES AND GOES LIKE THAT-->
<--MEANS A SWIFT END!>
< THE HIDDEN ONES...! THEY CAN... DIE!>
SHARE WITH ME... PLEASE...!
"SHARE...?"
LEETAH...! PLEASE...JUST ONCE...!

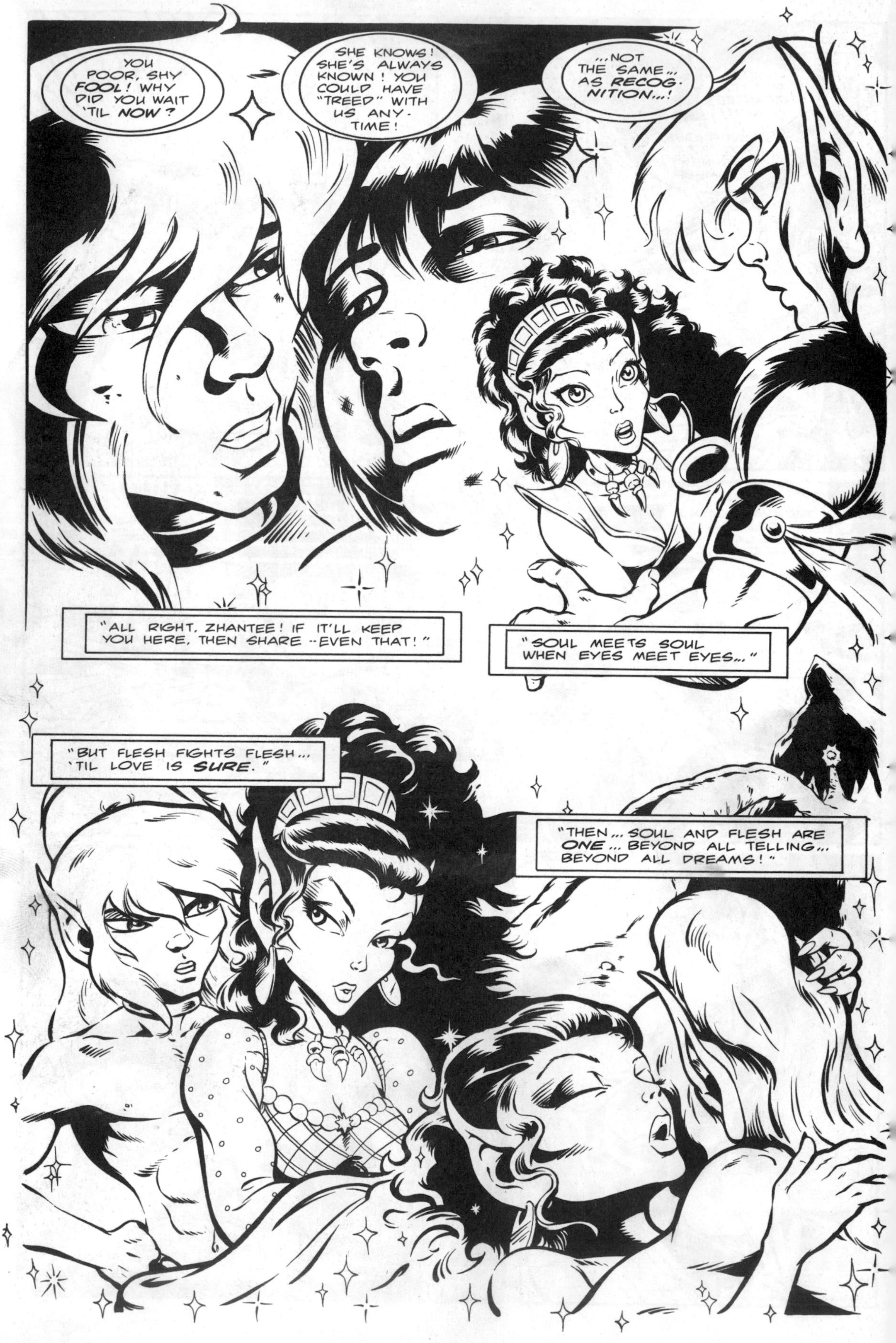
YOU POOR, SHY FOOL! WHY DID YOU WAIT 'TIL NOW?
SHE KNOWS! SHE'S ALWAYS KNOWN! YOU COULD HAVE "TREED" WITH US ANY-TIME!
...NOT THE SAME... AS RECOG-NITION...!
"ALL RIGHT, ZHANTEE! IF IT'LL KEEP YOU HERE, THEN SHARE --EVEN THAT!"
"SOUL MEETS SOUL WHEN EYES MEET EYES..."
"BUT FLESH FIGHTS FLESH... 'TIL LOVE IS SURE."
"THEN... SOUL AND FLESH ARE ONE... BEYOND ALL TELLING... BEYOND ALL DREAMS!"

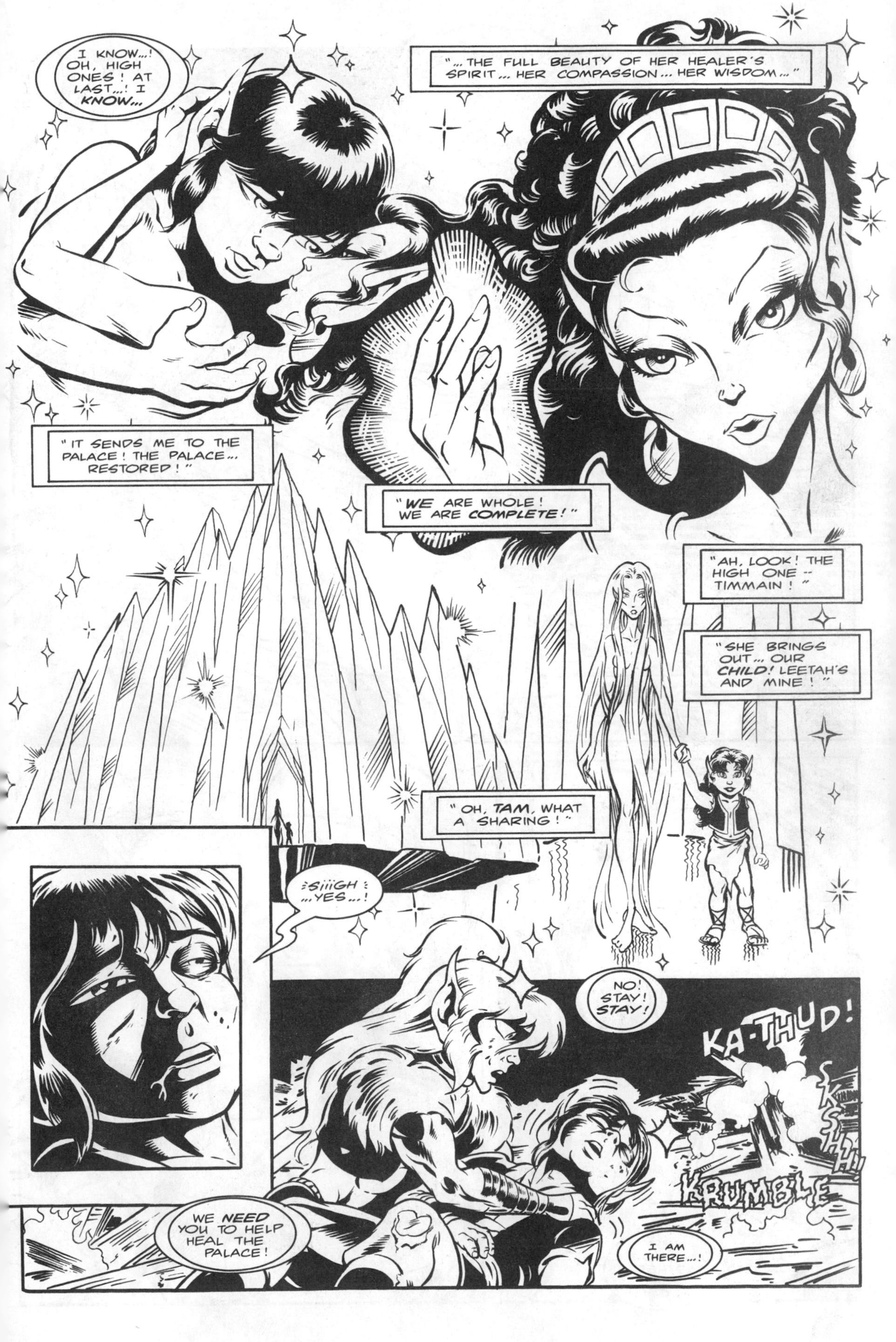
I KNOW...! OH, HIGH ONES! AT LAST...! I KNOW...
"...THE FULL BEAUTY OF HER HEALER'S SPIRIT... HER COMPASSION... HER WISDOM..."
"IT SENDS ME TO THE PALACE! THE PALACE... RESTORED!"
"WE ARE WHOLE! WE ARE COMPLETE!"
"AH, LOOK! THE HIGH ONE -- TIMMAIN!"
"SHE BRINGS OUT... OUR CHILD! LEETAH'S AND MINE!"
"OH, TAM, WHAT A SHARING!"
SIIIGH ...YES...!
NO! STAY! STAY!
KA-THUD!
KSSHH!
KRUMBLE
WE NEED YOU TO HELP HEAL THE PALACE!
I AM THERE...!

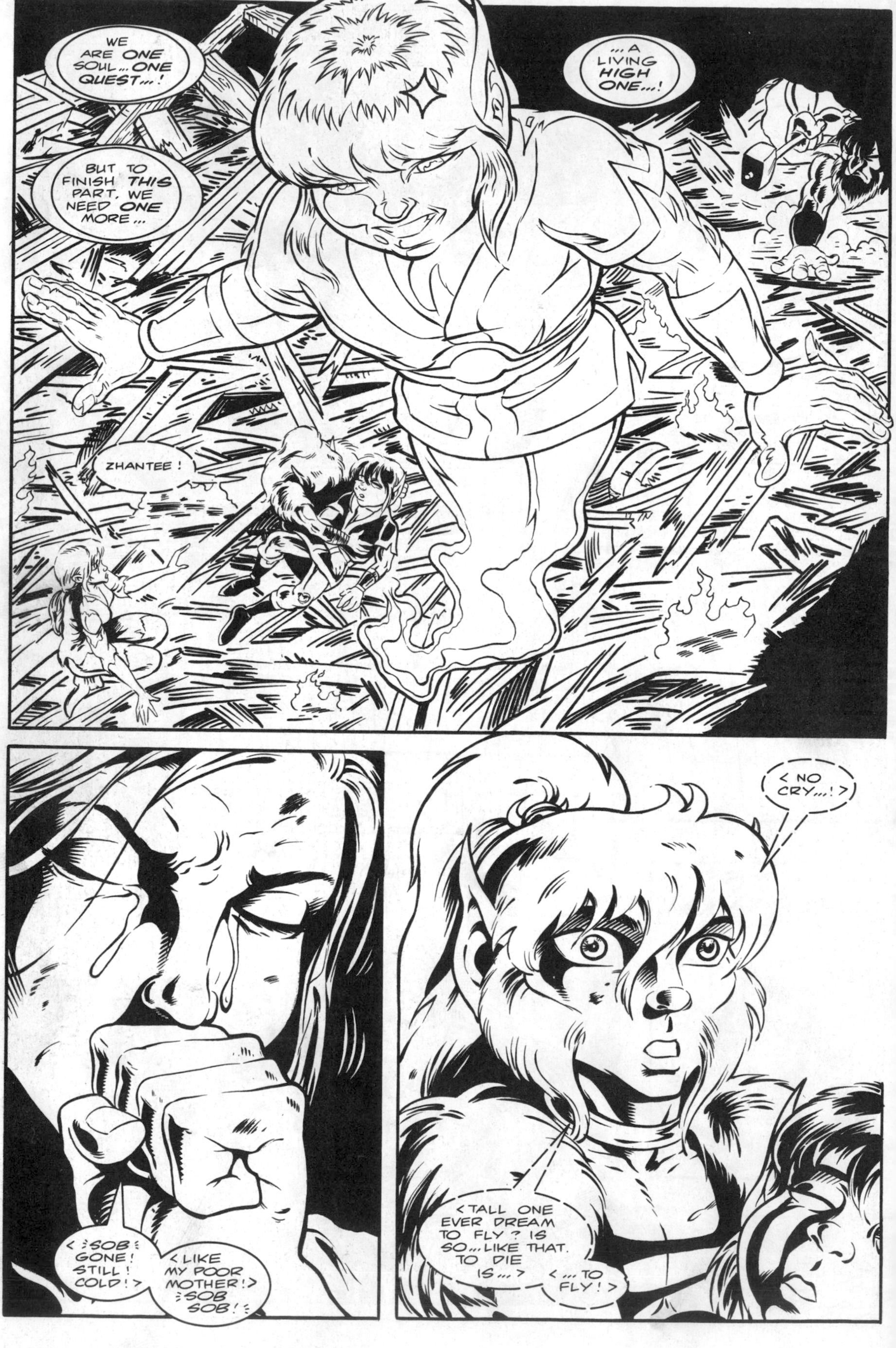
WE ARE ONE SOUL... ONE QUEST...!
BUT TO FINISH THIS PART, WE NEED ONE MORE...
...A LIVING HIGH ONE...!
ZHANTEE!
< :SOB: GONE! STILL! COLD! >
< LIKE MY POOR MOTHER! > :SOB SOB!:
< NO CRY...! >
< TALL ONE EVER DREAM TO FLY? IS SO... LIKE THAT. TO DIE IS... >
< ...TO FLY! >

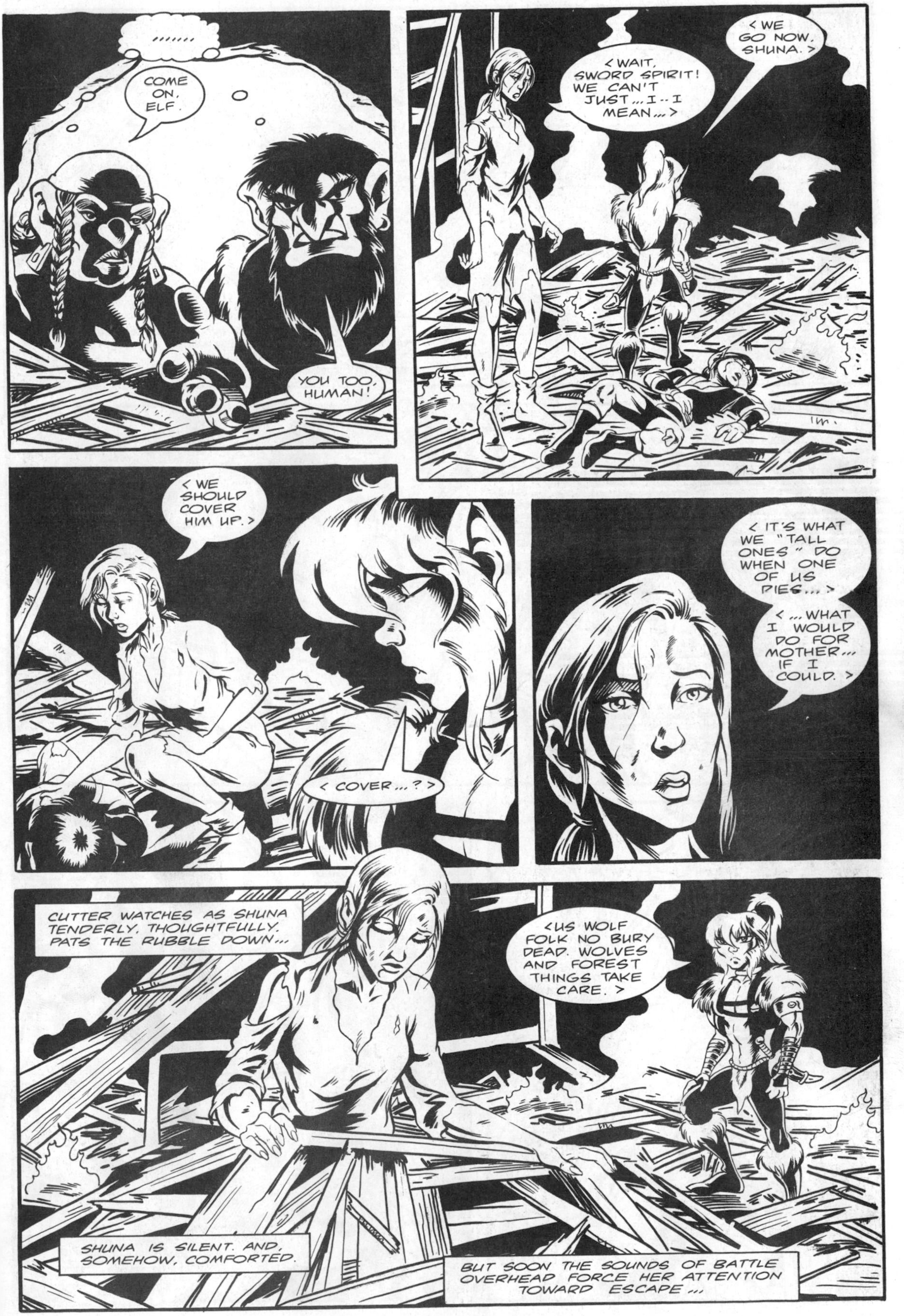
......
COME ON, ELF.
YOU TOO, HUMAN!
< WAIT, SWORD SPIRIT! WE CAN'T JUST... I--I MEAN... >
< WE GO NOW, SHUNA. >
< WE SHOULD COVER HIM UP. >
< COVER...? >
< IT'S WHAT WE "TALL ONES" DO WHEN ONE OF US DIES... >
< ...WHAT I WOULD DO FOR MOTHER... IF I COULD. >
CUTTER WATCHES AS SHUNA TENDERLY, THOUGHTFULLY, PATS THE RUBBLE DOWN...
<US WOLF FOLK NO BURY DEAD. WOLVES AND FOREST THINGS TAKE CARE. >
SHUNA IS SILENT. AND, SOMEHOW, COMFORTED.
BUT SOON THE SOUNDS OF BATTLE OVERHEAD FORCE HER ATTENTION TOWARD ESCAPE...

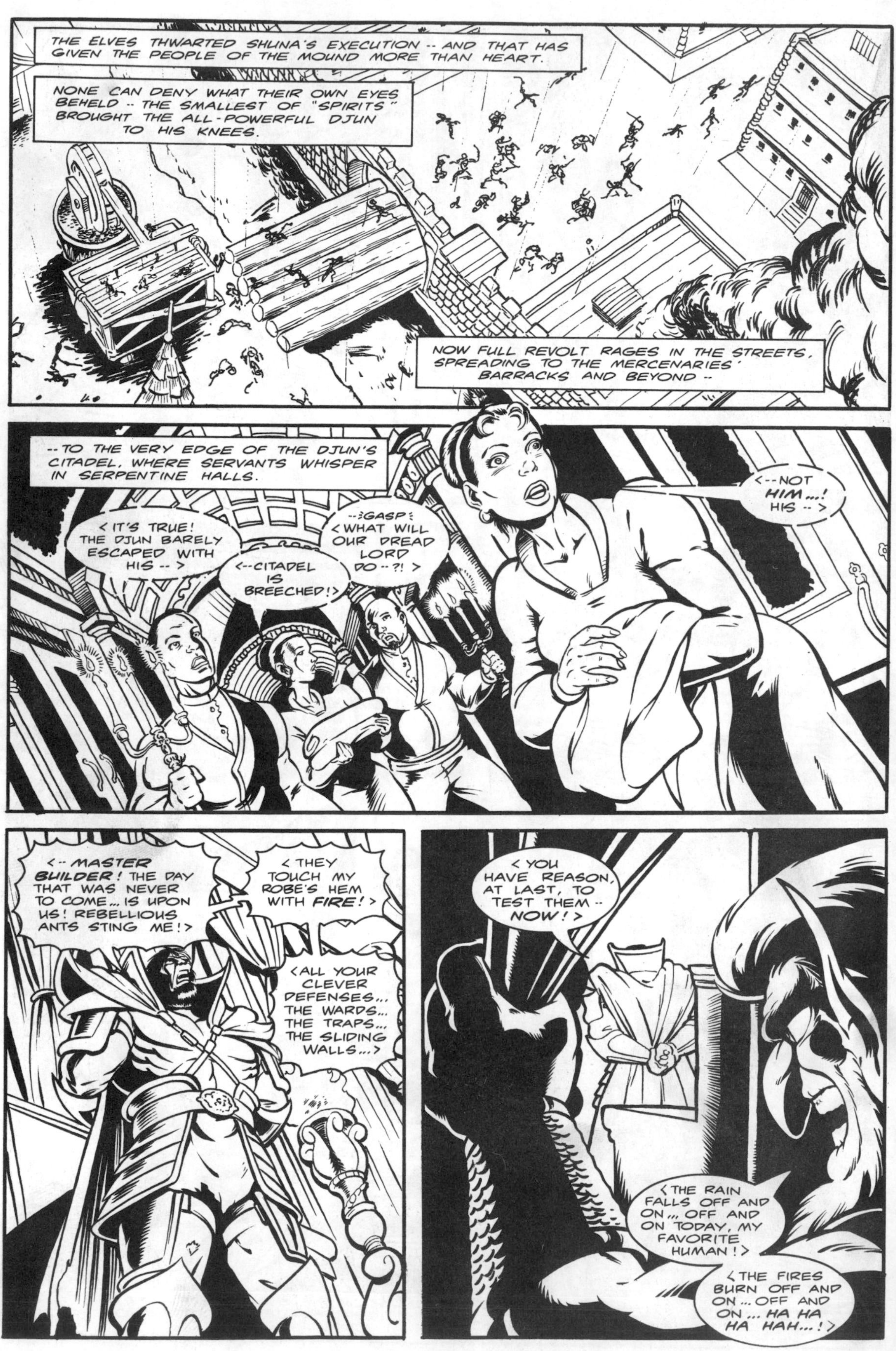

THE ELVES THWARTED SHUNA'S EXECUTION -- AND THAT HAS GIVEN THE PEOPLE OF THE MOUND MORE THAN HEART.
NONE CAN DENY WHAT THEIR OWN EYES BEHELD -- THE SMALLEST OF "SPIRITS" BROUGHT THE ALL-POWERFUL DJUN TO HIS KNEES.
NOW FULL REVOLT RAGES IN THE STREETS, SPREADING TO THE MERCENARIES' BARRACKS AND BEYOND --
-- TO THE VERY EDGE OF THE DJUN'S CITADEL, WHERE SERVANTS WHISPER IN SERPENTINE HALLS.
< IT'S TRUE! THE DJUN BARELY ESCAPED WITH HIS -- >
< --CITADEL IS BREECHED! >
--GASP-- < WHAT WILL OUR DREAD LORD DO --?! >
< --NOT HIM...! HIS -- >
< -- MASTER BUILDER! THE DAY THAT WAS NEVER TO COME... IS UPON US! REBELLIOUS ANTS STING ME! >
< THEY TOUCH MY ROBE'S HEM WITH FIRE! >
< ALL YOUR CLEVER DEFENSES... THE WARDS... THE TRAPS... THE SLIDING WALLS... >
< YOU HAVE REASON, AT LAST, TO TEST THEM -- NOW! >
< THE RAIN FALLS OFF AND ON... OFF AND ON TODAY, MY FAVORITE HUMAN! >
< THE FIRES BURN OFF AND ON... OFF AND ON... HA HA HA HAH...! >

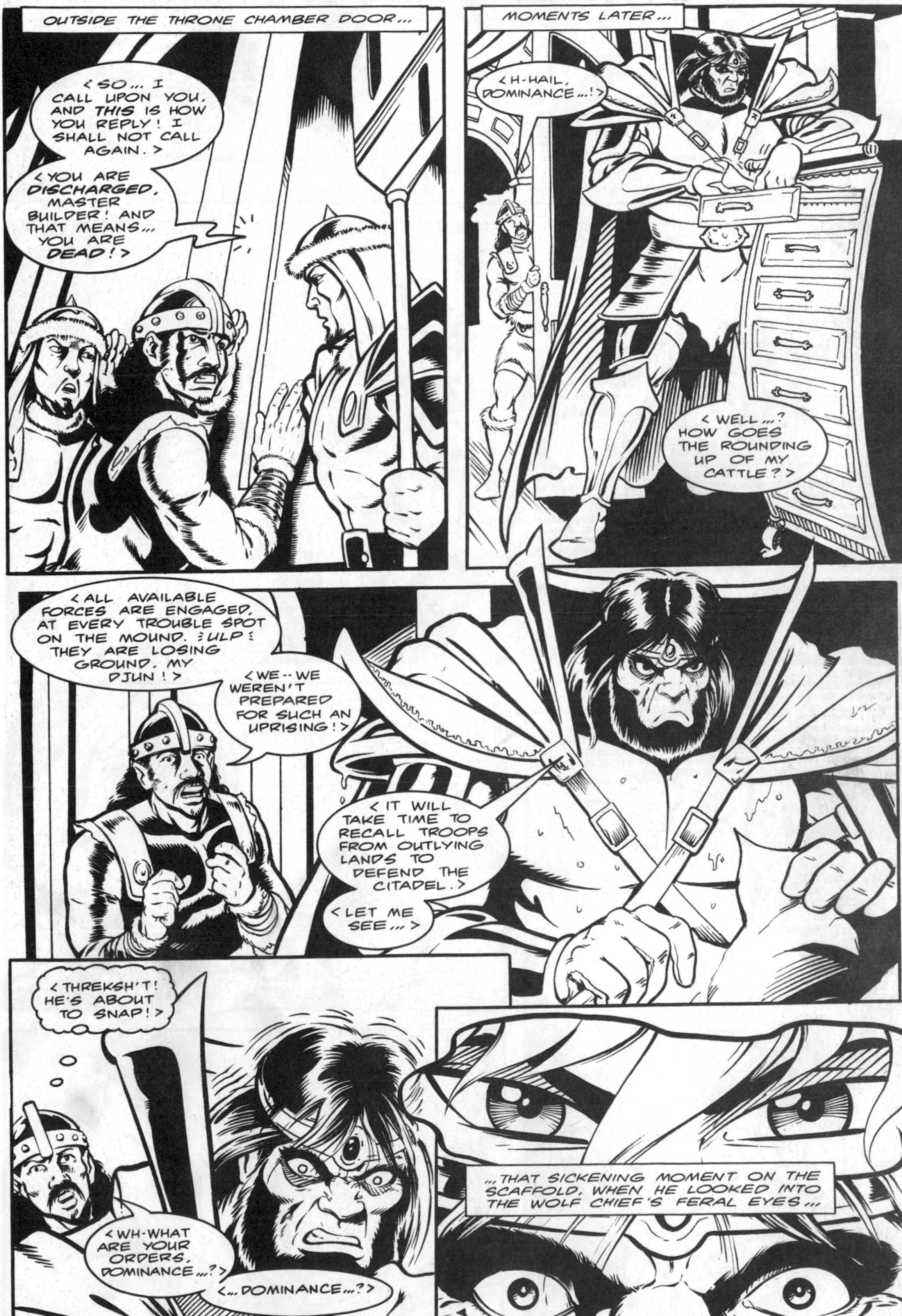
OUTSIDE THE THRONE CHAMBER DOOR...
< SO... I CALL UPON YOU, AND THIS IS HOW YOU REPLY! I SHALL NOT CALL AGAIN. >
< YOU ARE DISCHARGED, MASTER BUILDER! AND THAT MEANS... YOU ARE DEAD! >
MOMENTS LATER...
< H-HAIL, DOMINANCE...! >
< WELL...? HOW GOES THE ROUNDING UP OF MY CATTLE? >
< ALL AVAILABLE FORCES ARE ENGAGED, AT EVERY TROUBLE SPOT ON THE MOUND. :ULP: THEY ARE LOSING GROUND, MY DJUN! >
< WE -- WE WEREN'T PREPARED FOR SUCH AN UPRISING! >
< IT WILL TAKE TIME TO RECALL TROOPS FROM OUTLYING LANDS TO DEFEND THE CITADEL. >
< LET ME SEE... >
< THREKSH'T! HE'S ABOUT TO SNAP! >
< WH-WHAT ARE YOUR ORDERS, DOMINANCE...? >
< ...DOMINANCE...? >
BUT THE DJUN THINKS ONLY OF THAT MOMENT...
...THAT SICKENING MOMENT ON THE SCAFFOLD, WHEN HE LOOKED INTO THE WOLF CHIEF'S FERAL EYES...

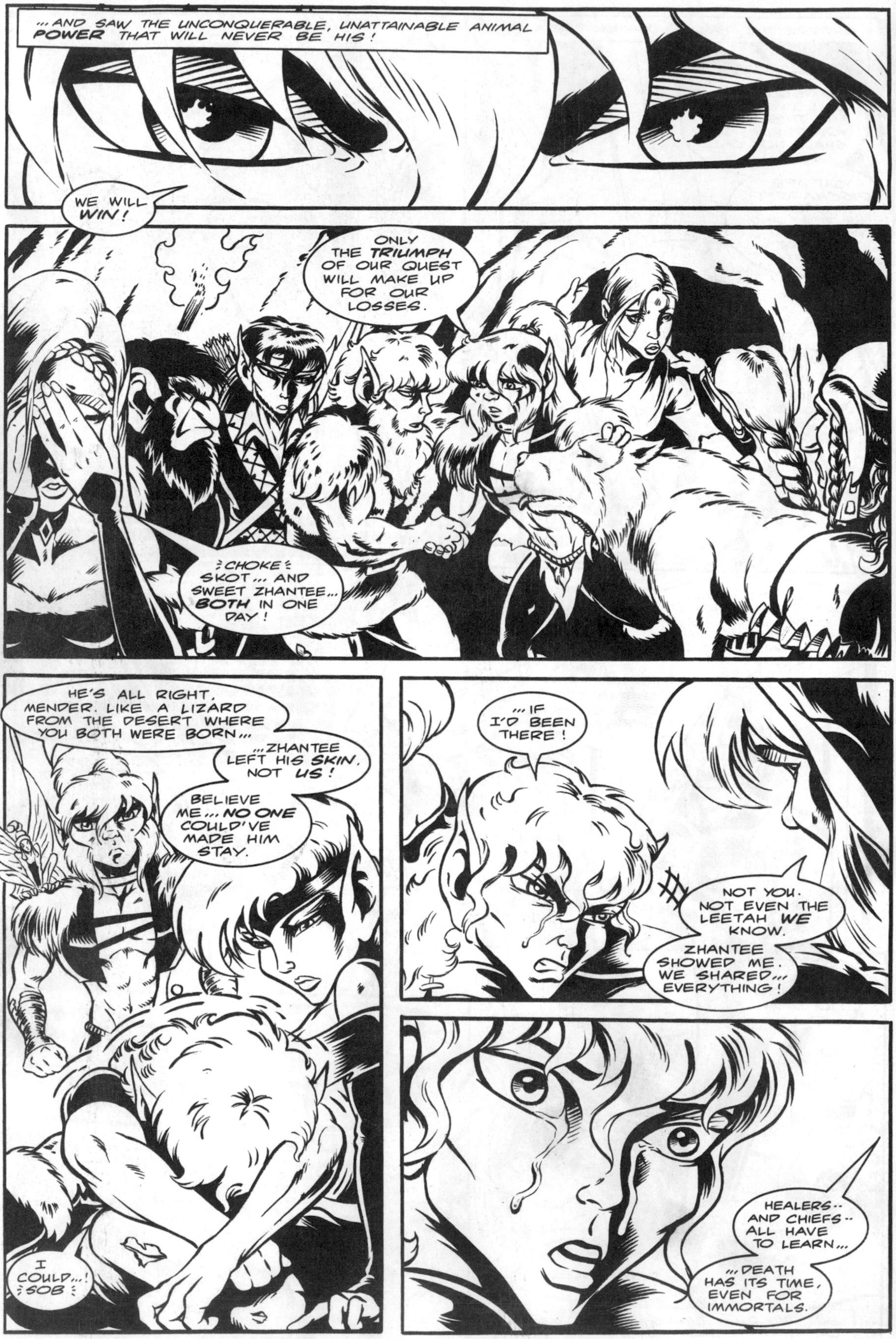
...AND SAW THE UNCONQUERABLE, UNATTAINABLE ANIMAL POWER THAT WILL NEVER BE HIS!
WE WILL WIN!
ONLY THE TRIUMPH OF OUR QUEST WILL MAKE UP FOR OUR LOSSES.
:CHOKE: SKOT... AND SWEET ZHANTEE... BOTH IN ONE DAY!
HE'S ALL RIGHT, MENDER. LIKE A LIZARD FROM THE DESERT WHERE YOU BOTH WERE BORN...
...ZHANTEE LEFT HIS SKIN, NOT US!
BELIEVE ME... NO ONE COULD'VE MADE HIM STAY.
I COULD...! :SOB:
...IF I'D BEEN THERE!
NOT YOU. NOT EVEN THE LEETAH WE KNOW.
ZHANTEE SHOWED ME. WE SHARED... EVERYTHING!
HEALERS.. AND CHIEFS.. ALL HAVE TO LEARN...
...DEATH HAS ITS TIME, EVEN FOR IMMORTALS.

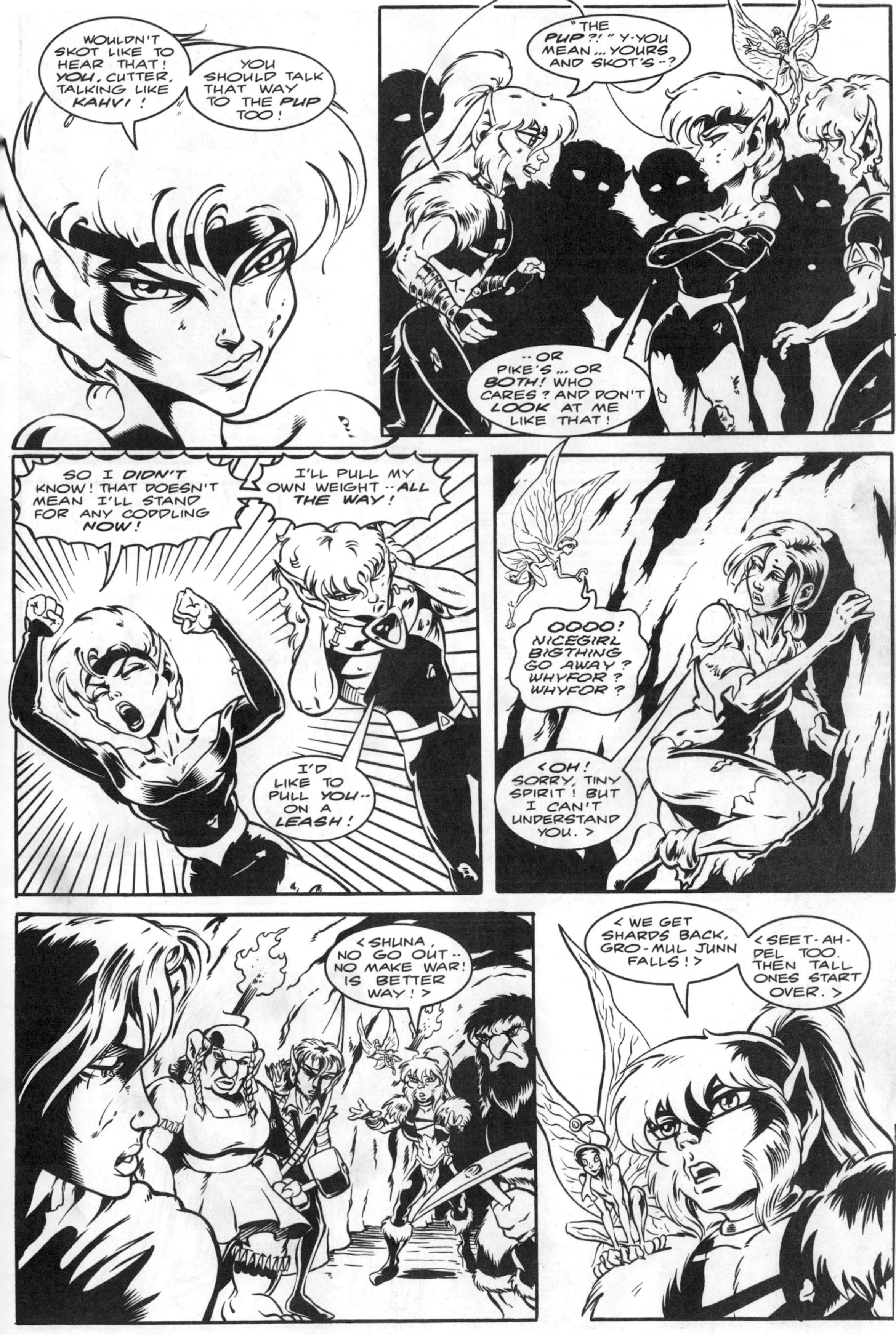
WOULDN'T SKOT LIKE TO HEAR THAT! YOU, CUTTER, TALKING LIKE KAHVI!
YOU SHOULD TALK THAT WAY TO THE PUP TOO!
"THE PUP?!" Y-YOU MEAN... YOURS AND SKOT'S--?
--OR PIKE'S... OR BOTH! WHO CARES? AND DON'T LOOK AT ME LIKE THAT!
SO I DIDN'T KNOW! THAT DOESN'T MEAN I'LL STAND FOR ANY CODDLING NOW!
I'LL PULL MY OWN WEIGHT--ALL THE WAY!
I'D LIKE TO PULL YOU--ON A LEASH!
OOOO! NICEGIRL BIGTHING GO AWAY? WHYFOR? WHYFOR?
<OH! SORRY, TINY SPIRIT! BUT I CAN'T UNDERSTAND YOU.>
<SHUNA, NO GO OUT-- NO MAKE WAR! IS BETTER WAY!>
<WE GET SHARDS BACK. GRO-MUL JUNN FALLS!>
<SEET-AH-DEL TOO. THEN TALL ONES START OVER.>

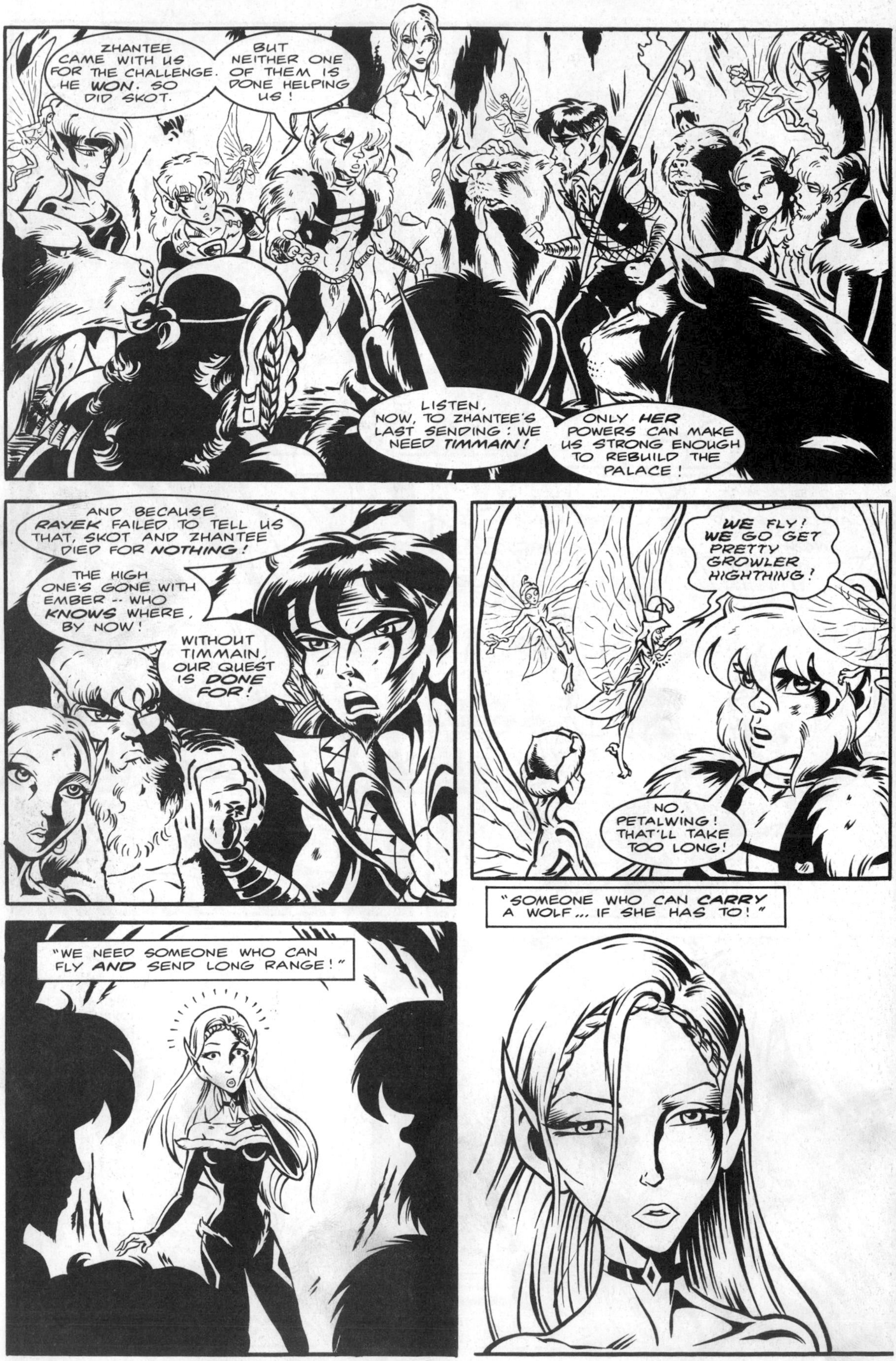
ZHANTEE CAME WITH US FOR THE CHALLENGE. HE WON. SO DID SKOT.
BUT NEITHER ONE OF THEM IS DONE HELPING US!
LISTEN, NOW, TO ZHANTEE'S LAST SENDING: WE NEED TIMMAIN!
ONLY HER POWERS CAN MAKE US STRONG ENOUGH TO REBUILD THE PALACE!
AND BECAUSE RAYEK FAILED TO TELL US THAT, SKOT AND ZHANTEE DIED FOR NOTHING!
THE HIGH ONE'S GONE WITH EMBER -- WHO KNOWS WHERE, BY NOW!
WITHOUT TIMMAIN, OUR QUEST IS DONE FOR!
WE FLY! WE GO GET PRETTY GROWLER HIGHTHING!
NO, PETALWING! THAT'LL TAKE TOO LONG!
"WE NEED SOMEONE WHO CAN FLY AND SEND LONG RANGE!"
"SOMEONE WHO CAN CARRY A WOLF... IF SHE HAS TO!"

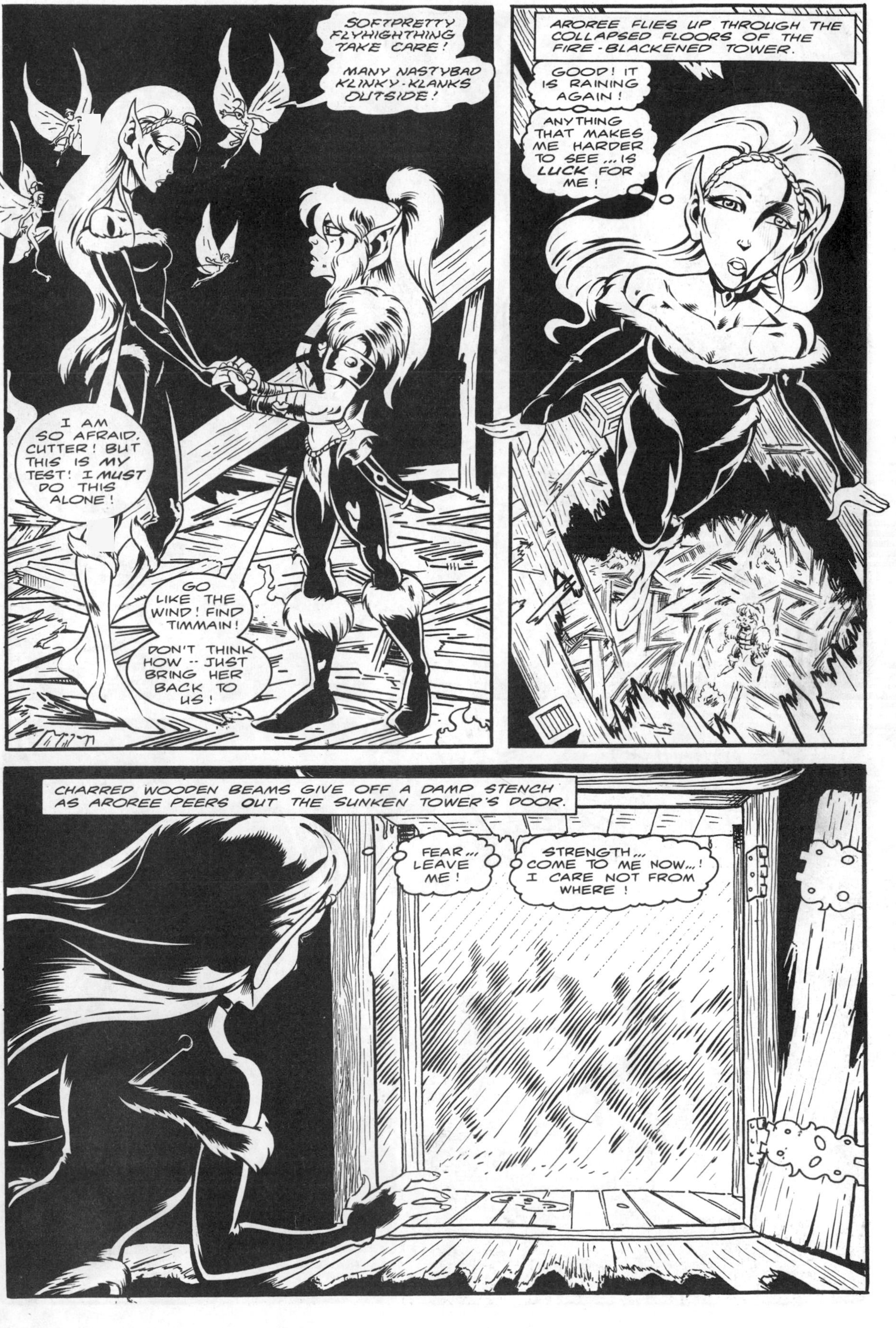
SOFTPRETTY FLYHIGHTHING TAKE CARE!
MANY NASTYBAD KLINKY-KLANKS OUTSIDE!
I AM SO AFRAID, CUTTER! BUT THIS IS MY TEST! I MUST DO THIS ALONE!
GO LIKE THE WIND! FIND TIMMAIN!
DON'T THINK HOW -- JUST BRING HER BACK TO US!
AROREE FLIES UP THROUGH THE COLLAPSED FLOORS OF THE FIRE-BLACKENED TOWER.
GOOD! IT IS RAINING AGAIN!
ANYTHING THAT MAKES ME HARDER TO SEE... IS LUCK FOR ME!
CHARRED WOODEN BEAMS GIVE OFF A DAMP STENCH AS AROREE PEERS OUT THE SUNKEN TOWER'S DOOR.
FEAR... LEAVE ME!
STRENGTH... COME TO ME NOW...! I CARE NOT FROM WHERE!

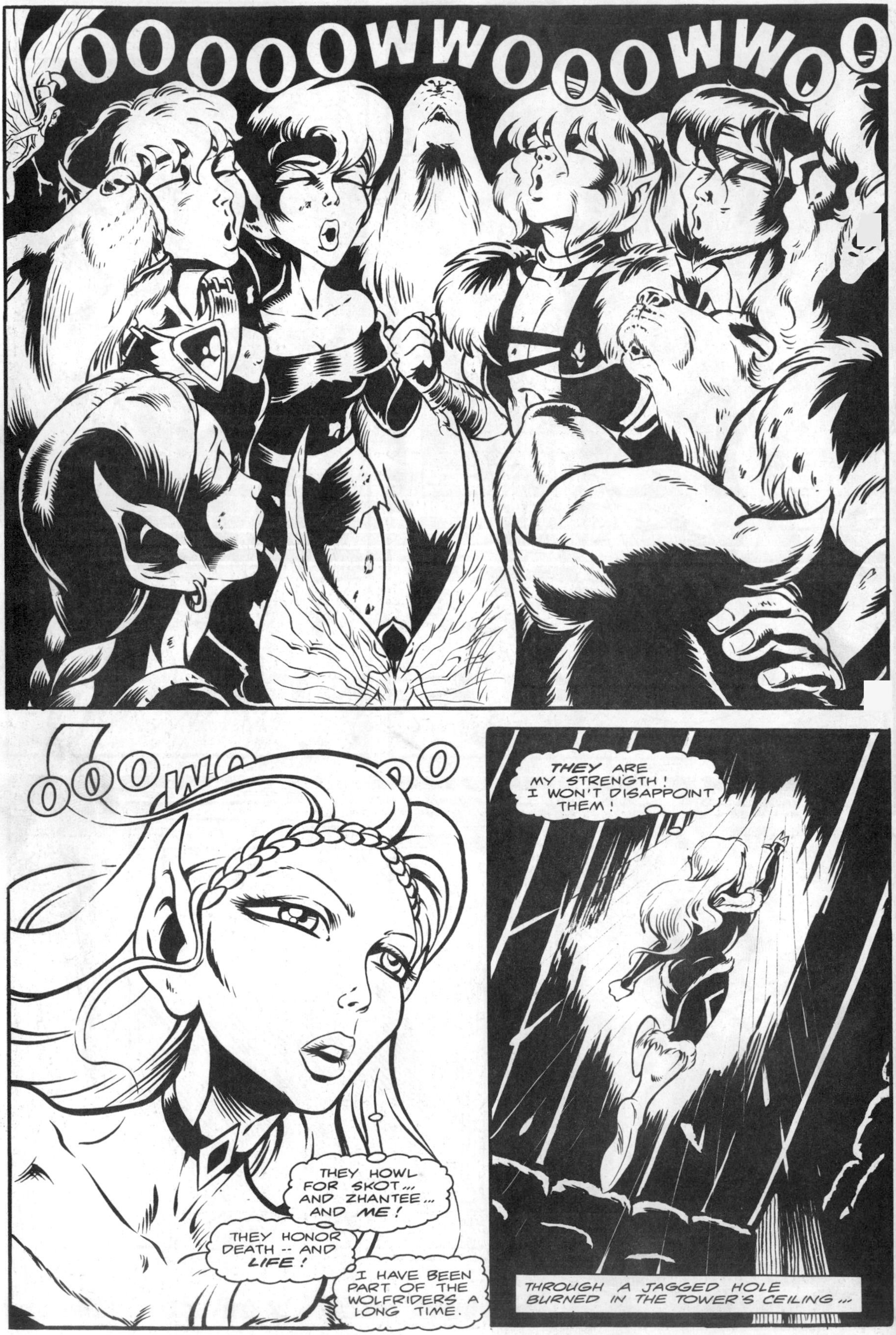

OOOOOWWWOOOWWOO
OOOWO
THEY HOWL FOR SKOT... AND ZHANTEE... AND ME!
THEY HONOR DEATH -- AND LIFE!
I HAVE BEEN PART OF THE WOLFRIDERS A LONG TIME.
THEY ARE MY STRENGTH! I WON'T DISAPPOINT THEM!
THROUGH A JAGGED HOLE BURNED IN THE TOWER'S CEILING...

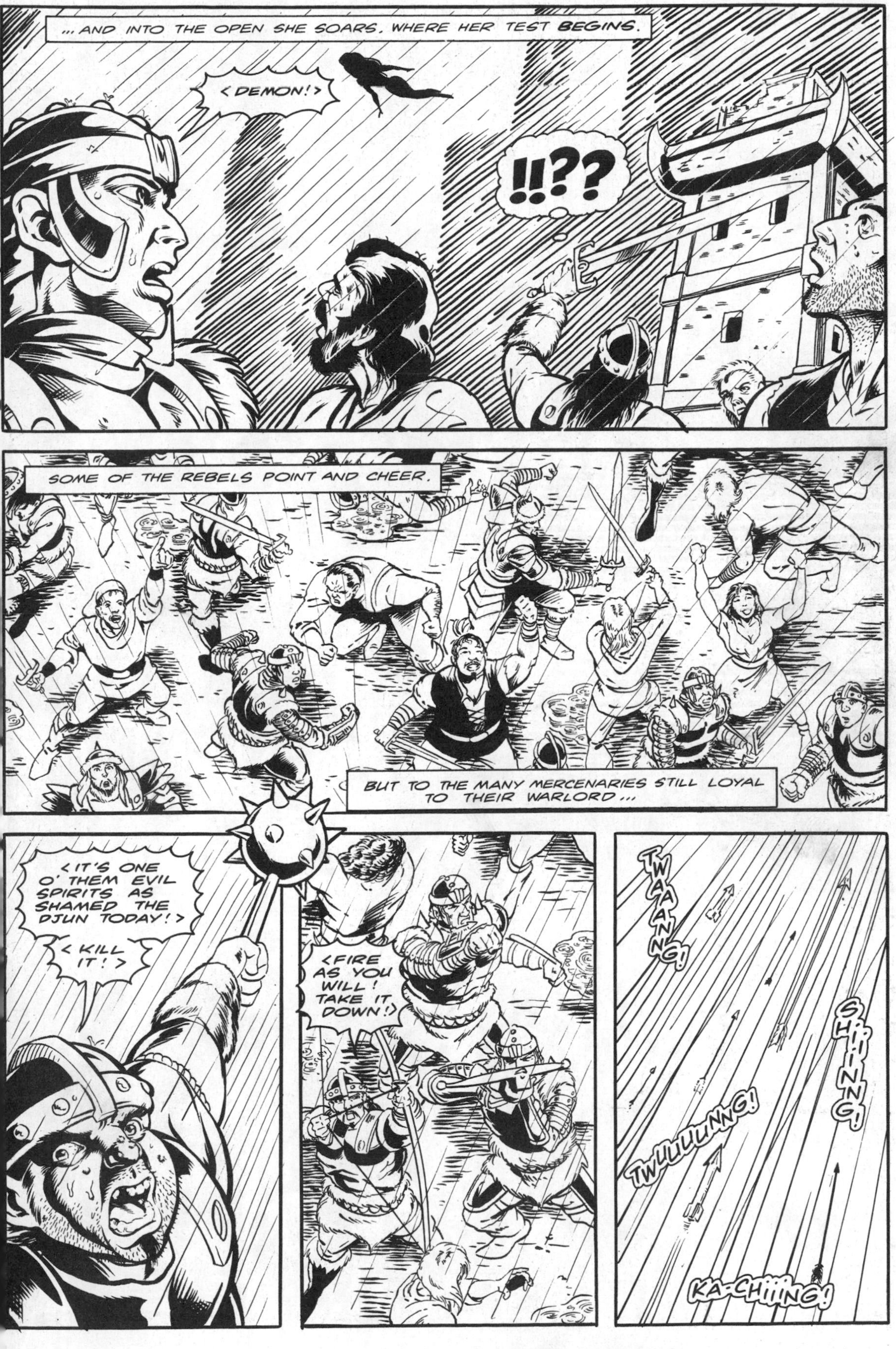
...AND INTO THE OPEN SHE SOARS, WHERE HER TEST BEGINS.
< DEMON! >
!!??
SOME OF THE REBELS POINT AND CHEER.
BUT TO THE MANY MERCENARIES STILL LOYAL TO THEIR WARLORD...
< IT'S ONE O' THEM EVIL SPIRITS AS SHAMED THE DJUN TODAY! >
< KILL IT! >
<FIRE AS YOU WILL! TAKE IT DOWN!>
TWAAANG!
SHIIINNG!
TWUUUUNNG!
KA-CHIIING!

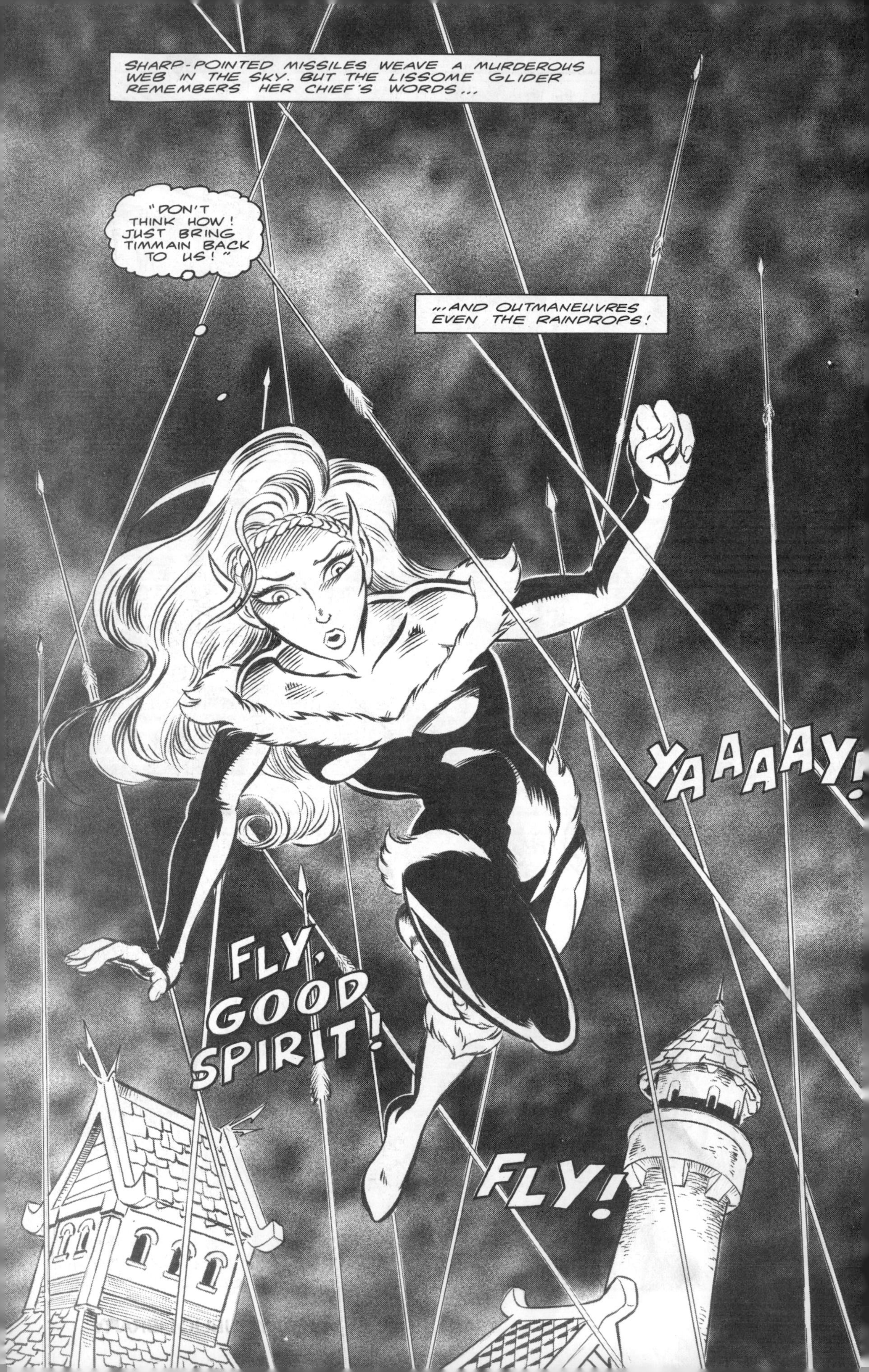
SHARP-POINTED MISSILES WEAVE A MURDEROUS WEB IN THE SKY. BUT THE LISSOME GLIDER REMEMBERS HER CHIEF'S WORDS...
"DON'T THINK HOW! JUST BRING TIMMAIN BACK TO US!"
...AND OUTMANEUVRES EVEN THE RAINDROPS!
YAAAAY!
FLY, GOOD SPIRIT!
FLY!

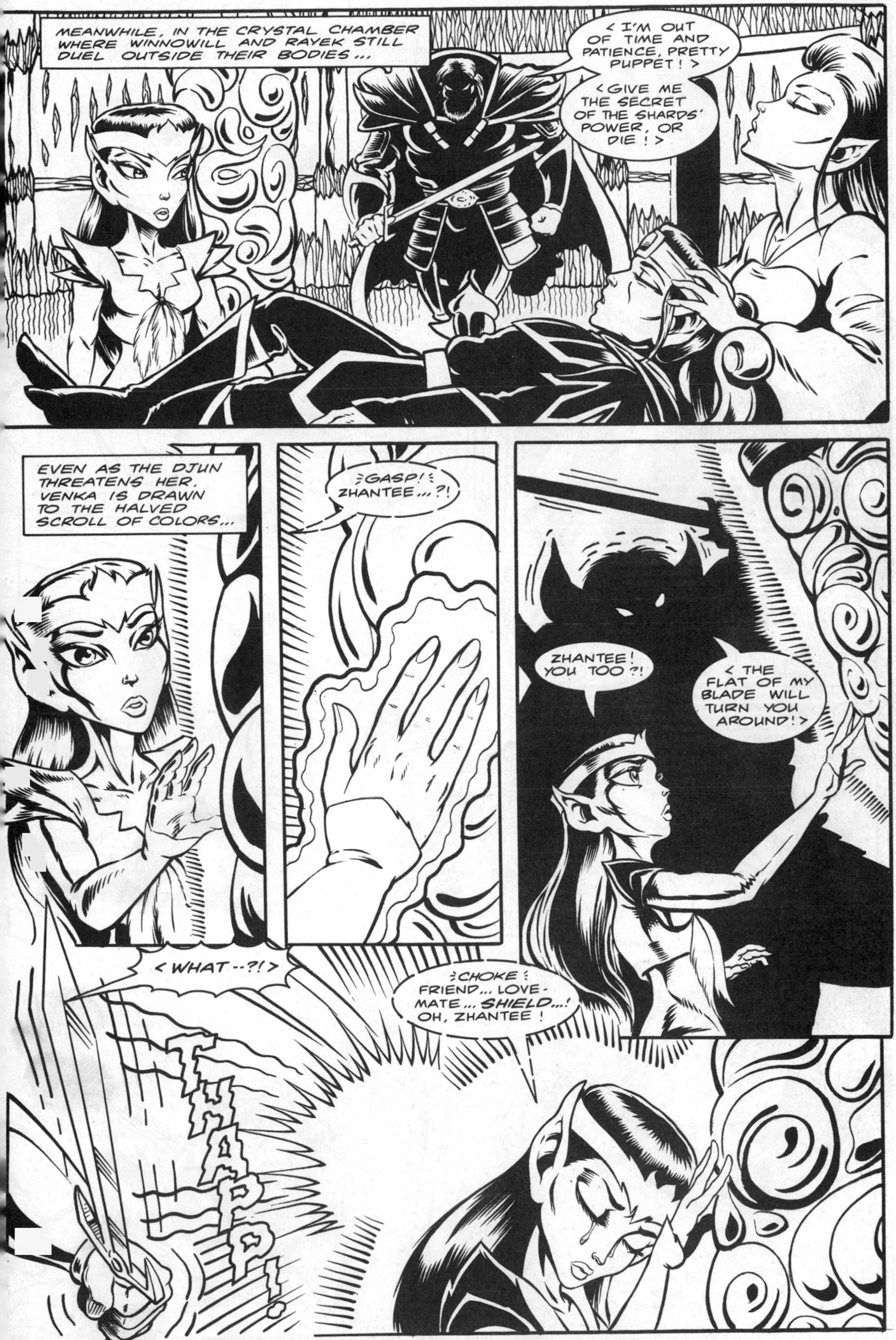
MEANWHILE, IN THE CRYSTAL CHAMBER WHERE WINNOWILL AND RAYEK STILL DUEL OUTSIDE THEIR BODIES...
< I'M OUT OF TIME AND PATIENCE, PRETTY PUPPET! >
< GIVE ME THE SECRET OF THE SHARDS' POWER, OR DIE! >
EVEN AS THE DJUN THREATENS HER, VENKA IS DRAWN TO THE HALVED SCROLL OF COLORS...
:GASP!: ZHANTEE...?!
ZHANTEE! YOU TOO ?!
< THE FLAT OF MY BLADE WILL TURN YOU AROUND! >
< WHAT--?! >
:CHOKE: FRIEND... LOVE-MATE... SHIELD...! OH, ZHANTEE!
THAPP!

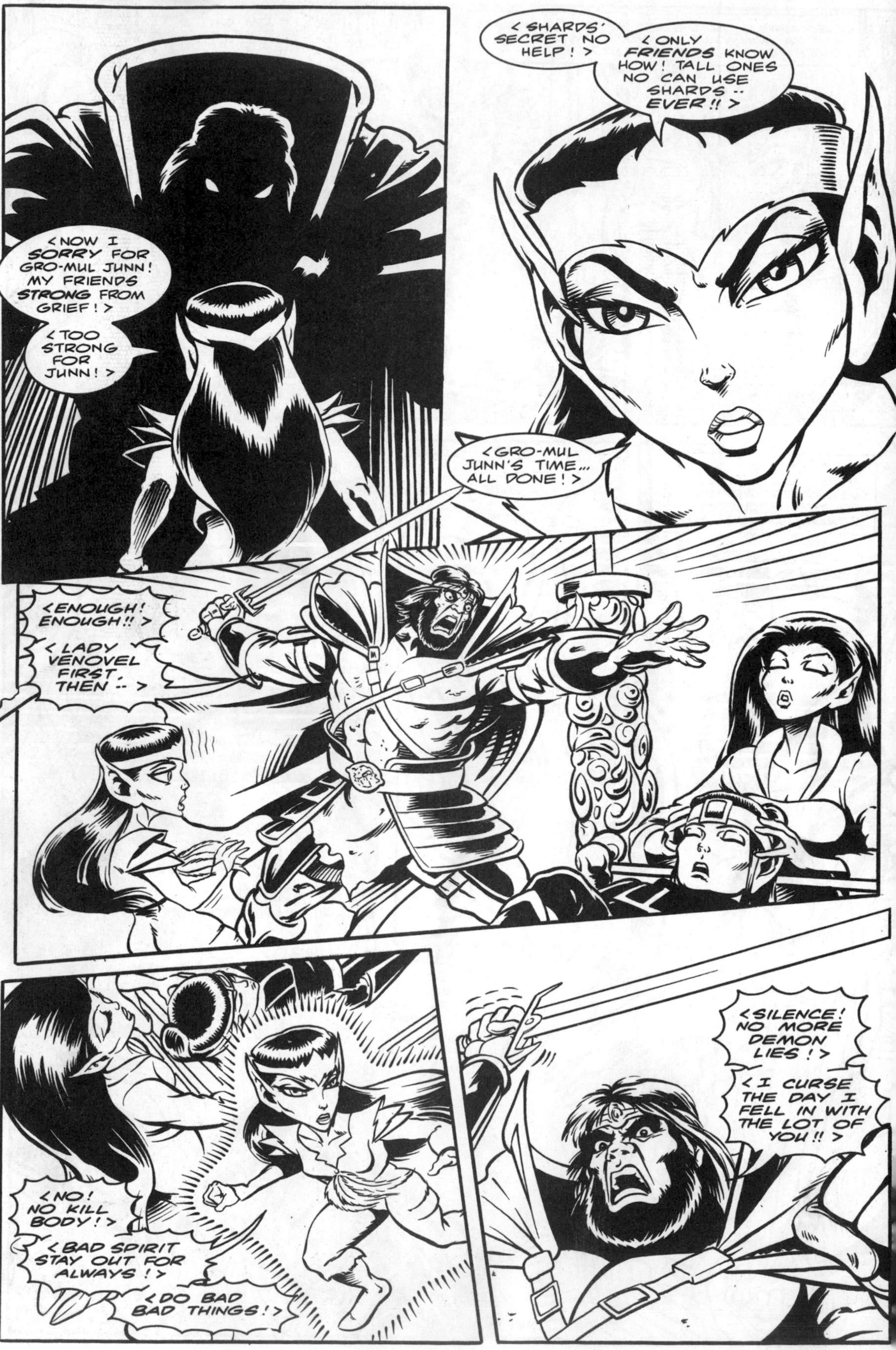
<NOW I SORRY FOR GRO-MUL JUNN! MY FRIENDS STRONG FROM GRIEF!>
<TOO STRONG FOR JUNN!>
<SHARDS' SECRET NO HELP!>
<ONLY FRIENDS KNOW HOW! TALL ONES NO CAN USE SHARDS -- EVER!!>
<GRO-MUL JUNN'S TIME... ALL DONE!>
<ENOUGH! ENOUGH!!>
<LADY VENOVEL FIRST. THEN -->
<NO! NO KILL BODY!>
<BAD SPIRIT STAY OUT FOR ALWAYS!>
<DO BAD BAD THINGS!>
<SILENCE! NO MORE DEMON LIES!>
<I CURSE THE DAY I FELL IN WITH THE LOT OF YOU!!>

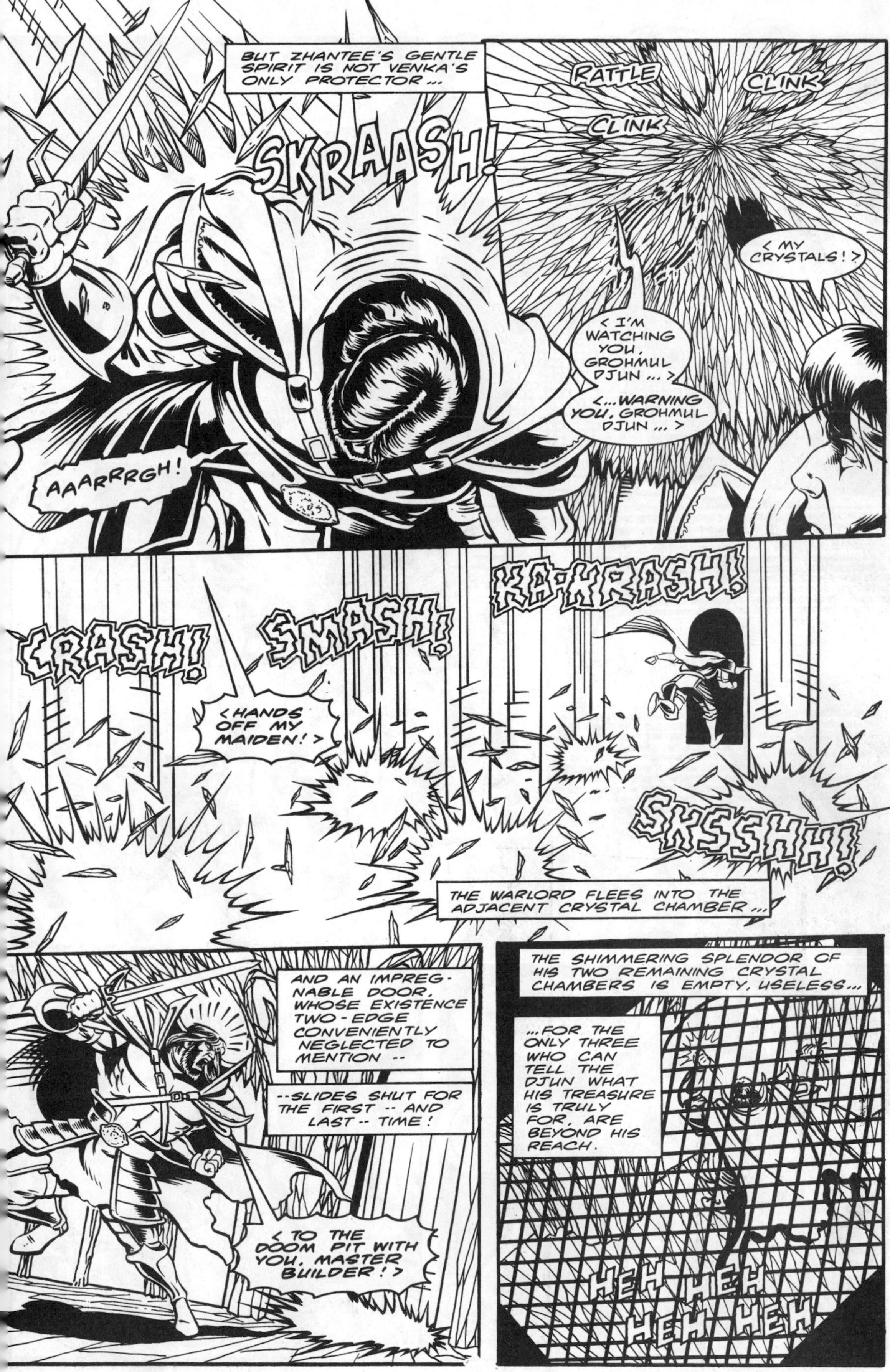
BUT ZHANTEE'S GENTLE SPIRIT IS NOT VENKA'S ONLY PROTECTOR ...
SKRAASH!
AAARRRGH!
RATTLE
CLINK
CLINK
< MY CRYSTALS! >
< I'M WATCHING YOU, GROHMUL DJUN ... >
< ... WARNING YOU, GROHMUL DJUN ... >
CRASH!
SMASH!
KA-KRASH!
< HANDS OFF MY MAIDEN! >
SKSSHH!
THE WARLORD FLEES INTO THE ADJACENT CRYSTAL CHAMBER ...
AND AN IMPREGNABLE DOOR, WHOSE EXISTENCE TWO-EDGE CONVENIENTLY NEGLECTED TO MENTION --
--SLIDES SHUT FOR THE FIRST -- AND LAST -- TIME!
< TO THE DOOM PIT WITH YOU, MASTER BUILDER! >
THE SHIMMERING SPLENDOR OF HIS TWO REMAINING CRYSTAL CHAMBERS IS EMPTY, USELESS ...
... FOR THE ONLY THREE WHO CAN TELL THE DJUN WHAT HIS TREASURE IS TRULY FOR, ARE BEYOND HIS REACH.
HEH HEH
HEH HEH

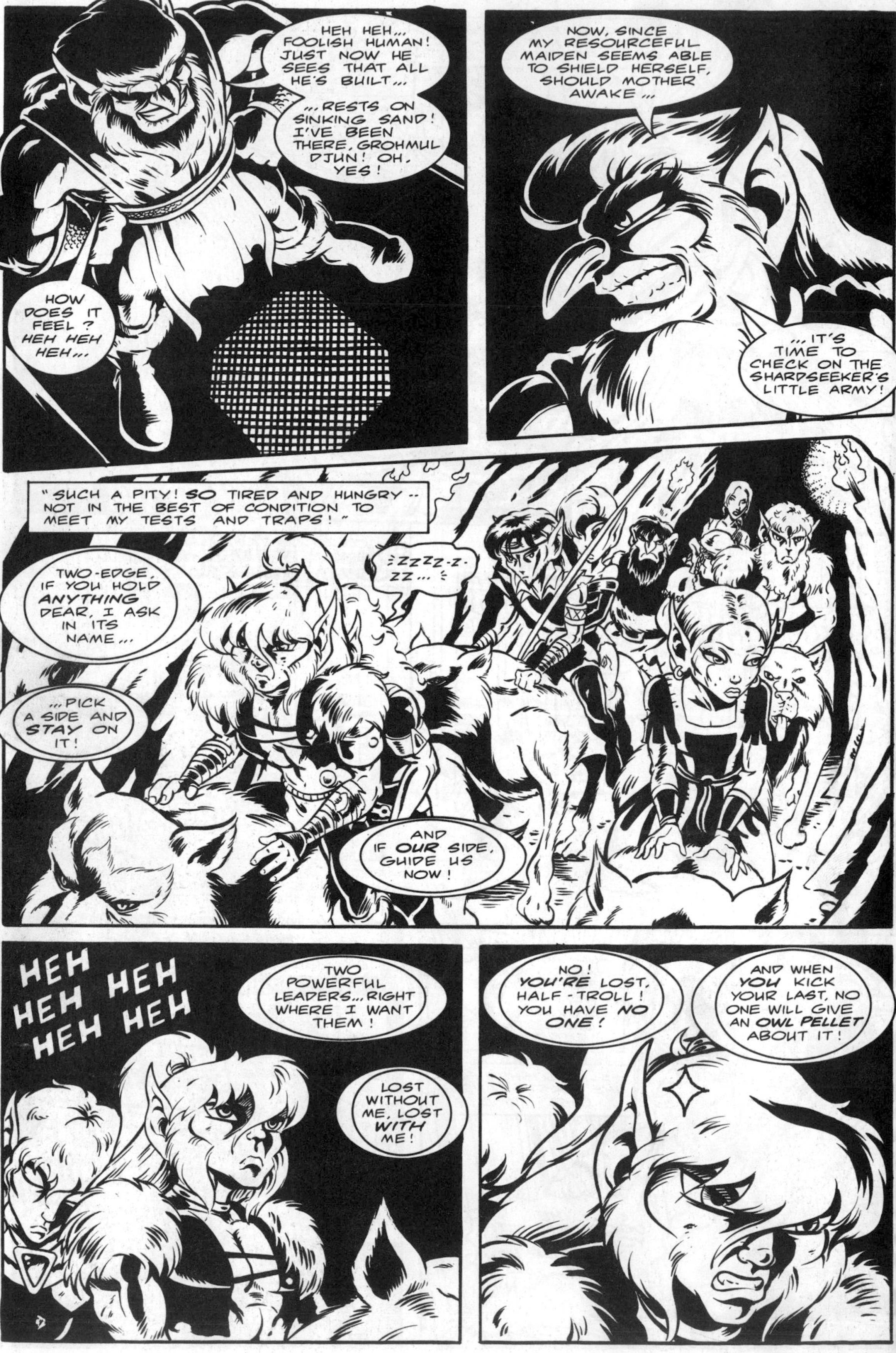
HEH HEH... FOOLISH HUMAN! JUST NOW HE SEES THAT ALL HE'S BUILT...
...RESTS ON SINKING SAND! I'VE BEEN THERE, GROHMUL DJUN! OH, YES!
HOW DOES IT FEEL? HEH HEH HEH...
NOW, SINCE MY RESOURCEFUL MAIDEN SEEMS ABLE TO SHIELD HERSELF, SHOULD MOTHER AWAKE...
...IT'S TIME TO CHECK ON THE SHARDSEEKER'S LITTLE ARMY!
"SUCH A PITY! SO TIRED AND HUNGRY -- NOT IN THE BEST OF CONDITION TO MEET MY TESTS AND TRAPS!"
TWO-EDGE, IF YOU HOLD ANYTHING DEAR, I ASK IN ITS NAME...
ZZZZ-Z-ZZ...
...PICK A SIDE AND STAY ON IT!
AND IF OUR SIDE, GUIDE US NOW!
HEH HEH HEH HEH HEH HEH
TWO POWERFUL LEADERS... RIGHT WHERE I WANT THEM!
LOST WITHOUT ME, LOST WITH ME!
NO! YOU'RE LOST, HALF-TROLL! YOU HAVE NO ONE!
AND WHEN YOU KICK YOUR LAST, NO ONE WILL GIVE AN OWL PELLET ABOUT IT!

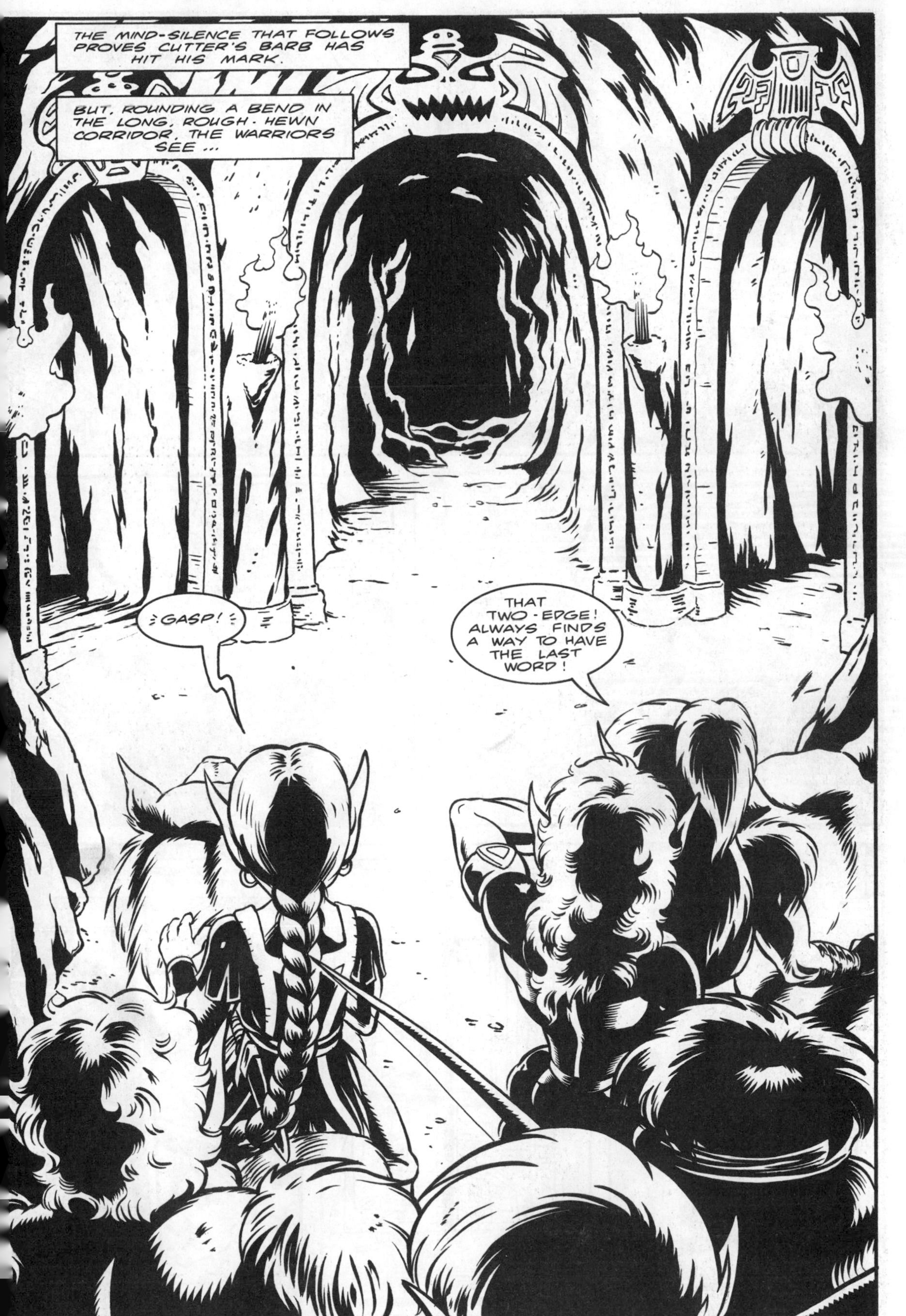
THE MIND-SILENCE THAT FOLLOWS PROVES CUTTER'S BARB HAS HIT HIS MARK.
BUT, ROUNDING A BEND IN THE LONG, ROUGH-HEWN CORRIDOR, THE WARRIORS SEE...
GASP!
THAT TWO-EDGE! ALWAYS FINDS A WAY TO HAVE THE LAST WORD!

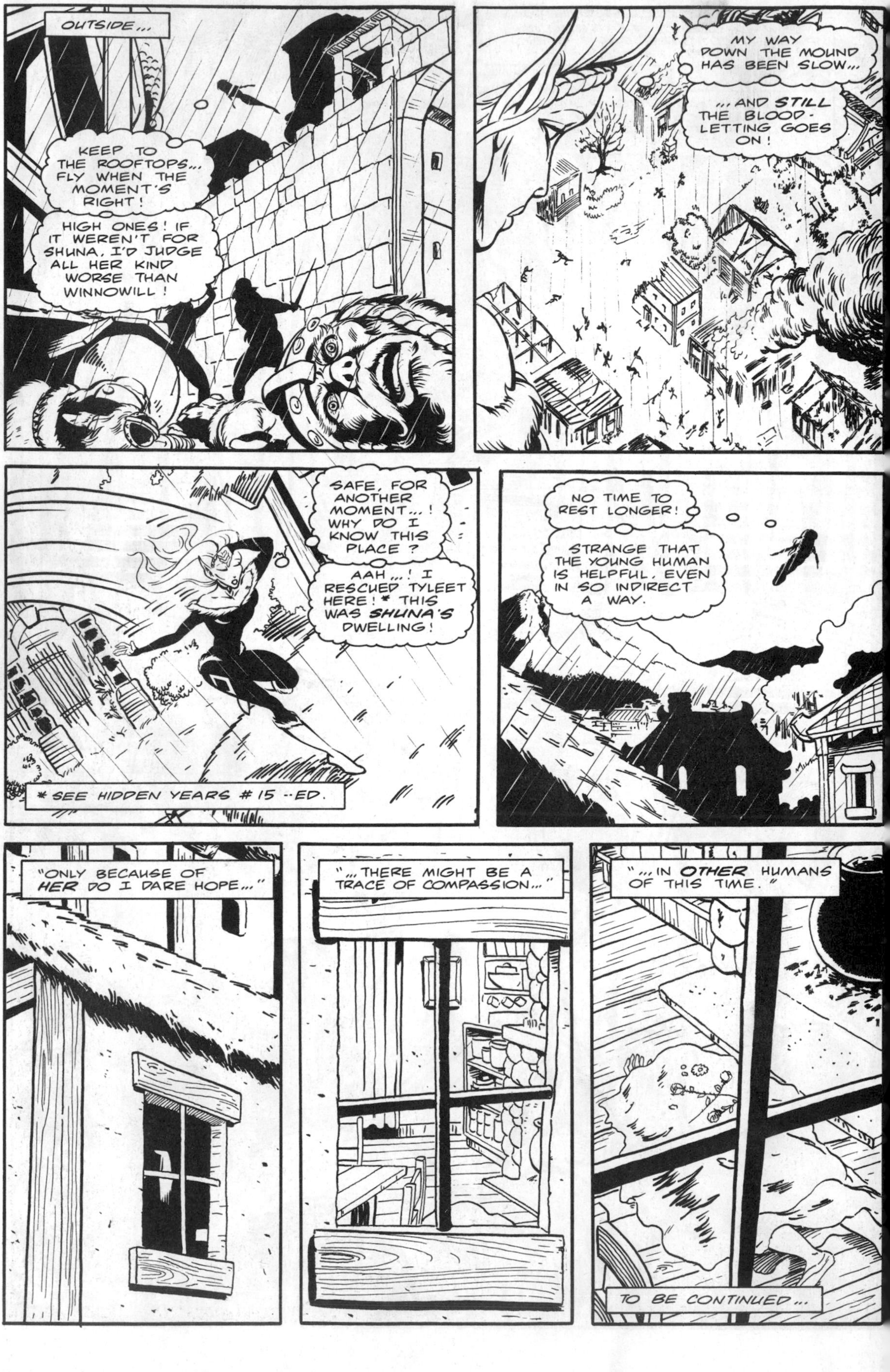
OUTSIDE...
KEEP TO THE ROOFTOPS... FLY WHEN THE MOMENT'S RIGHT!
HIGH ONES! IF IT WEREN'T FOR SHUNA, I'D JUDGE ALL HER KIND WORSE THAN WINNOWILL!
MY WAY DOWN THE MOUND HAS BEEN SLOW...
...AND STILL THE BLOOD-LETTING GOES ON!
SAFE, FOR ANOTHER MOMENT...! WHY DO I KNOW THIS PLACE?
AAH...! I RESCUED TYLEET HERE! * THIS WAS SHUNA'S DWELLING!
* SEE HIDDEN YEARS #15 --ED.
NO TIME TO REST LONGER!
STRANGE THAT THE YOUNG HUMAN IS HELPFUL, EVEN IN SO INDIRECT A WAY.
"ONLY BECAUSE OF HER DO I DARE HOPE..."
"...THERE MIGHT BE A TRACE OF COMPASSION..."
"...IN OTHER HUMANS OF THIS TIME."
TO BE CONTINUED...

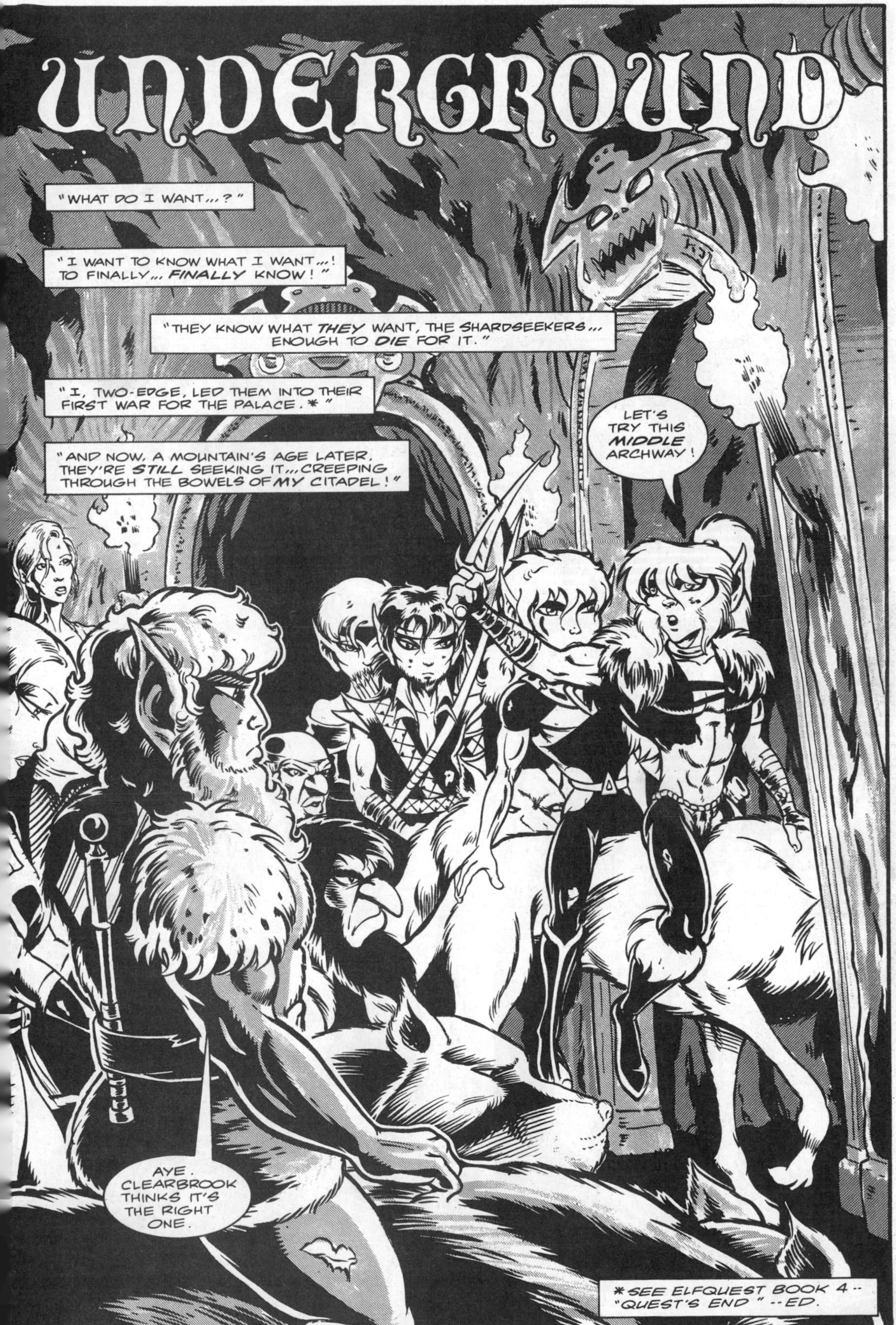
UNDERGROUND
"WHAT DO I WANT...?"
"I WANT TO KNOW WHAT I WANT...! TO FINALLY... FINALLY KNOW!"
"THEY KNOW WHAT THEY WANT, THE SHARDSEEKERS... ENOUGH TO DIE FOR IT."
"I, TWO-EDGE, LED THEM INTO THEIR FIRST WAR FOR THE PALACE.*"
"AND NOW, A MOUNTAIN'S AGE LATER, THEY'RE STILL SEEKING IT... CREEPING THROUGH THE BOWELS OF MY CITADEL!"
LET'S TRY THIS MIDDLE ARCHWAY!
AYE. CLEARBROOK THINKS IT'S THE RIGHT ONE.
*SEE ELFQUEST BOOK 4 -- "QUEST'S END" --ED.

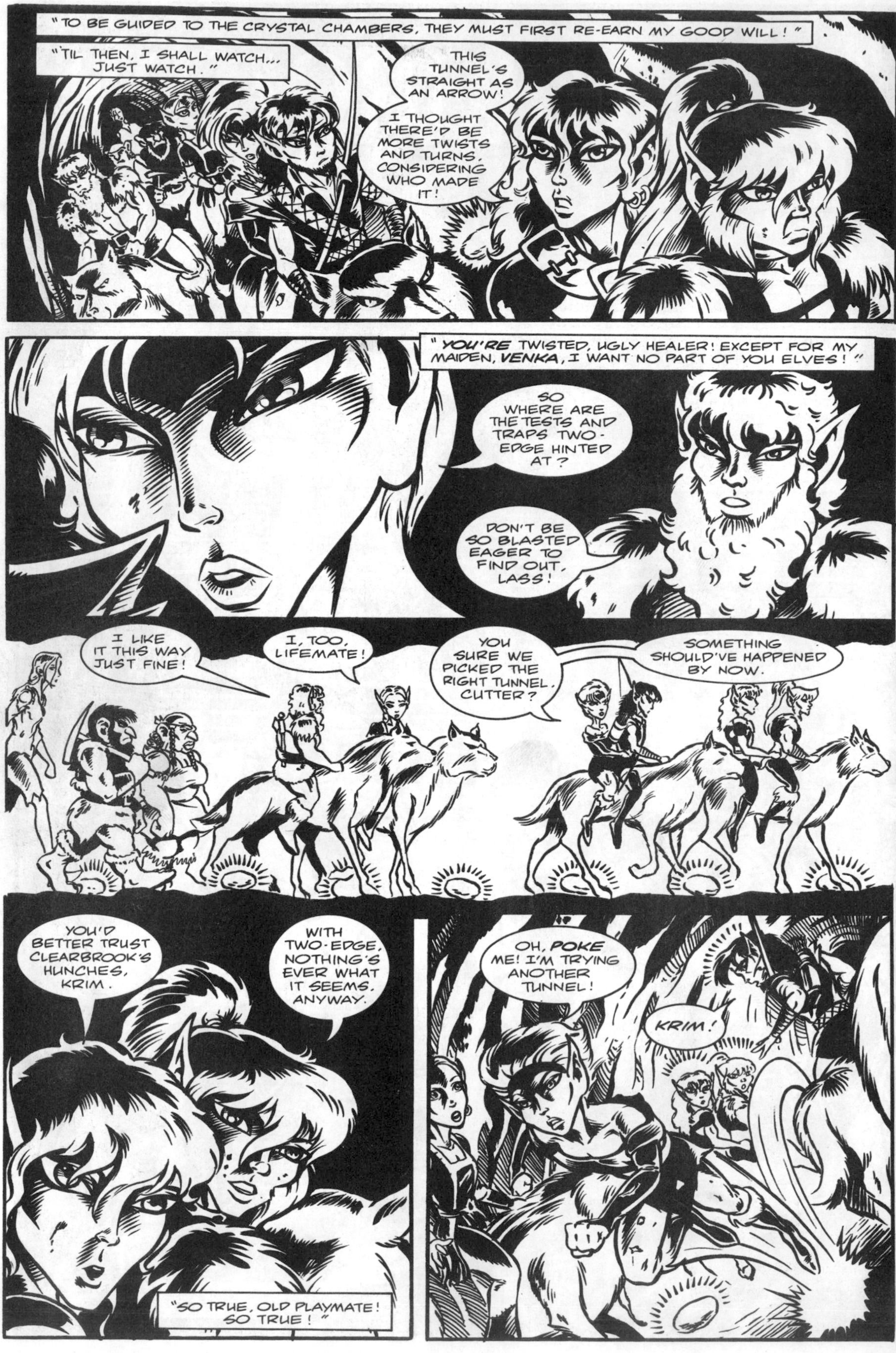
"TO BE GUIDED TO THE CRYSTAL CHAMBERS, THEY MUST FIRST RE-EARN MY GOOD WILL!"
"'TIL THEN, I SHALL WATCH... JUST WATCH."
THIS TUNNEL'S STRAIGHT AS AN ARROW!
I THOUGHT THERE'D BE MORE TWISTS AND TURNS, CONSIDERING WHO MADE IT!
"YOU'RE TWISTED, UGLY HEALER! EXCEPT FOR MY MAIDEN, VENKA, I WANT NO PART OF YOU ELVES!"
SO WHERE ARE THE TESTS AND TRAPS TWO-EDGE HINTED AT?
DON'T BE SO BLASTED EAGER TO FIND OUT, LASS!
I LIKE IT THIS WAY JUST FINE!
I, TOO, LIFEMATE!
YOU SURE WE PICKED THE RIGHT TUNNEL, CUTTER?
SOMETHING SHOULD'VE HAPPENED BY NOW.
YOU'D BETTER TRUST CLEARBROOK'S HUNCHES, KRIM.
WITH TWO-EDGE, NOTHING'S EVER WHAT IT SEEMS, ANYWAY.
"SO TRUE, OLD PLAYMATE! SO TRUE!"
OH, POKE ME! I'M TRYING ANOTHER TUNNEL!
KRIM!

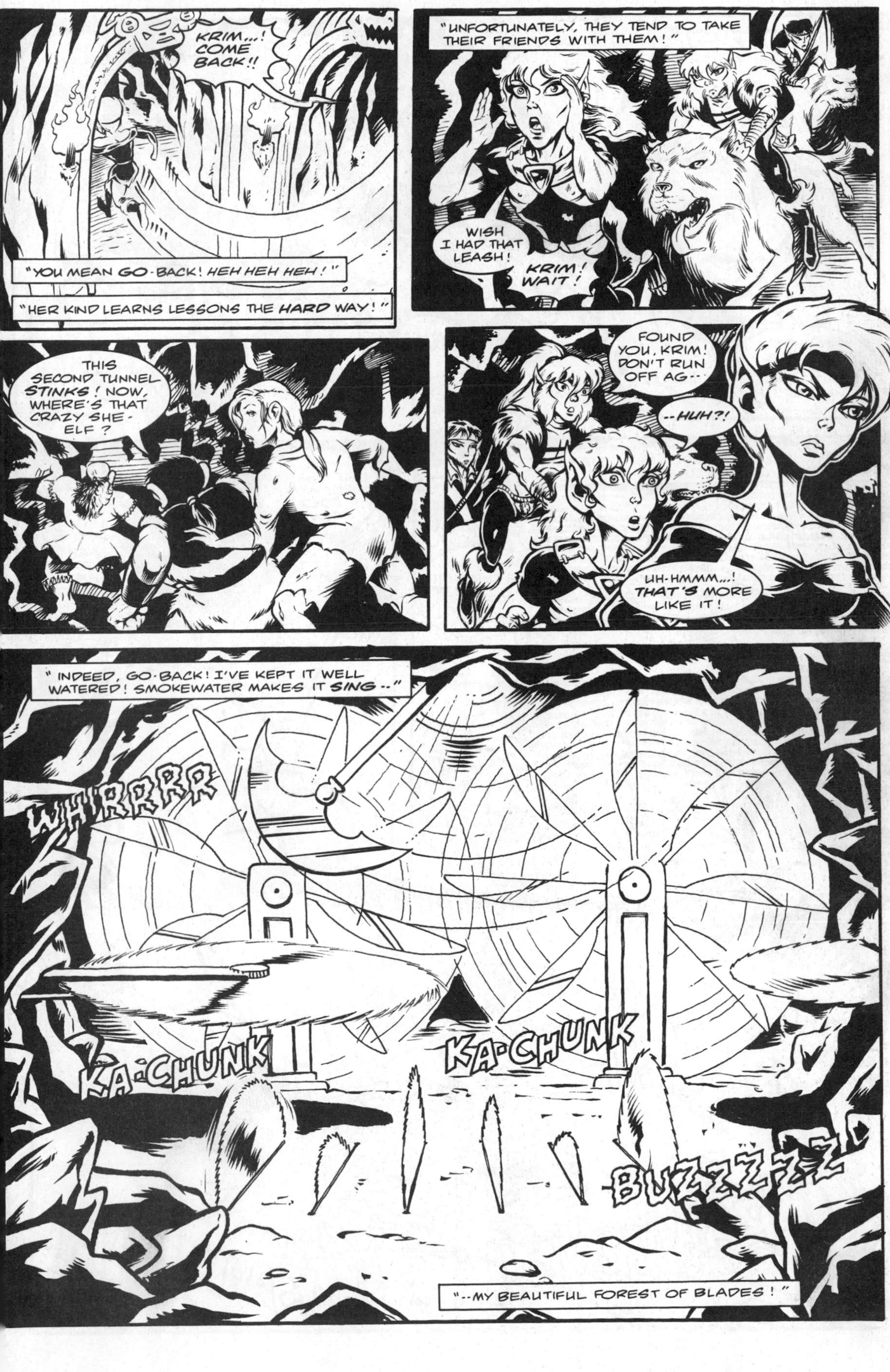
KRIM...! COME BACK!!
"YOU MEAN GO-BACK! HEH HEH HEH!"
"HER KIND LEARNS LESSONS THE HARD WAY!"
"UNFORTUNATELY, THEY TEND TO TAKE THEIR FRIENDS WITH THEM!"
WISH I HAD THAT LEASH!
KRIM! WAIT!
THIS SECOND TUNNEL STINKS! NOW, WHERE'S THAT CRAZY SHE-ELF?
FOUND YOU, KRIM! DON'T RUN OFF AG--
--HUH?!
UH-HMMM...! THAT'S MORE LIKE IT!
" INDEED, GO-BACK! I'VE KEPT IT WELL WATERED! SMOKEWATER MAKES IT SING--"
WHRRRR
KA-CHUNK
KA-CHUNK
BUZZZZZZ
"--MY BEAUTIFUL FOREST OF BLADES!"

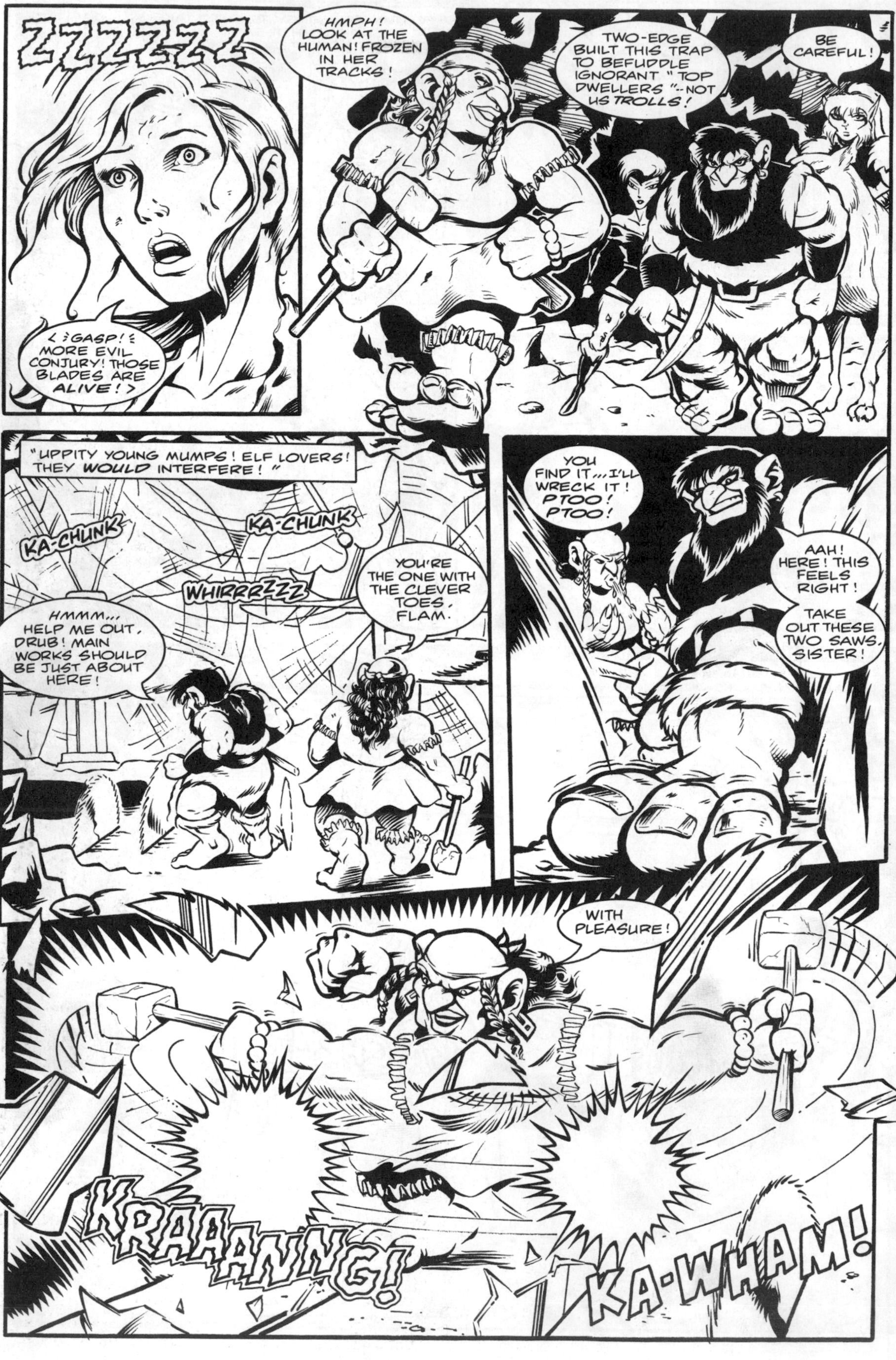
ZZZZZZ
HMPH! LOOK AT THE HUMAN! FROZEN IN HER TRACKS!
TWO-EDGE BUILT THIS TRAP TO BEFUDDLE IGNORANT "TOP DWELLERS"--NOT US TROLLS!
BE CAREFUL!
< GASP! MORE EVIL CONJURY! THOSE BLADES ARE ALIVE! >
"UPPITY YOUNG MUMPS! ELF LOVERS! THEY WOULD INTERFERE!"
KA-CHUNK
KA-CHUNK
WHIRRRZZZ
HMMM... HELP ME OUT, DRUB! MAIN WORKS SHOULD BE JUST ABOUT HERE!
YOU'RE THE ONE WITH THE CLEVER TOES, FLAM.
YOU FIND IT... I'LL WRECK IT! PTOO! PTOO!
AAH! HERE! THIS FEELS RIGHT!
TAKE OUT THESE TWO SAWS, SISTER!
WITH PLEASURE!
KRAAANNG!
KA-WHAM!

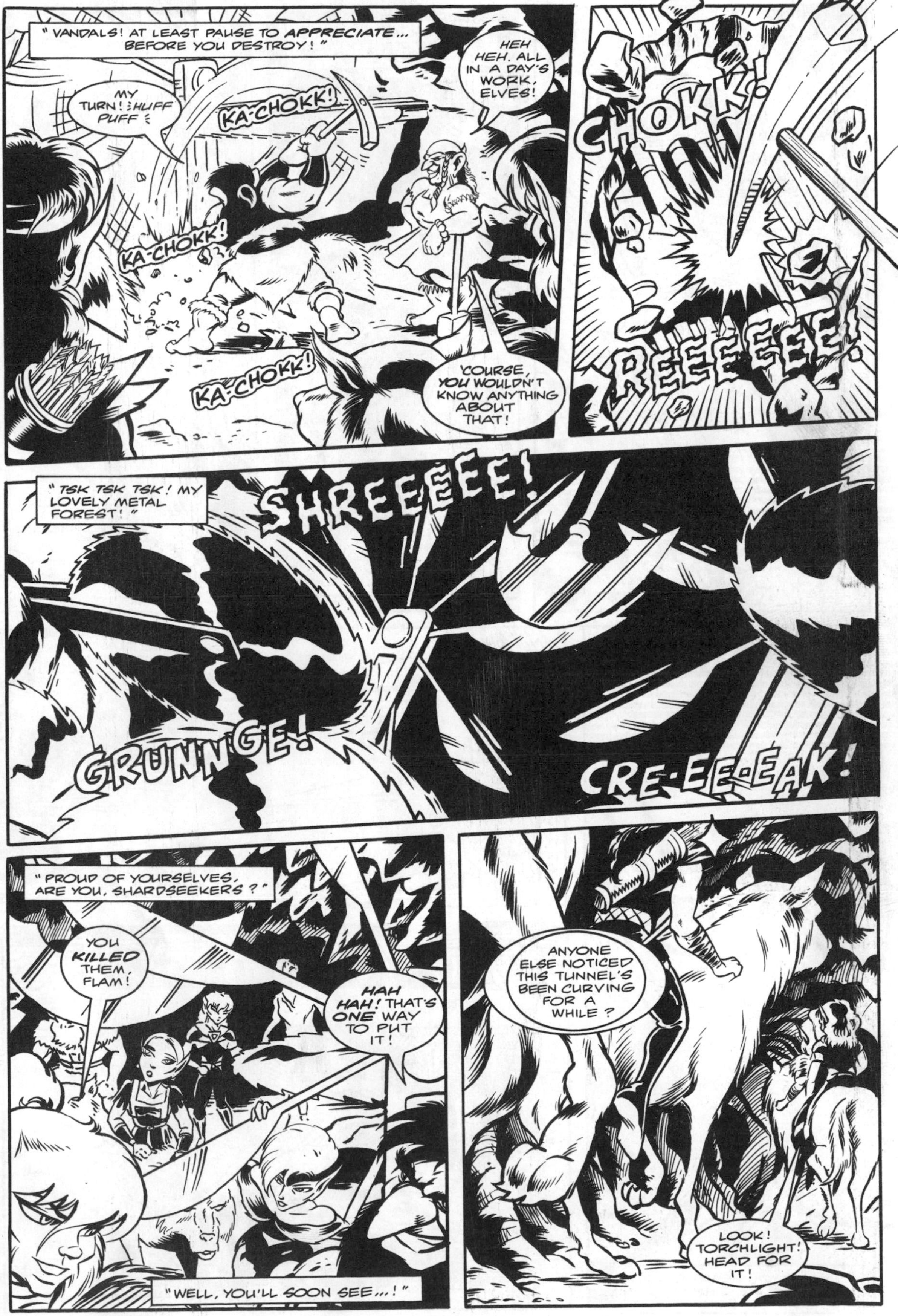
"VANDALS! AT LEAST PAUSE TO APPRECIATE... BEFORE YOU DESTROY!"
MY TURN! HUFF PUFF
KA-CHOKK!
HEH HEH. ALL IN A DAY'S WORK, ELVES!
KA-CHOKK!
KA-CHOKK!
'COURSE, YOU WOULDN'T KNOW ANYTHING ABOUT THAT!
CHOKK!
REEEEEEE!
"TSK TSK TSK! MY LOVELY METAL FOREST!"
SHREEEEEE!
GRUNNGE!
CRE-EE-EAK!
"PROUD OF YOURSELVES, ARE YOU, SHARDSEEKERS?"
YOU KILLED THEM, FLAM!
HAH HAH! THAT'S ONE WAY TO PUT IT!
"WELL, YOU'LL SOON SEE...!"
ANYONE ELSE NOTICED THIS TUNNEL'S BEEN CURVING FOR A WHILE?
LOOK! TORCHLIGHT! HEAD FOR IT!

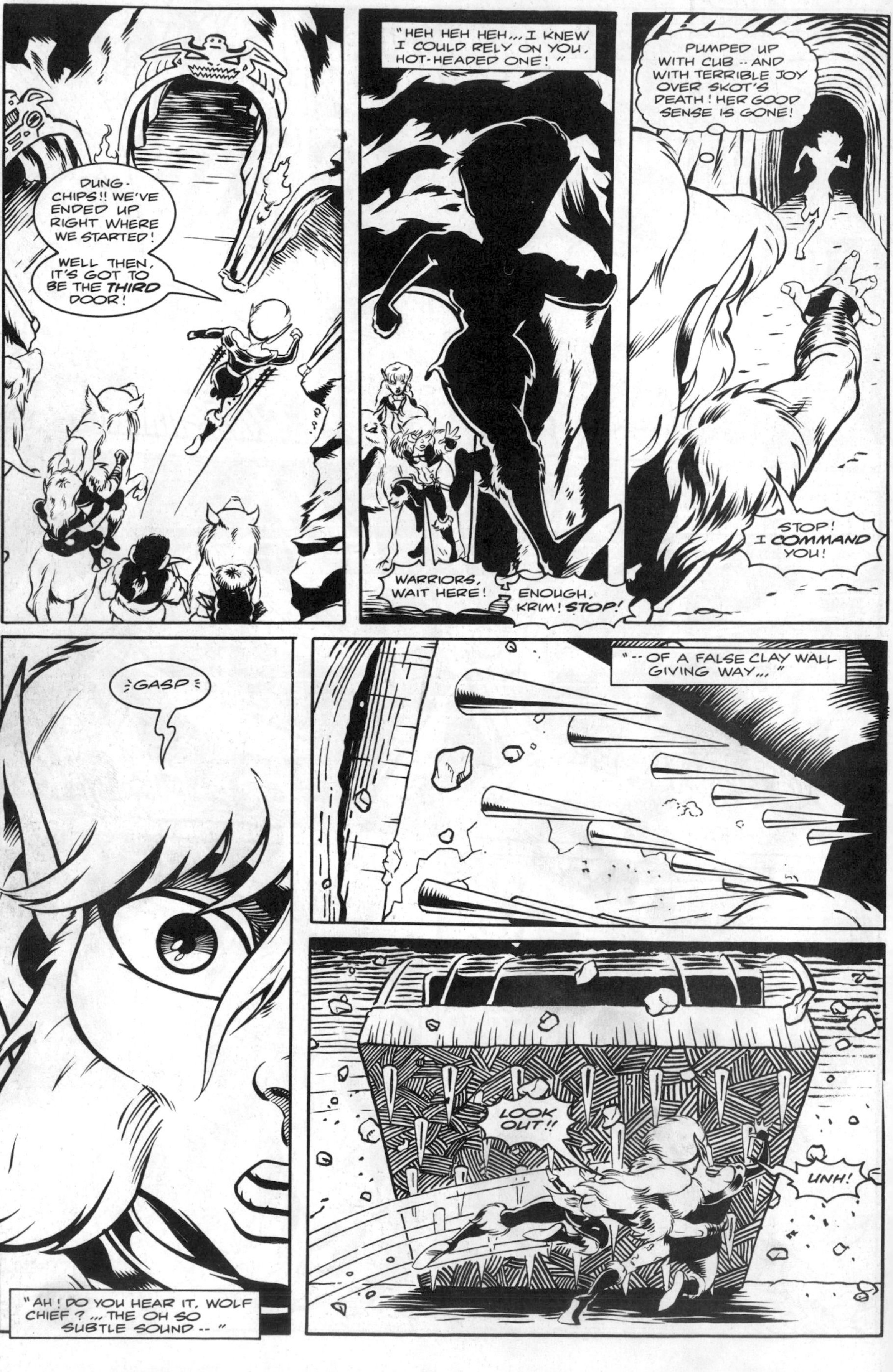

DUNG-CHIPS!! WE'VE ENDED UP RIGHT WHERE WE STARTED!
WELL THEN, IT'S GOT TO BE THE THIRD DOOR!
"HEH HEH HEH... I KNEW I COULD RELY ON YOU, HOT-HEADED ONE!"
WARRIORS, WAIT HERE!
ENOUGH, KRIM! STOP!
PUMPED UP WITH CUB -- AND WITH TERRIBLE JOY OVER SKOT'S DEATH! HER GOOD SENSE IS GONE!
STOP! I COMMAND YOU!
GASP
"AH! DO YOU HEAR IT, WOLF CHIEF? ... THE OH SO SUBTLE SOUND --"
"-- OF A FALSE CLAY WALL GIVING WAY..."
LOOK OUT!!
UNH!

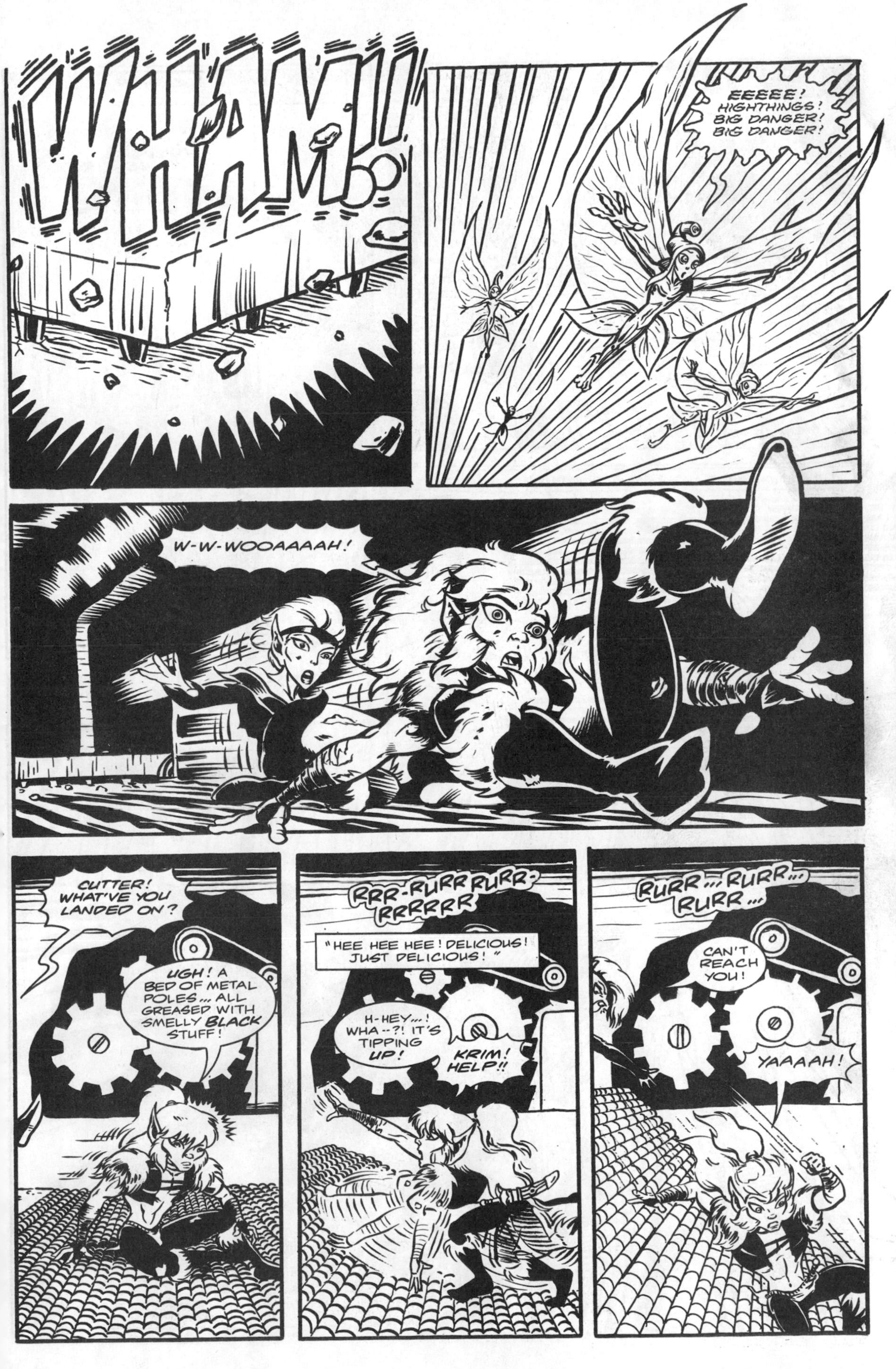
WHAM!!
EEEEE! HIGHTHINGS! BIG DANGER! BIG DANGER!
W-W-WOOAAAAAH!
CUTTER! WHAT'VE YOU LANDED ON?
UGH! A BED OF METAL POLES... ALL GREASED WITH SMELLY BLACK STUFF!
RRR-RURR RURR-RRRRRR
"HEE HEE HEE! DELICIOUS! JUST DELICIOUS!"
H-HEY...! WHA--?! IT'S TIPPING UP!
KRIM! HELP!!
RURR... RURR... RURR...
CAN'T REACH YOU!
YAAAAH!

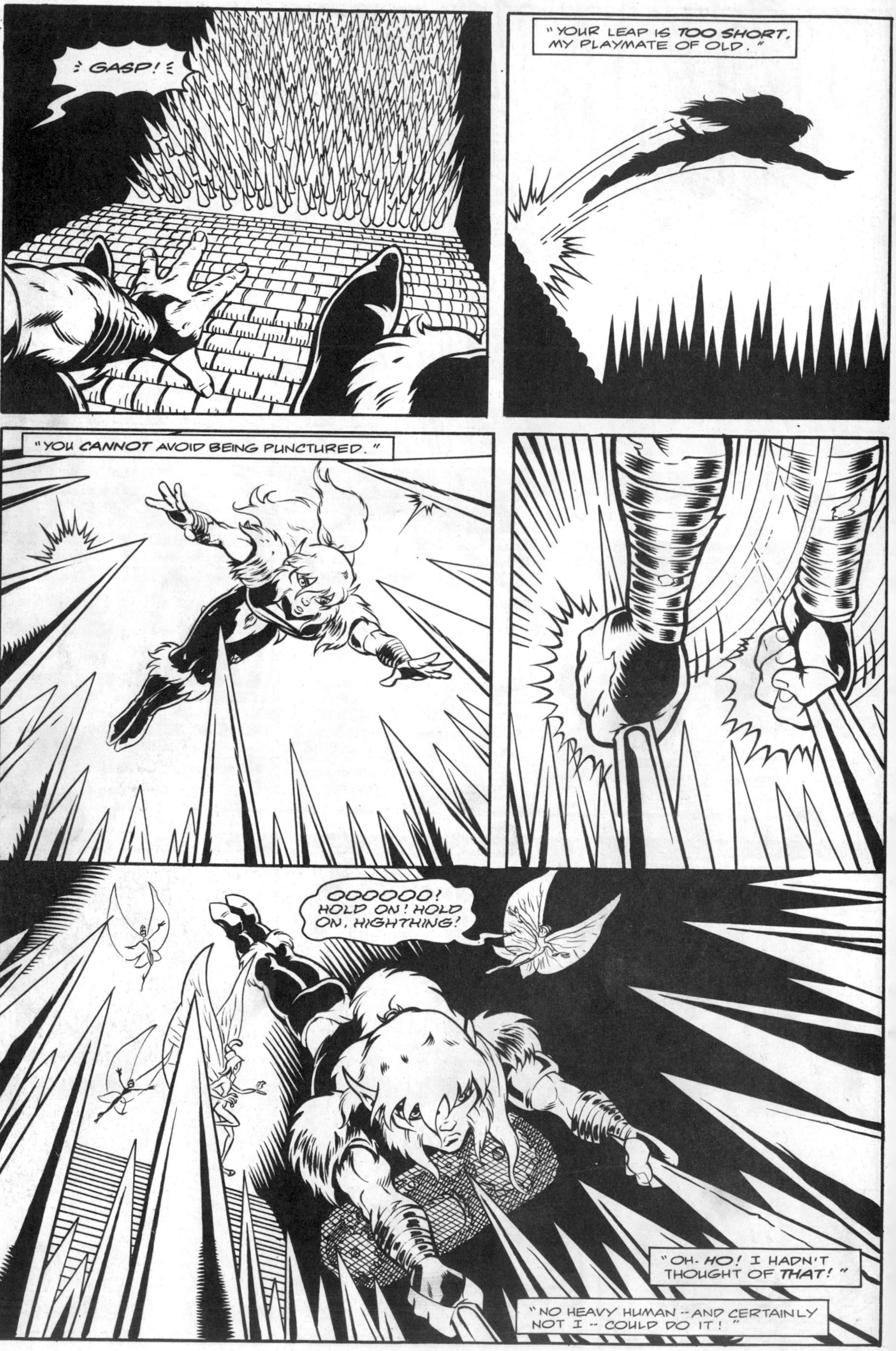
GASP!
"YOUR LEAP IS TOO SHORT, MY PLAYMATE OF OLD."
"YOU CANNOT AVOID BEING PUNCTURED."
OOOOOOO! HOLD ON! HOLD ON, HIGHTHING!
"OH- HO! I HADN'T THOUGHT OF THAT!"
"NO HEAVY HUMAN -- AND CERTAINLY NOT I -- COULD DO IT!"

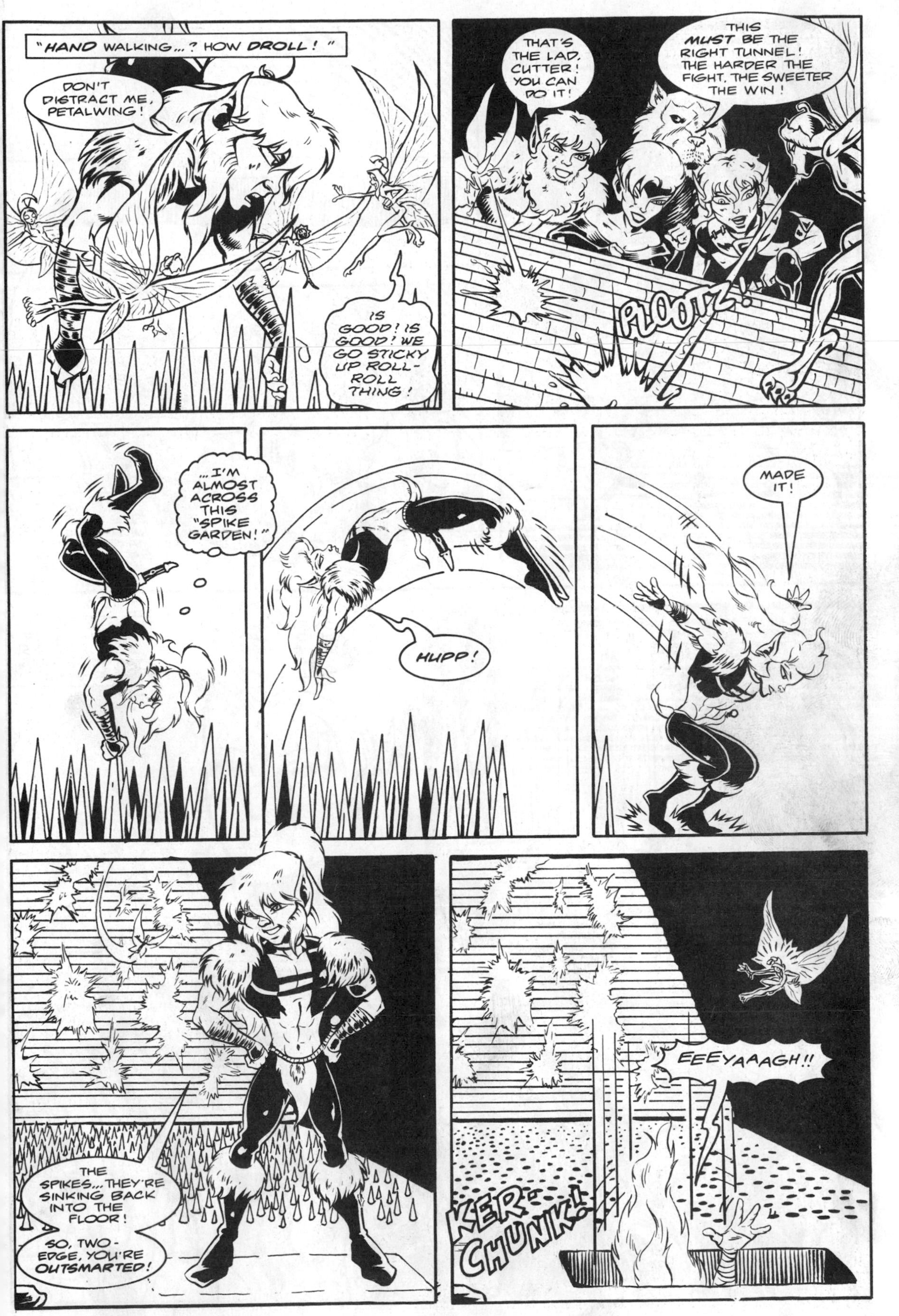
"HAND WALKING...? HOW DROLL!"
DON'T DISTRACT ME, PETALWING!
IS GOOD! IS GOOD! WE GO STICKY UP ROLL-ROLL THING!
THAT'S THE LAD, CUTTER! YOU CAN DO IT!
THIS MUST BE THE RIGHT TUNNEL! THE HARDER THE FIGHT, THE SWEETER THE WIN!
PLOOTZ!
...I'M ALMOST ACROSS THIS "SPIKE GARDEN!"
HUPP!
MADE IT!
THE SPIKES... THEY'RE SINKING BACK INTO THE FLOOR!
SO, TWO-EDGE, YOU'RE OUTSMARTED!
EEEYAAAGH!!
KER-CHUNK!

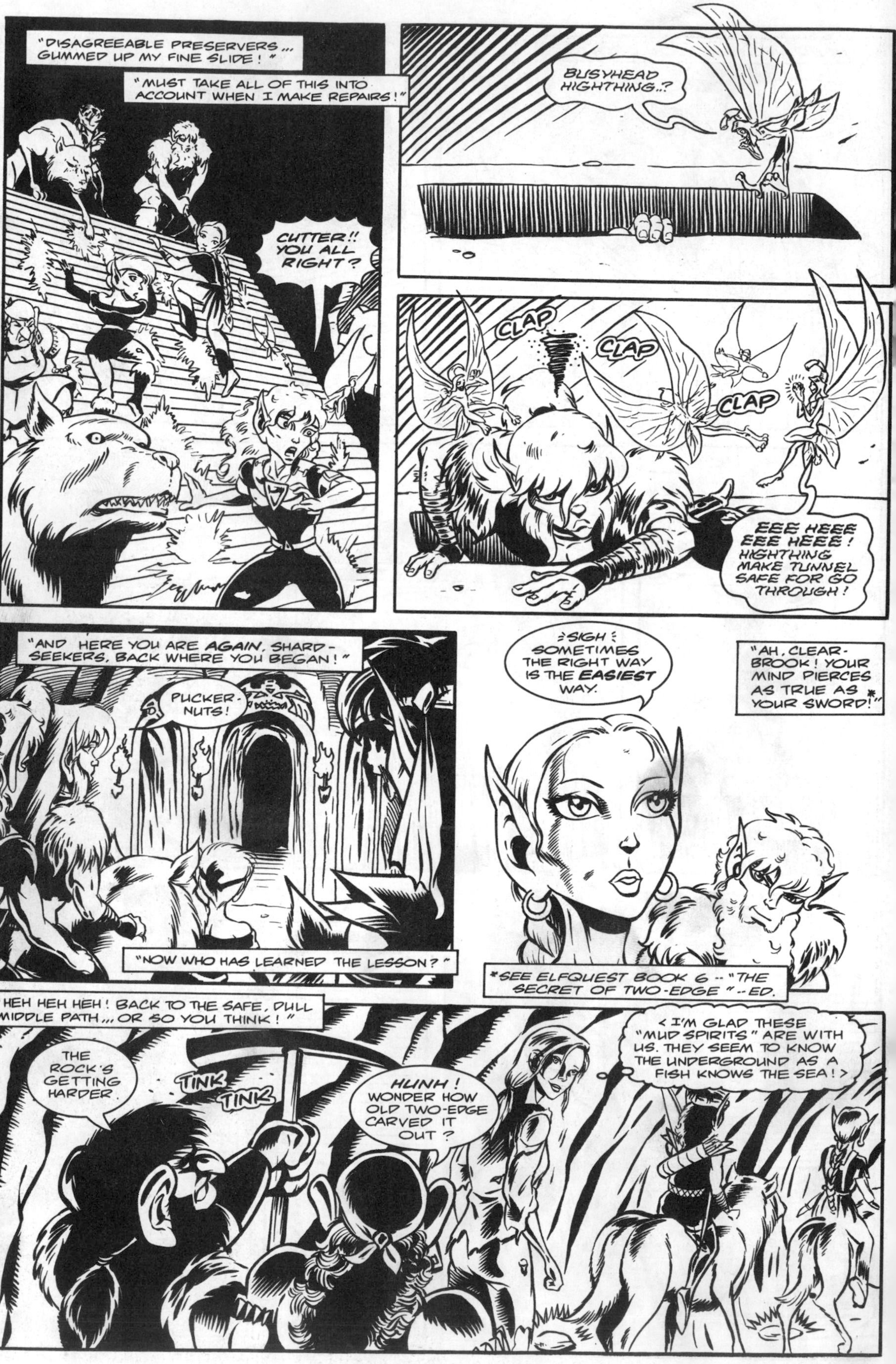
"DISAGREEABLE PRESERVERS... GUMMED UP MY FINE SLIDE!"
"MUST TAKE ALL OF THIS INTO ACCOUNT WHEN I MAKE REPAIRS!"
CUTTER!! YOU ALL RIGHT?
BUSYHEAD HIGHTHING..?
CLAP
CLAP
CLAP
EEE HEEE EEE HEEE! HIGHTHING MAKE TUNNEL SAFE FOR GO THROUGH!
"AND HERE YOU ARE AGAIN, SHARD-SEEKERS, BACK WHERE YOU BEGAN!"
PUCKER-NUTS!
"NOW WHO HAS LEARNED THE LESSON?"
SIGH SOMETIMES THE RIGHT WAY IS THE EASIEST WAY.
"AH, CLEAR-BROOK! YOUR MIND PIERCES AS TRUE AS YOUR SWORD!*"
*SEE ELFQUEST BOOK 6 -- "THE SECRET OF TWO-EDGE" -- ED.
"HEH HEH HEH! BACK TO THE SAFE, DULL MIDDLE PATH... OR SO YOU THINK!"
THE ROCK'S GETTING HARDER.
TINK
TINK
HUNH! WONDER HOW OLD TWO-EDGE CARVED IT OUT?
<I'M GLAD THESE "MUD SPIRITS" ARE WITH US. THEY SEEM TO KNOW THE UNDERGROUND AS A FISH KNOWS THE SEA!>

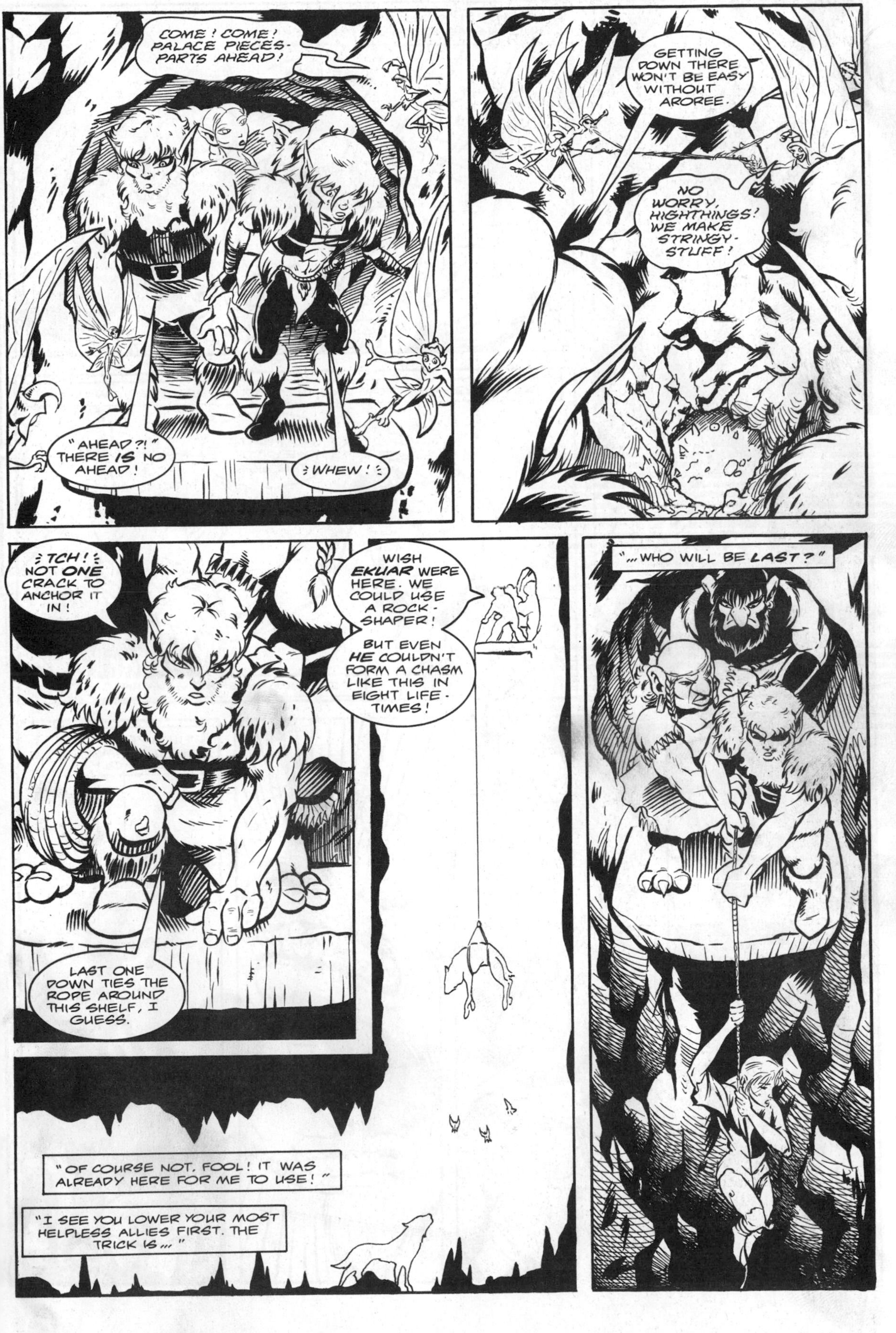
COME! COME! PALACE PIECES-PARTS AHEAD!
"AHEAD?!" THERE IS NO AHEAD!
WHEW!
GETTING DOWN THERE WON'T BE EASY WITHOUT AROREE.
NO WORRY, HIGHTHINGS! WE MAKE STRINGY-STUFF!
TCH! NOT ONE CRACK TO ANCHOR IT IN!
LAST ONE DOWN TIES THE ROPE AROUND THIS SHELF, I GUESS.
WISH EKUAR WERE HERE. WE COULD USE A ROCK-SHAPER!
BUT EVEN HE COULDN'T FORM A CHASM LIKE THIS IN EIGHT LIFE-TIMES!
"OF COURSE NOT, FOOL! IT WAS ALREADY HERE FOR ME TO USE!"
"I SEE YOU LOWER YOUR MOST HELPLESS ALLIES FIRST. THE TRICK IS...,"
"...WHO WILL BE LAST?"

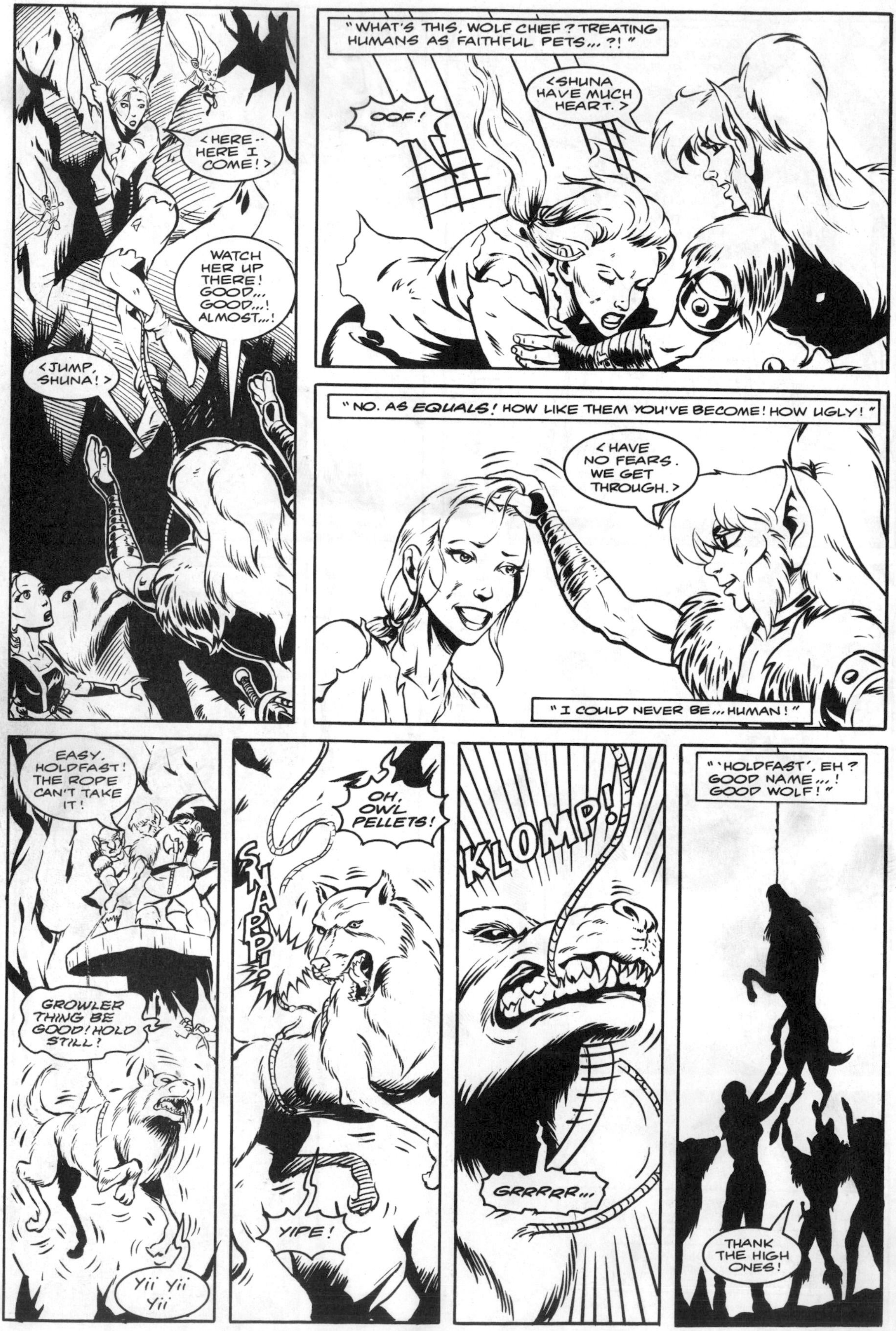
<HERE-- HERE I COME!>
WATCH HER UP THERE! GOOD... GOOD...! ALMOST...!
<JUMP, SHUNA!>
"WHAT'S THIS, WOLF CHIEF? TREATING HUMANS AS FAITHFUL PETS...?!"
OOF!
<SHUNA HAVE MUCH HEART.>
"NO. AS EQUALS! HOW LIKE THEM YOU'VE BECOME! HOW UGLY!"
<HAVE NO FEARS. WE GET THROUGH.>
"I COULD NEVER BE... HUMAN!"
EASY, HOLDFAST! THE ROPE CAN'T TAKE IT!
GROWLER THING BE GOOD! HOLD STILL!
Yii Yii Yii
OH, OWL PELLETS!
SNAPP!
YIPE!
KLOMP!
GRRRRR...
"'HOLDFAST', EH? GOOD NAME...! GOOD WOLF!"
THANK THE HIGH ONES!

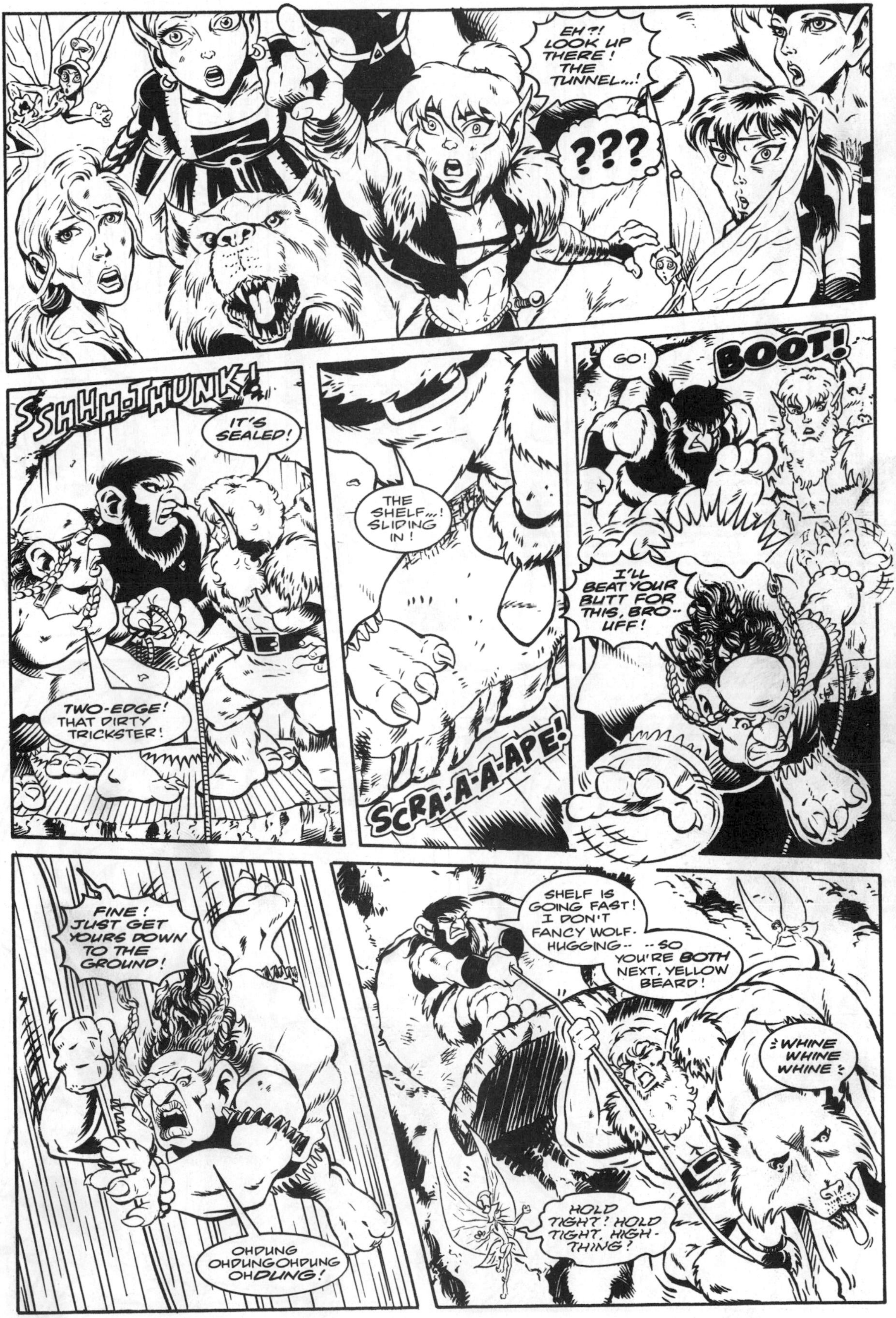
EH?! LOOK UP THERE! THE TUNNEL...!
???
SSHHH-THUNK!
IT'S SEALED!
TWO-EDGE! THAT DIRTY TRICKSTER!
THE SHELF...! SLIDING IN!
SCRA-A-A-APE!
GO!
BOOT!
I'LL BEAT YOUR BUTT FOR THIS, BRO-- UFF!
FINE! JUST GET YOURS DOWN TO THE GROUND!
OHDUNG OHDUNGOHDUNG OHDUNG!
SHELF IS GOING FAST! I DON'T FANCY WOLF-HUGGING-- --SO YOU'RE BOTH NEXT, YELLOW BEARD!
WHINE WHINE WHINE
HOLD TIGHT! HOLD TIGHT, HIGH-THING!

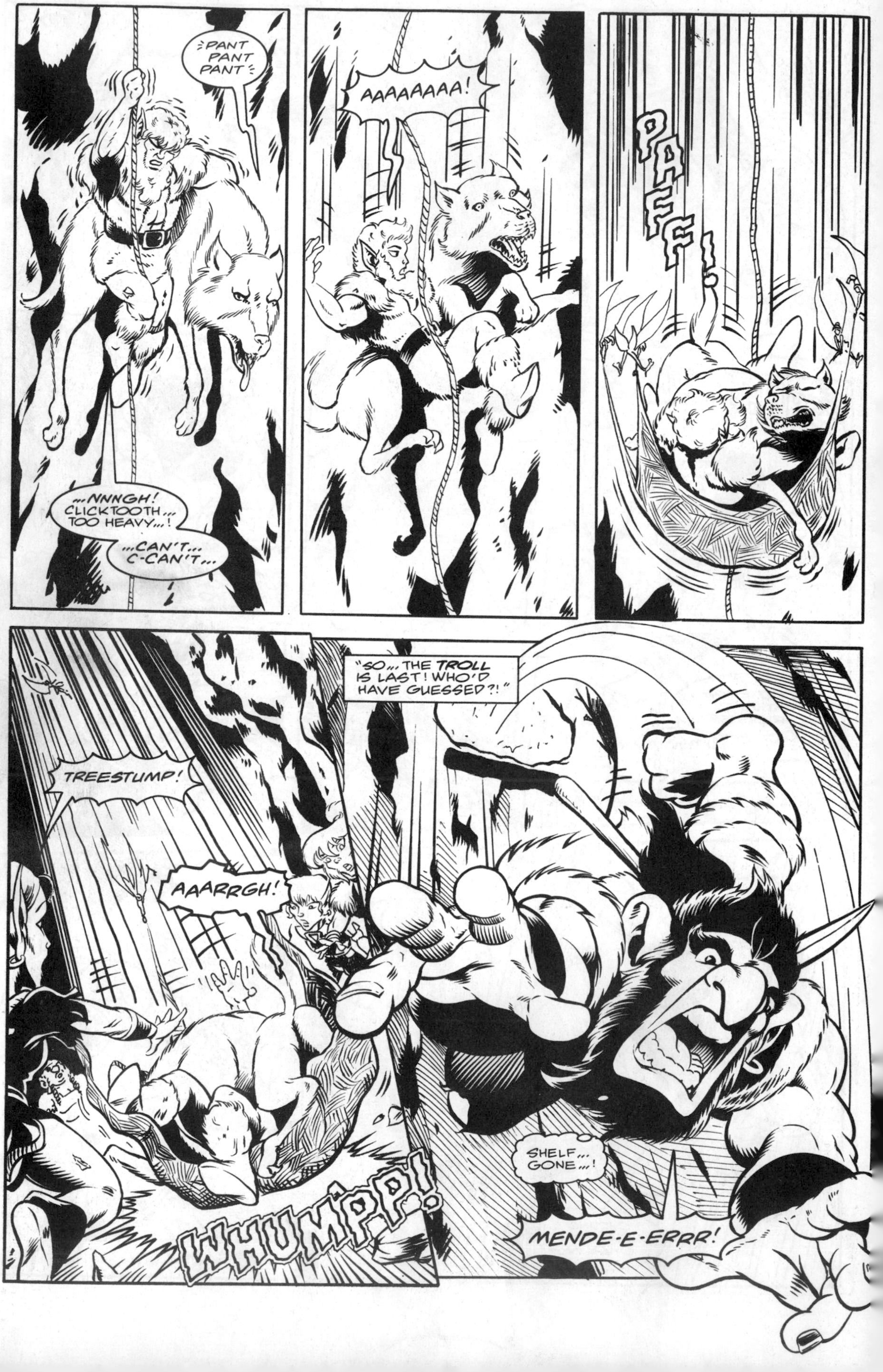

PANT PANT PANT
...NNNGH! CLICKTOOTH... TOO HEAVY...!
...CAN'T... C-CAN'T...
AAAAAAAA!
PAFFF!
"SO... THE TROLL IS LAST! WHO'D HAVE GUESSED?!"
TREESTUMP!
AAARRGH!
WHUMPP!
SHELF... GONE...!
MENDE-E-ERRR!

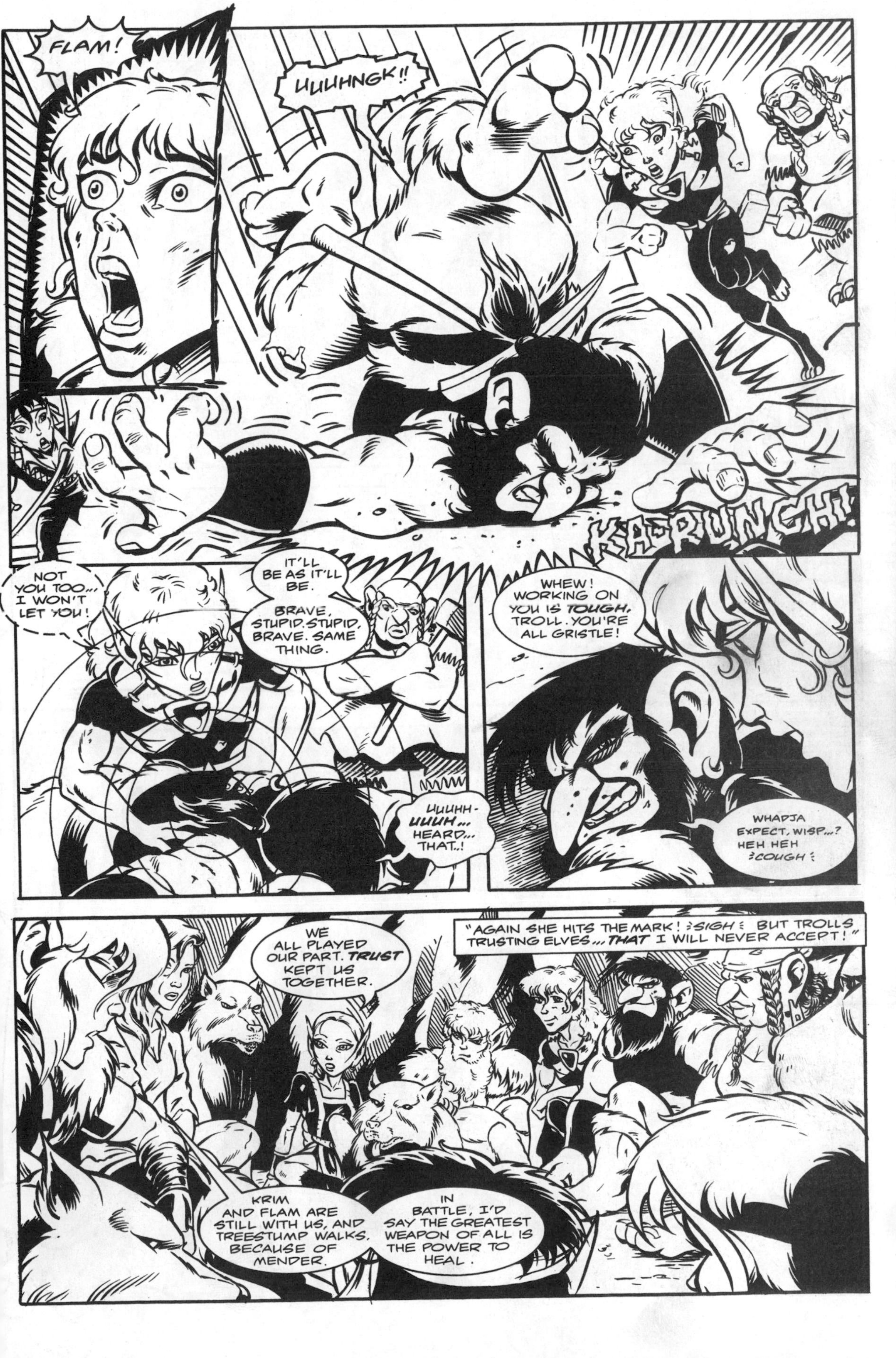
FLAM!
UUUHNGK!!
KA-RUNCH!!
NOT YOU TOO... I WON'T LET YOU!
IT'LL BE AS IT'LL BE.
BRAVE, STUPID. STUPID, BRAVE. SAME THING.
UUUHH-UUUH... HEARD... THAT..!
WHEW! WORKING ON YOU IS TOUGH, TROLL. YOU'RE ALL GRISTLE!
WHADJA EXPECT, WISP...? HEH HEH ⁝COUGH⁝
"AGAIN SHE HITS THE MARK! ⁝SIGH⁝ BUT TROLLS TRUSTING ELVES... THAT I WILL NEVER ACCEPT!"
WE ALL PLAYED OUR PART. TRUST KEPT US TOGETHER.
KRIM AND FLAM ARE STILL WITH US, AND TREESTUMP WALKS, BECAUSE OF MENDER.
IN BATTLE, I'D SAY THE GREATEST WEAPON OF ALL IS THE POWER TO HEAL.

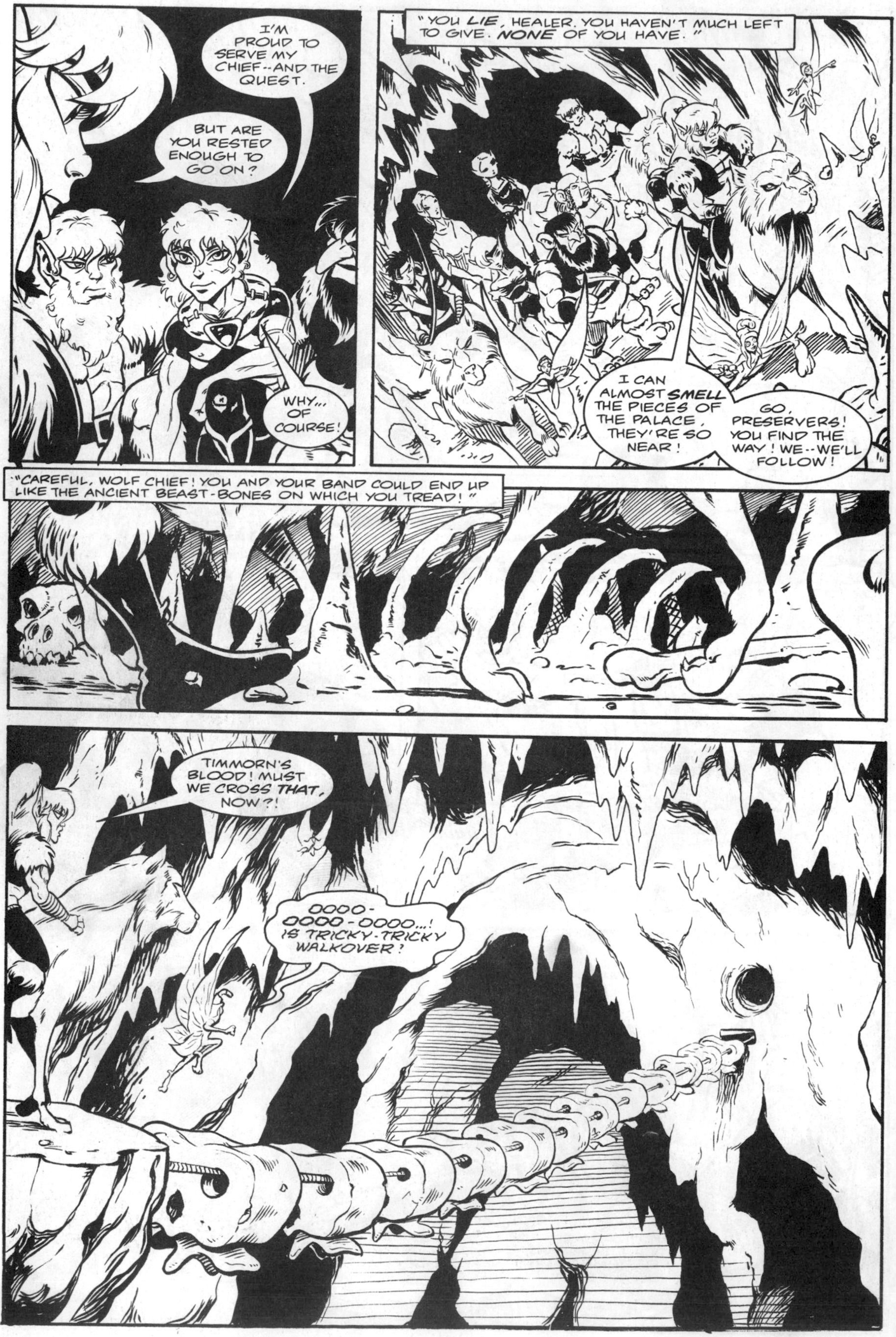
I'M PROUD TO SERVE MY CHIEF--AND THE QUEST.
BUT ARE YOU RESTED ENOUGH TO GO ON?
WHY... OF COURSE!
"YOU LIE, HEALER. YOU HAVEN'T MUCH LEFT TO GIVE. NONE OF YOU HAVE."
I CAN ALMOST SMELL THE PIECES OF THE PALACE, THEY'RE SO NEAR!
GO, PRESERVERS! YOU FIND THE WAY! WE--WE'LL FOLLOW!
"CAREFUL, WOLF CHIEF! YOU AND YOUR BAND COULD END UP LIKE THE ANCIENT BEAST-BONES ON WHICH YOU TREAD!"
TIMMORN'S BLOOD! MUST WE CROSS THAT, NOW?!
OOOO-OOOO-OOOO...! IS TRICKY-TRICKY WALKOVER?

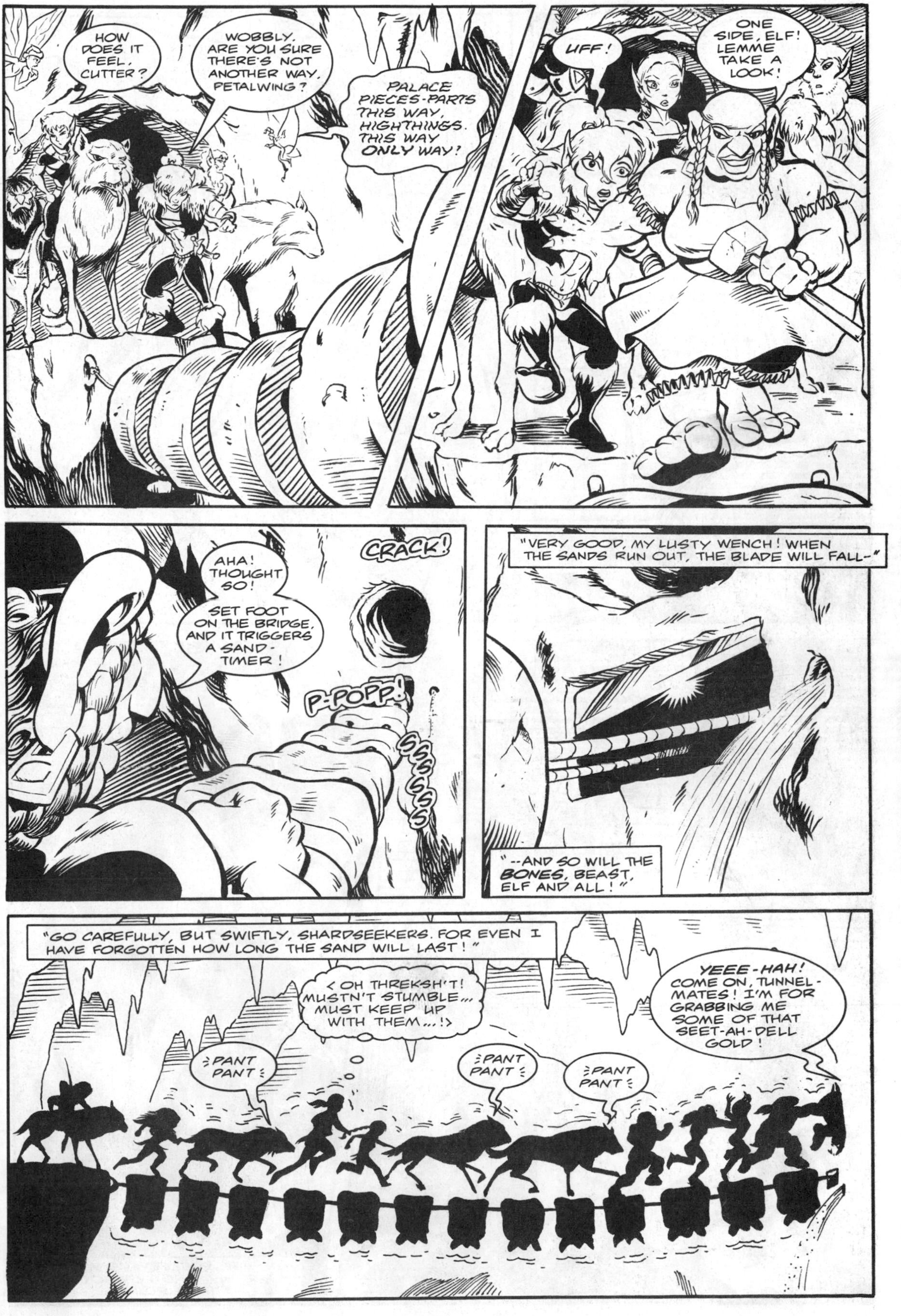
HOW DOES IT FEEL, CUTTER?
WOBBLY. ARE YOU SURE THERE'S NOT ANOTHER WAY, PETALWING?
PALACE PIECES-PARTS THIS WAY, HIGHTHINGS. THIS WAY ONLY WAY!
UFF!
ONE SIDE, ELF! LEMME TAKE A LOOK!
CRACK!
AHA! THOUGHT SO!
SET FOOT ON THE BRIDGE, AND IT TRIGGERS A SAND-TIMER!
P-POPP!
SSSSSS
"VERY GOOD, MY LUSTY WENCH! WHEN THE SANDS RUN OUT, THE BLADE WILL FALL-"
"--AND SO WILL THE BONES, BEAST, ELF AND ALL!"
"GO CAREFULLY, BUT SWIFTLY, SHARDSEEKERS. FOR EVEN I HAVE FORGOTTEN HOW LONG THE SAND WILL LAST!"
< OH THREKSH'T! MUSTN'T STUMBLE... MUST KEEP UP WITH THEM...!>
YEEE-HAH! COME ON, TUNNEL-MATES! I'M FOR GRABBING ME SOME OF THAT SEET-AH-DELL GOLD!
PANT PANT
PANT PANT
PANT PANT

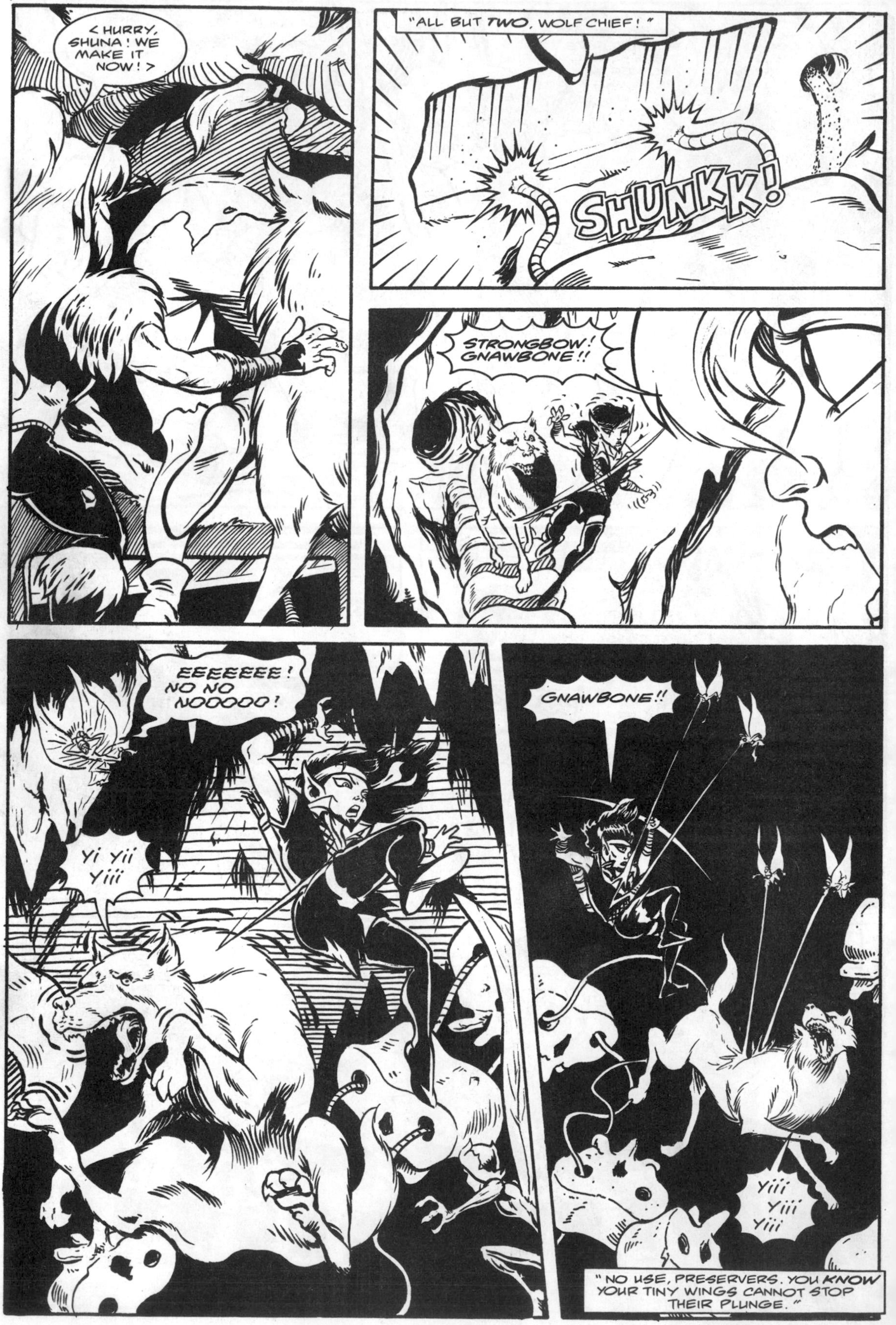
< HURRY, SHUNA! WE MAKE IT NOW! >
"ALL BUT *TWO*, WOLF CHIEF!"
SHUNKK!
STRONGBOW! GNAWBONE!!
EEEEEEE! NO NO NOOOOO!
Yi Yii Yiii
GNAWBONE!!
Yiii Yiii Yiii
"NO USE, PRESERVERS. YOU *KNOW* YOUR TINY WINGS CANNOT STOP THEIR PLUNGE."

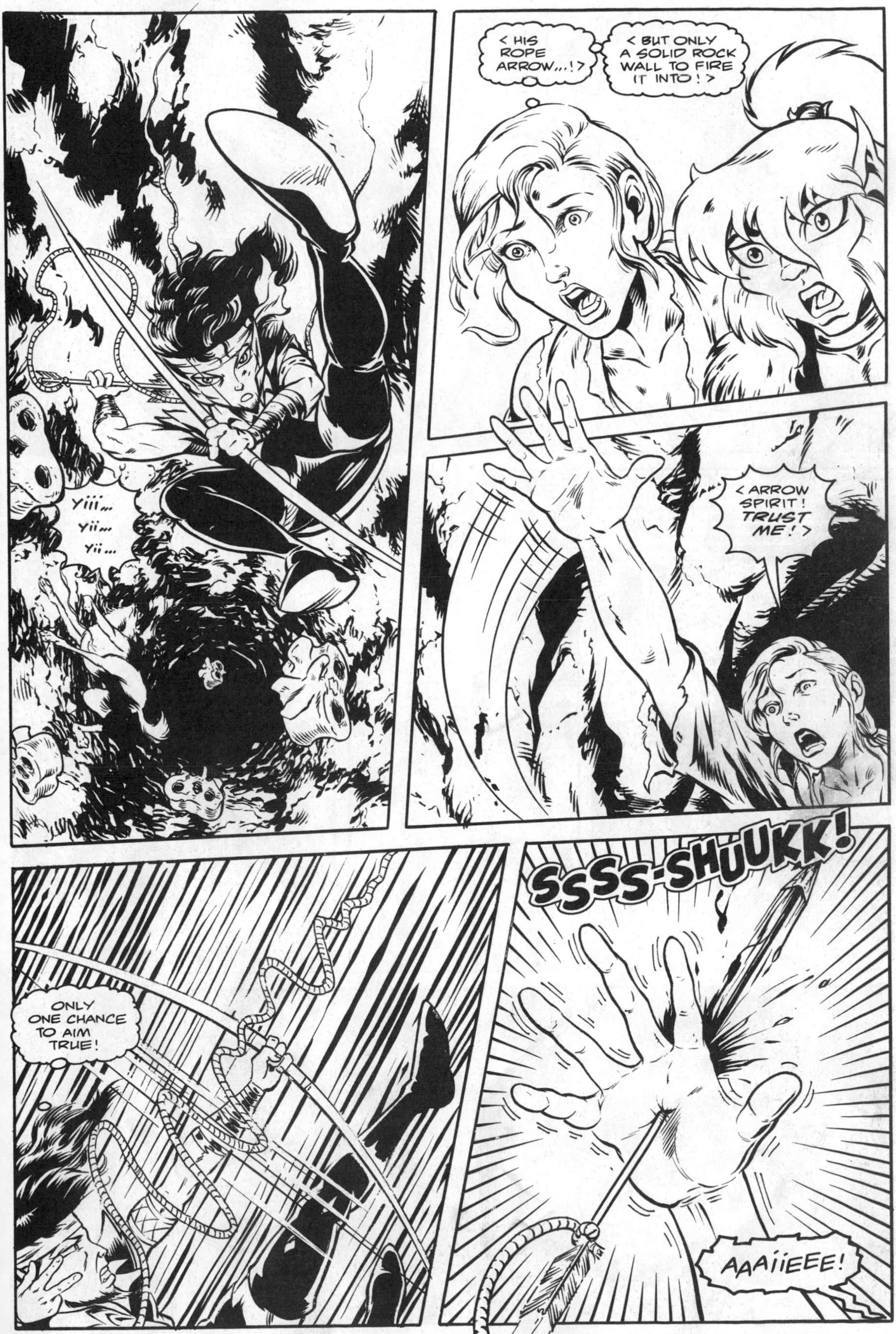
Yiii...
Yii...
Yii...
< HIS ROPE ARROW...! >
< BUT ONLY A SOLID ROCK WALL TO FIRE IT INTO! >
< ARROW SPIRIT! TRUST ME! >
ONLY ONE CHANCE TO AIM TRUE!
SSSS-SHUUKK!
AAAiiEEE!

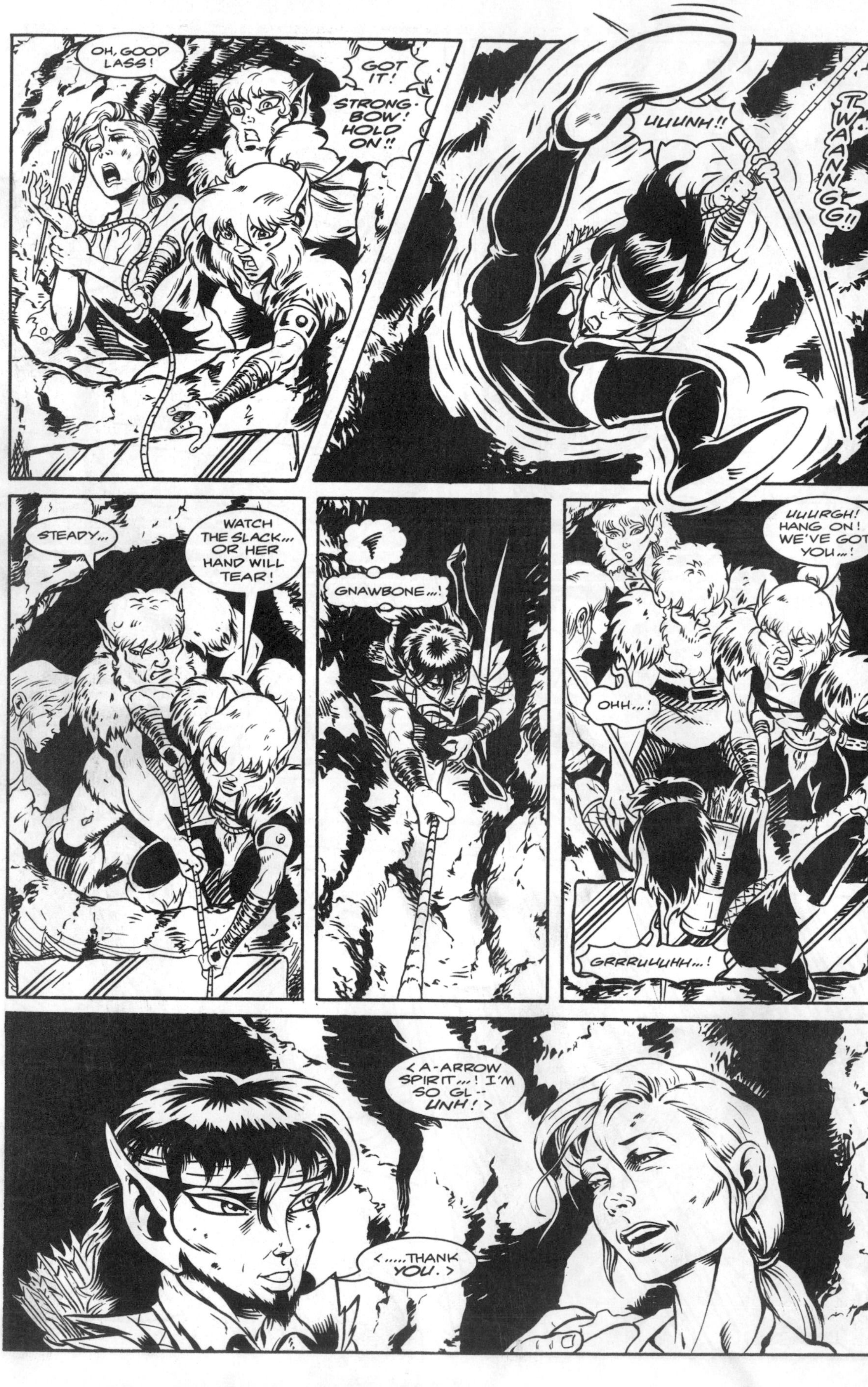
OH, GOOD LASS!
GOT IT! STRONGBOW! HOLD ON!!
UUUNH!!
TWAANNGG!!
STEADY...
WATCH THE SLACK... OR HER HAND WILL TEAR!
!
GNAWBONE...!
UUURGH! HANG ON! WE'VE GOT YOU...!
OHH...!
GRRRUUUHH...!
< A-ARROW SPIRIT...! I'M SO GL-- UNH! >
< .....THANK YOU. >

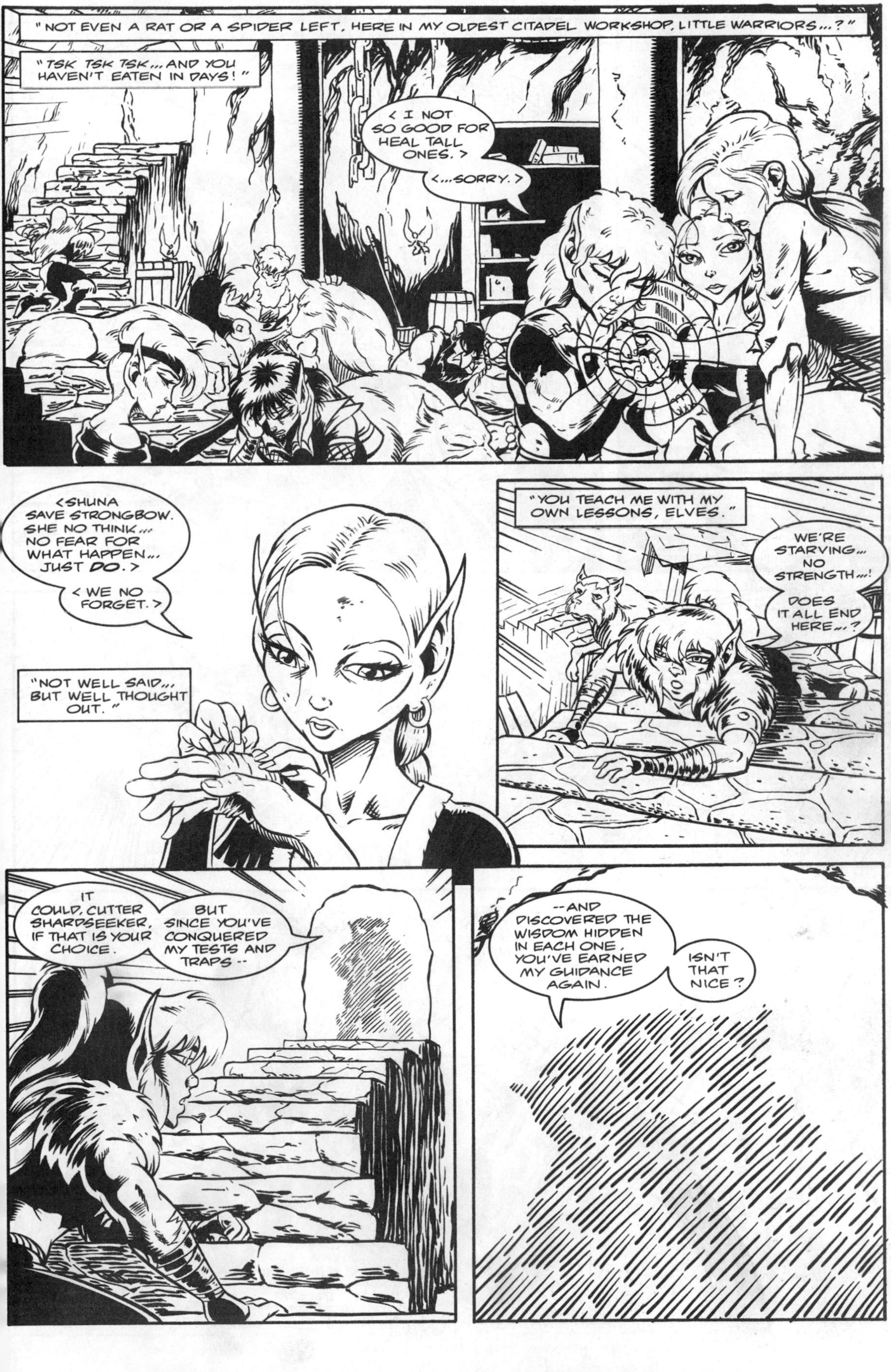
"NOT EVEN A RAT OR A SPIDER LEFT, HERE IN MY OLDEST CITADEL WORKSHOP, LITTLE WARRIORS...?"
"TSK TSK TSK... AND YOU HAVEN'T EATEN IN DAYS!"
< I NOT SO GOOD FOR HEAL TALL ONES. >
<...SORRY.>
<SHUNA SAVE STRONGBOW. SHE NO THINK... NO FEAR FOR WHAT HAPPEN... JUST DO.>
< WE NO FORGET. >
"NOT WELL SAID... BUT WELL THOUGHT OUT."
"YOU TEACH ME WITH MY OWN LESSONS, ELVES."
WE'RE STARVING... NO STRENGTH...!
DOES IT ALL END HERE...?
IT COULD, CUTTER SHARDSEEKER, IF THAT IS YOUR CHOICE.
BUT SINCE YOU'VE CONQUERED MY TESTS AND TRAPS --
--AND DISCOVERED THE WISDOM HIDDEN IN EACH ONE, YOU'VE EARNED MY GUIDANCE AGAIN.
ISN'T THAT NICE?

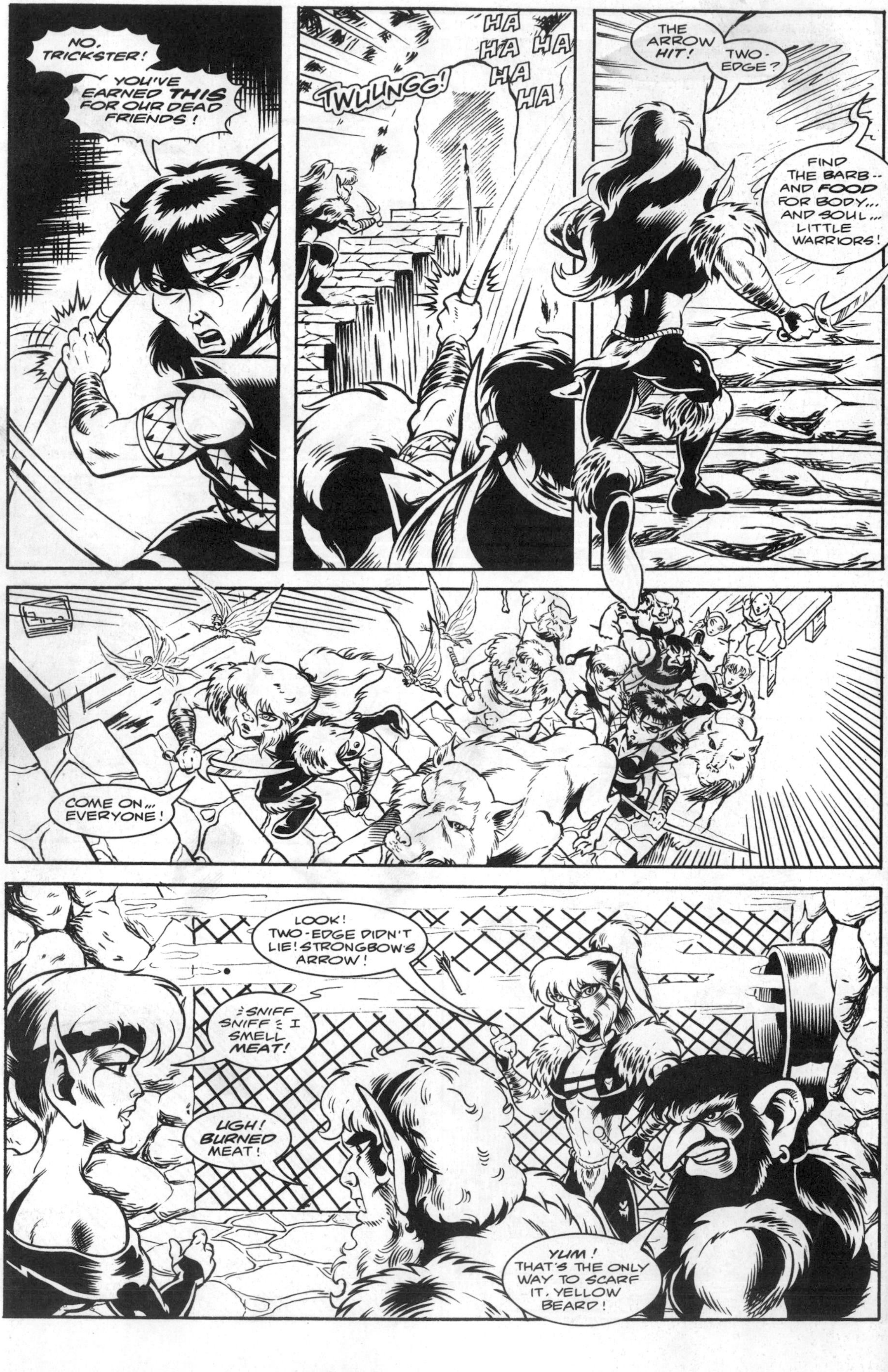
NO, TRICKSTER!
YOU'VE EARNED THIS FOR OUR DEAD FRIENDS!
HA HA HA HA HA HA
TWUUNGG!
THE ARROW HIT!
TWO-EDGE?
FIND THE BARB-- AND FOOD FOR BODY... AND SOUL... LITTLE WARRIORS!
COME ON... EVERYONE!
LOOK! TWO-EDGE DIDN'T LIE! STRONGBOW'S ARROW!
SNIFF SNIFF I SMELL MEAT!
UGH! BURNED MEAT!
YUM! THAT'S THE ONLY WAY TO SCARF IT, YELLOW BEARD!

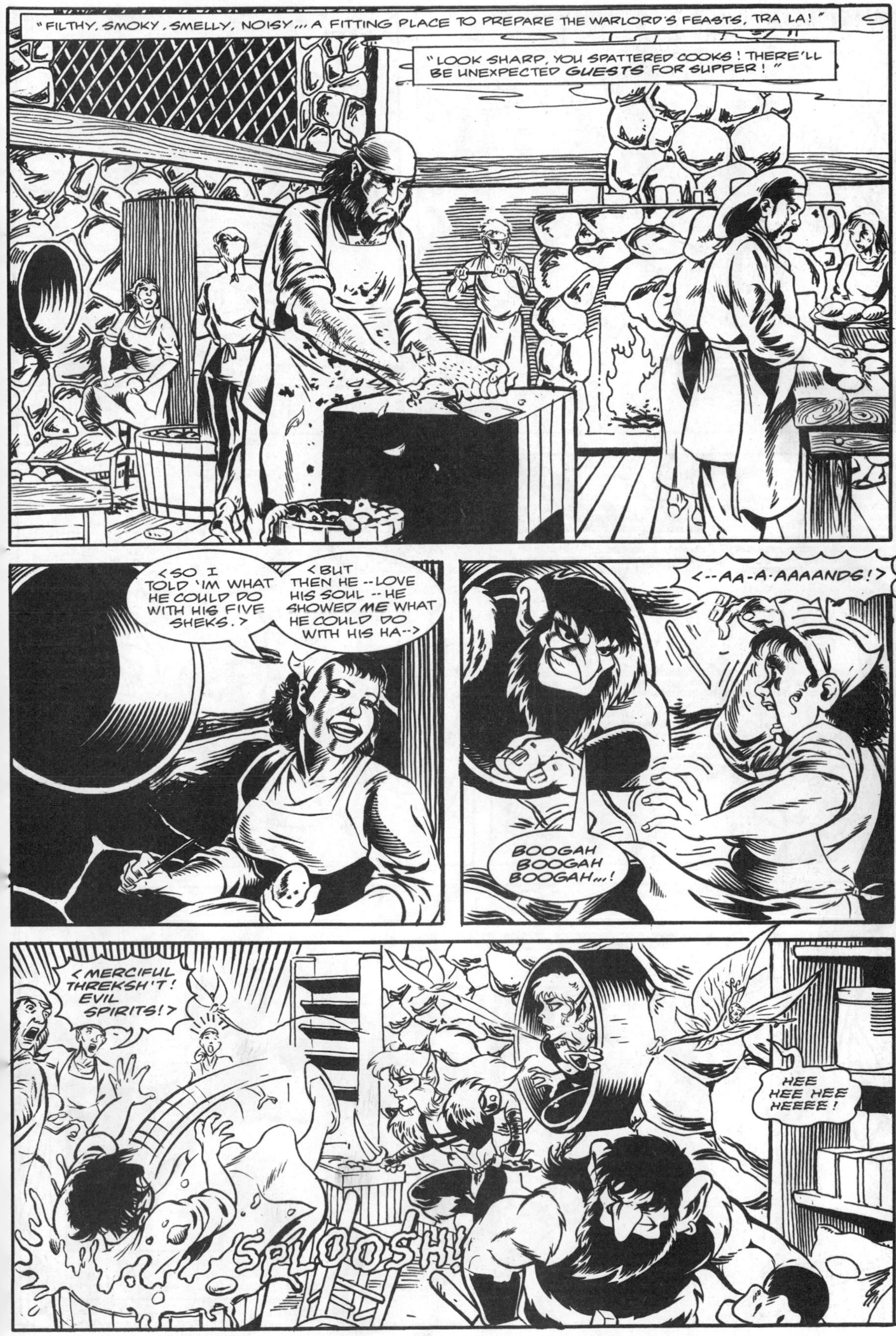
"FILTHY, SMOKY, SMELLY, NOISY... A FITTING PLACE TO PREPARE THE WARLORD'S FEASTS, TRA LA!"
"LOOK SHARP, YOU SPATTERED COOKS! THERE'LL BE UNEXPECTED GUESTS FOR SUPPER!"
<SO I TOLD 'IM WHAT HE COULD DO WITH HIS FIVE SHEKS.>
<BUT THEN HE --LOVE HIS SOUL --HE SHOWED ME WHAT HE COULD DO WITH HIS HA-->
<--AA-A-AAAANDS!>
BOOGAH BOOGAH BOOGAH...!
<MERCIFUL THREKSH'T! EVIL SPIRITS!>
HEE HEE HEE HEEEE!
SPLOOSH!

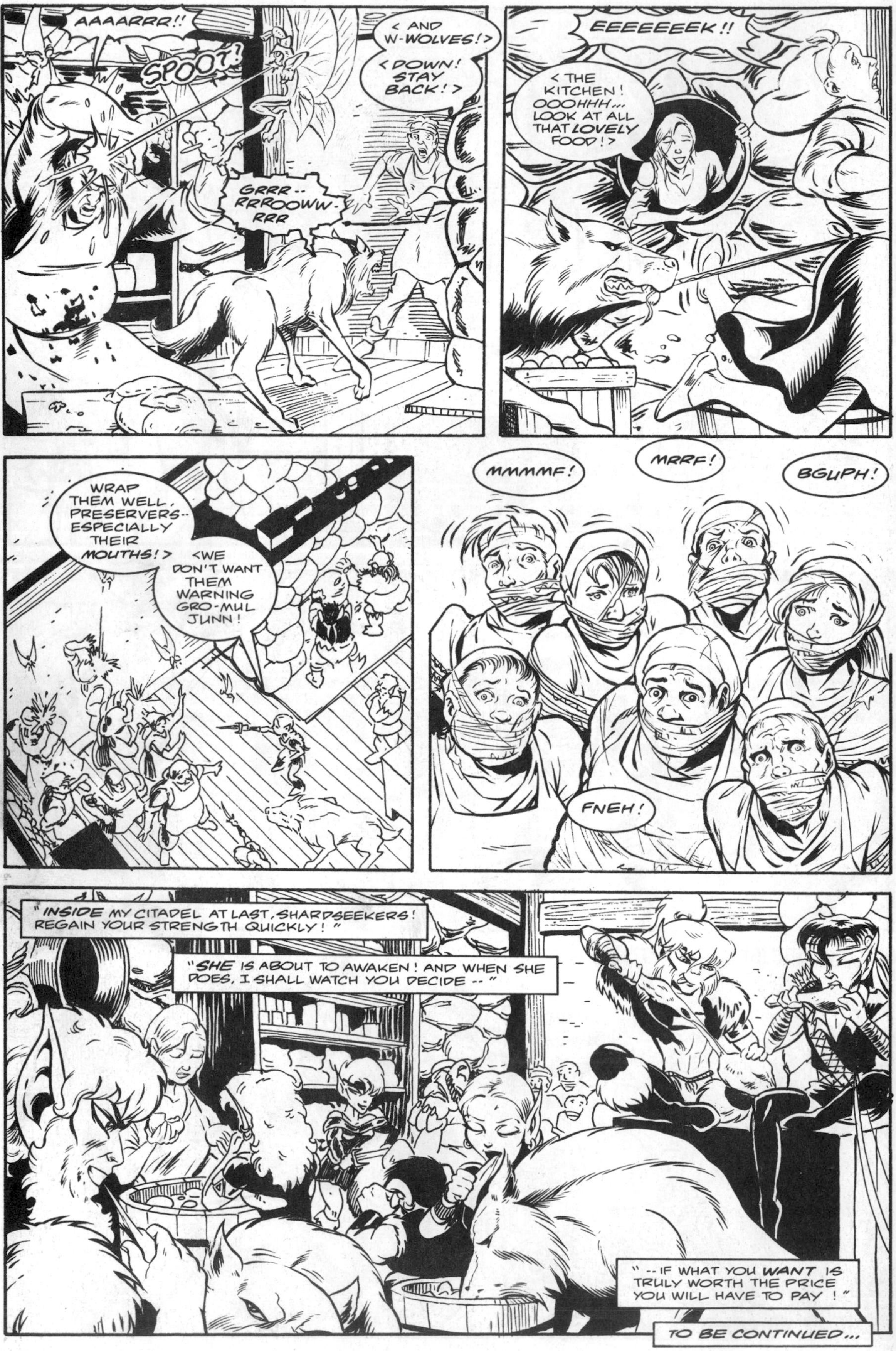
AAAARRR!!
SPOOT!
< AND W-WOLVES! >
< DOWN! STAY BACK! >
GRRR-- RRROOWW-RRR
EEEEEEEK!!
< THE KITCHEN! OOOHHH... LOOK AT ALL THAT LOVELY FOOD! >
< WRAP THEM WELL, PRESERVERS-- ESPECIALLY THEIR MOUTHS! >
< WE DON'T WANT THEM WARNING GRO-MUL JUNN! >
MMMMF!
MRRF!
BGUPH!
FNEH!
" INSIDE MY CITADEL AT LAST, SHARDSEEKERS! REGAIN YOUR STRENGTH QUICKLY! "
" SHE IS ABOUT TO AWAKEN! AND WHEN SHE DOES, I SHALL WATCH YOU DECIDE -- "
" -- IF WHAT YOU WANT IS TRULY WORTH THE PRICE YOU WILL HAVE TO PAY! "
TO BE CONTINUED...

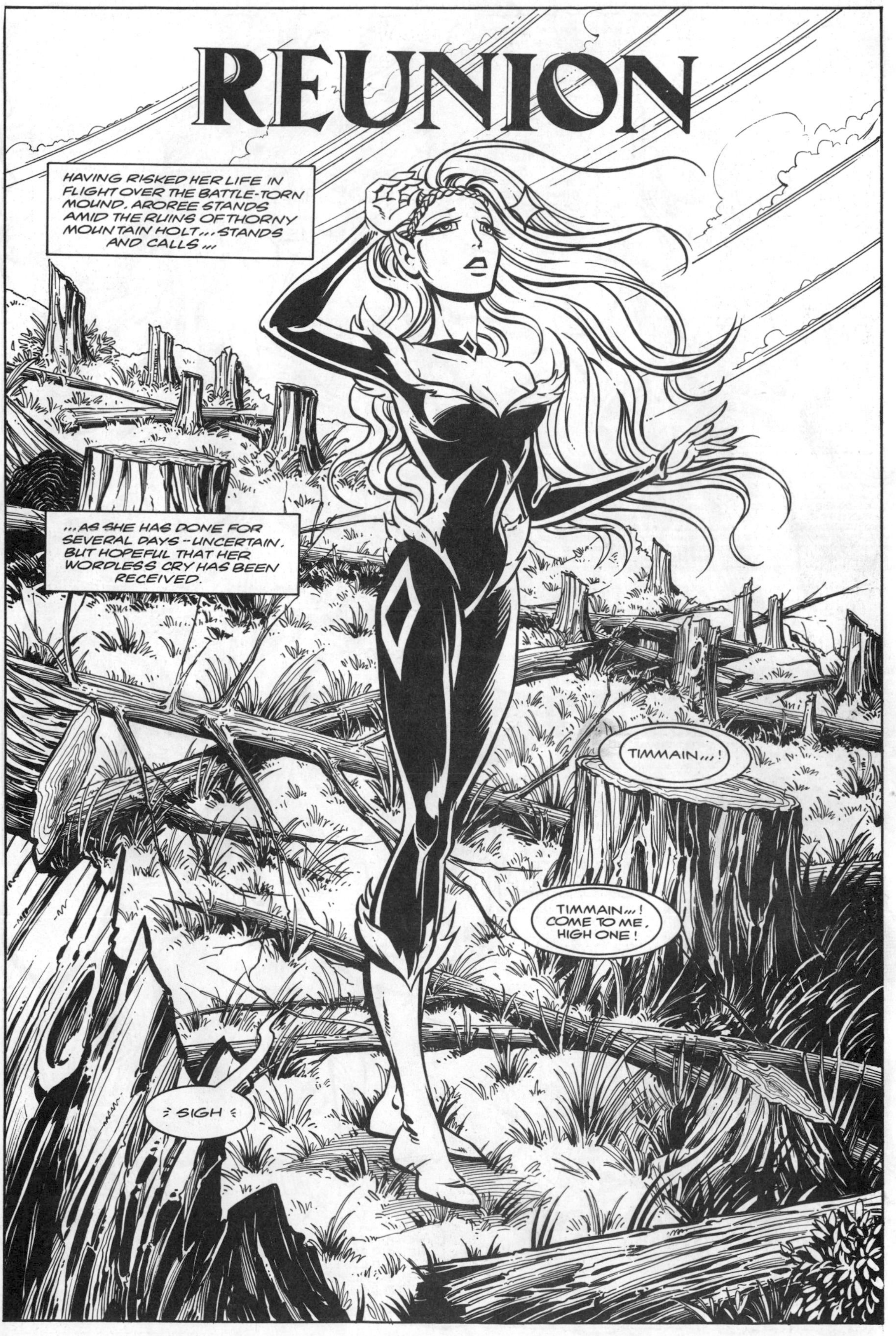
REUNION
HAVING RISKED HER LIFE IN FLIGHT OVER THE BATTLE-TORN MOUND, AROREE STANDS AMID THE RUINS OF THORNY MOUNTAIN HOLT... STANDS AND CALLS...
...AS SHE HAS DONE FOR SEVERAL DAYS--UNCERTAIN, BUT HOPEFUL THAT HER WORDLESS CRY HAS BEEN RECEIVED.
TIMMAIN...!
TIMMAIN...! COME TO ME, HIGH ONE!
SIGH

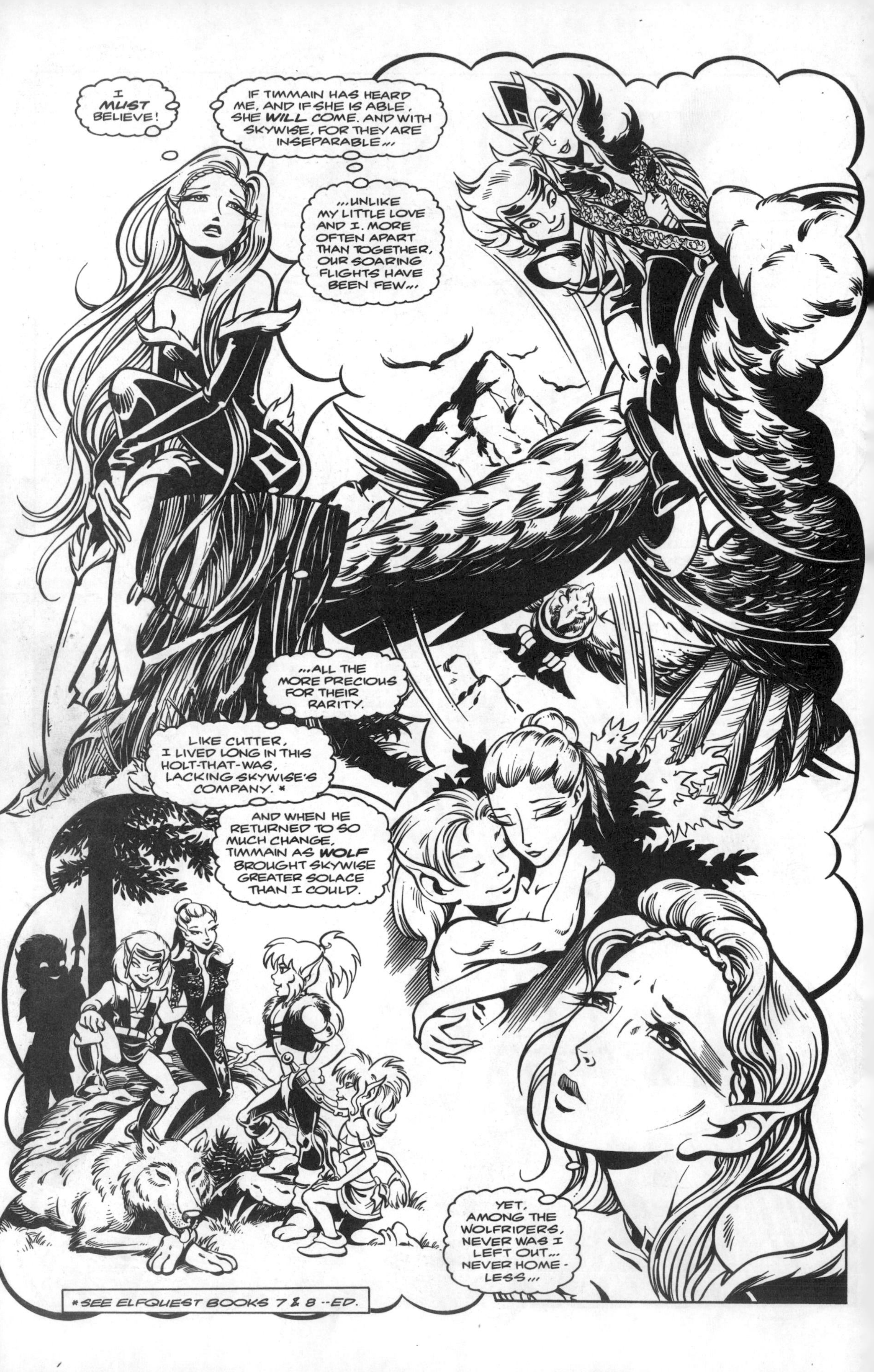
I MUST BELIEVE!
IF TIMMAIN HAS HEARD ME, AND IF SHE IS ABLE, SHE WILL COME. AND WITH SKYWISE, FOR THEY ARE INSEPARABLE...
...UNLIKE MY LITTLE LOVE AND I. MORE OFTEN APART THAN TOGETHER, OUR SOARING FLIGHTS HAVE BEEN FEW...
...ALL THE MORE PRECIOUS FOR THEIR RARITY.
LIKE CUTTER, I LIVED LONG IN THIS HOLT-THAT-WAS, LACKING SKYWISE'S COMPANY. *
AND WHEN HE RETURNED TO SO MUCH CHANGE, TIMMAIN AS WOLF BROUGHT SKYWISE GREATER SOLACE THAN I COULD.
YET, AMONG THE WOLFRIDERS, NEVER WAS I LEFT OUT... NEVER HOME-LESS...
* SEE ELFQUEST BOOKS 7 & 8 --ED.

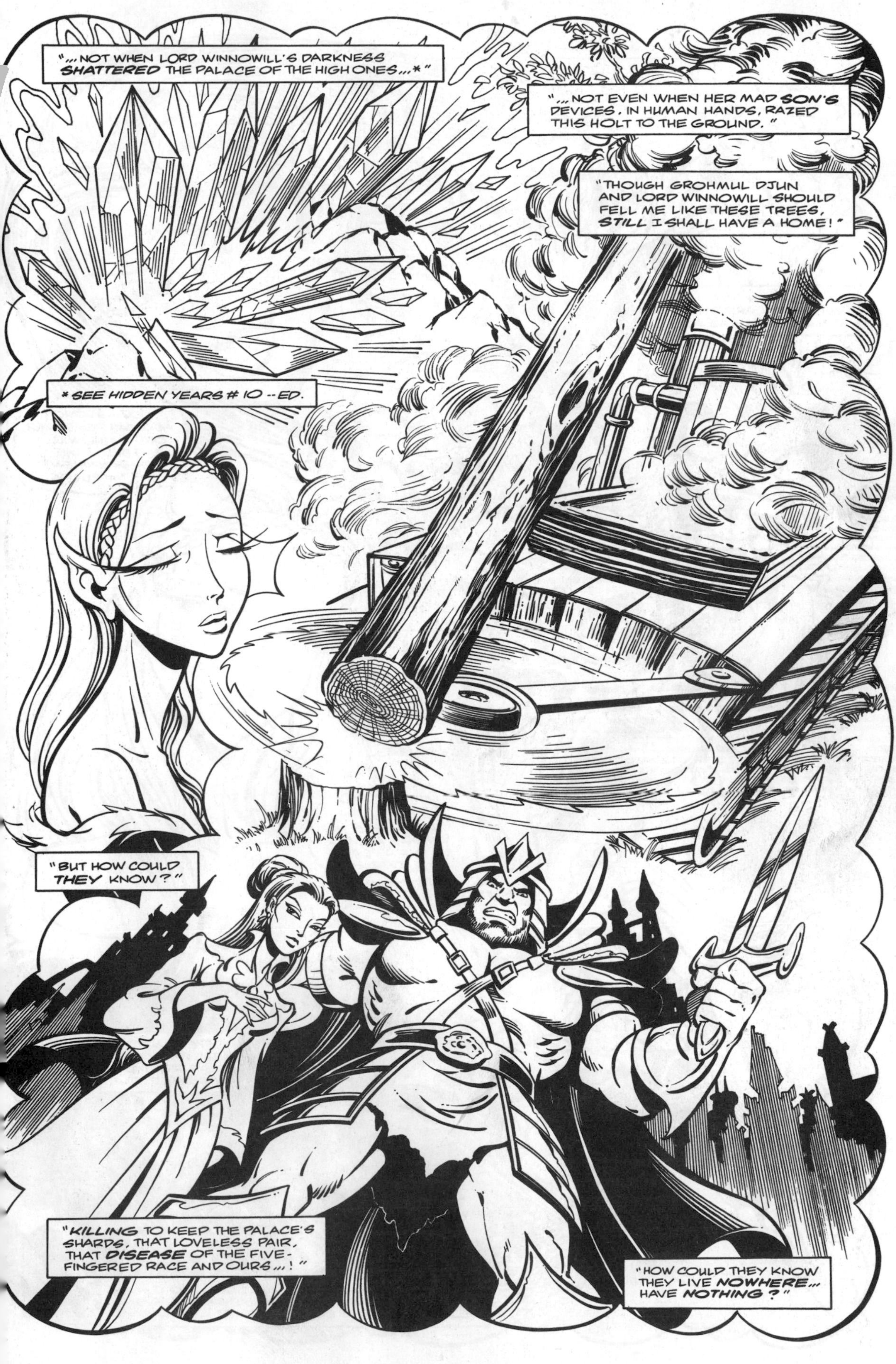
"...NOT WHEN LORD WINNOWILL'S DARKNESS SHATTERED THE PALACE OF THE HIGH ONES...*"
"...NOT EVEN WHEN HER MAD SON'S DEVICES, IN HUMAN HANDS, RAZED THIS HOLT TO THE GROUND."
"THOUGH GROHMUL DJUN AND LORD WINNOWILL SHOULD FELL ME LIKE THESE TREES, STILL I SHALL HAVE A HOME!"
* SEE HIDDEN YEARS # 10 --ED.
"BUT HOW COULD THEY KNOW?"
"KILLING TO KEEP THE PALACE'S SHARDS, THAT LOVELESS PAIR, THAT DISEASE OF THE FIVE-FINGERED RACE AND OURS...!"
"HOW COULD THEY KNOW THEY LIVE NOWHERE... HAVE NOTHING?"

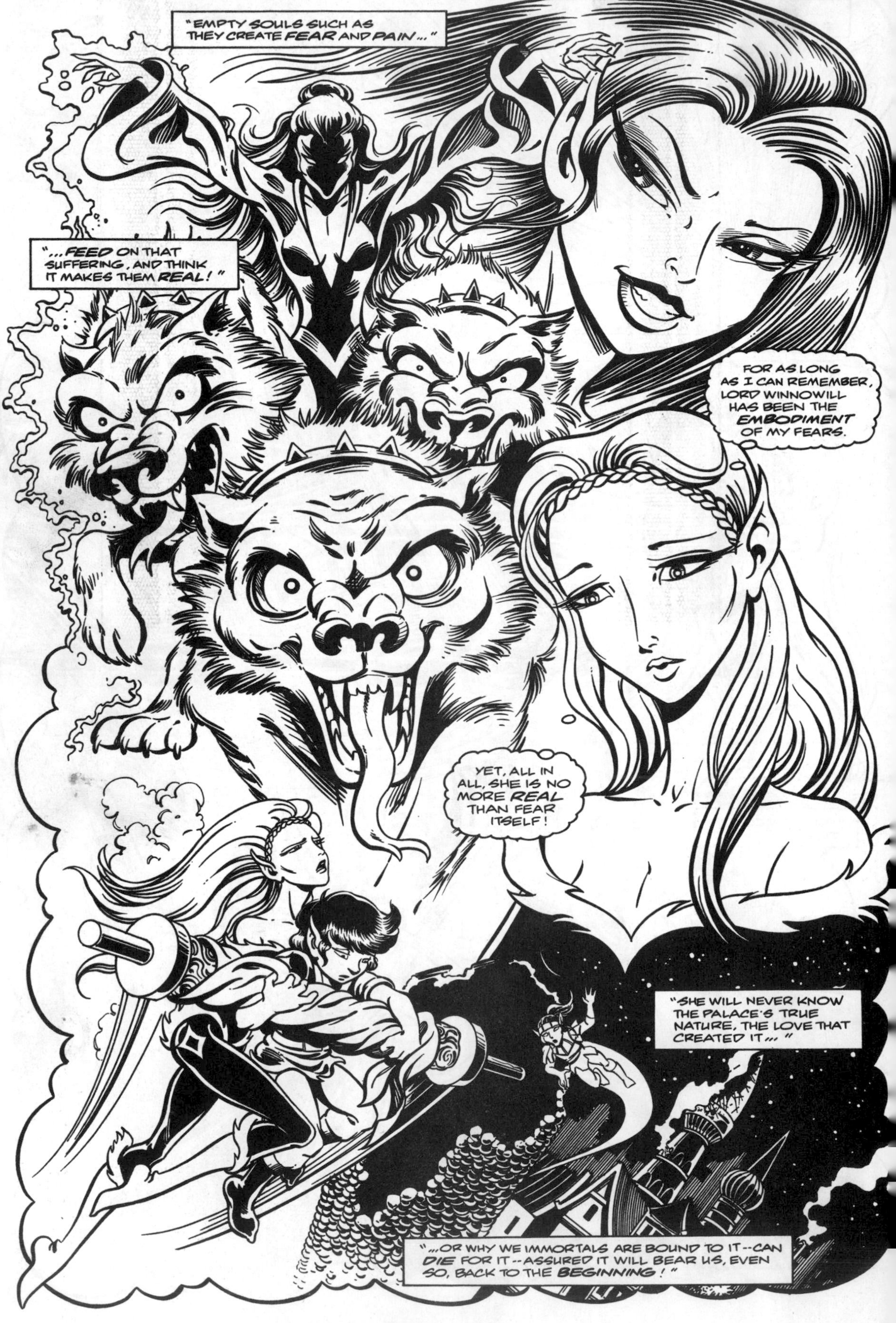
"EMPTY SOULS SUCH AS THEY CREATE FEAR AND PAIN..."
"...FEED ON THAT SUFFERING, AND THINK IT MAKES THEM REAL!"
FOR AS LONG AS I CAN REMEMBER, LORD WINNOWILL HAS BEEN THE EMBODIMENT OF MY FEARS.
YET, ALL IN ALL, SHE IS NO MORE REAL THAN FEAR ITSELF!
"SHE WILL NEVER KNOW THE PALACE'S TRUE NATURE, THE LOVE THAT CREATED IT..."
"...OR WHY WE IMMORTALS ARE BOUND TO IT--CAN DIE FOR IT--ASSURED IT WILL BEAR US, EVEN SO, BACK TO THE BEGINNING!"

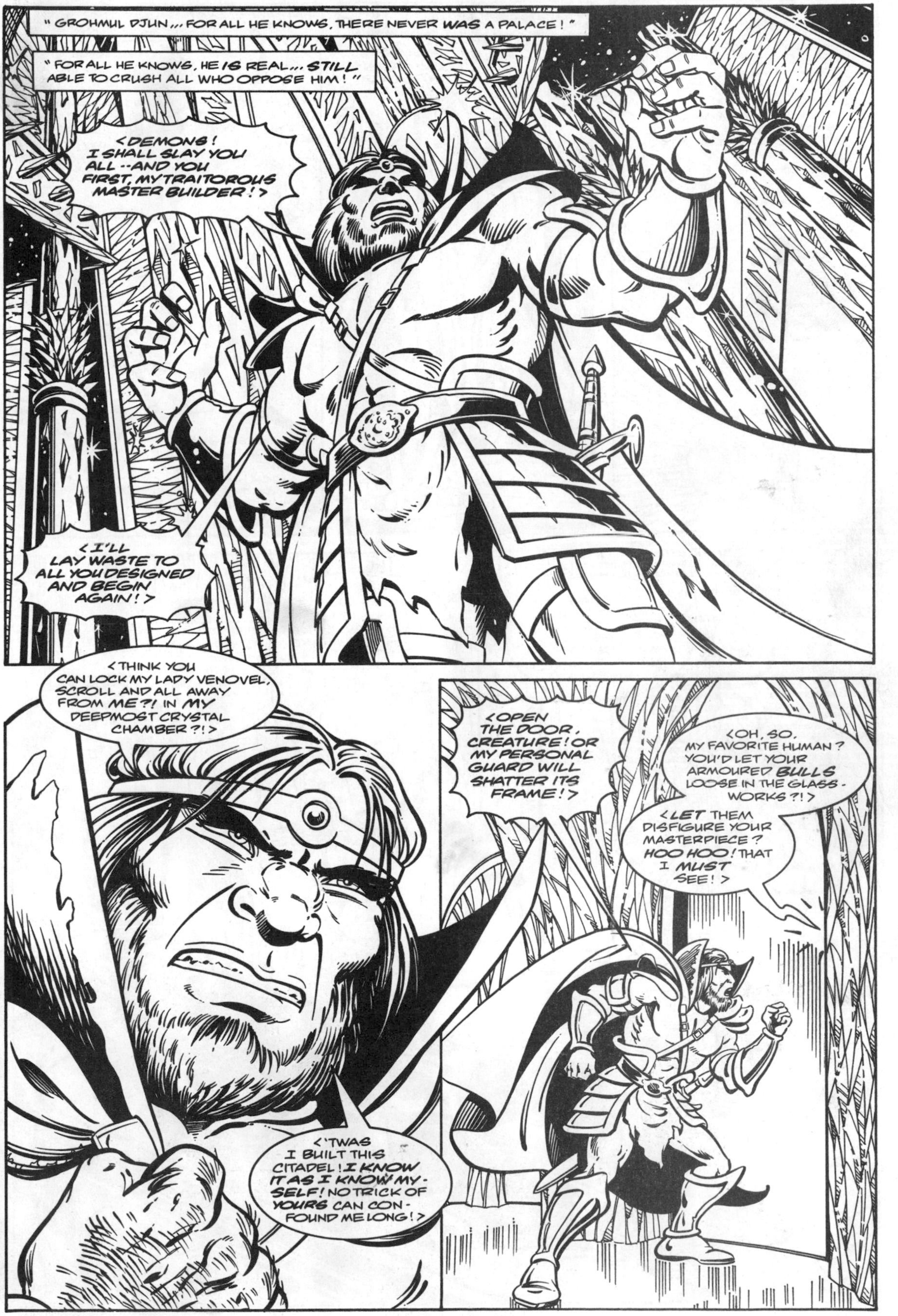
"GROHMUL DJUN... FOR ALL HE KNOWS, THERE NEVER WAS A PALACE!"
"FOR ALL HE KNOWS, HE IS REAL... STILL ABLE TO CRUSH ALL WHO OPPOSE HIM!"
<DEMONS! I SHALL SLAY YOU ALL --AND YOU FIRST, MY TRAITOROUS MASTER BUILDER!>
<I'LL LAY WASTE TO ALL YOU DESIGNED AND BEGIN AGAIN!>
<THINK YOU CAN LOCK MY LADY VENOVEL, SCROLL AND ALL AWAY FROM ME?! IN MY DEEPMOST CRYSTAL CHAMBER?!>
<'TWAS I BUILT THIS CITADEL! I KNOW IT AS I KNOW MY-SELF! NO TRICK OF YOURS CAN CON-FOUND ME LONG!>
<OPEN THE DOOR, CREATURE! OR MY PERSONAL GUARD WILL SHATTER ITS FRAME!>
<OH, SO, MY FAVORITE HUMAN? YOU'D LET YOUR ARMOURED BULLS LOOSE IN THE GLASS-WORKS?!>
<LET THEM DISFIGURE YOUR MASTERPIECE? HOO HOO! THAT I MUST SEE!>

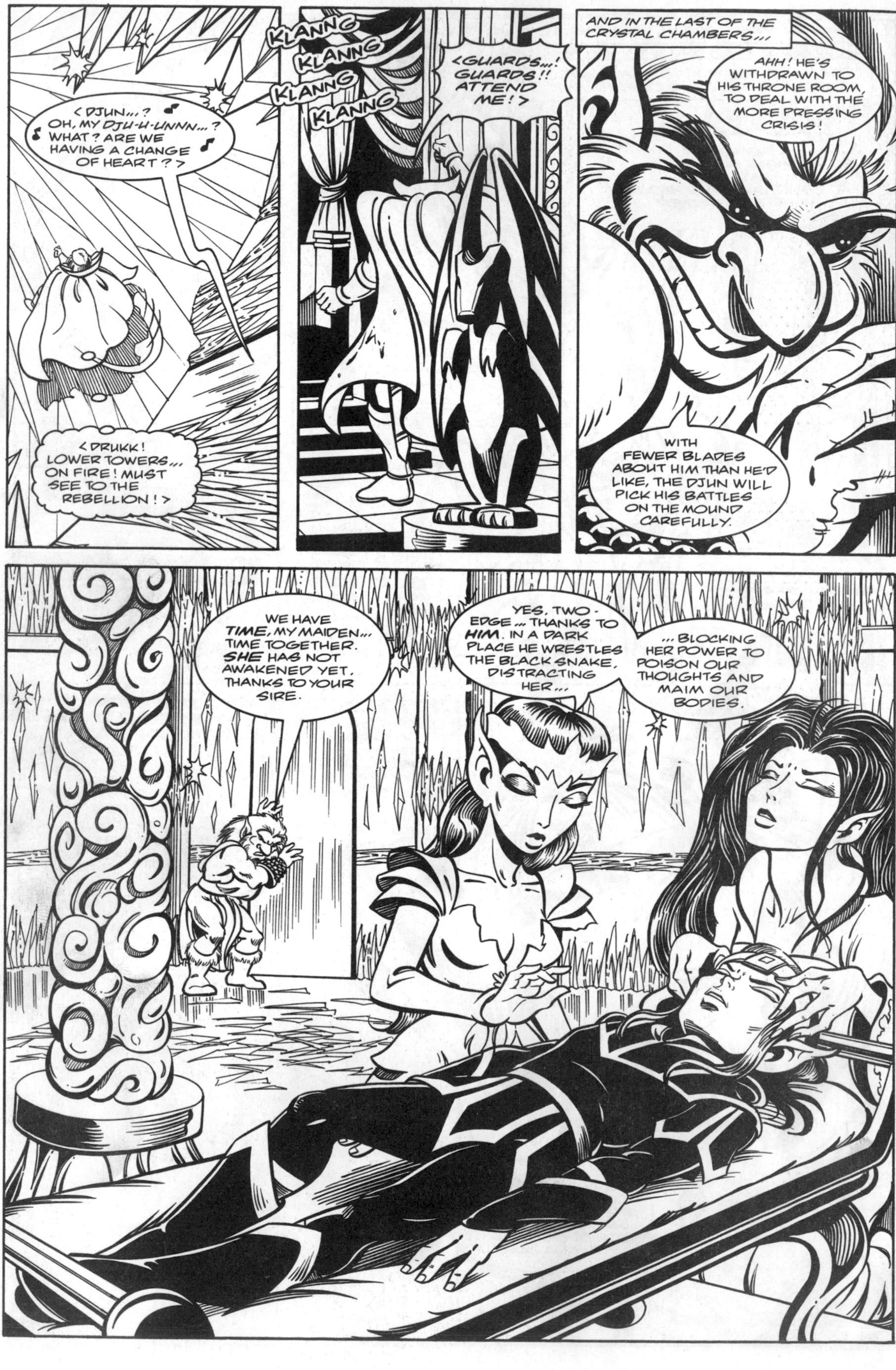

< DJUN...? OH, MY DJU-U-UNNN...? WHAT? ARE WE HAVING A CHANGE OF HEART? >
< DRUKK! LOWER TOWERS... ON FIRE! MUST SEE TO THE REBELLION! >
KLANNG KLANNG KLANNG KLANNG
< GUARDS...! GUARDS!! ATTEND ME! >
AND IN THE LAST OF THE CRYSTAL CHAMBERS...
AHH! HE'S WITHDRAWN TO HIS THRONE ROOM, TO DEAL WITH THE MORE PRESSING CRISIS!
WITH FEWER BLADES ABOUT HIM THAN HE'D LIKE, THE DJUN WILL PICK HIS BATTLES ON THE MOUND CAREFULLY.
WE HAVE TIME, MY MAIDEN... TIME TOGETHER. SHE HAS NOT AWAKENED YET, THANKS TO YOUR SIRE.
YES, TWO-EDGE... THANKS TO HIM. IN A DARK PLACE HE WRESTLES THE BLACK SNAKE, DISTRACTING HER...
...BLOCKING HER POWER TO POISON OUR THOUGHTS AND MAIM OUR BODIES.

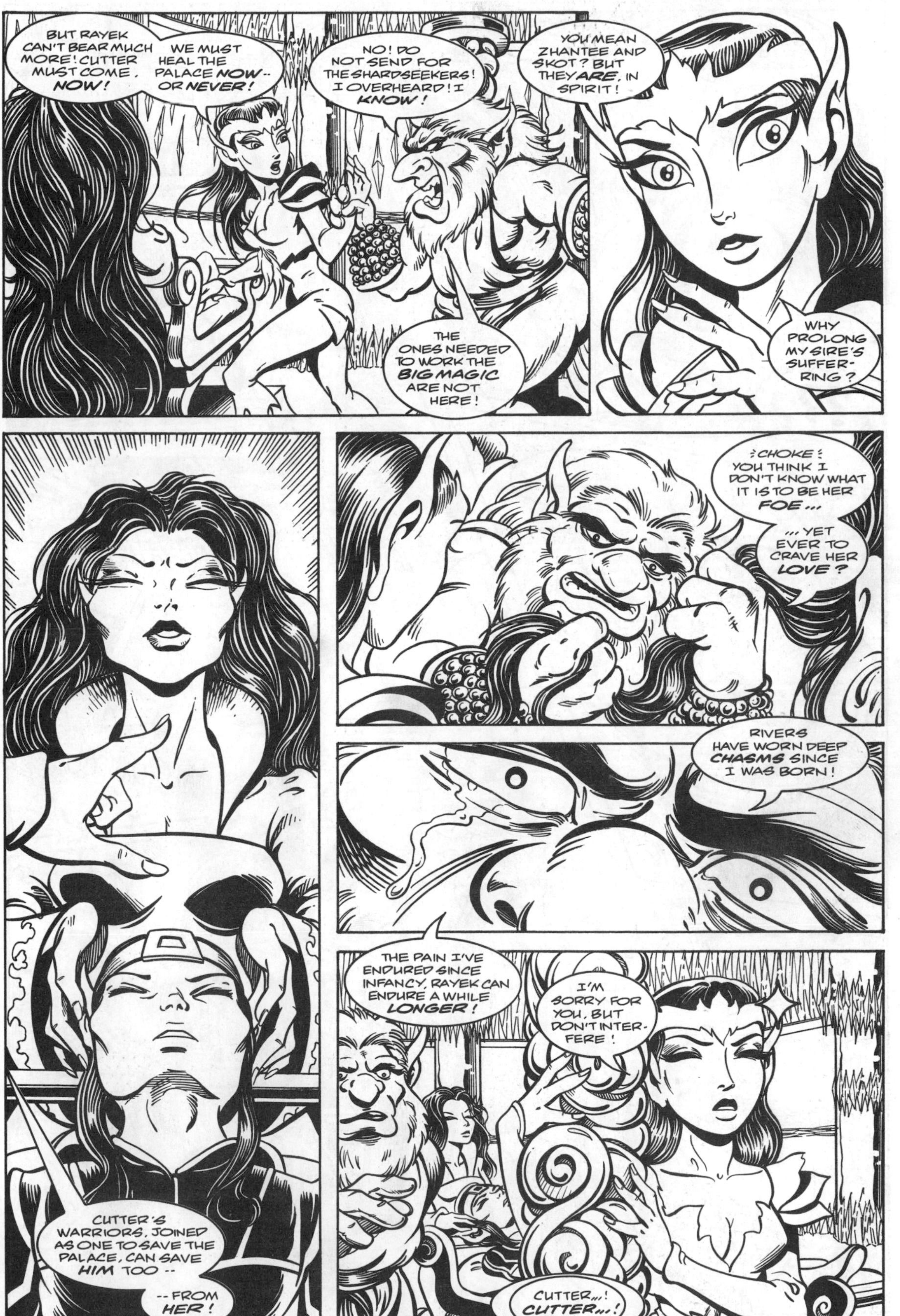
BUT RAYEK CAN'T BEAR MUCH MORE! CUTTER MUST COME, NOW!
WE MUST HEAL THE PALACE NOW -- OR NEVER!
NO! DO NOT SEND FOR THE SHARDSEEKERS! I OVERHEARD! I KNOW!
THE ONES NEEDED TO WORK THE BIG MAGIC ARE NOT HERE!
YOU MEAN ZHANTEE AND SKOT? BUT THEY ARE, IN SPIRIT!
WHY PROLONG MY SIRE'S SUFFER-RING?
CUTTER'S WARRIORS, JOINED AS ONE TO SAVE THE PALACE, CAN SAVE HIM TOO --
-- FROM HER!
CHOKE! YOU THINK I DON'T KNOW WHAT IT IS TO BE HER FOE...
...YET EVER TO CRAVE HER LOVE?
RIVERS HAVE WORN DEEP CHASMS SINCE I WAS BORN!
THE PAIN I'VE ENDURED SINCE INFANCY, RAYEK CAN ENDURE A WHILE LONGER!
I'M SORRY FOR YOU, BUT DON'T INTER-FERE!
CUTTER...! CUTTER...!

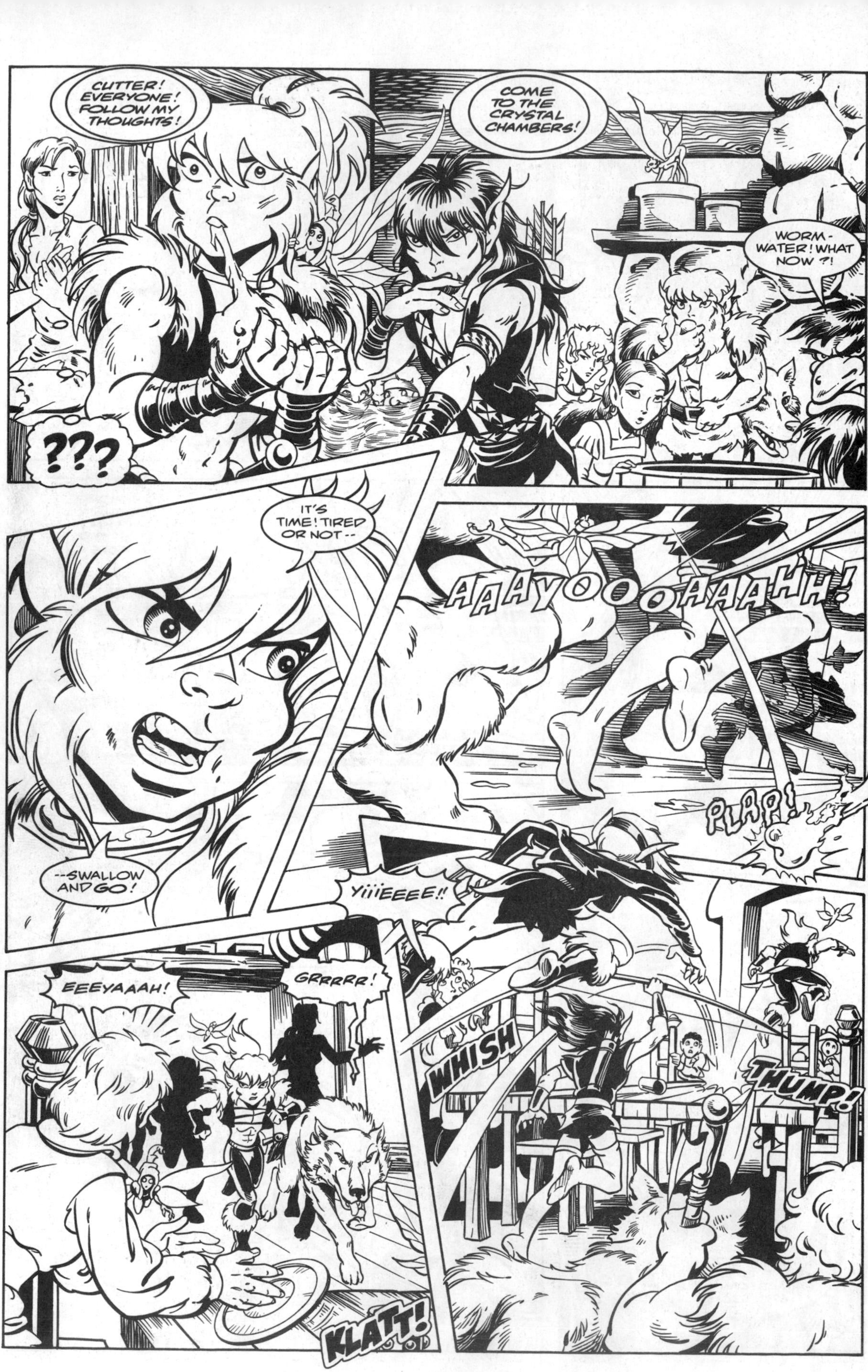
CUTTER! EVERYONE! FOLLOW MY THOUGHTS!
???
COME TO THE CRYSTAL CHAMBERS!
WORM-WATER! WHAT NOW ?!
IT'S TIME! TIRED OR NOT--
--SWALLOW AND GO!
AAAYOOOOHAAAHH!
PLAP!
YiiiEEEE!!
EEEYAAAH!
GRRRRR!
KLATT!
WHISH
THUMP!

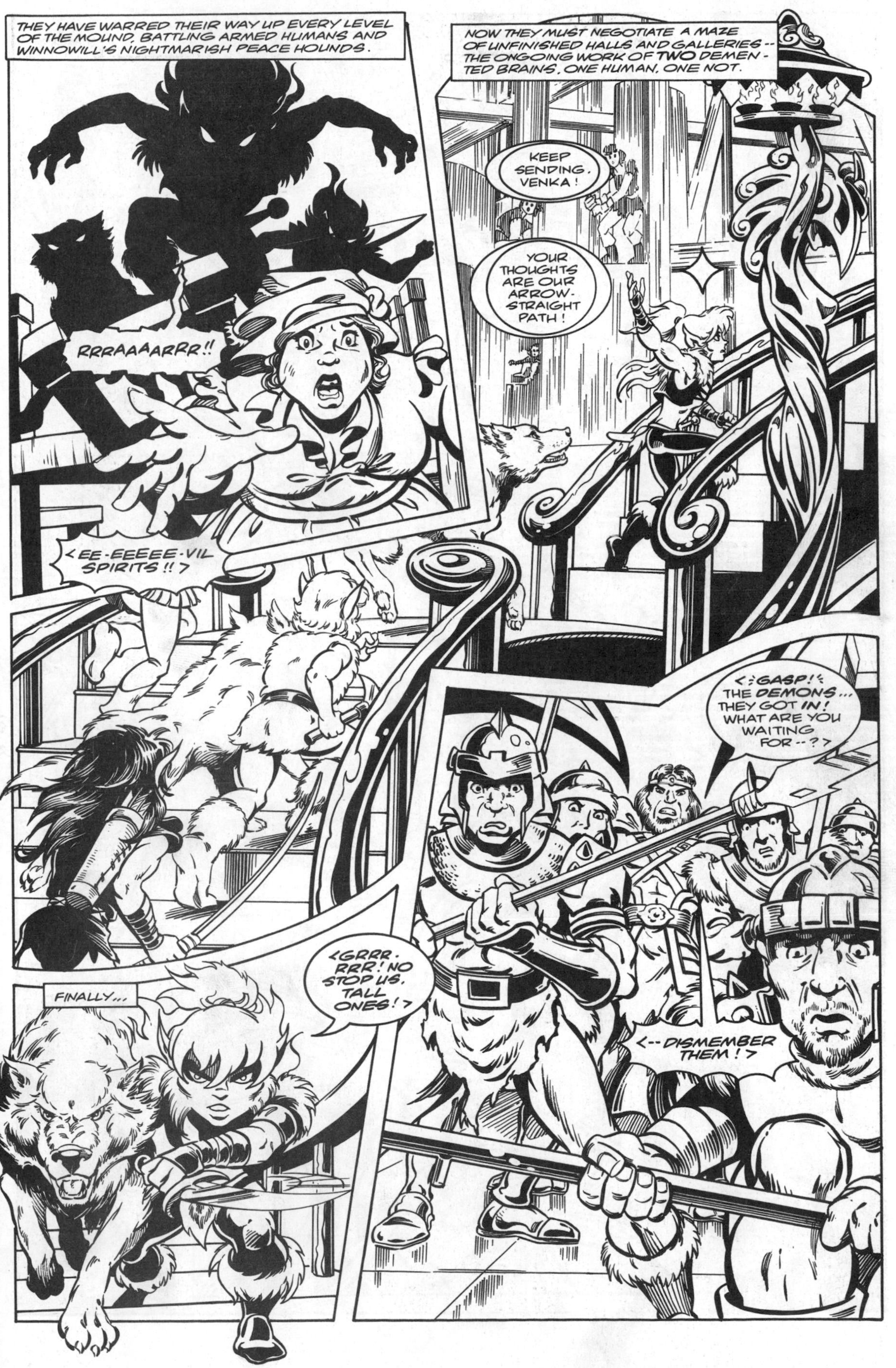
THEY HAVE WARRED THEIR WAY UP EVERY LEVEL OF THE MOUND, BATTLING ARMED HUMANS AND WINNOWILL'S NIGHTMARISH PEACE HOUNDS.
RRRAAAARRR!!
<EE-EEEEE-VIL SPIRITS!!>
NOW THEY MUST NEGOTIATE A MAZE OF UNFINISHED HALLS AND GALLERIES -- THE ONGOING WORK OF TWO DEMENTED BRAINS, ONE HUMAN, ONE NOT.
KEEP SENDING, VENKA!
YOUR THOUGHTS ARE OUR ARROW-STRAIGHT PATH!
<GASP! THE DEMONS... THEY GOT IN! WHAT ARE YOU WAITING FOR --?>
<--DISMEMBER THEM!>
FINALLY...
<GRRR-RRR! NO STOP US, TALL ONES!>

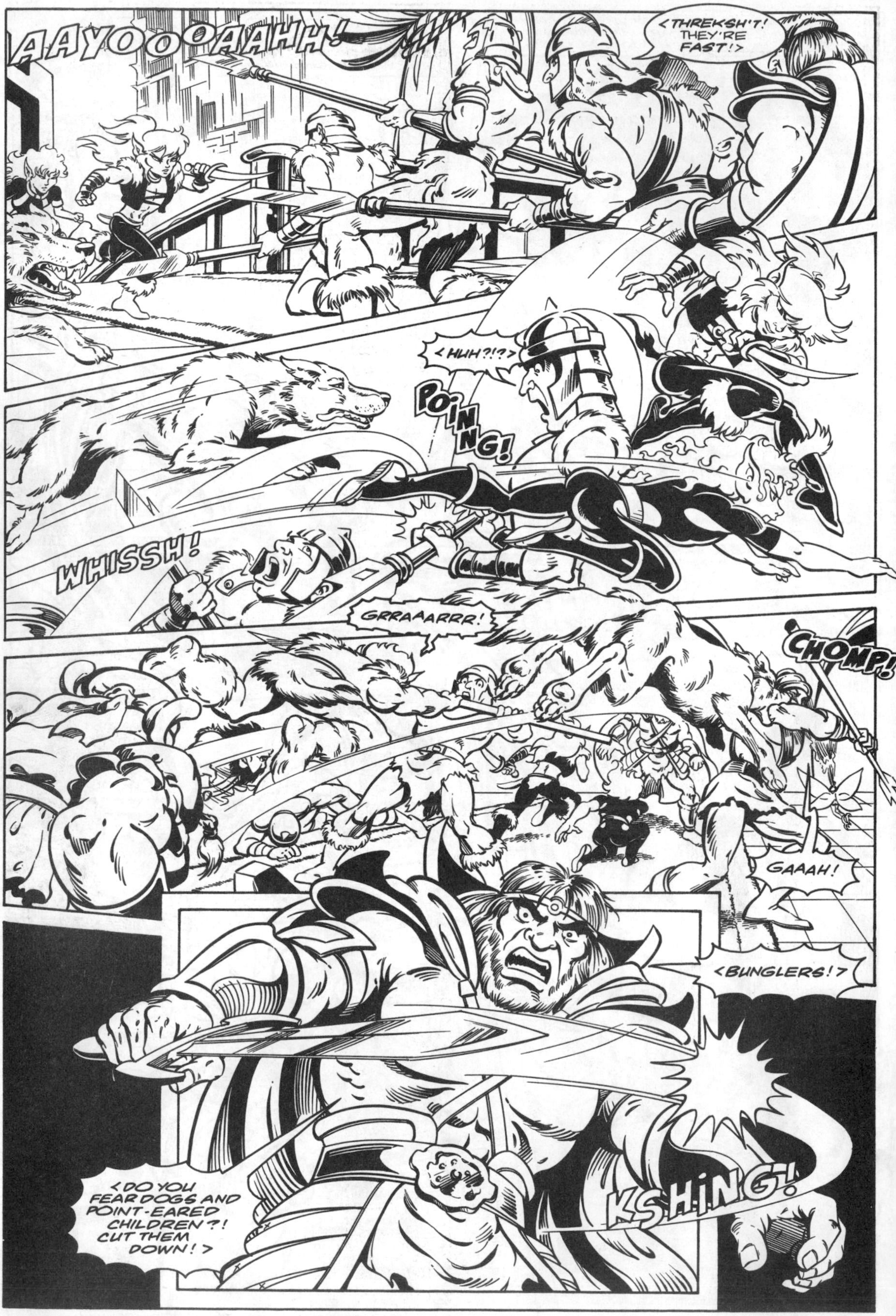
AAYOOOAAHH!
<THREKSH'T! THEY'RE FAST!>
<HUH?!?>
POINNG!
WHISSH!
GRRAAARRR!
CHOMP!
GAAAH!
<BUNGLERS!>
<DO YOU FEAR DOGS AND POINT-EARED CHILDREN?! CUT THEM DOWN!>
KSHING!

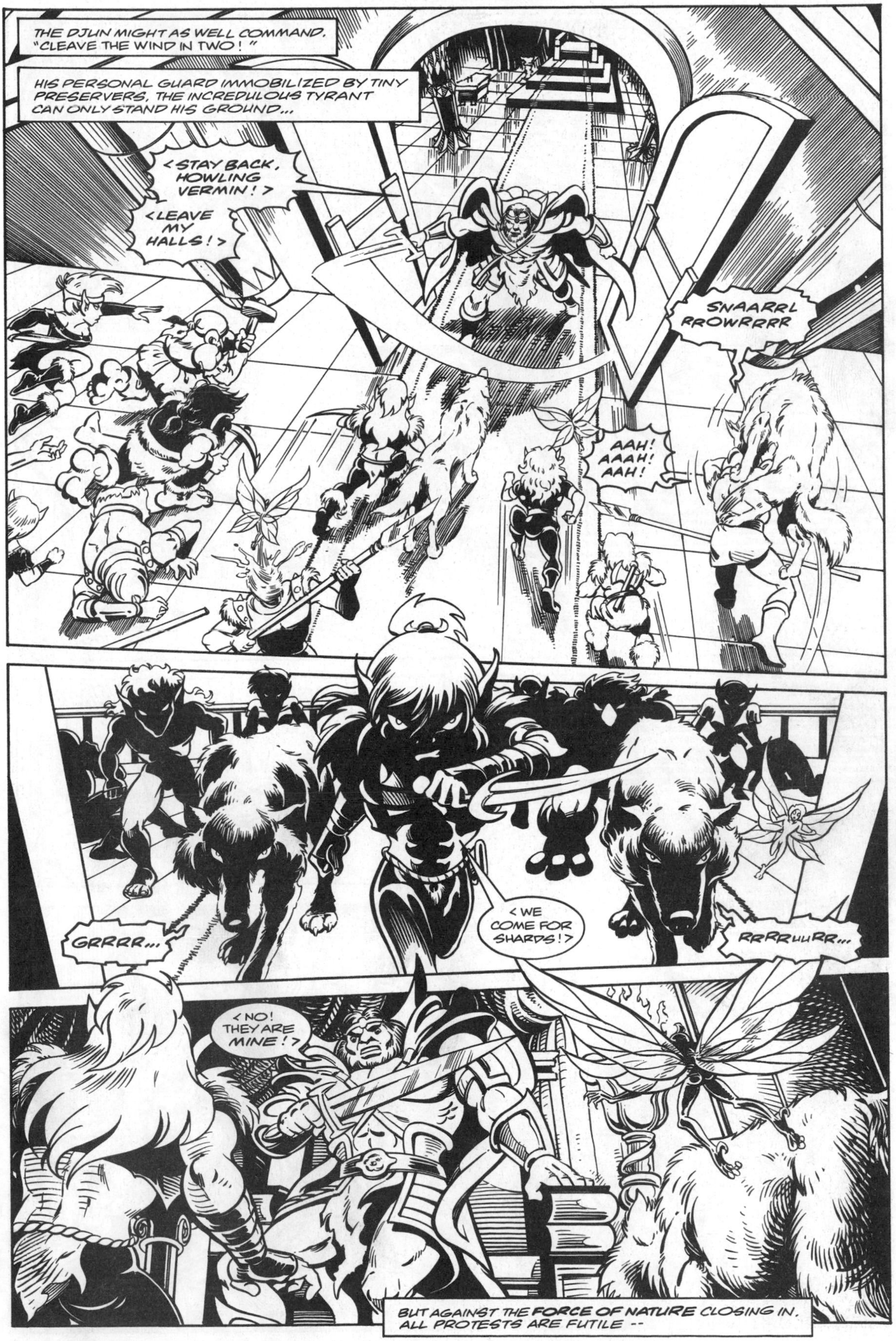

THE DJUN MIGHT AS WELL COMMAND, "CLEAVE THE WIND IN TWO!"
HIS PERSONAL GUARD IMMOBILIZED BY TINY PRESERVERS, THE INCREDULOUS TYRANT CAN ONLY STAND HIS GROUND...
<STAY BACK, HOWLING VERMIN!>
<LEAVE MY HALLS!>
SNAARRL RROWRRRR
AAH! AAAH! AAH!
GRRRR...
<WE COME FOR SHARDS!>
RRRRuuRR...
<NO! THEY ARE MINE!>
BUT AGAINST THE FORCE OF NATURE CLOSING IN, ALL PROTESTS ARE FUTILE --

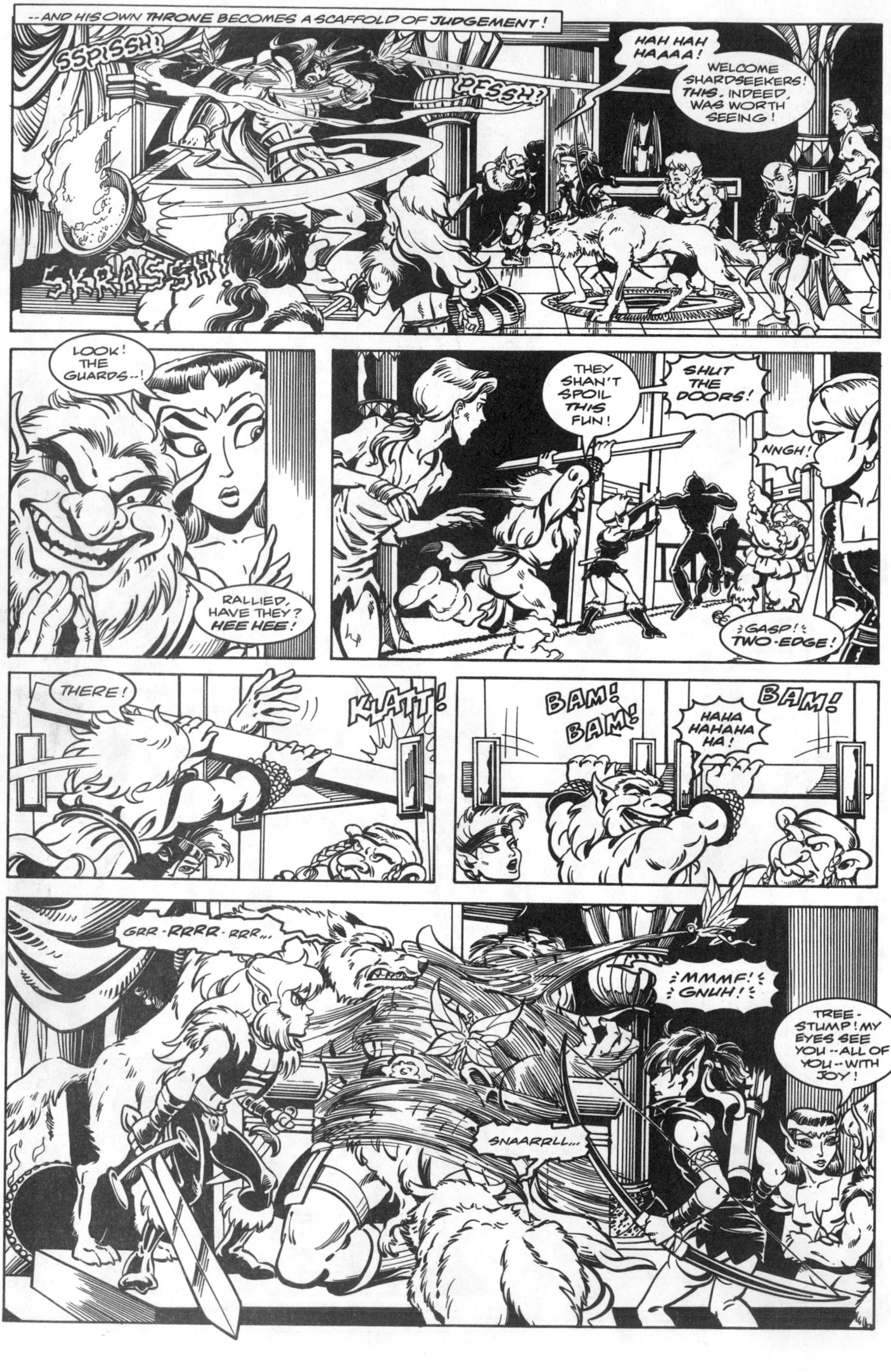
--AND HIS OWN THRONE BECOMES A SCAFFOLD OF JUDGEMENT!
SSPISSH!
PFSSH!
HAH HAH HAAAA!
WELCOME SHARDSEEKERS! THIS, INDEED, WAS WORTH SEEING!
SKRASSH!
LOOK! THE GUARDS--!
RALLIED, HAVE THEY? HEE HEE!
THEY SHAN'T SPOIL THIS FUN!
SHUT THE DOORS!
NNGH!
GASP! TWO-EDGE!
THERE!
KLATT!
BAM! BAM!
HAHA HAHAHA HA!
BAM!
GRR-RRRR-RRR...
MMMF! GNUH!
TREE-STUMP! MY EYES SEE YOU--ALL OF YOU--WITH JOY!
SNAARRLL...

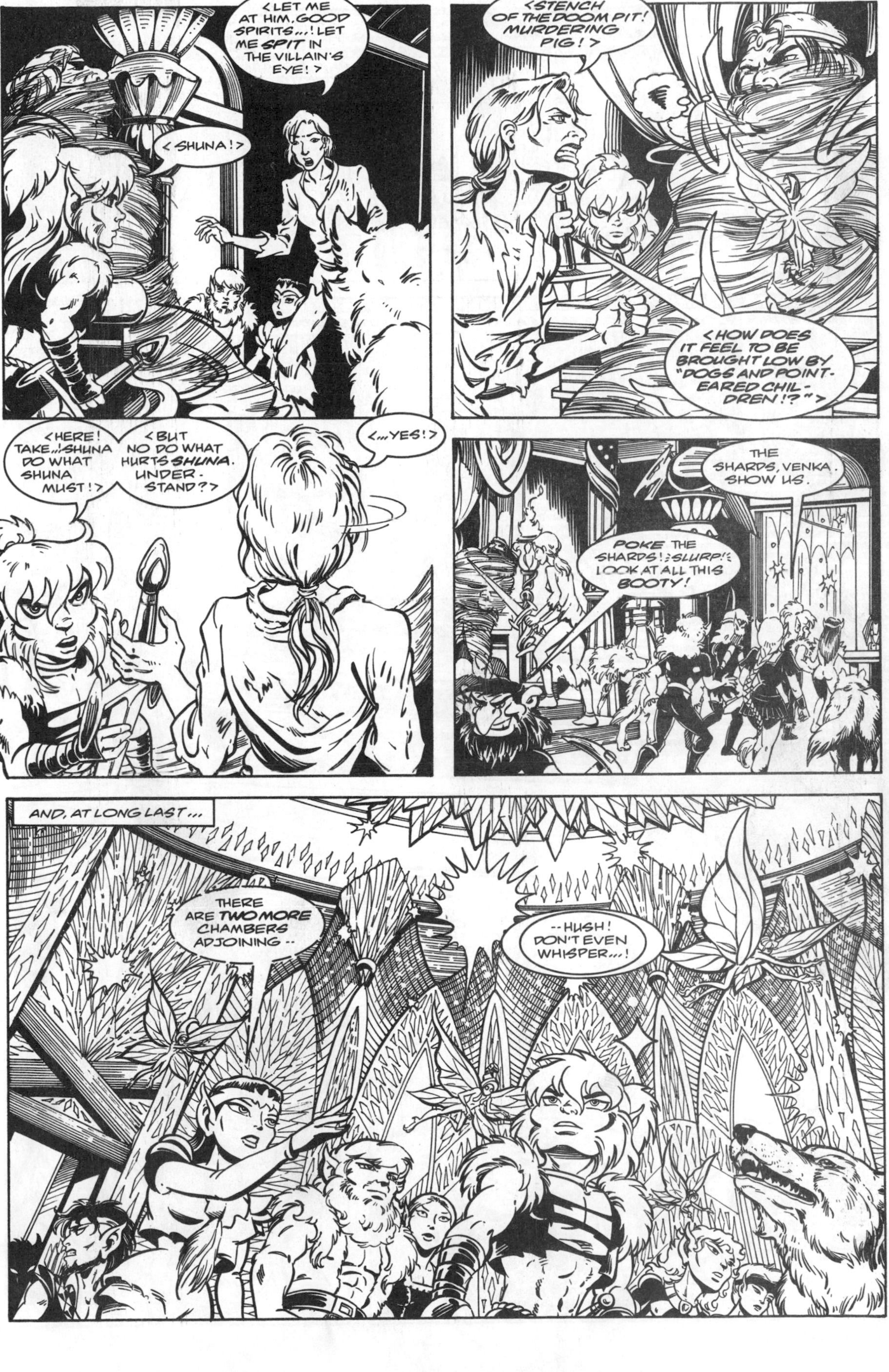
<LET ME AT HIM, GOOD SPIRITS...! LET ME SPIT IN THE VILLAIN'S EYE!>
<SHUNA!>
<STENCH OF THE DOOM PIT! MURDERING PIG!>
<HOW DOES IT FEEL TO BE BROUGHT LOW BY "DOGS AND POINT-EARED CHIL-DREN!?">
<HERE! TAKE...! SHUNA DO WHAT SHUNA MUST!>
<BUT NO DO WHAT HURTS SHUNA. UNDER-STAND?>
<...YES!>
THE SHARDS, VENKA. SHOW US.
POKE THE SHARDS! SLURP! LOOK AT ALL THIS BOOTY!
AND, AT LONG LAST...
THERE ARE TWO MORE CHAMBERS ADJOINING --
--HUSH! DON'T EVEN WHISPER...!

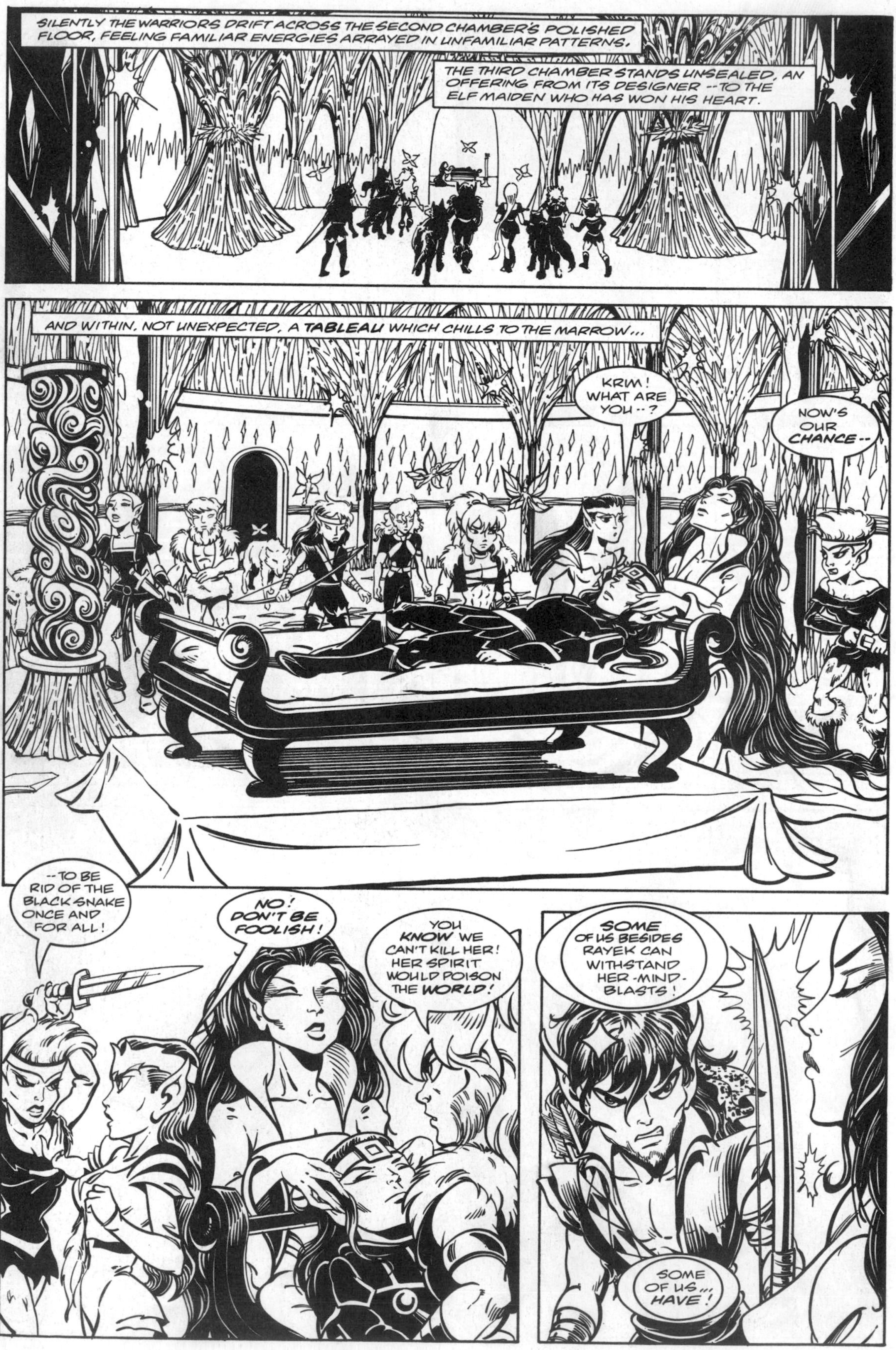
SILENTLY THE WARRIORS DRIFT ACROSS THE SECOND CHAMBER'S POLISHED FLOOR, FEELING FAMILIAR ENERGIES ARRAYED IN UNFAMILIAR PATTERNS.
THE THIRD CHAMBER STANDS UNSEALED, AN OFFERING FROM ITS DESIGNER --TO THE ELF MAIDEN WHO HAS WON HIS HEART.
AND WITHIN, NOT UNEXPECTED, A TABLEAU WHICH CHILLS TO THE MARROW...
KRIM! WHAT ARE YOU--?
NOW'S OUR CHANCE--
--TO BE RID OF THE BLACK SNAKE ONCE AND FOR ALL!
NO! DON'T BE FOOLISH!
YOU KNOW WE CAN'T KILL HER! HER SPIRIT WOULD POISON THE WORLD!
SOME OF US BESIDES RAYEK CAN WITHSTAND HER MIND-BLASTS!
SOME OF US... HAVE!

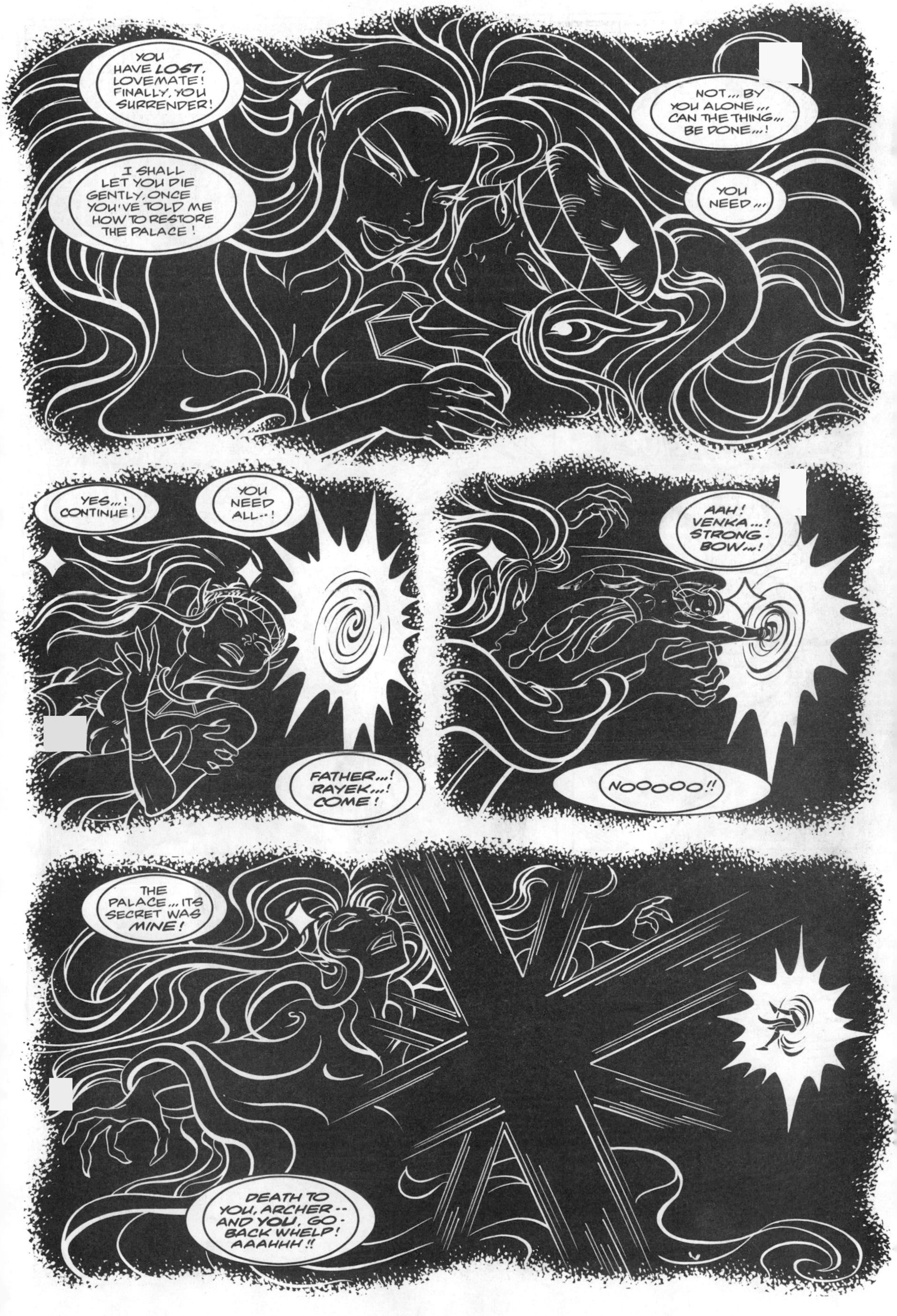
YOU HAVE LOST, LOVEMATE! FINALLY, YOU SURRENDER!
I SHALL LET YOU DIE GENTLY, ONCE YOU'VE TOLD ME HOW TO RESTORE THE PALACE!
NOT... BY YOU ALONE... CAN THE THING... BE DONE...!
YOU NEED...
YES...! CONTINUE!
YOU NEED ALL--!
FATHER...! RAYEK...! COME!
AAH! VENKA...! STRONG-BOW...!
NOOOOO!!
THE PALACE... ITS SECRET WAS MINE!
DEATH TO YOU, ARCHER-- AND YOU, GO-BACK WHELP! AAAHHH!!

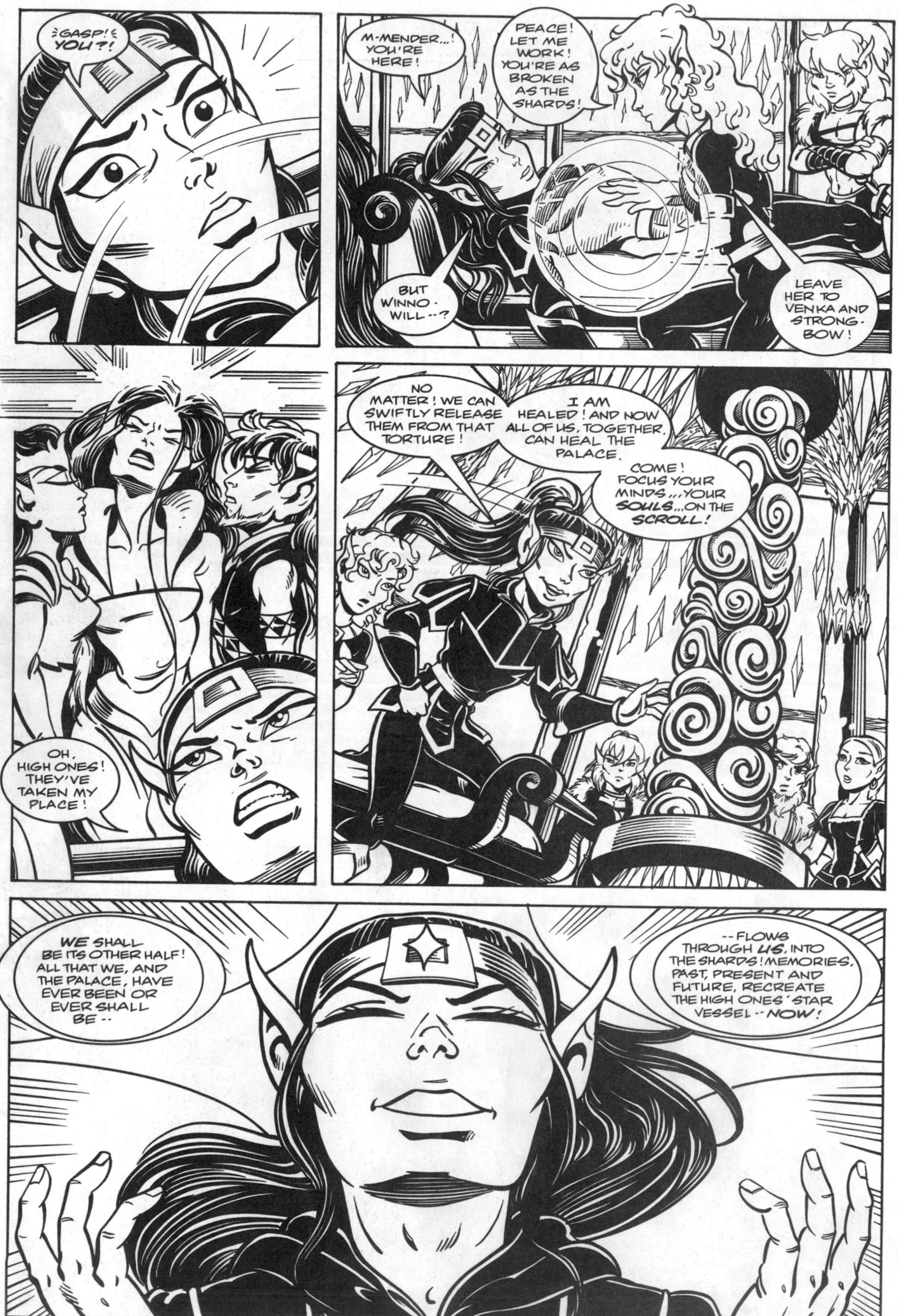
GASP! YOU?!
M-MENDER...! YOU'RE HERE!
PEACE! LET ME WORK! YOU'RE AS BROKEN AS THE SHARDS!
BUT WINNO-WILL--?
LEAVE HER TO VENKA AND STRONG-BOW!
OH, HIGH ONES! THEY'VE TAKEN MY PLACE!
NO MATTER! WE CAN SWIFTLY RELEASE THEM FROM THAT TORTURE!
I AM HEALED! AND NOW ALL OF US, TOGETHER, CAN HEAL THE PALACE.
COME! FOCUS YOUR MINDS... YOUR SOULS... ON THE SCROLL!
WE SHALL BE ITS OTHER HALF! ALL THAT WE, AND THE PALACE, HAVE EVER BEEN OR EVER SHALL BE--
--FLOWS THROUGH US, INTO THE SHARDS! MEMORIES, PAST, PRESENT AND FUTURE, RECREATE THE HIGH ONES' STAR VESSEL--NOW!

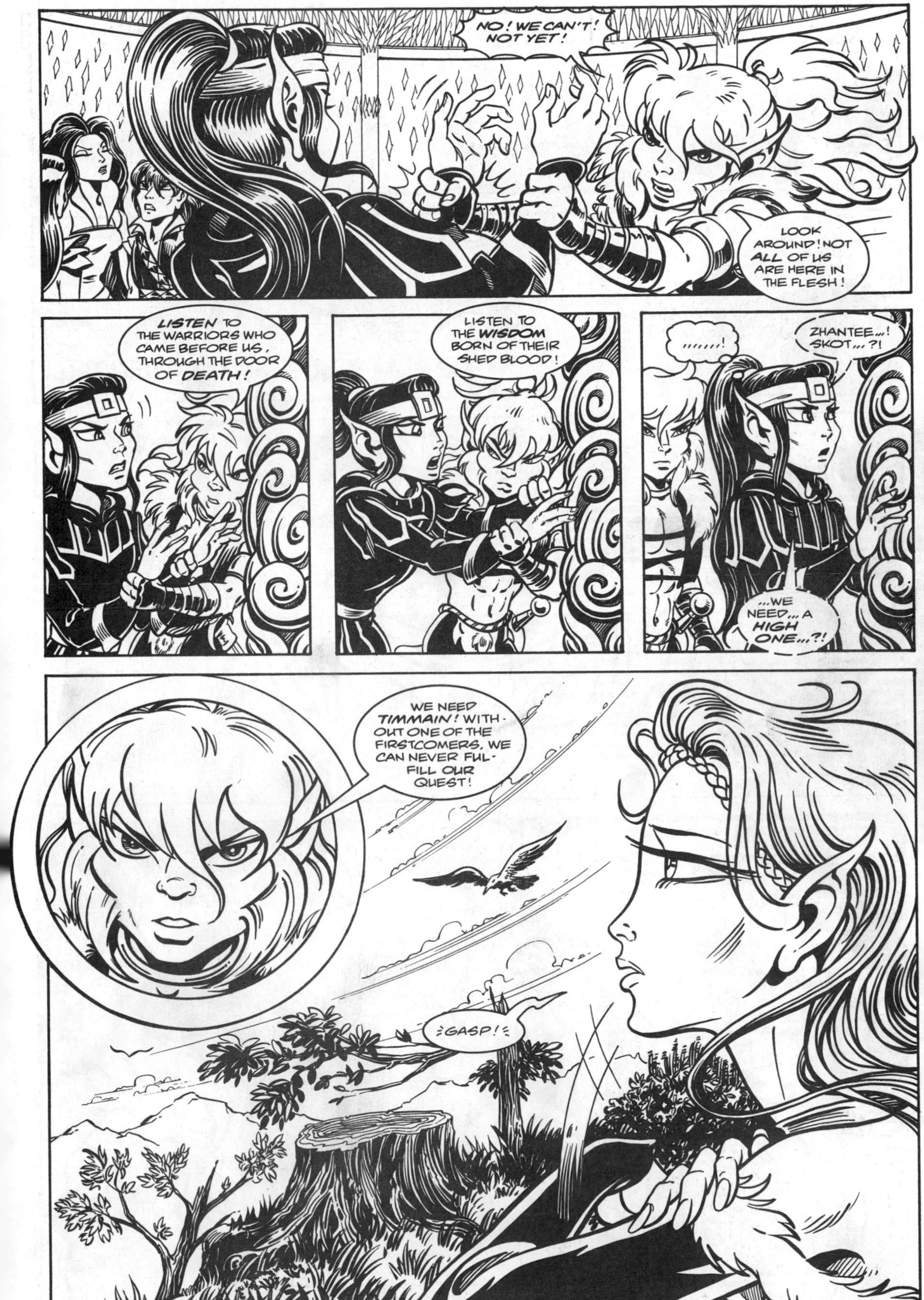
NO! WE CAN'T! NOT YET!
LOOK AROUND! NOT ALL OF US ARE HERE IN THE FLESH!
LISTEN TO THE WARRIORS WHO CAME BEFORE US, THROUGH THE DOOR OF DEATH!
LISTEN TO THE WISDOM BORN OF THEIR SHED BLOOD!
......!
ZHANTEE...! SKOT...?!
...WE NEED... A HIGH ONE...?!
WE NEED TIMMAIN! WITHOUT ONE OF THE FIRSTCOMERS, WE CAN NEVER FULFILL OUR QUEST!
GASP!

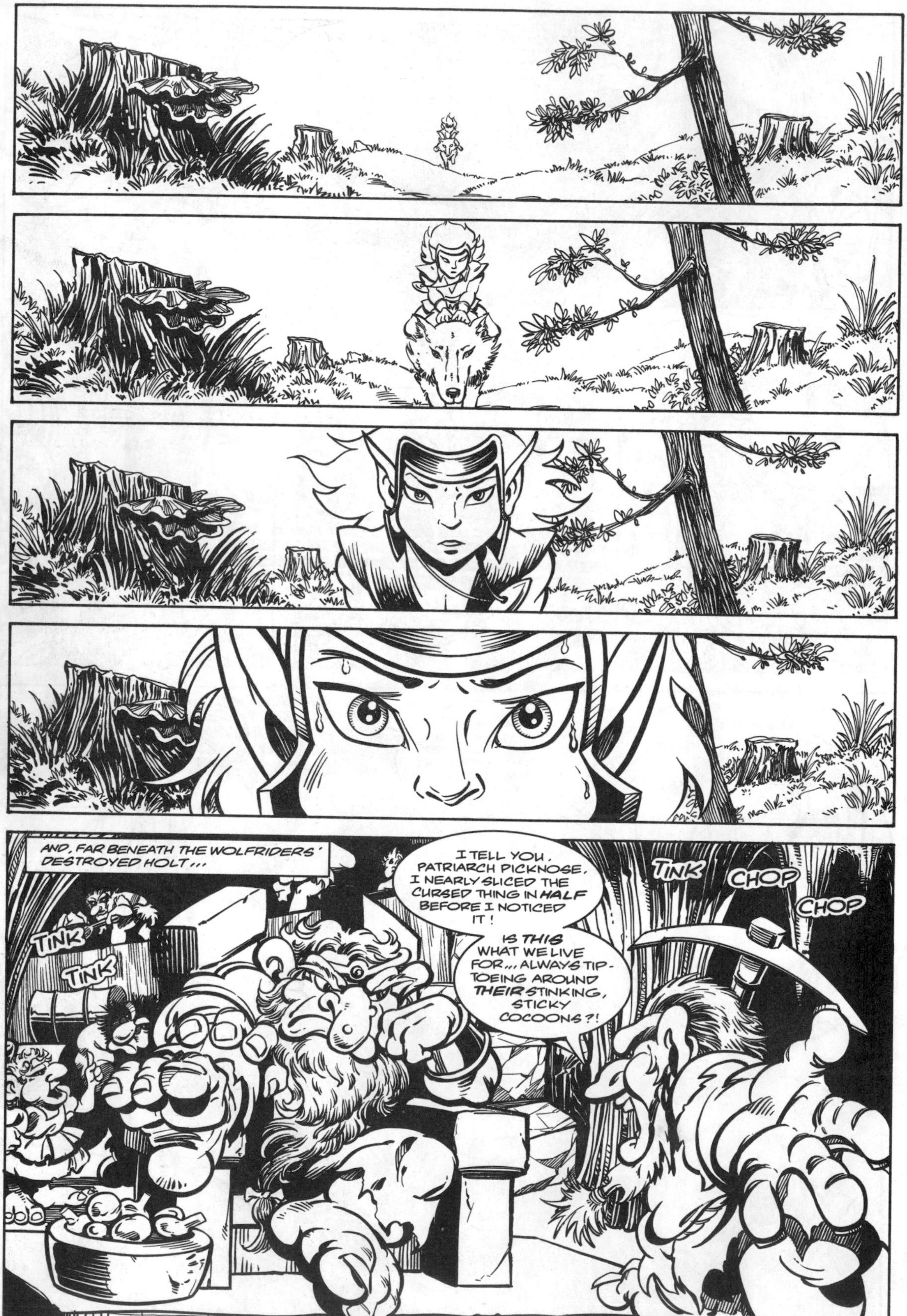
AND, FAR BENEATH THE WOLFRIDERS' DESTROYED HOLT...
I TELL YOU, PATRIARCH PICKNOSE, I NEARLY SLICED THE CURSED THING IN HALF BEFORE I NOTICED IT!
IS THIS WHAT WE LIVE FOR... ALWAYS TIP-TOEING AROUND THEIR STINKING, STICKY COCOONS?!
TINK
CHOP
CHOP
TINK
TINK

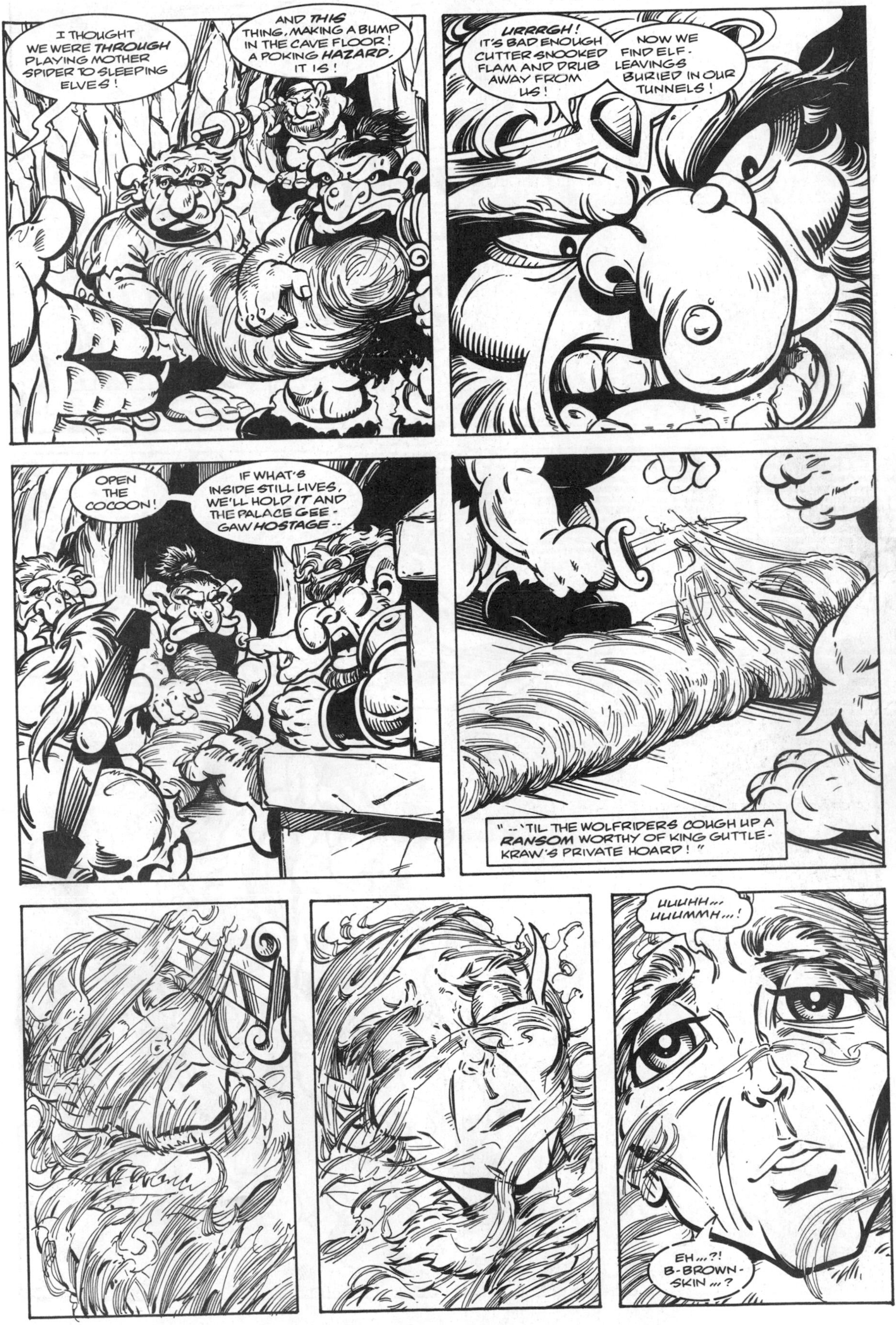
I THOUGHT WE WERE THROUGH PLAYING MOTHER SPIDER TO SLEEPING ELVES!
AND THIS THING, MAKING A BUMP IN THE CAVE FLOOR! A POKING HAZARD, IT IS!
URRRGH! IT'S BAD ENOUGH CUTTER SNOOKED FLAM AND DRUB AWAY FROM US!
NOW WE FIND ELF-LEAVINGS BURIED IN OUR TUNNELS!
OPEN THE COCOON!
IF WHAT'S INSIDE STILL LIVES, WE'LL HOLD IT AND THE PALACE GEE-GAW HOSTAGE--
"--'TIL THE WOLFRIDERS COUGH UP A RANSOM WORTHY OF KING GUTTLE-KRAW'S PRIVATE HOARD!"
UUUHH...UUUMMH...!
EH...?! B-BROWN-SKIN...?

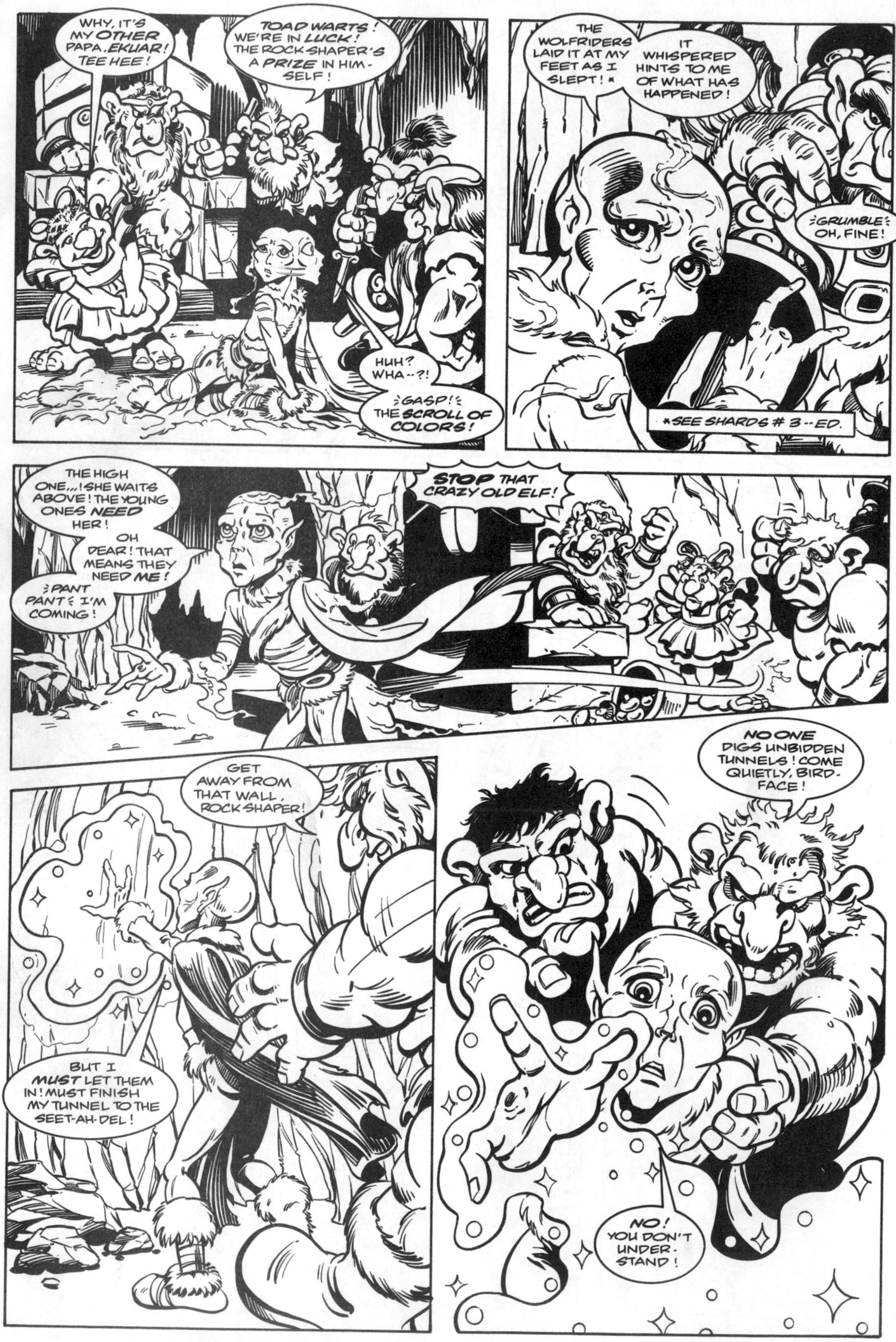
WHY, IT'S MY OTHER PAPA, EKUAR! TEE HEE!
TOAD WARTS! WE'RE IN LUCK! THE ROCK SHAPER'S A PRIZE IN HIMSELF!
HUH? WHA--?!
GASP! THE SCROLL OF COLORS!
THE WOLFRIDERS LAID IT AT MY FEET AS I SLEPT! *
IT WHISPERED HINTS TO ME OF WHAT HAS HAPPENED!
GRUMBLE! OH, FINE!
* SEE SHARDS # 3 -- ED.
THE HIGH ONE...! SHE WAITS ABOVE! THE YOUNG ONES NEED HER!
OH DEAR! THAT MEANS THEY NEED ME!
PANT PANT! I'M COMING!
STOP THAT CRAZY OLD ELF!
GET AWAY FROM THAT WALL, ROCK SHAPER!
BUT I MUST LET THEM IN! MUST FINISH MY TUNNEL TO THE SEET-AH-DEL!
NO ONE DIGS UNBIDDEN TUNNELS! COME QUIETLY, BIRD-FACE!
NO! YOU DON'T UNDERSTAND!

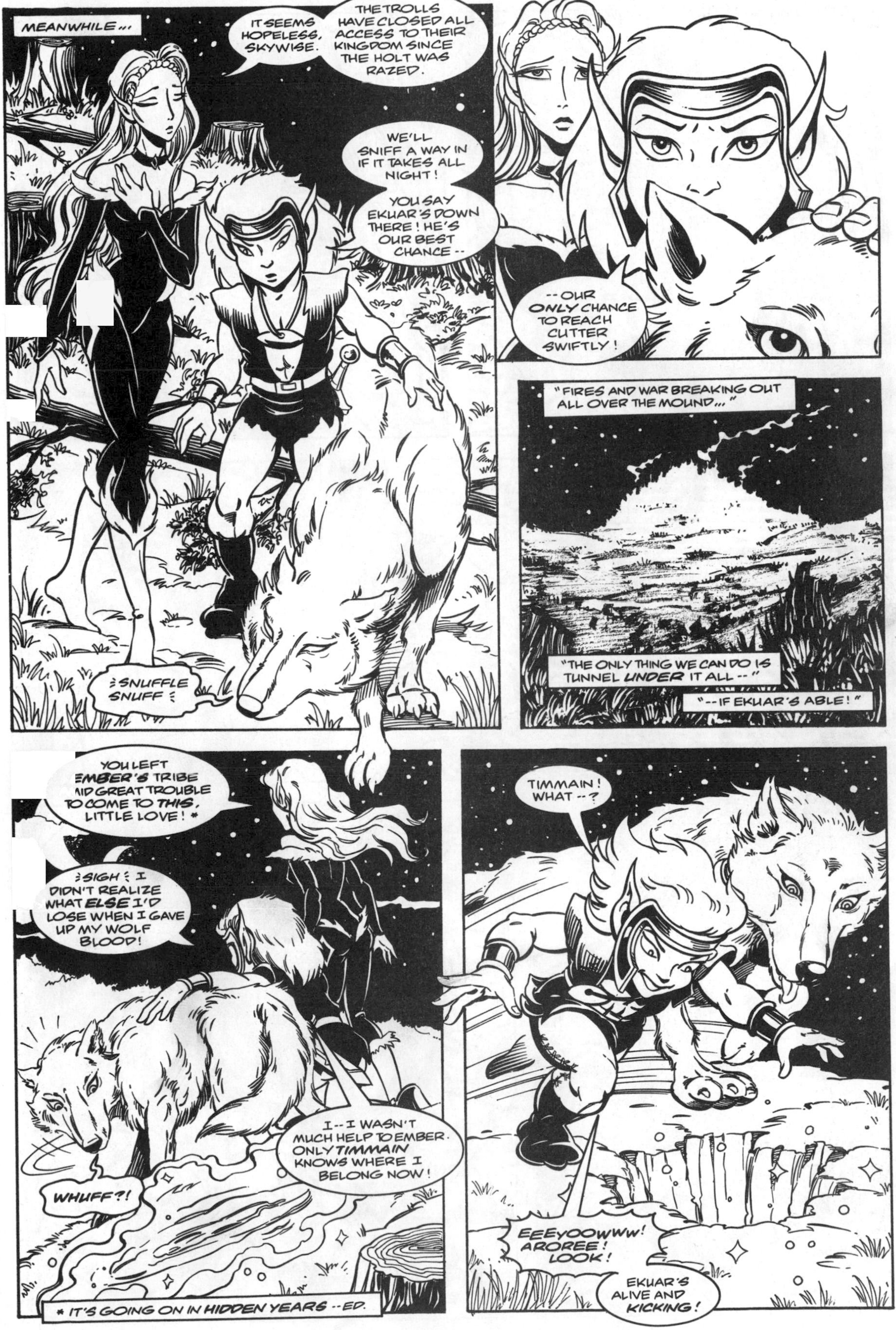

MEANWHILE...
IT SEEMS HOPELESS, SKYWISE.
THE TROLLS HAVE CLOSED ALL ACCESS TO THEIR KINGDOM SINCE THE HOLT WAS RAZED.
WE'LL SNIFF A WAY IN IF IT TAKES ALL NIGHT!
YOU SAY EKUAR'S DOWN THERE! HE'S OUR BEST CHANCE --
SNUFFLE SNUFF
--OUR ONLY CHANCE TO REACH CUTTER SWIFTLY!
"FIRES AND WAR BREAKING OUT ALL OVER THE MOUND..."
"THE ONLY THING WE CAN DO IS TUNNEL UNDER IT ALL --"
"--IF EKUAR'S ABLE!"
YOU LEFT EMBER'S TRIBE MID GREAT TROUBLE TO COME TO THIS, LITTLE LOVE! *
SIGH I DIDN'T REALIZE WHAT ELSE I'D LOSE WHEN I GAVE UP MY WOLF BLOOD!
I--I WASN'T MUCH HELP TO EMBER. ONLY TIMMAIN KNOWS WHERE I BELONG NOW!
WHUFF?!
* IT'S GOING ON IN HIDDEN YEARS --ED.
TIMMAIN! WHAT --?
EEEYOOWWW! AROREE! LOOK!
EKUAR'S ALIVE AND KICKING!

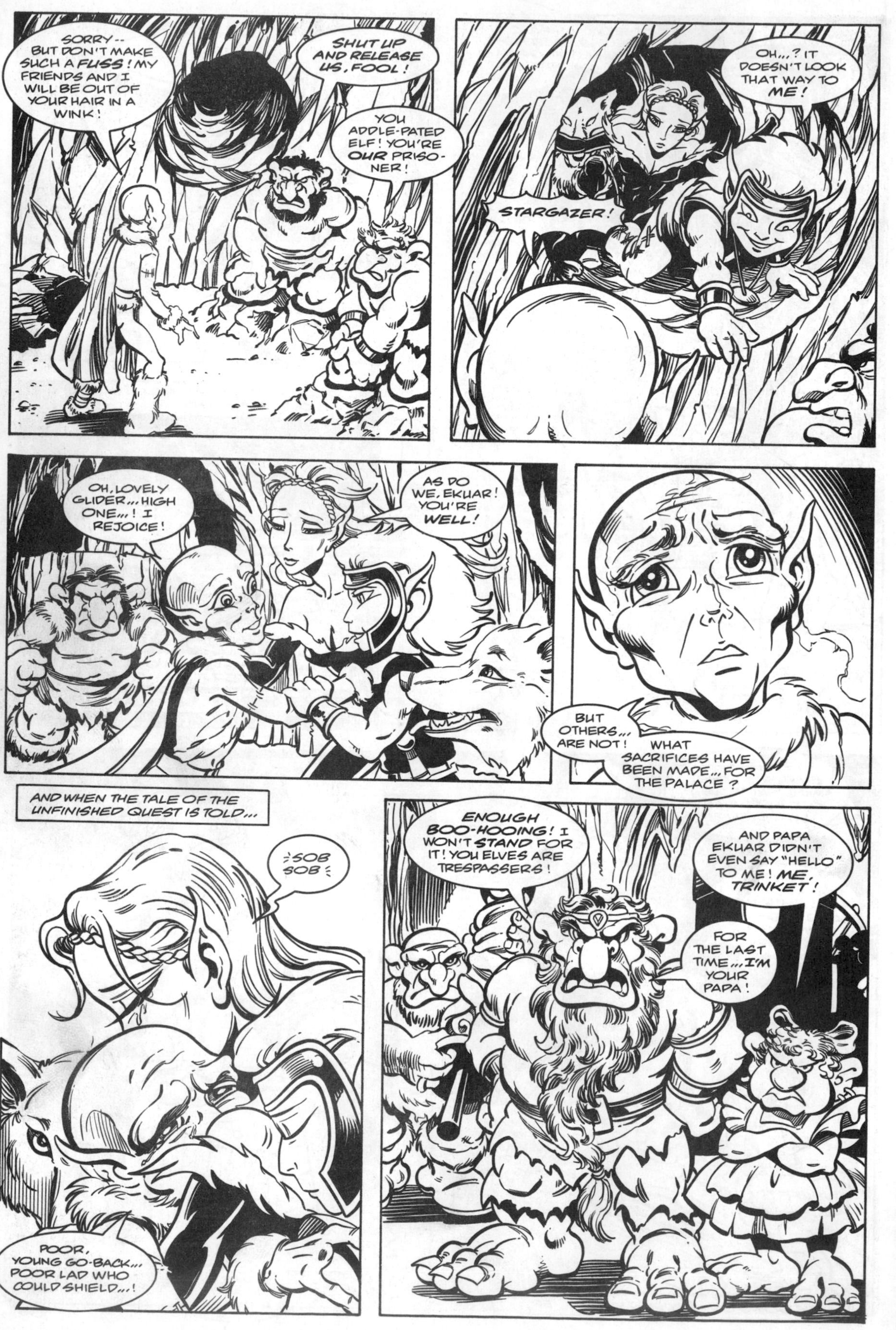
SORRY -- BUT DON'T MAKE SUCH A FUSS! MY FRIENDS AND I WILL BE OUT OF YOUR HAIR IN A WINK!
SHUT UP AND RELEASE US, FOOL!
YOU ADDLE-PATED ELF! YOU'RE OUR PRISONER!
OH...? IT DOESN'T LOOK THAT WAY TO ME!
STARGAZER!
OH, LOVELY GLIDER... HIGH ONE...! I REJOICE!
AS DO WE, EKUAR! YOU'RE WELL!
BUT OTHERS... ARE NOT!
WHAT SACRIFICES HAVE BEEN MADE... FOR THE PALACE?
AND WHEN THE TALE OF THE UNFINISHED QUEST IS TOLD...
SOB SOB
POOR, YOUNG GO-BACK... POOR LAD WHO COULD SHIELD...!
ENOUGH BOO-HOOING! I WON'T STAND FOR IT! YOU ELVES ARE TRESPASSERS!
AND PAPA EKUAR DIDN'T EVEN SAY "HELLO" TO ME! ME, TRINKET!
FOR THE LAST TIME... I'M YOUR PAPA!

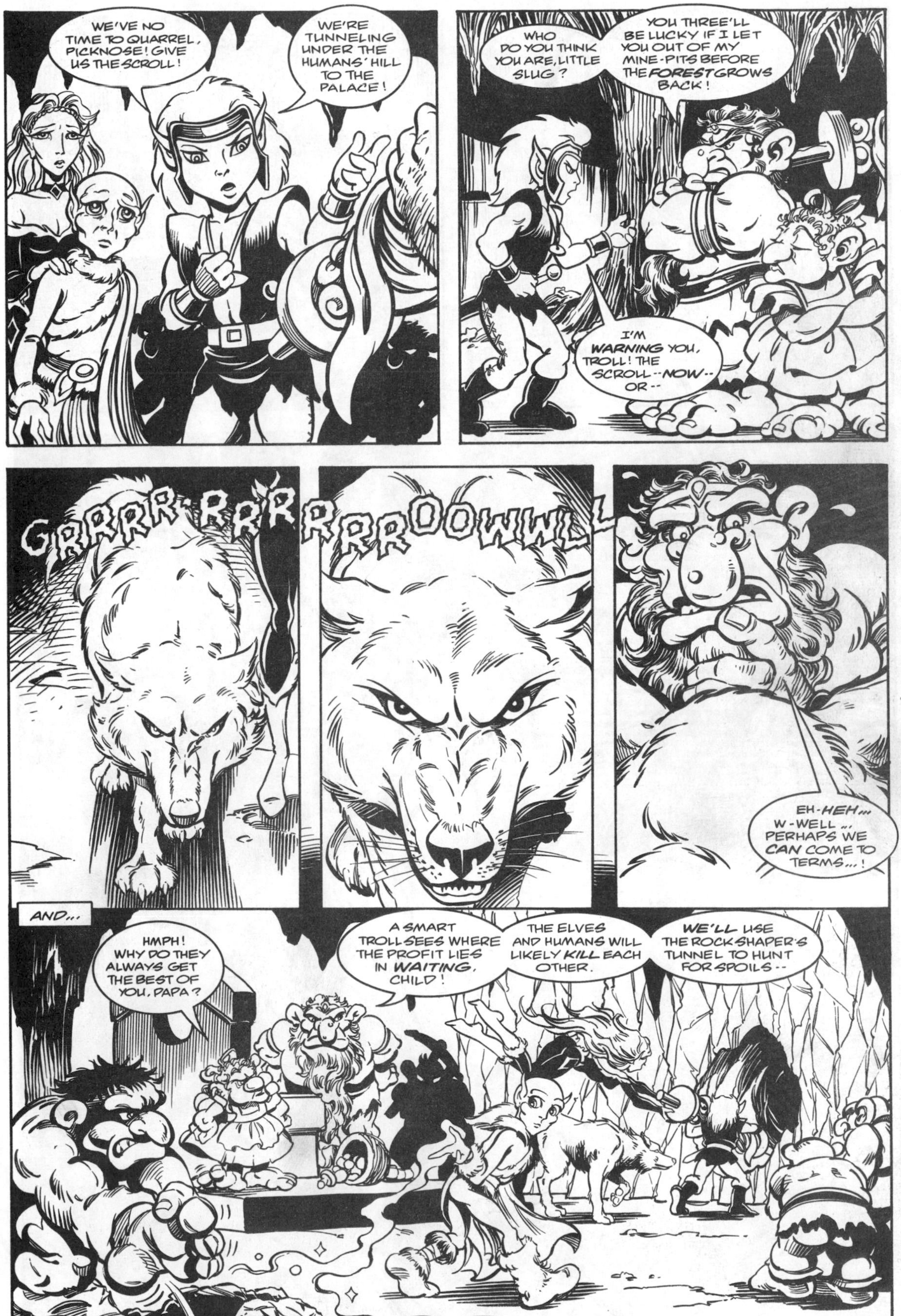

WE'VE NO TIME TO QUARREL, PICKNOSE! GIVE US THE SCROLL!
WE'RE TUNNELING UNDER THE HUMANS' HILL TO THE PALACE!
WHO DO YOU THINK YOU ARE, LITTLE SLUG?
YOU THREE'LL BE LUCKY IF I LET YOU OUT OF MY MINE-PITS BEFORE THE FOREST GROWS BACK!
I'M WARNING YOU, TROLL! THE SCROLL--NOW--OR--
GRRRR-RRRRRRROOWWLL
EH-HEH... W-WELL... PERHAPS WE CAN COME TO TERMS...!
AND...
HMPH! WHY DO THEY ALWAYS GET THE BEST OF YOU, PAPA?
A SMART TROLL SEES WHERE THE PROFIT LIES IN WAITING, CHILD!
THE ELVES AND HUMANS WILL LIKELY KILL EACH OTHER.
WE'LL USE THE ROCKSHAPER'S TUNNEL TO HUNT FOR SPOILS--

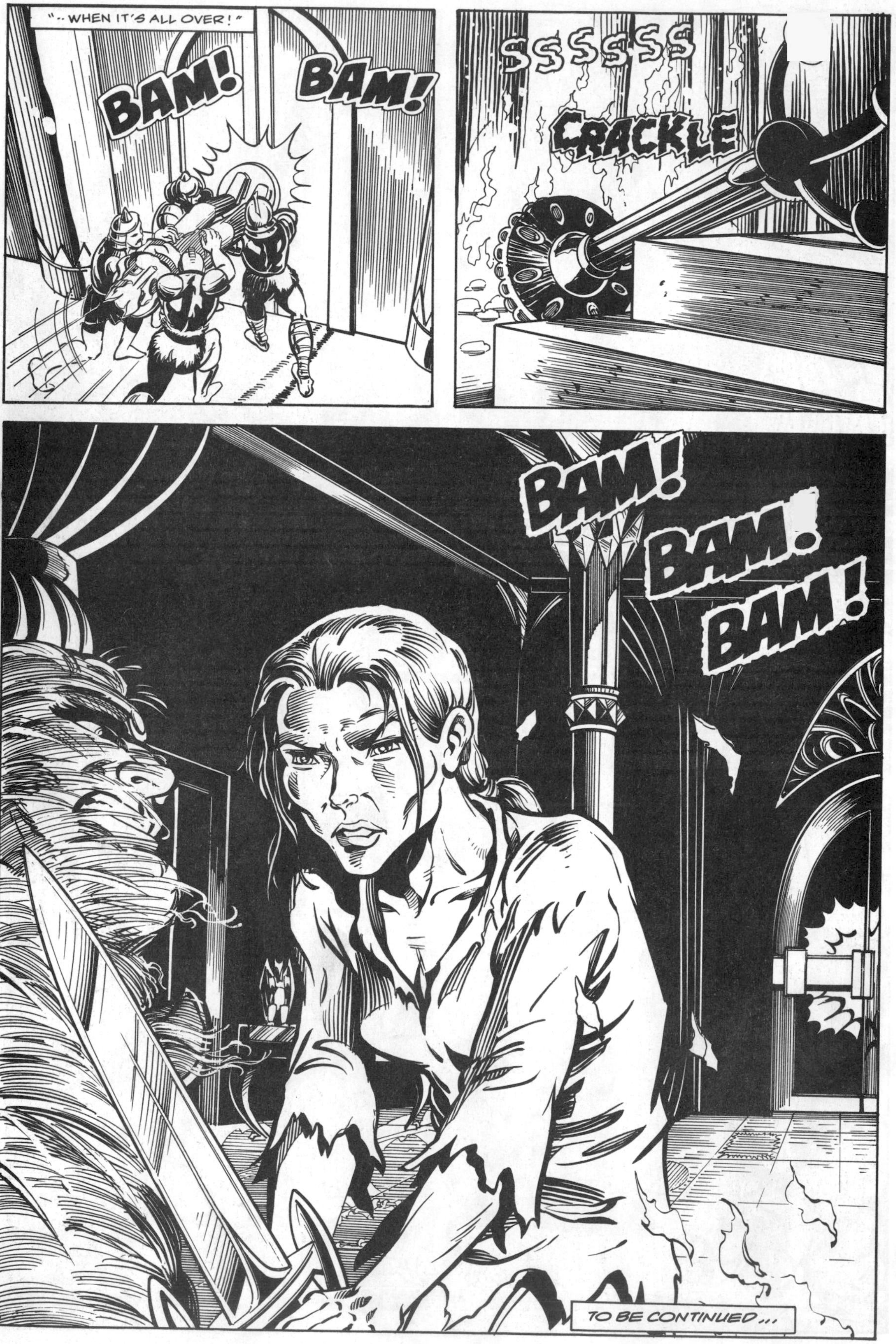
"..WHEN IT'S ALL OVER!"
BAM!
BAM!
SSSSSS
CRACKLE
BAM!
BAM!
BAM!
TO BE CONTINUED...

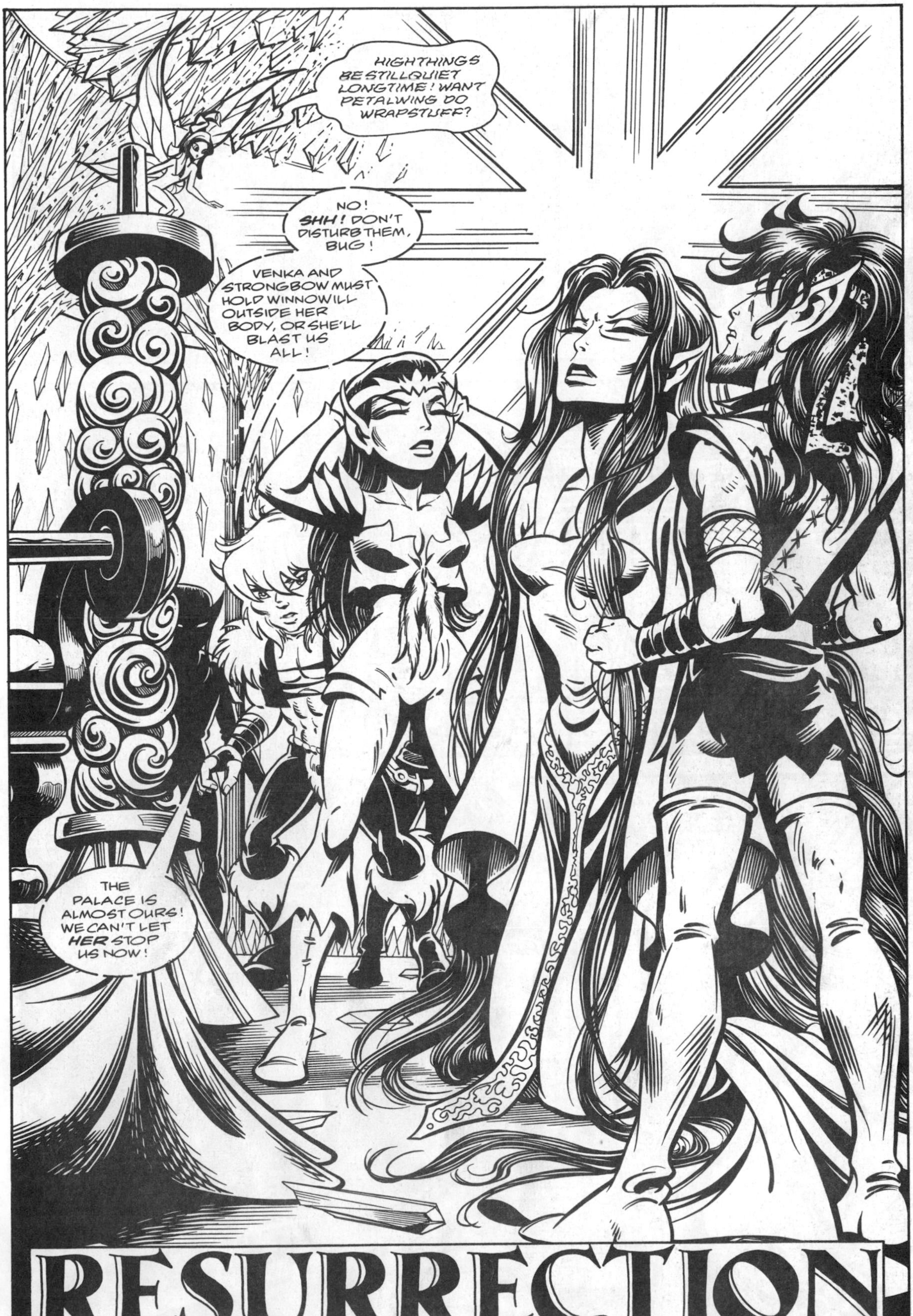
HIGHTHINGS BE STILLQUIET LONGTIME! WANT PETALWING DO WRAPSTUFF?
NO! SHH! DON'T DISTURB THEM, BUG!
VENKA AND STRONGBOW MUST HOLD WINNOWILL OUTSIDE HER BODY, OR SHE'LL BLAST US ALL!
THE PALACE IS ALMOST OURS! WE CAN'T LET HER STOP US NOW!
RESURRECTION

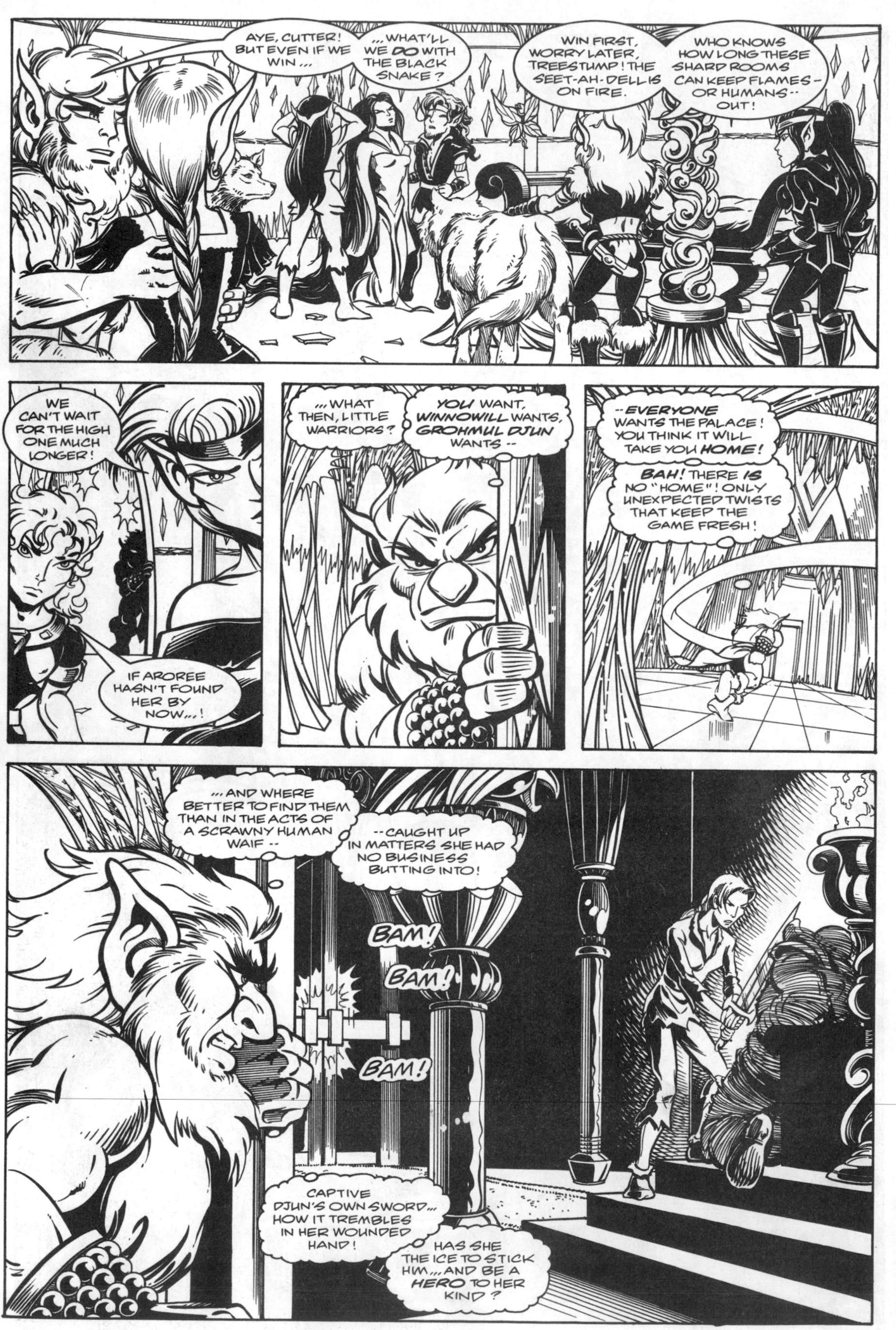
AYE, CUTTER! BUT EVEN IF WE WIN...
...WHAT'LL WE DO WITH THE BLACK SNAKE?
WIN FIRST, WORRY LATER, TREESTUMP! THE SEET-AH-DELL IS ON FIRE.
WHO KNOWS HOW LONG THESE SHARD ROOMS CAN KEEP FLAMES -- OR HUMANS -- OUT!
WE CAN'T WAIT FOR THE HIGH ONE MUCH LONGER!
IF AROREE HASN'T FOUND HER BY NOW...!
...WHAT THEN, LITTLE WARRIORS?
YOU WANT, WINNOWILL WANTS, GROHMUL DJUN WANTS --
--EVERYONE WANTS THE PALACE! YOU THINK IT WILL TAKE YOU HOME!
BAH! THERE IS NO "HOME"! ONLY UNEXPECTED TWISTS THAT KEEP THE GAME FRESH!
...AND WHERE BETTER TO FIND THEM THAN IN THE ACTS OF A SCRAWNY HUMAN WAIF --
--CAUGHT UP IN MATTERS SHE HAD NO BUSINESS BUTTING INTO!
BAM!
BAM!
BAM!
CAPTIVE DJUN'S OWN SWORD... HOW IT TREMBLES IN HER WOUNDED HAND!
HAS SHE THE ICE TO STICK HIM... AND BE A HERO TO HER KIND?

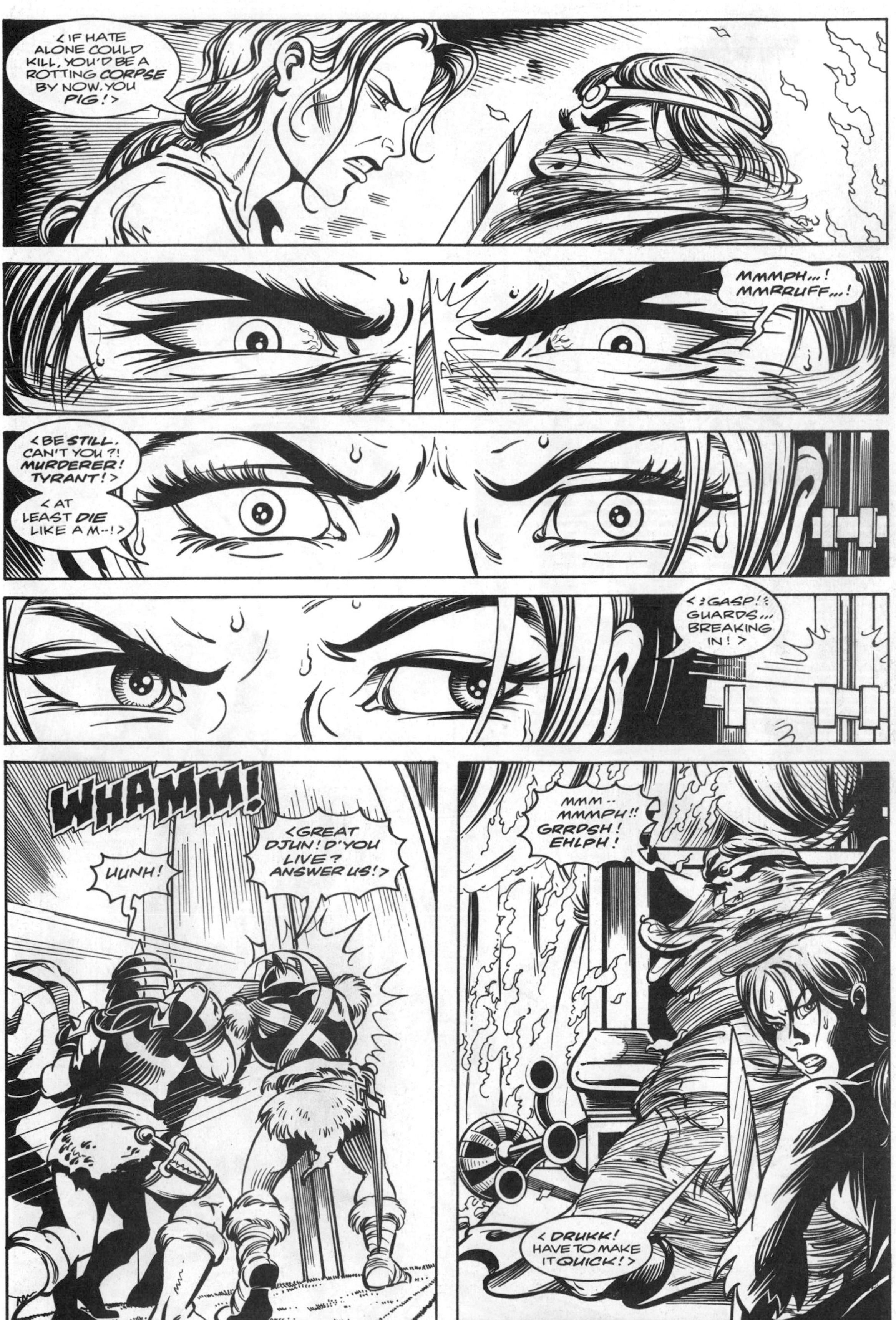

< IF HATE ALONE COULD KILL, YOU'D BE A ROTTING CORPSE BY NOW, YOU PIG! >
MMMPH...! MMRRUFF...!
< BE STILL, CAN'T YOU ?! MURDERER! TYRANT! >
< AT LEAST DIE LIKE A M--! >
< GASP! GUARDS... BREAKING IN! >
WHAMM!
UUNH!
< GREAT DJUN! D'YOU LIVE? ANSWER US! >
MMM.. MMMPH!! GRRDSH! EHLPH!
< DRUKK! HAVE TO MAKE IT QUICK! >

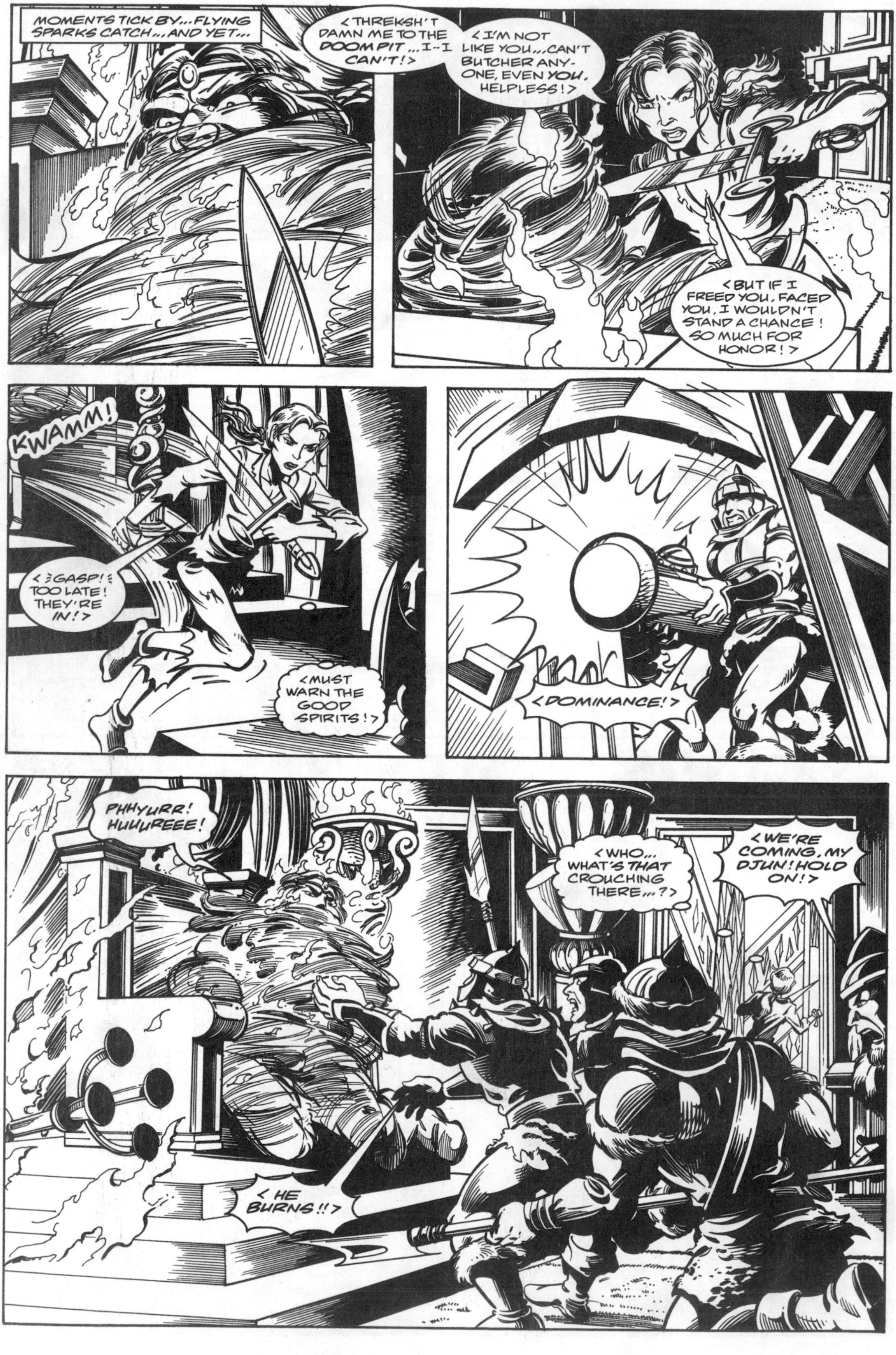
MOMENTS TICK BY... FLYING SPARKS CATCH... AND YET...
< THREKSH'T DAMN ME TO THE DOOM PIT ... I-- I CAN'T! >
< I'M NOT LIKE YOU... CAN'T BUTCHER ANY-ONE, EVEN YOU. HELPLESS! >
< BUT IF I FREED YOU, FACED YOU, I WOULDN'T STAND A CHANCE! SO MUCH FOR HONOR! >
KWAMM!
< GASP! TOO LATE! THEY'RE IN! >
< MUST WARN THE GOOD SPIRITS! >
< DOMINANCE! >
PHHYURR! HUUUREEE!
< WHO... WHAT'S THAT CROUCHING THERE...? >
< WE'RE COMING, MY DJUN! HOLD ON! >
< HE BURNS!! >

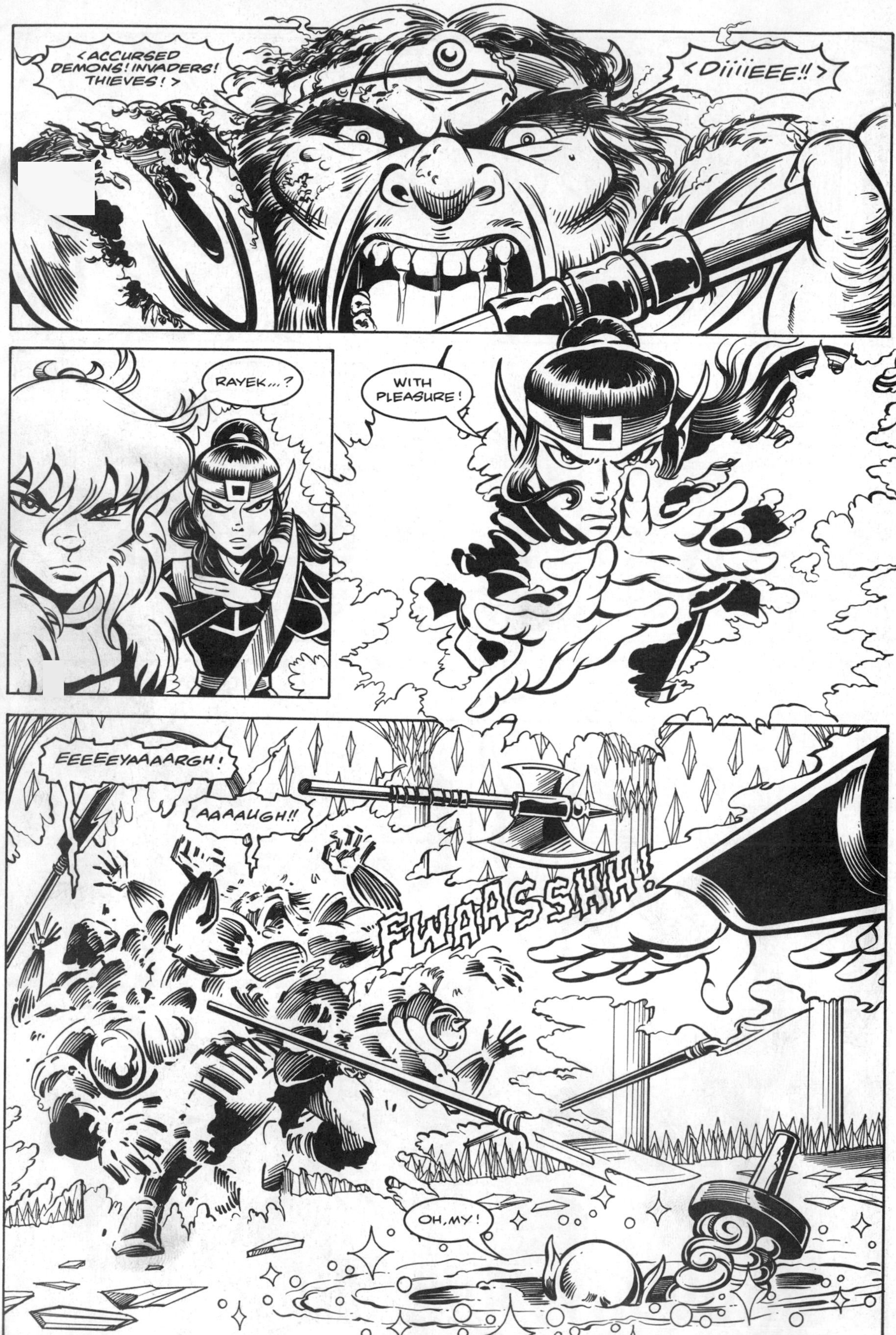
<ACCURSED DEMONS! INVADERS! THIEVES!>
<DIIIIEEE!!>
RAYEK...?
WITH PLEASURE!
EEEEEYAAAARGH!
AAAAUGH!!
FWAASSHH!
OH, MY!

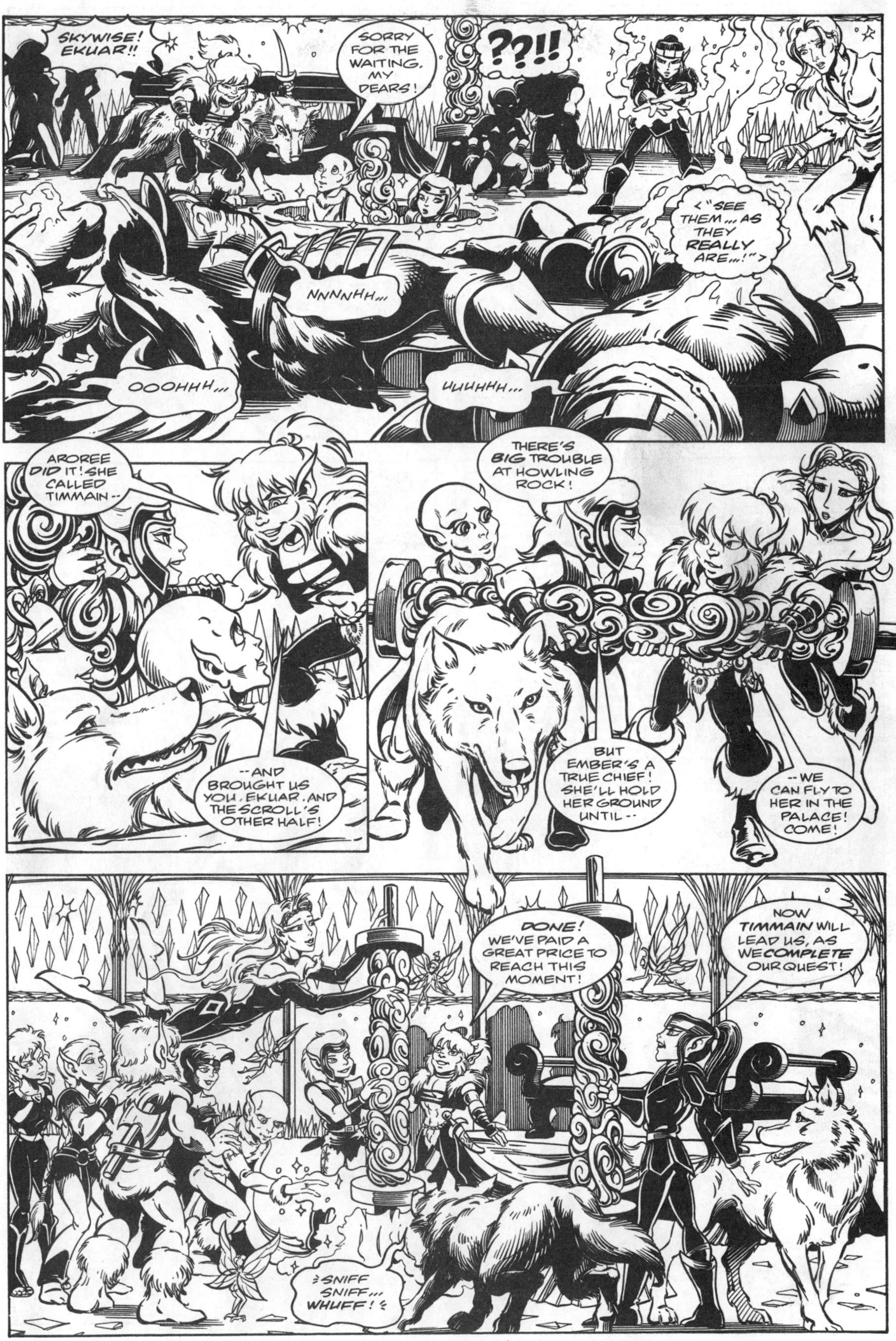
SKYWISE! EKUAR!!
SORRY FOR THE WAITING, MY DEARS!
??!!
<"SEE THEM... AS THEY REALLY ARE...!">
NNNNHH...
OOOHHH...
UUUHHH...
AROREE DID IT! SHE CALLED TIMMAIN--
--AND BROUGHT US YOU, EKUAR, AND THE SCROLL'S OTHER HALF!
THERE'S BIG TROUBLE AT HOWLING ROCK!
BUT EMBER'S A TRUE CHIEF! SHE'LL HOLD HER GROUND UNTIL--
--WE CAN FLY TO HER IN THE PALACE! COME!
DONE! WE'VE PAID A GREAT PRICE TO REACH THIS MOMENT!
NOW TIMMAIN WILL LEAD US, AS WE COMPLETE OUR QUEST!
SNIFF SNIFF... WHUFF!

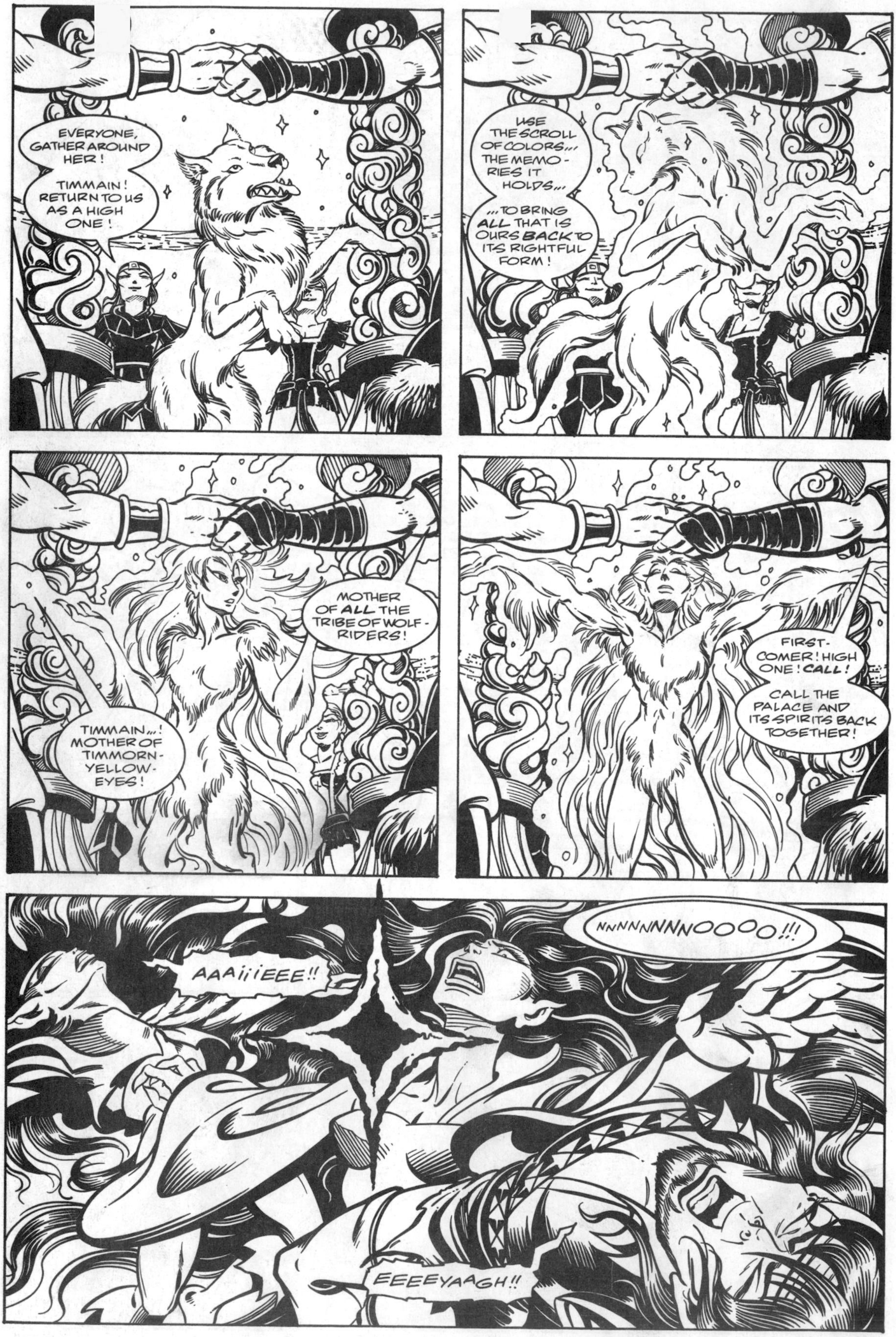
EVERYONE, GATHER AROUND HER!
TIMMAIN! RETURN TO US AS A HIGH ONE!
USE THE SCROLL OF COLORS... THE MEMORIES IT HOLDS...
...TO BRING ALL THAT IS OURS BACK TO ITS RIGHTFUL FORM!
MOTHER OF ALL THE TRIBE OF WOLF-RIDERS!
TIMMAIN...! MOTHER OF TIMMORN-YELLOW-EYES!
FIRST-COMER! HIGH ONE! CALL!
CALL THE PALACE AND ITS SPIRITS BACK TOGETHER!
NNNNNNNNOOOOO!!!
AAAiiiEEE!!
EEEEYAAGH!!

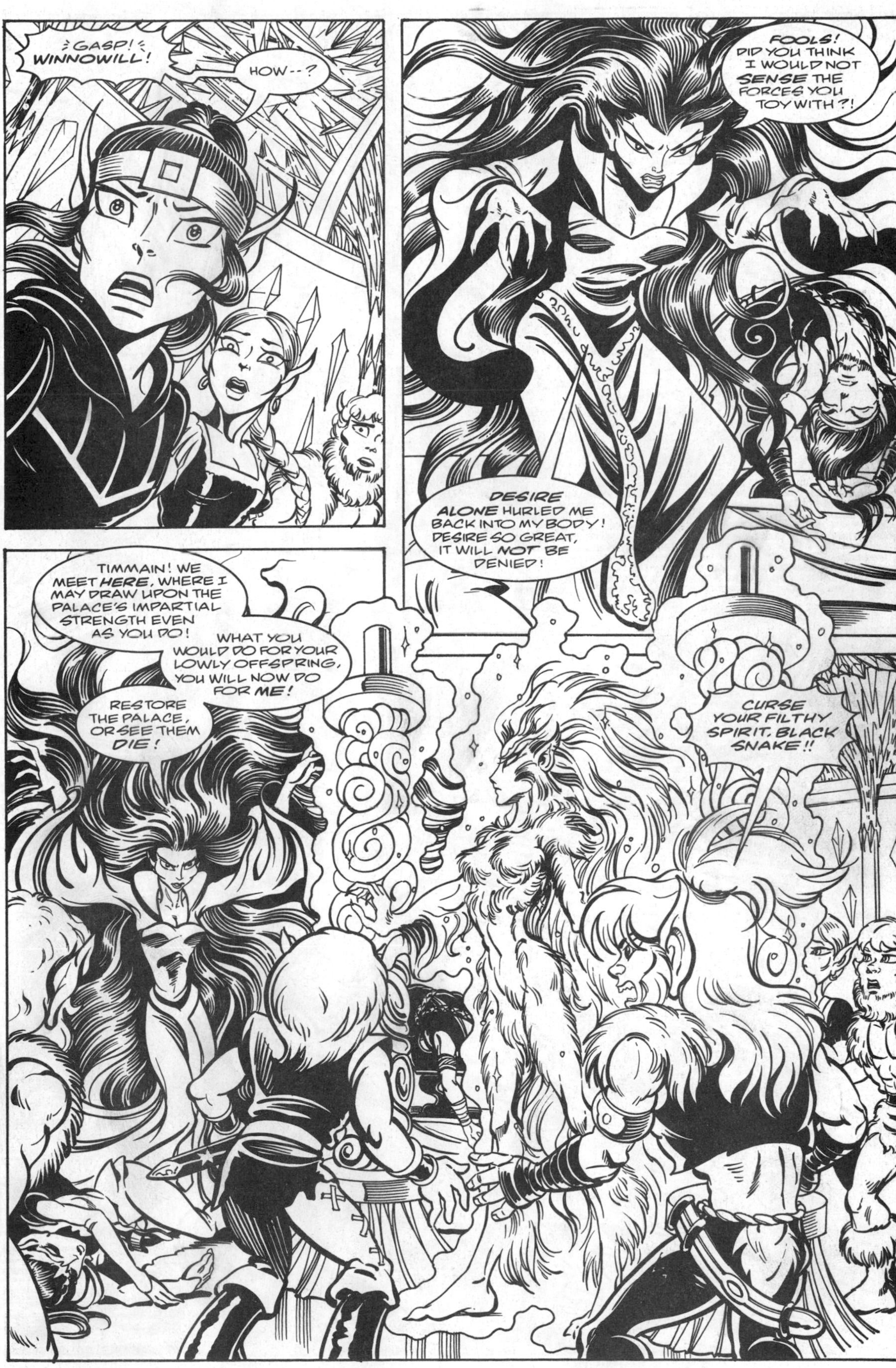

GASP! WINNOWILL!
HOW--?
FOOLS! DID YOU THINK I WOULD NOT SENSE THE FORCES YOU TOY WITH?!
DESIRE ALONE HURLED ME BACK INTO MY BODY! DESIRE SO GREAT, IT WILL NOT BE DENIED!
TIMMAIN! WE MEET HERE, WHERE I MAY DRAW UPON THE PALACE'S IMPARTIAL STRENGTH EVEN AS YOU DO!
WHAT YOU WOULD DO FOR YOUR LOWLY OFFSPRING, YOU WILL NOW DO FOR ME!
RESTORE THE PALACE, OR SEE THEM DIE!
CURSE YOUR FILTHY SPIRIT, BLACK SNAKE!!

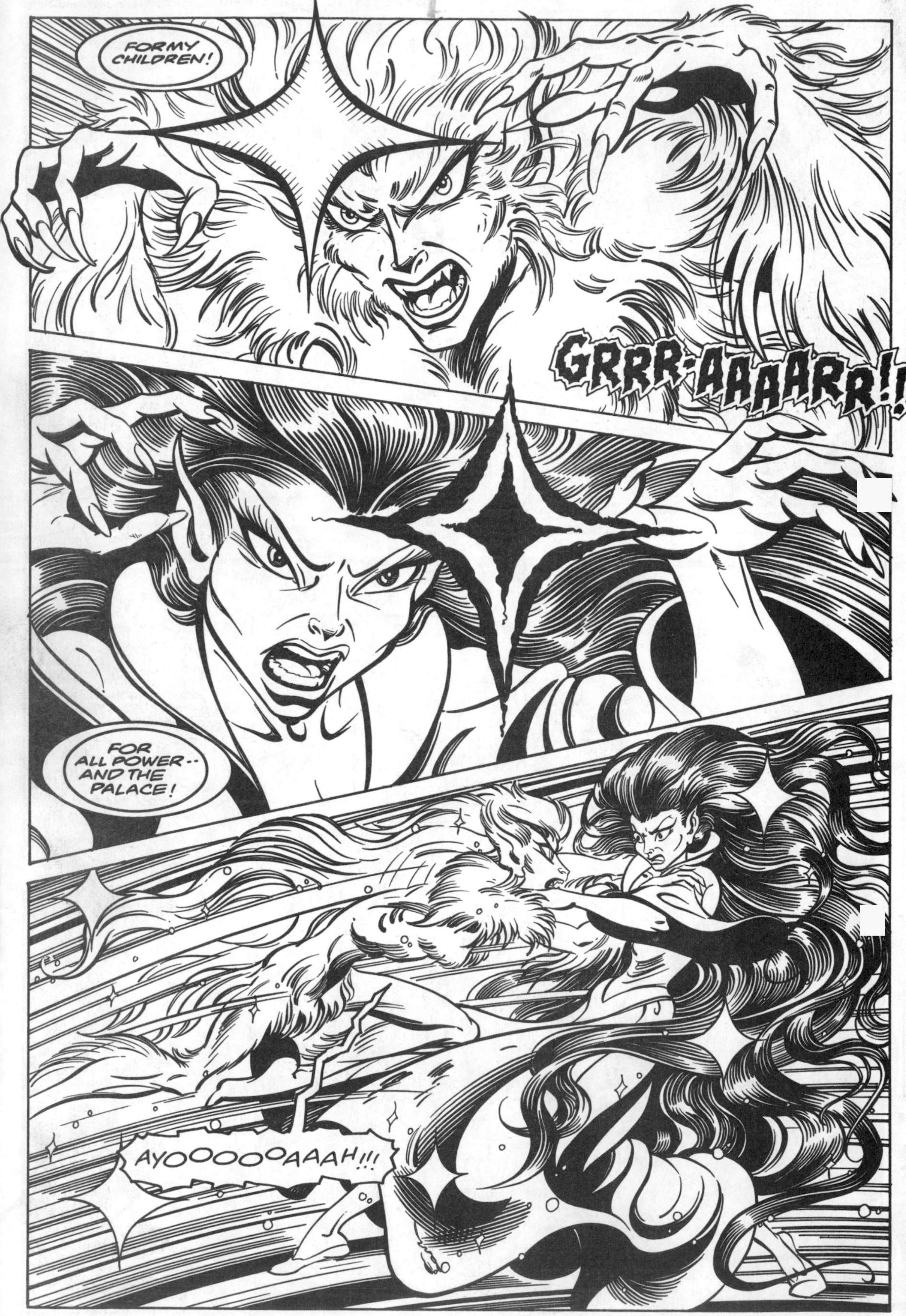
FOR MY CHILDREN!
GRRR-AAAAARR!!
FOR ALL POWER-- AND THE PALACE!
AYOOOOOAAAH!!!

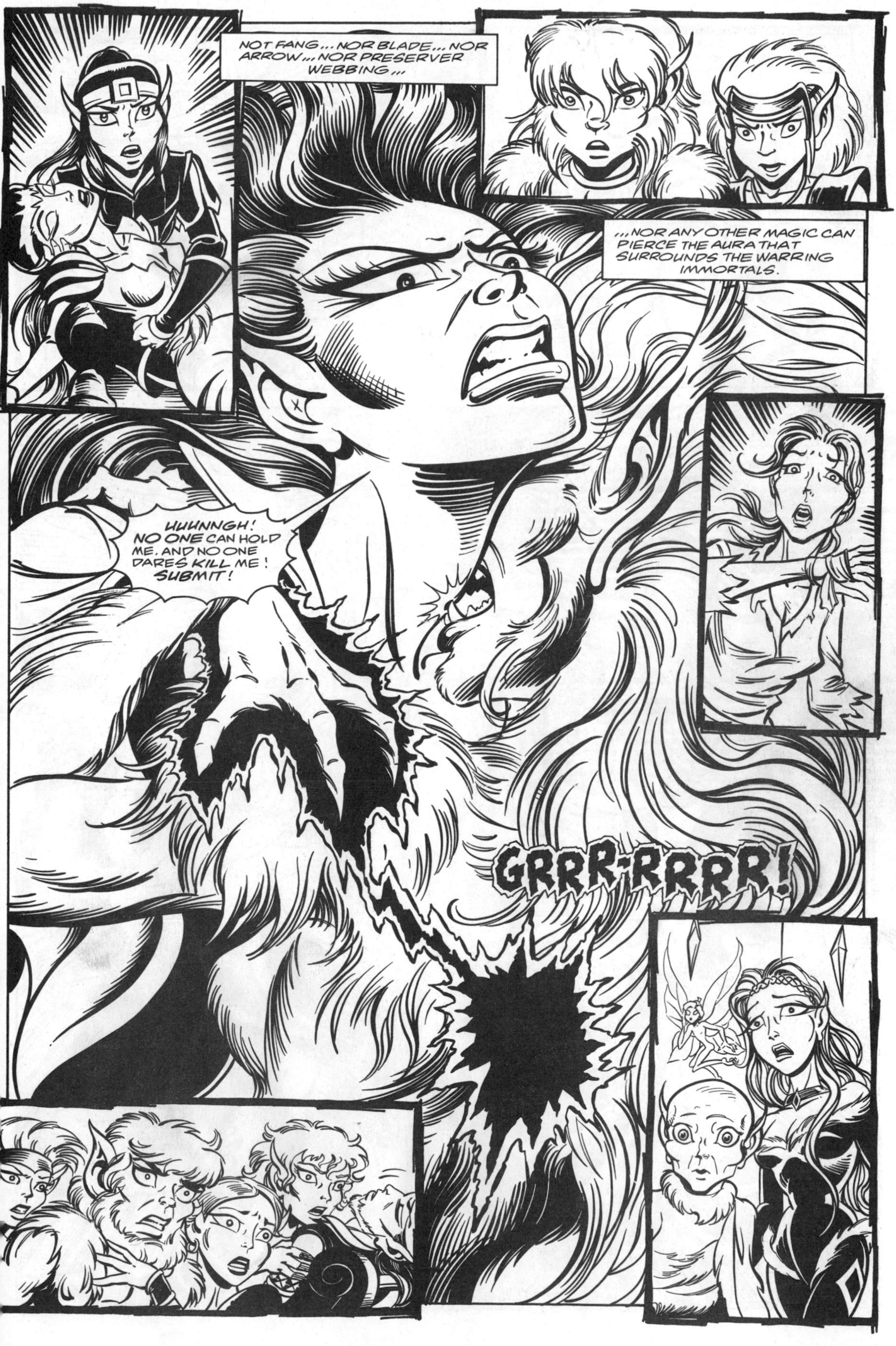
NOT FANG... NOR BLADE... NOR ARROW... NOR PRESERVER WEBBING...
...NOR ANY OTHER MAGIC CAN PIERCE THE AURA THAT SURROUNDS THE WARRING IMMORTALS.
UUUNNGH! NO ONE CAN HOLD ME. AND NO ONE DARES KILL ME! SUBMIT!
GRRR-RRRRR!

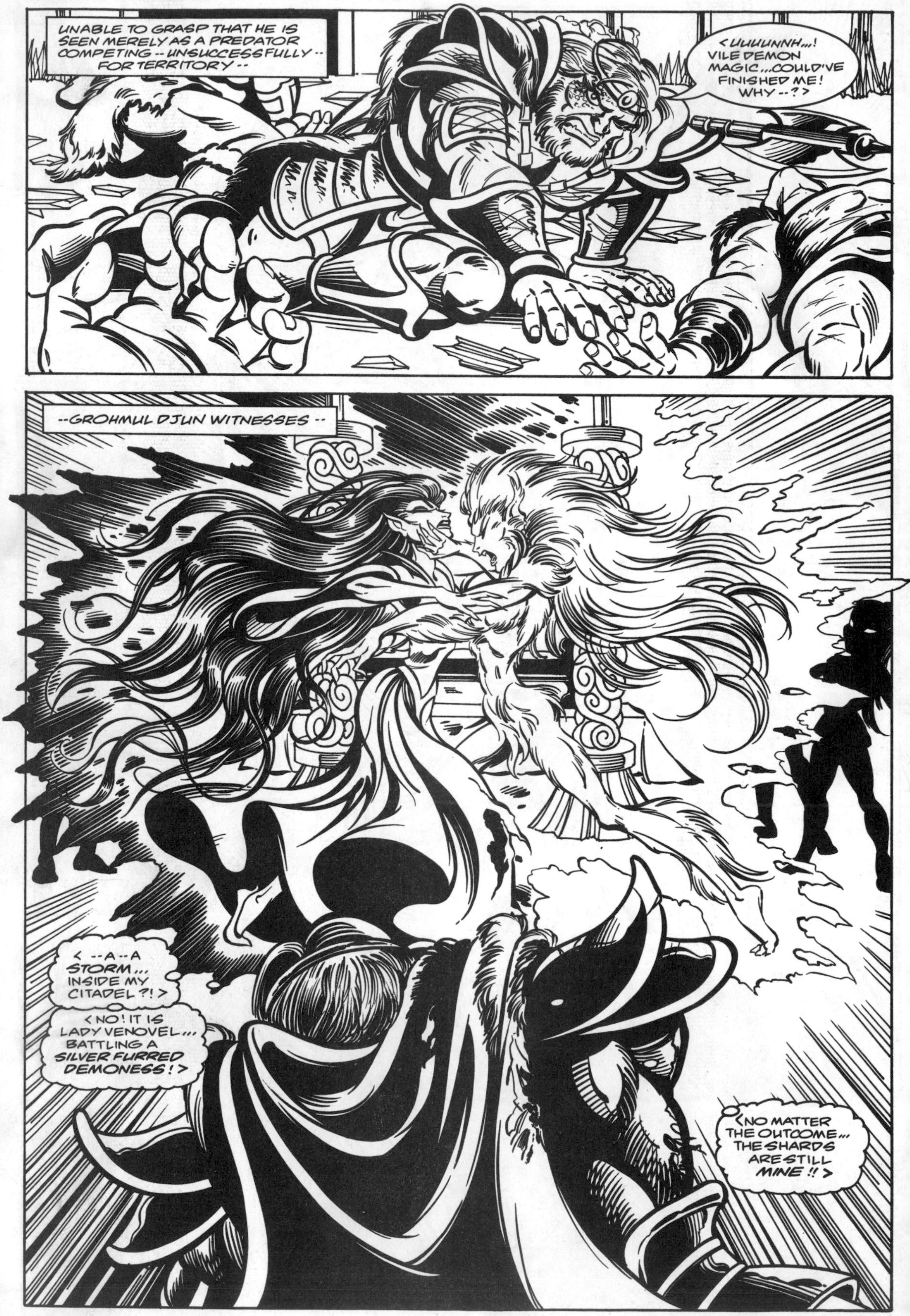
UNABLE TO GRASP THAT HE IS SEEN MERELY AS A PREDATOR COMPETING -- UNSUCCESSFULLY -- FOR TERRITORY --
<UUUUUNNH...! VILE DEMON MAGIC... COULD'VE FINISHED ME! WHY --?>
--GROHMUL DJUN WITNESSES --
< --A--A STORM... INSIDE MY CITADEL?!>
<NO! IT IS LADY VENOVEL... BATTLING A SILVER FURRED DEMONESS!>
<NO MATTER THE OUTCOME... THE SHARDS ARE STILL MINE!!>

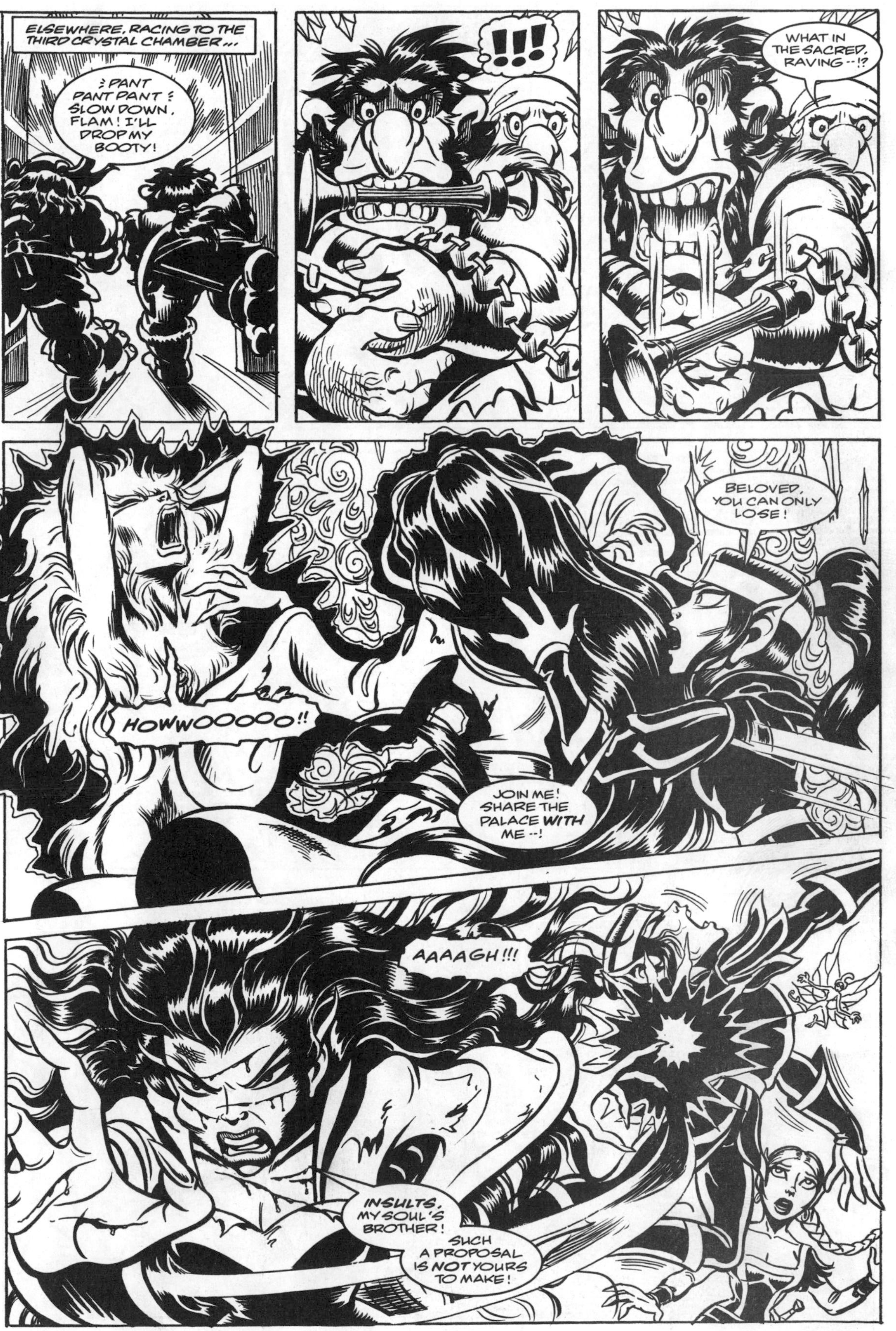
ELSEWHERE, RACING TO THE THIRD CRYSTAL CHAMBER...
PANT PANT PANT SLOW DOWN, FLAM! I'LL DROP MY BOOTY!
!!!
WHAT IN THE SACRED, RAVING --!?
BELOVED, YOU CAN ONLY LOSE!
HOWWOOOOO!!
JOIN ME! SHARE THE PALACE WITH ME--!
AAAAGH!!!
INSULTS, MY SOUL'S BROTHER!
SUCH A PROPOSAL IS NOT YOURS TO MAKE!

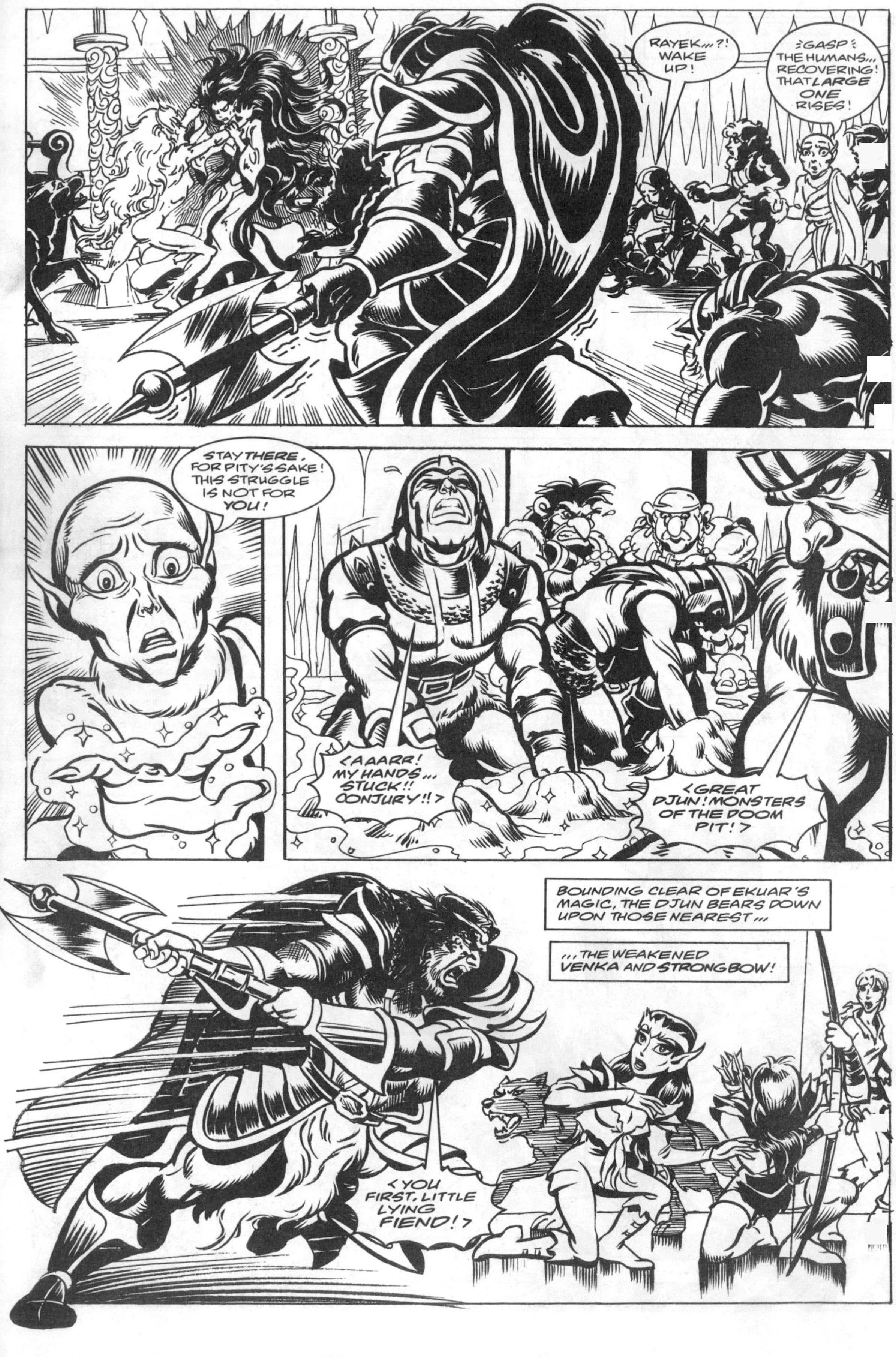
RAYEK...?! WAKE UP!
GASP THE HUMANS... RECOVERING! THAT LARGE ONE RISES!
STAY THERE, FOR PITY'S SAKE! THIS STRUGGLE IS NOT FOR YOU!
<AAARR! MY HANDS... STUCK!! CONJURY!!>
<GREAT DJUN! MONSTERS OF THE DOOM PIT!>
BOUNDING CLEAR OF EKUAR'S MAGIC, THE DJUN BEARS DOWN UPON THOSE NEAREST...
...THE WEAKENED VENKA AND STRONGBOW!
<YOU FIRST, LITTLE LYING FIEND!>

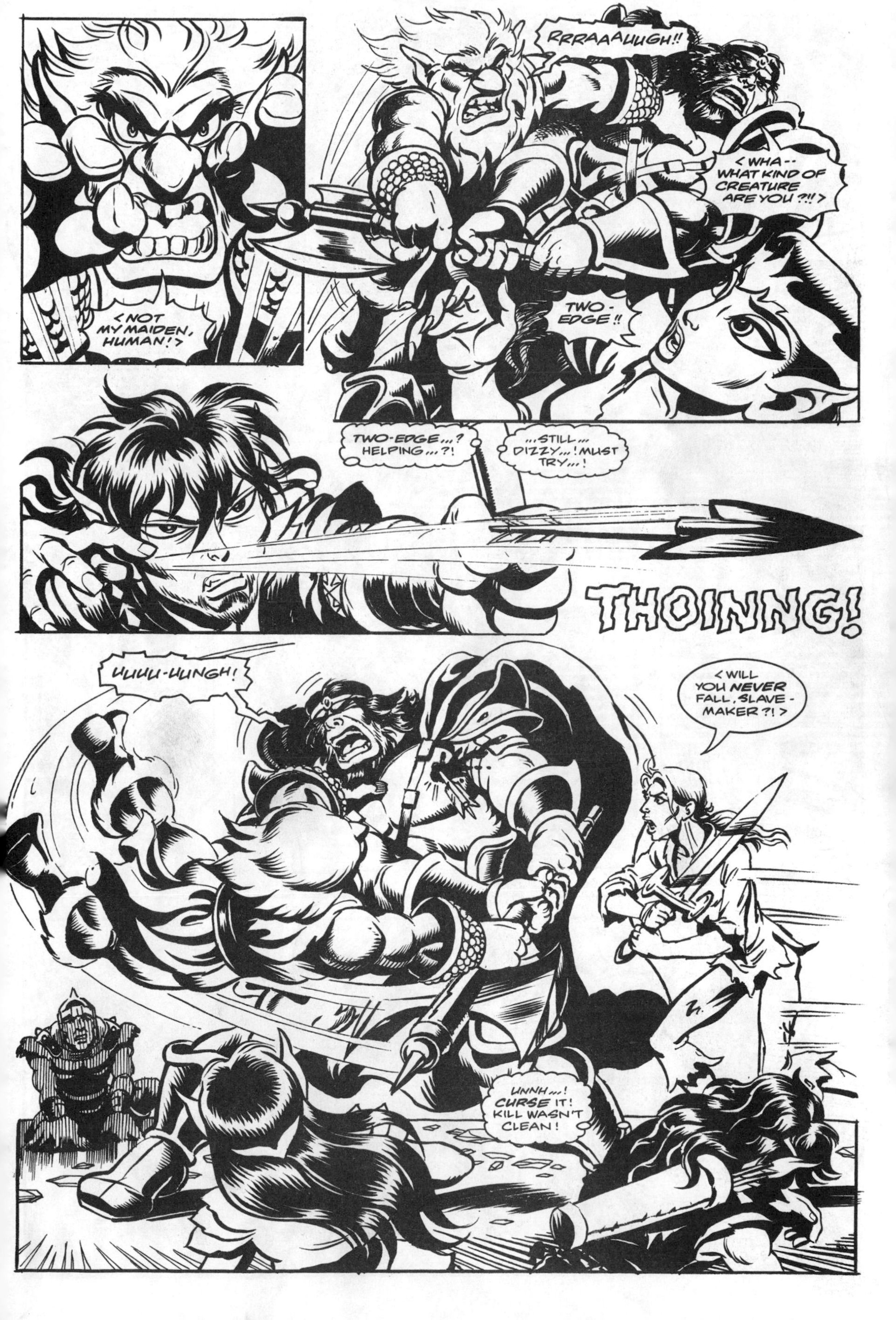

RRRAAAUUGH!!
< NOT MY MAIDEN, HUMAN! >
< WHA-- WHAT KIND OF CREATURE ARE YOU ?!! >
TWO-EDGE!!
TWO-EDGE...? HELPING...?!
...STILL... DIZZY...! MUST TRY...!
THOINNG!
UUUU-UUNGH!
< WILL YOU NEVER FALL, SLAVE-MAKER ?! >
UNNH...! CURSE IT! KILL WASN'T CLEAN!

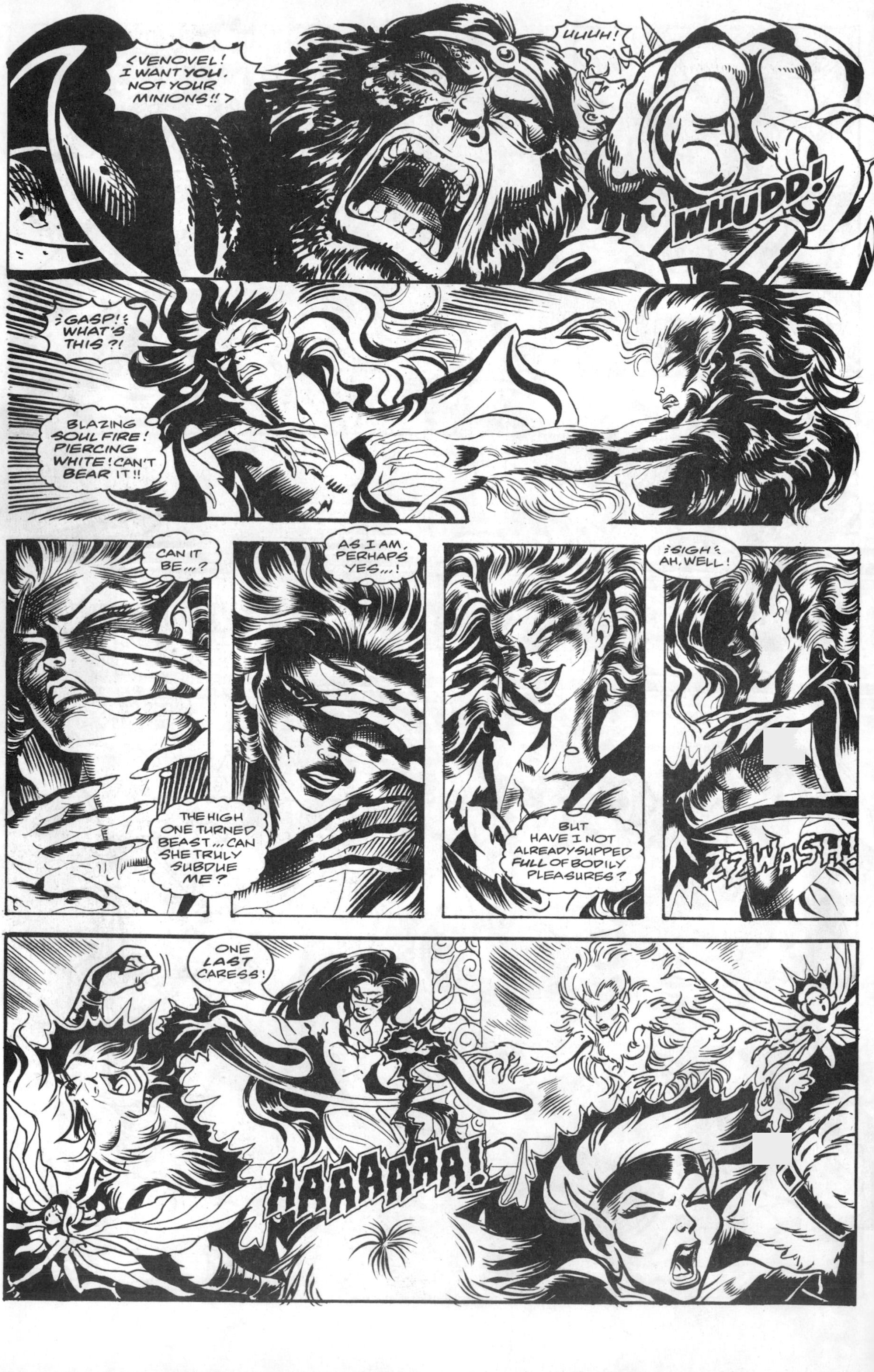
<VENOVEL! I WANT YOU. NOT YOUR MINIONS!!>
UUUH!
WHUDD!
GASP! WHAT'S THIS?!
BLAZING SOUL FIRE! PIERCING WHITE! CAN'T BEAR IT!!
CAN IT BE...?
THE HIGH ONE TURNED BEAST... CAN SHE TRULY SUBDUE ME?
AS I AM, PERHAPS YES...!
BUT HAVE I NOT ALREADY SUPPED FULL OF BODILY PLEASURES?
SIGH AH, WELL!
ZZWASH!
ONE LAST CARESS!
AAAAAAA!

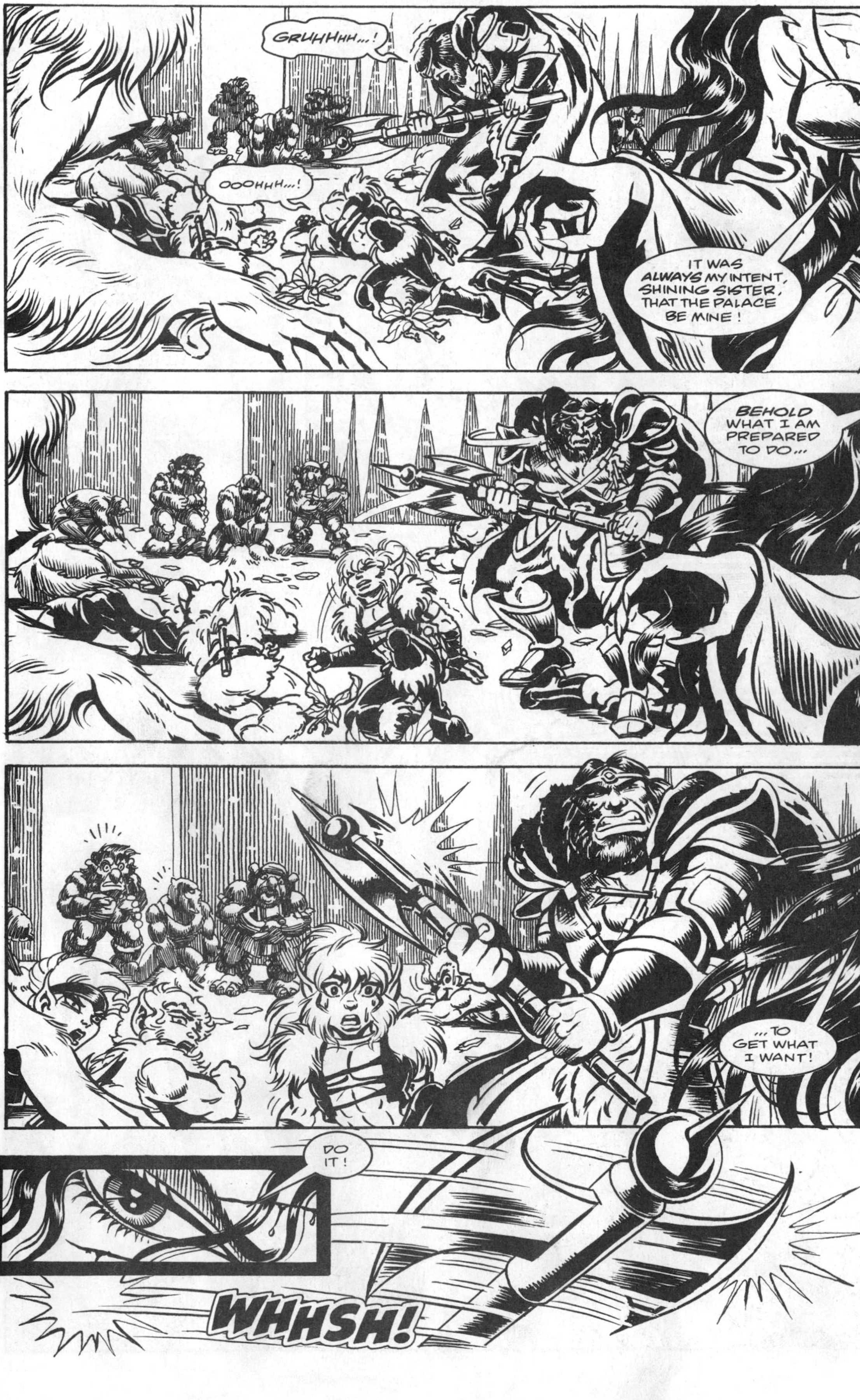
GRUHHHH...!
OOOHHH...!
IT WAS ALWAYS MY INTENT, SHINING SISTER, THAT THE PALACE BE MINE!
BEHOLD WHAT I AM PREPARED TO DO...
...TO GET WHAT I WANT!
DO IT!
WHHSH!

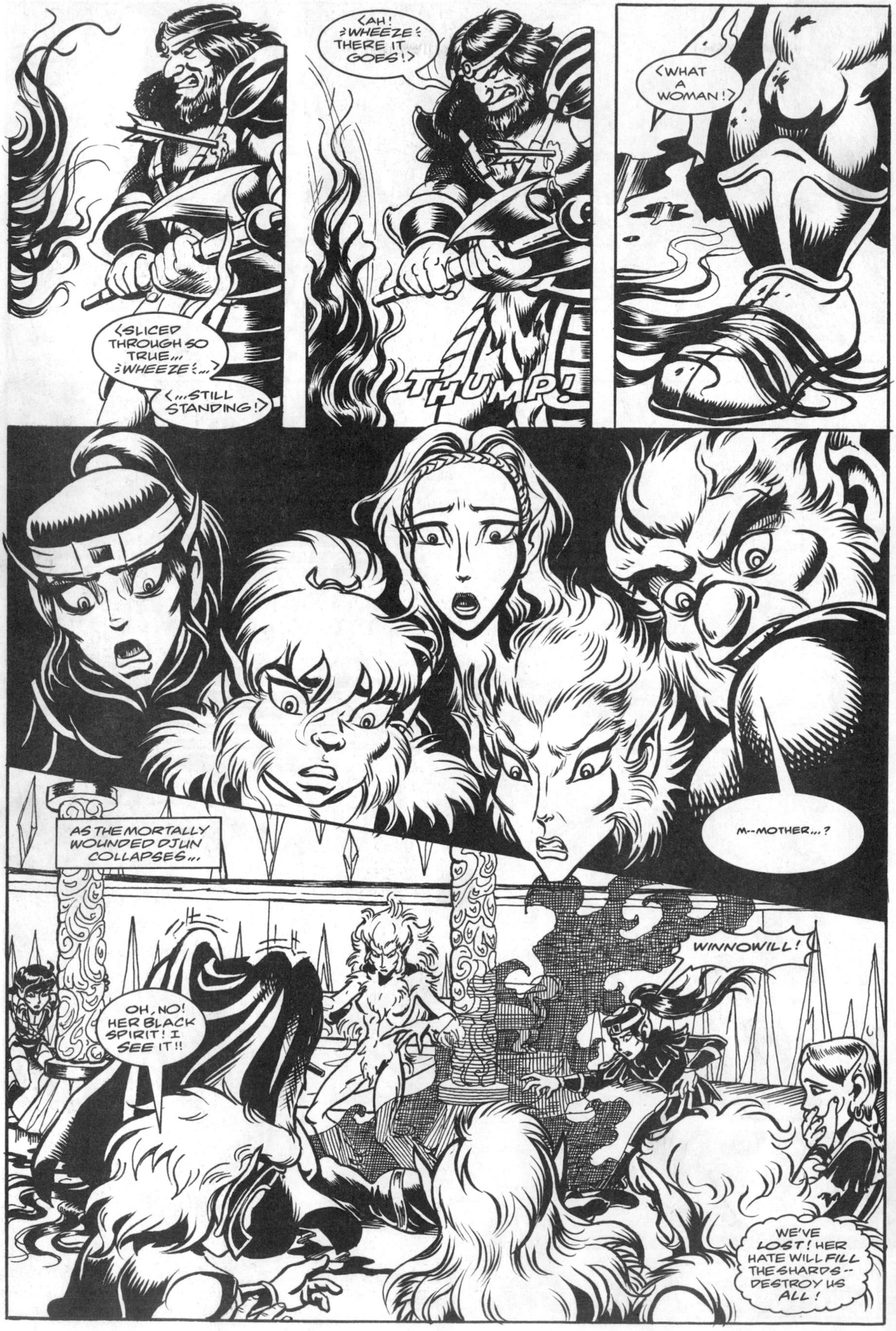

<SLICED THROUGH SO TRUE... ≷WHEEZE≶...>
<...STILL STANDING!>
<AH! ≷WHEEZE≶ THERE IT GOES!>
THUMP!
<WHAT A WOMAN!>
M--MOTHER...?
AS THE MORTALLY WOUNDED DJUN COLLAPSES...
WINNOWILL!
OH, NO! HER BLACK SPIRIT! I SEE IT!!
WE'VE LOST! HER HATE WILL FILL THE SHARDS-- DESTROY US ALL!

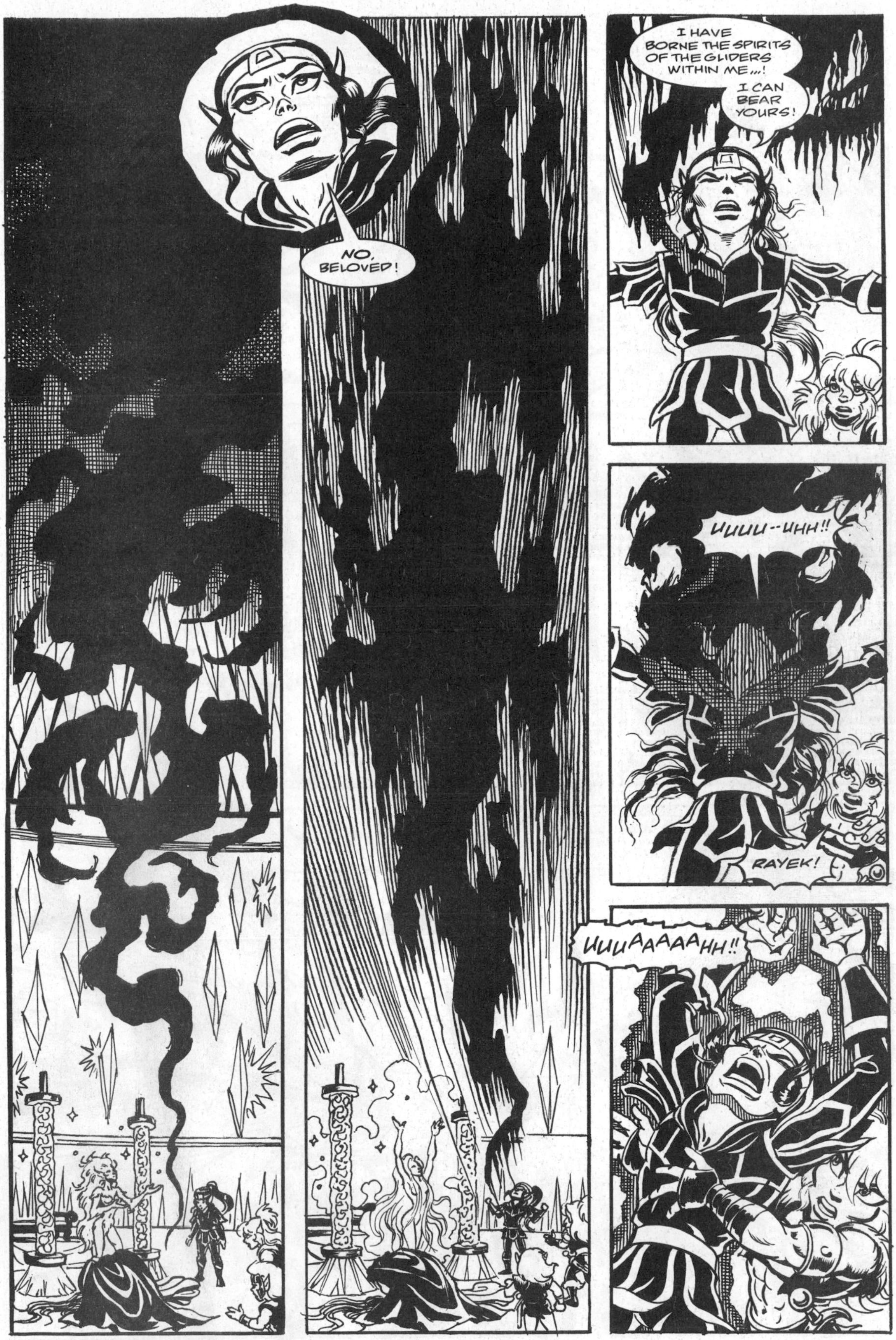
NO, BELOVED!
I HAVE BORNE THE SPIRITS OF THE GLIDERS WITHIN ME...!
I CAN BEAR YOURS!
UUUU--UHH!!
RAYEK!
UUUAAAAAHH!!

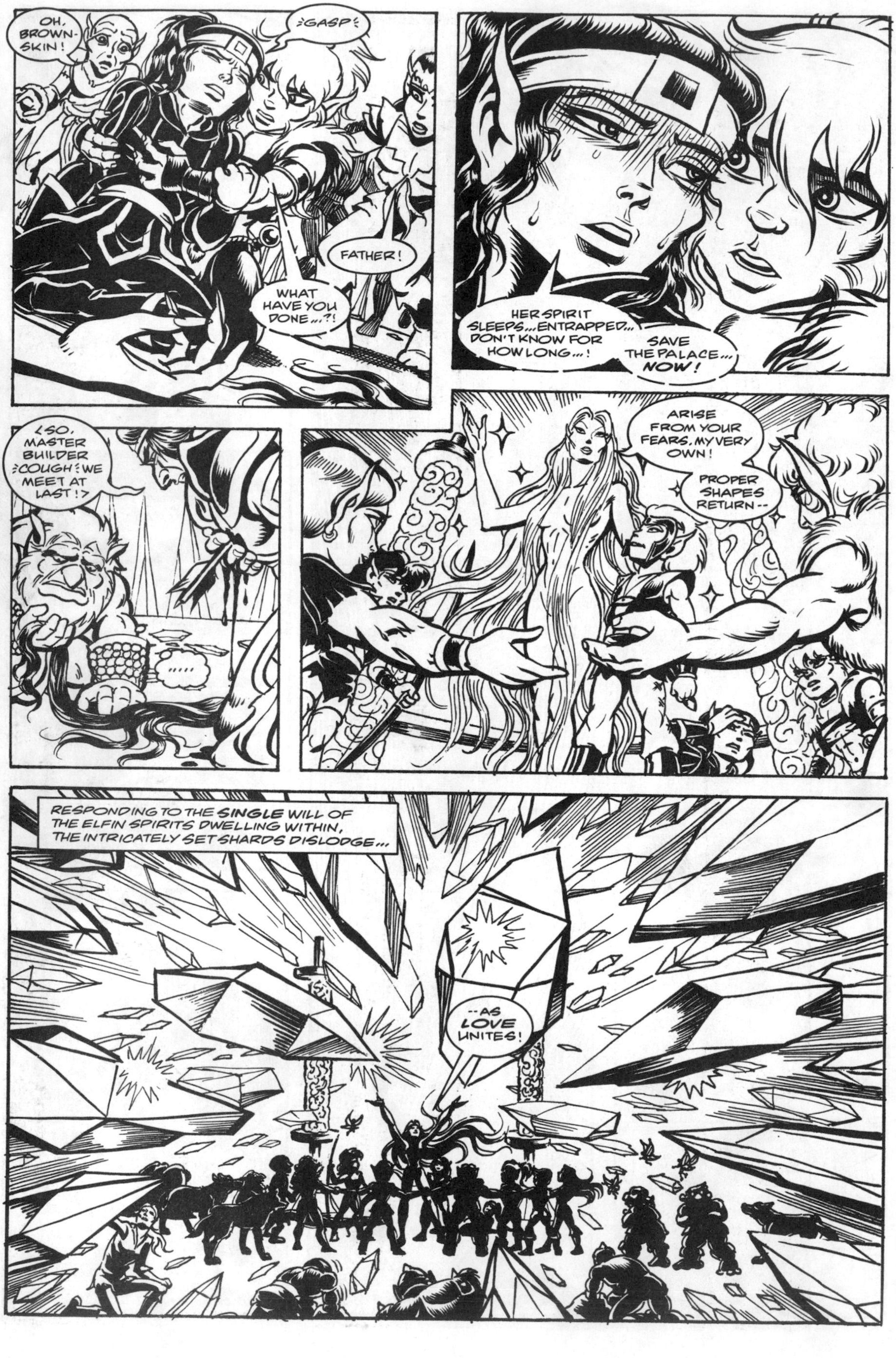
OH, BROWN-SKIN!
GASP
FATHER!
WHAT HAVE YOU DONE...?!
HER SPIRIT SLEEPS... ENTRAPPED... DON'T KNOW FOR HOW LONG...!
SAVE THE PALACE... NOW!
<SO, MASTER BUILDER COUGH WE MEET AT LAST!>
.....
ARISE FROM YOUR FEARS, MY VERY OWN!
PROPER SHAPES RETURN--
RESPONDING TO THE SINGLE WILL OF THE ELFIN SPIRITS DWELLING WITHIN, THE INTRICATELY SET SHARDS DISLODGE...
--AS LOVE UNITES!

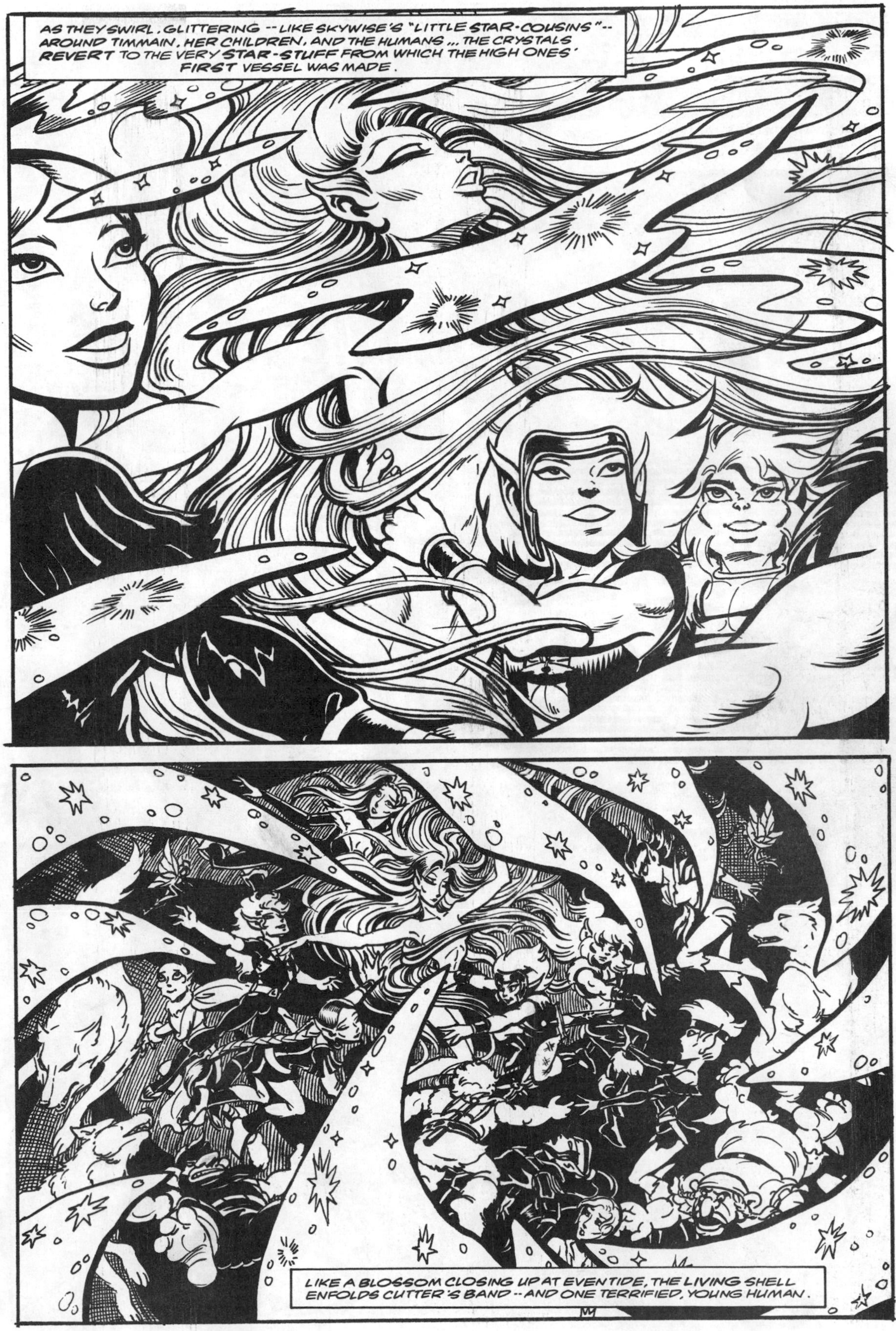
AS THEY SWIRL, GLITTERING -- LIKE SKYWISE'S "LITTLE STAR-COUSINS" -- AROUND TIMMAIN, HER CHILDREN, AND THE HUMANS ... THE CRYSTALS REVERT TO THE VERY STAR-STUFF FROM WHICH THE HIGH ONES' FIRST VESSEL WAS MADE.
LIKE A BLOSSOM CLOSING UP AT EVENTIDE, THE LIVING SHELL ENFOLDS CUTTER'S BAND -- AND ONE TERRIFIED, YOUNG HUMAN.

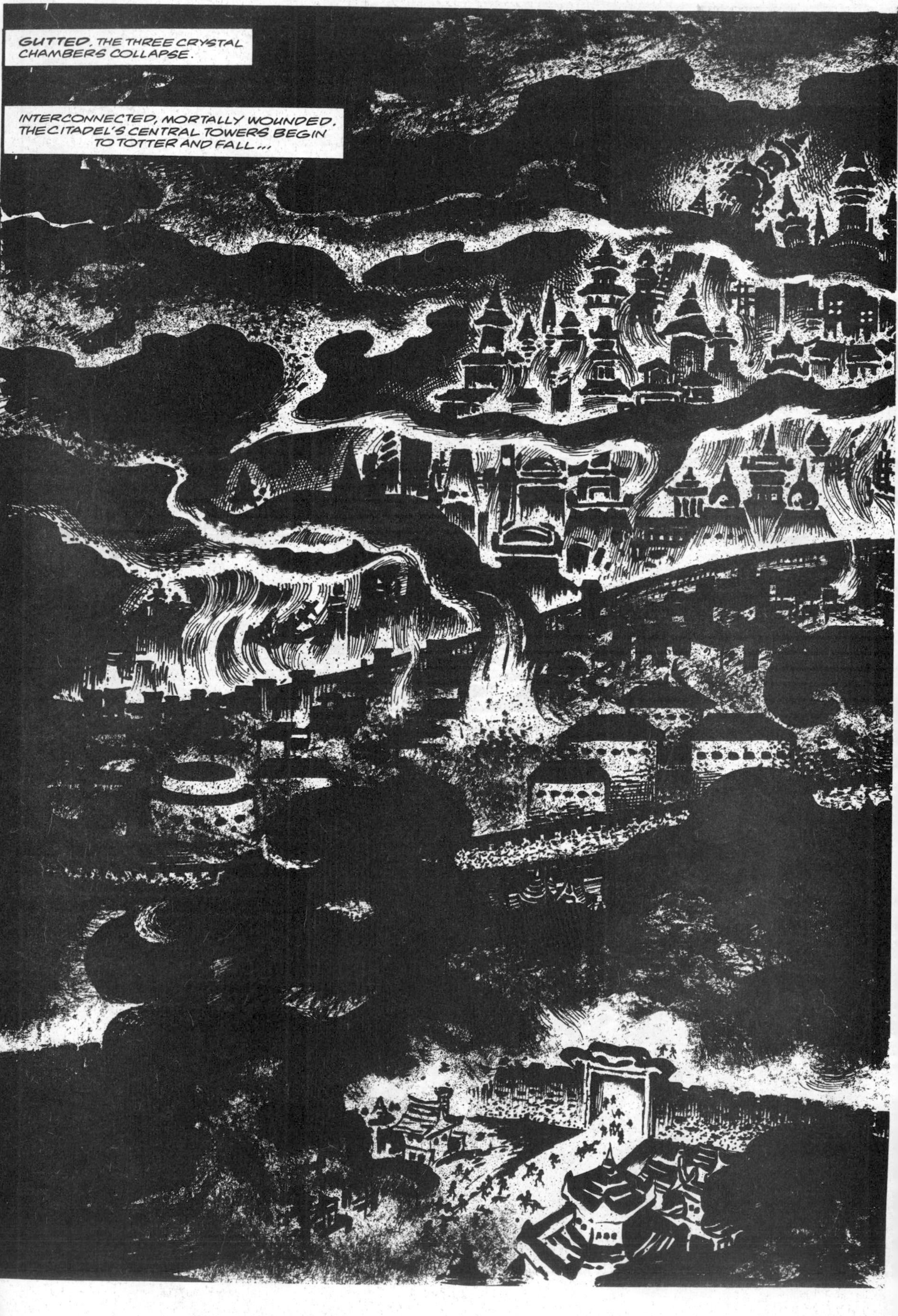
GUTTED. THE THREE CRYSTAL CHAMBERS COLLAPSE.
INTERCONNECTED, MORTALLY WOUNDED. THE CITADEL'S CENTRAL TOWERS BEGIN TO TOTTER AND FALL...

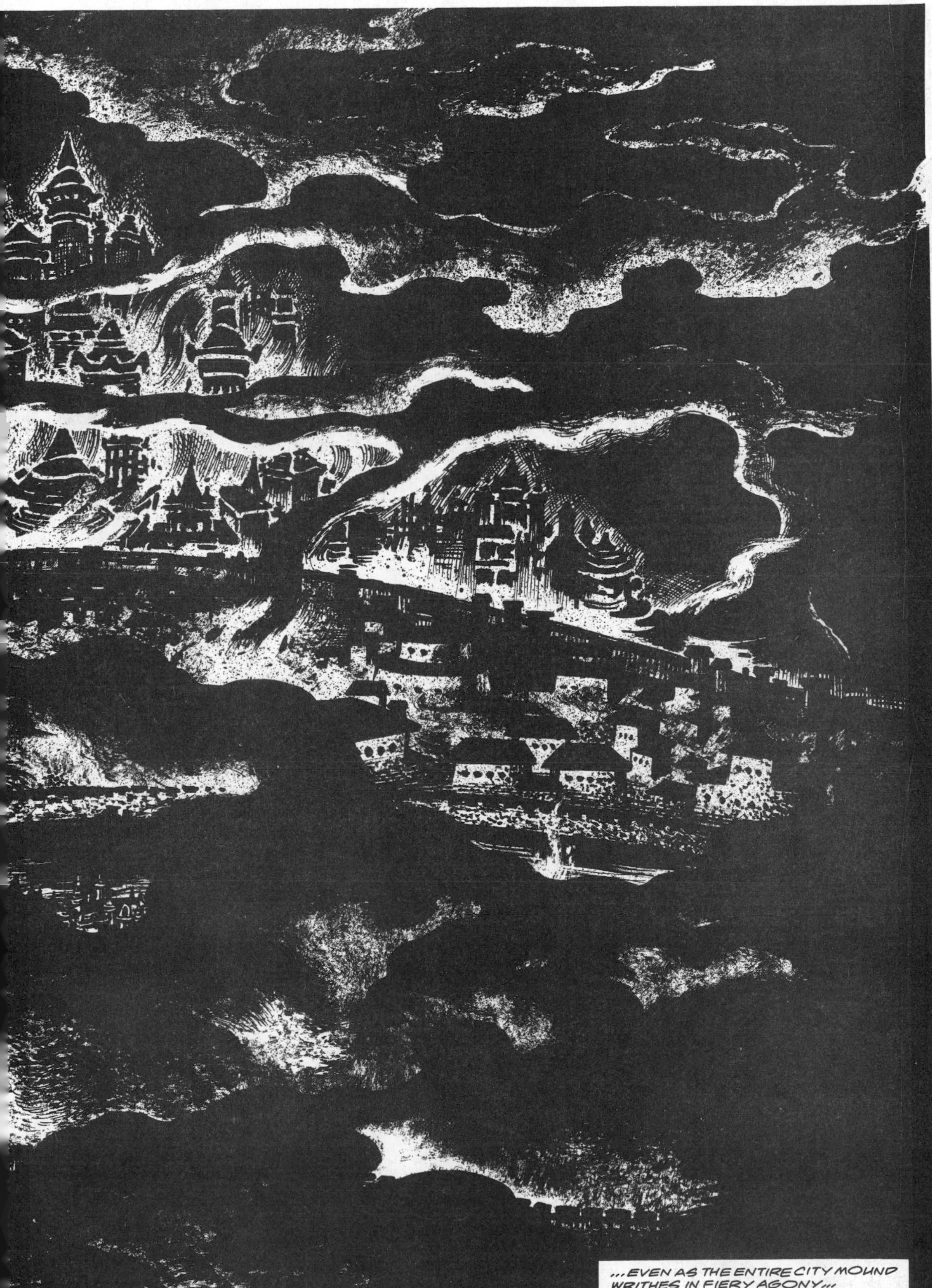
...EVEN AS THE ENTIRE CITY MOUND WRITHES IN FIERY AGONY...

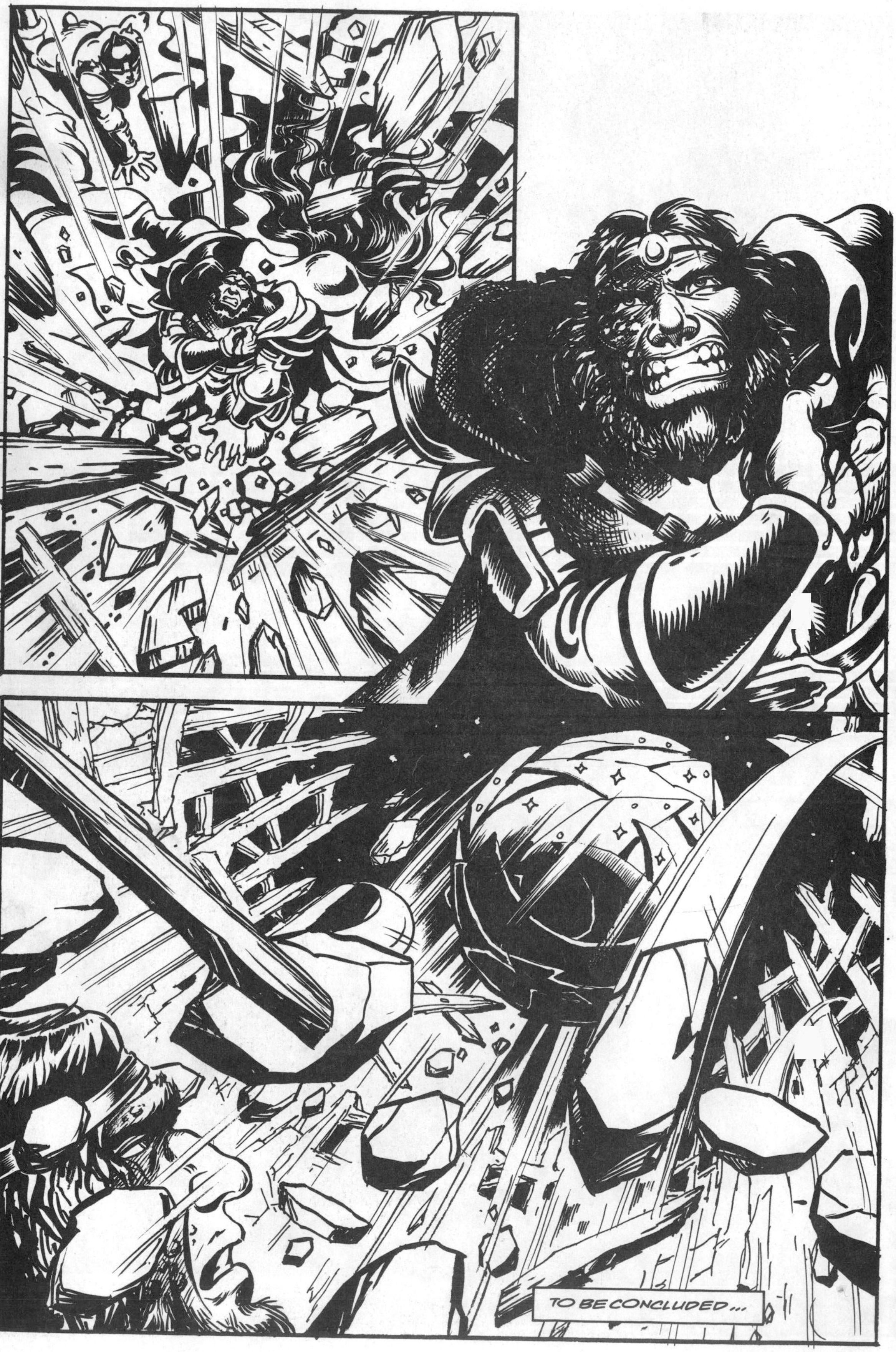
TO BE CONCLUDED...

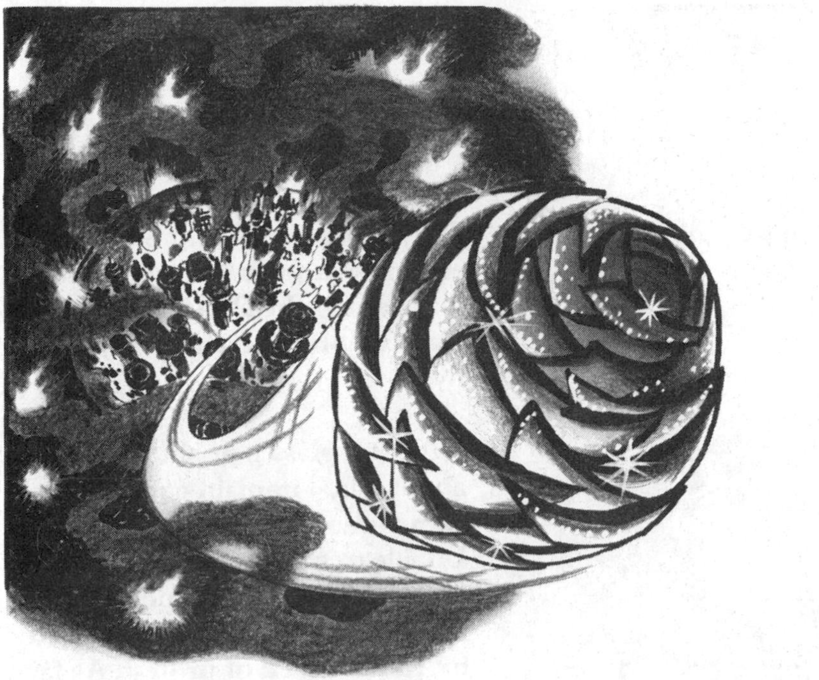

Free and whole again, the Palace of the High Ones has taken its original form, that of a great flying shell. Jubilant, it soars through the acrid smoke, high into the overcast sky, leaving Grohmul Djun's crumbling Citadel far below.

Shielded from the destruction wrought by their escape, Cutter's warriors howl in triumph. Their quest is complete; what was theirs, is theirs once more. Only Rayek, braced against the shell's curving wall, remains silent, choked with deepest pain. Inside him crawls the imprisoned spirit of the Black Snake, restless, apt to strike at his first unguarded moment.

"I can no longer be Master of the Palace." His mournful voice quiets the revelers. "Who will guide it now?"

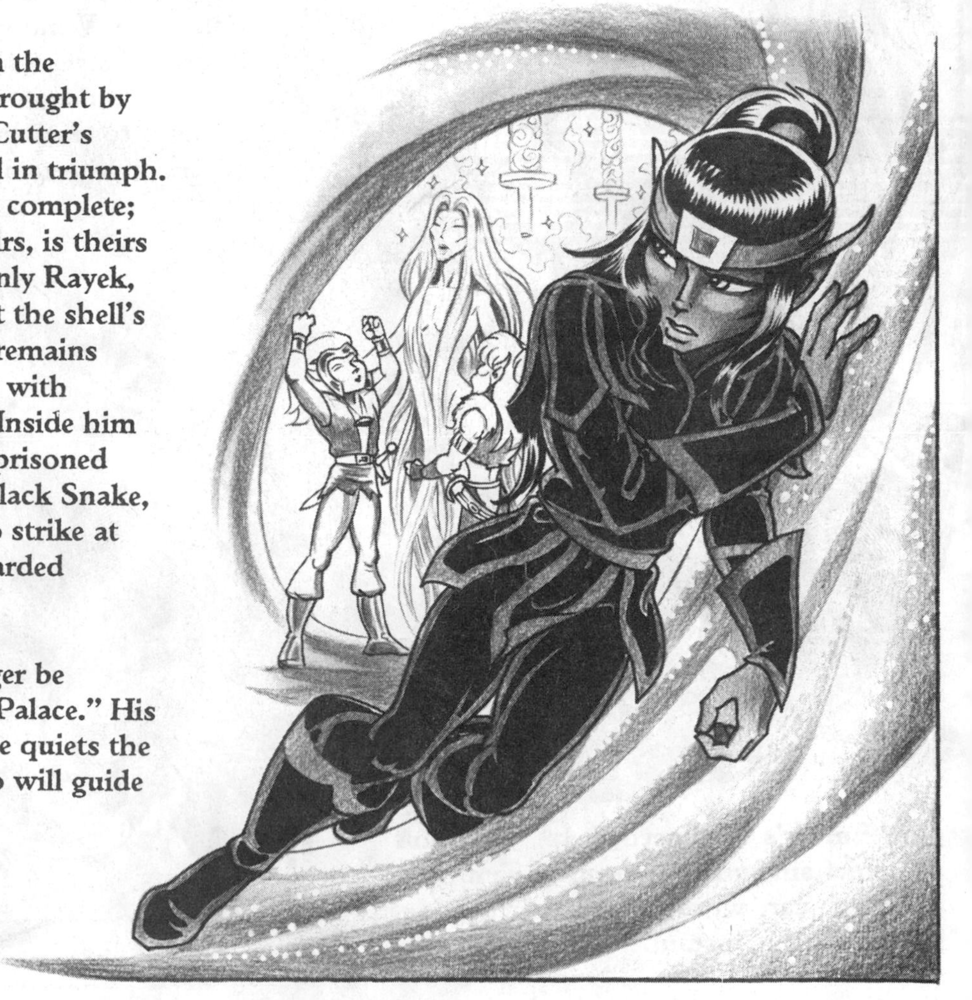

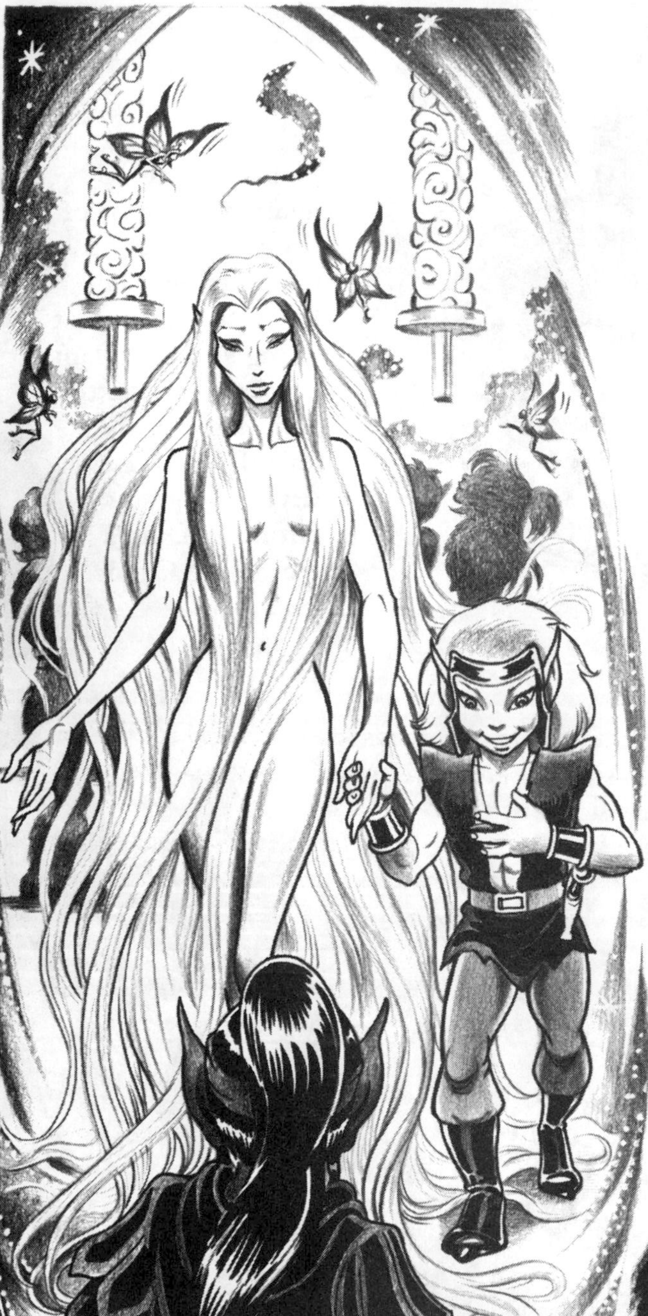

"We will," Skywise smiles. "The Palace belonged to the High Ones when the World of Two Moons was fresh born. Timmain was among the Palace's first Masters. She'll teach us all to fly."

Her spun glass hair shimmering about her, Timmain gazes compassionately at Rayek. Unable to meet her eyes, he lowers his head and nods. Nearby, Cutter frowns, disturbed by Rayek's lack of protest. As far as Cutter knows, only two things obsess his old rival: the Palace and Winnowill. Yet now, it seems, Rayek must surrender the one, to devote all his strength to restraining the other... a grim fate indeed!

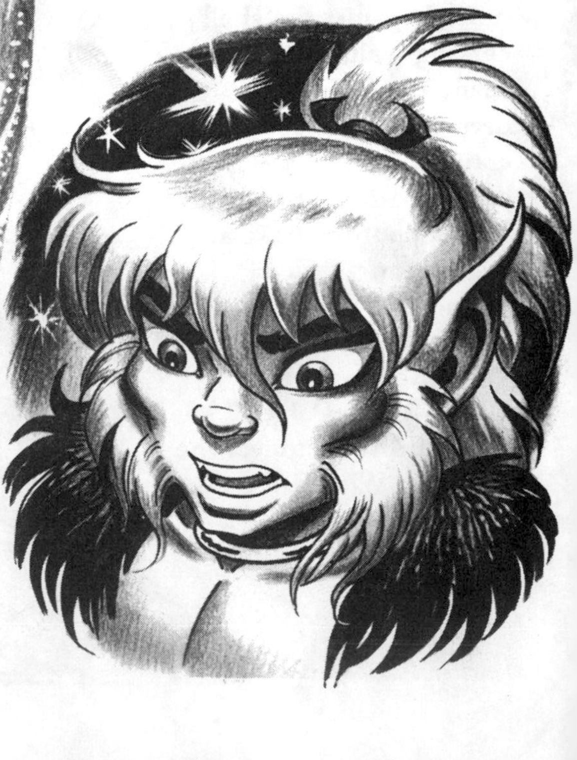

"Ember's tribe needs help." The wolf chieftain suddenly turns to Timmain. "I don't care who takes us there, so long as it's this instant!"

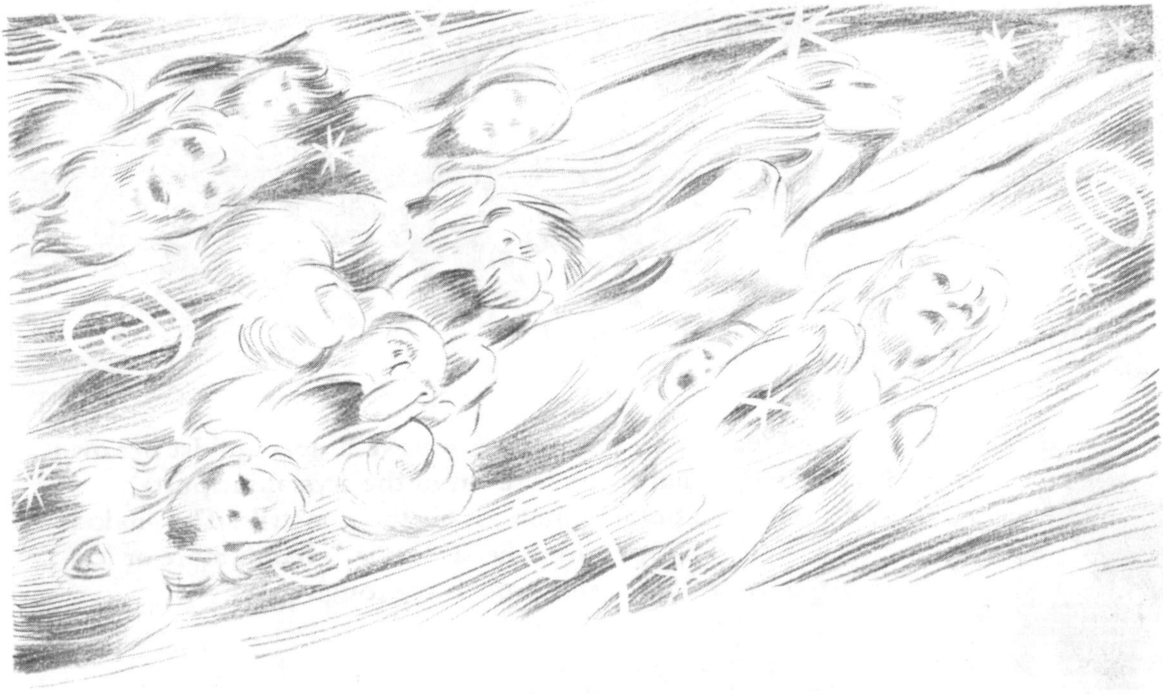

"An instant is all we shall need." The High One reaches for the Scroll of Colors spinning above her head. "But let us arrive in a form familiar to those we seek!"

Timmain's will feeds the aura which crackles between the Scrolls, illuminating the chamber. A strange buzzing fills the sensitive ears of elves and wolves alike. All within the magical vessel feel the sudden pull of weightless, timeless flight. The troll siblings, Flam and Drub, cling to one another, terrified of the weird sensation. In the form of a crystal Palace, and in less time than it takes to draw a single breath, the flying shell appears and settles to ground near Howling Rock.

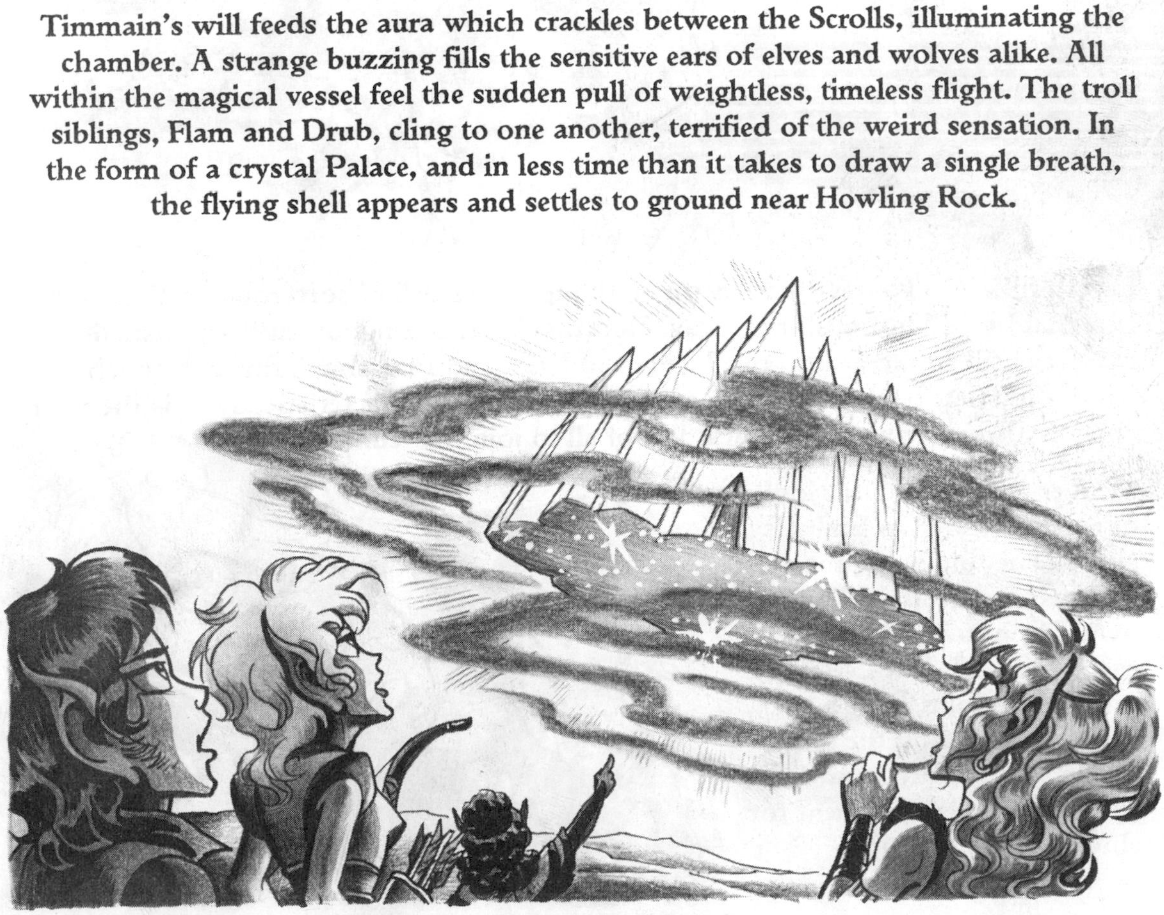

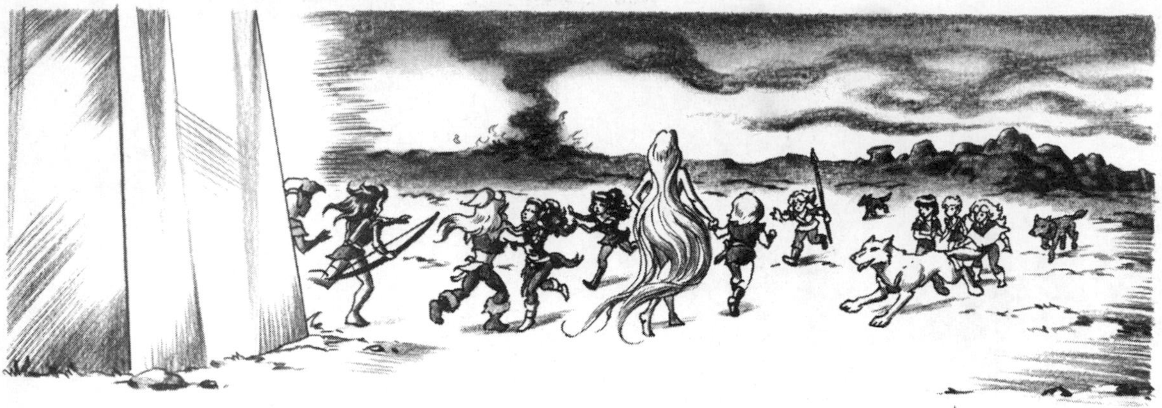

Because, to save the Palace, they were forced to leave Ember amidst her own crisis, Skywise and Timmain are first out of the crystalline portal. Unexpectedly, the stench of burning flesh assails their nostrils. The anxious stargazer and the High One sigh with relief as Ember's band, more or less intact, dash toward them through the rough grass.

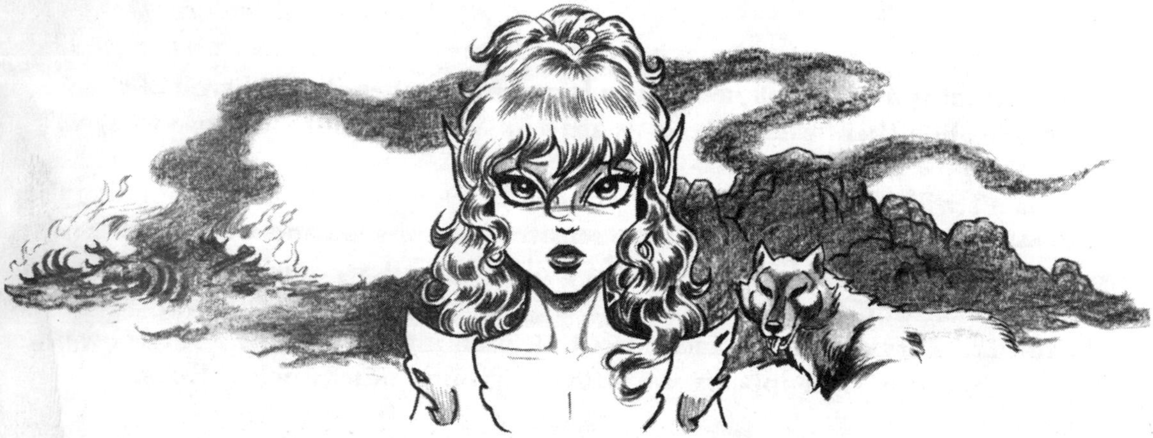

Leetah flies into Cutter's arms assured, though the smell of sorcerous death is upon her, that he will not push her away. Moments later, Strongbow and Moonshade embrace as if to merge into one being, and Krim and Pike share, through touch and tears, a lifemate's loss and a new cub's beginning. Uncharacteristically, it is the young chieftess Ember who hangs back, last of all to join the reunion.

Mender fails to note the look of recent farewell in Ember's eyes as she finally approaches. The warrior-healer, full of his own adventures, reaches eagerly for her. But Leetah gently takes him aside as Ember's arms find the only one who can truly know her heart. **This is a moment for chiefs,** Leetah sends.

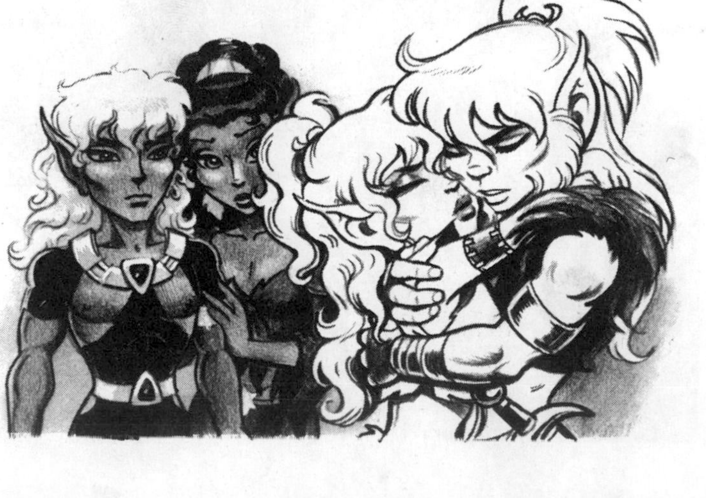

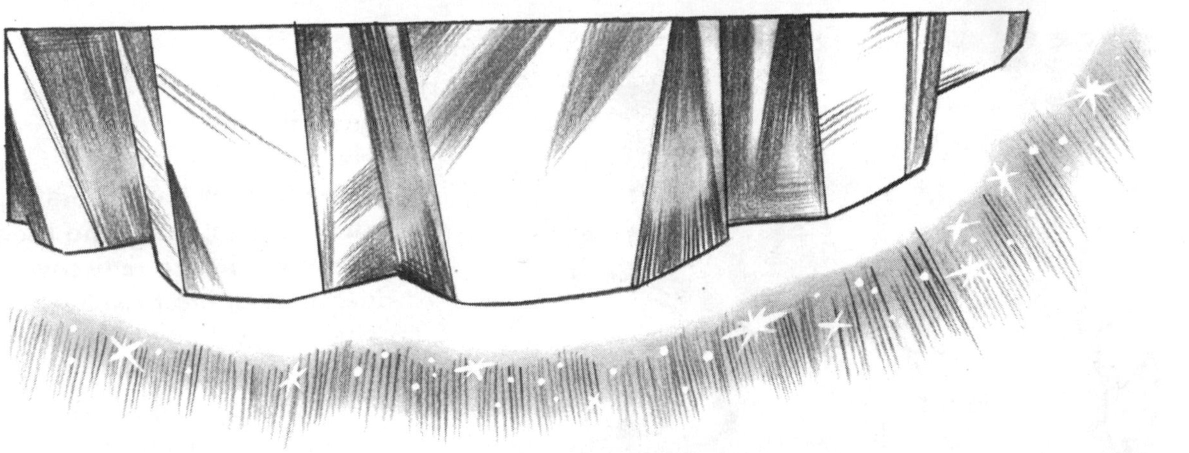

There is little time wasted at Howling Rock as the reunited elves realize the entire World of Two Moons is theirs to roam at will. Before poor Drub and Flam have even recovered from their first flight, the Palace streaks off for the other side of the planet, seeking Dart's small band of young warriors.

Ember's twin brother Suntop provides the psychic beacon which guides the Palace over the devastated Forevergreen jungle. His is the first - and most powerful - of elfin minds to send out a call. In what seems no time at all, the great, glowing vessel arrives to sweep Dart's band away from the ruins of what was once a beleaguered human city.

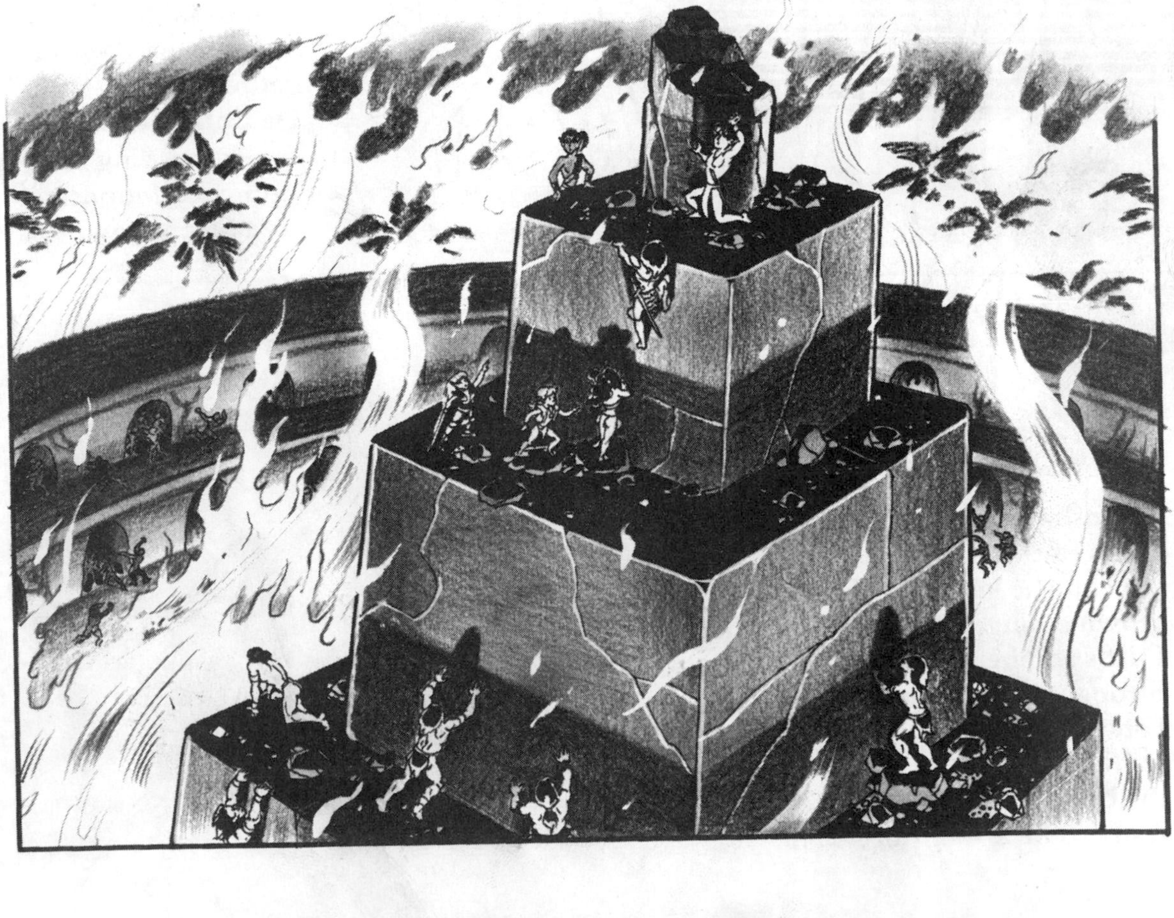

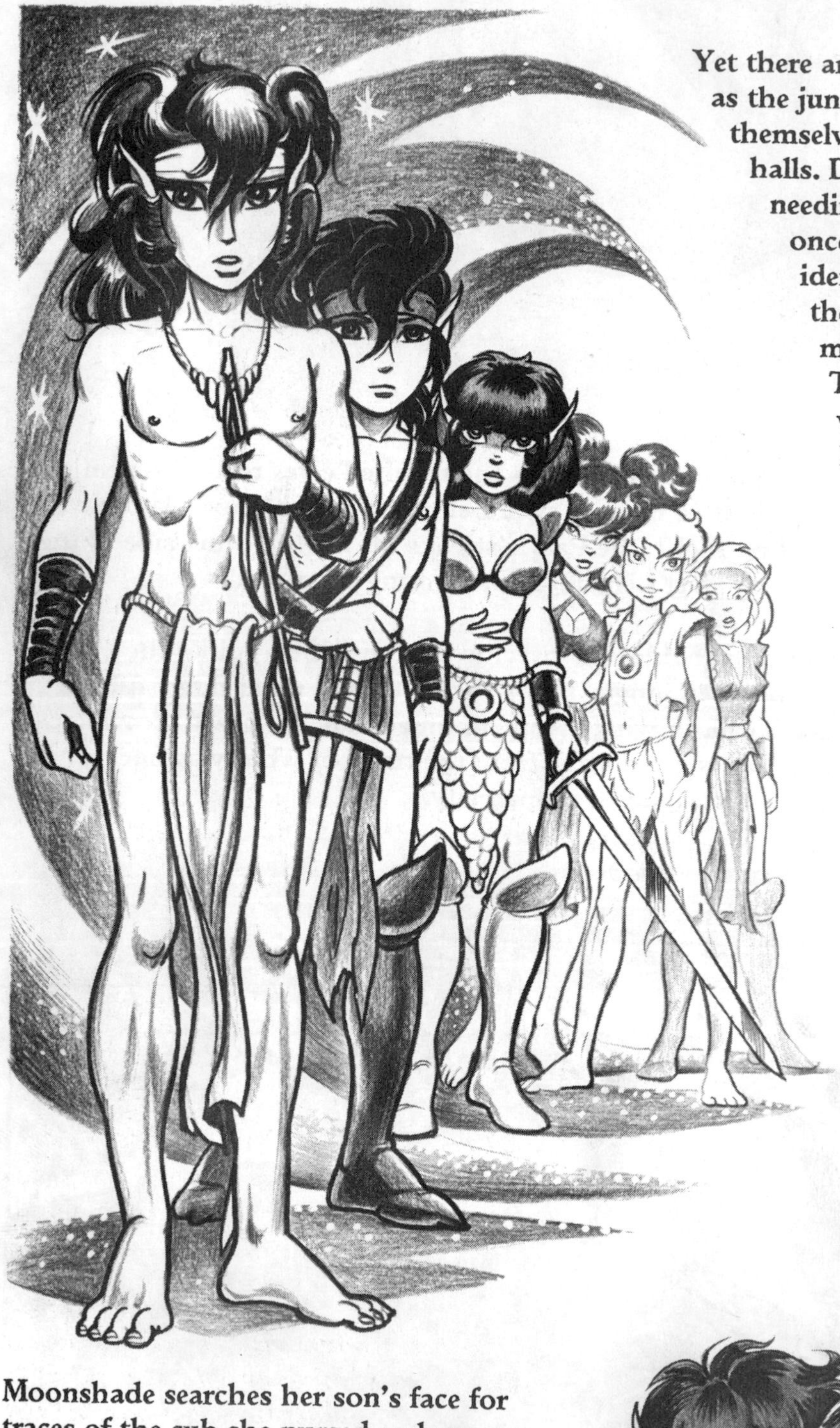

Yet there are no howls of celebration as the jungle warriors suddenly find themselves standing in the Palace's halls. Dazed, they look about, needing time to recall who they once were, time to rediscover identities all but dissolved in the primeval ooze of that most ancient of forests. There they found humans who yearned to be elves, led by a mad, immortal Glider almost as poisonous as the Black Snake herself. To come from that... to the Palace's womb-like interior where their race began... is a challenge to everything Dart and his warriors have come to call reality.

At last Suntop breaks into a smile, "Mother! Father! Ember! Hello!" He trots over to join his family, moving Dart to approach Moonshade and Strongbow.

Moonshade searches her son's face for traces of the cub she nursed so long ago, the cub she knows far better than the grown stranger standing before her. Dart's somber gaze shifts from her to Strongbow. "Down there in the Forevergreen, I lost myself," he murmurs to his sire. "But, in the losing, I found the Now of Wolf Thought. I think I'm ready to be a Wolfrider again."

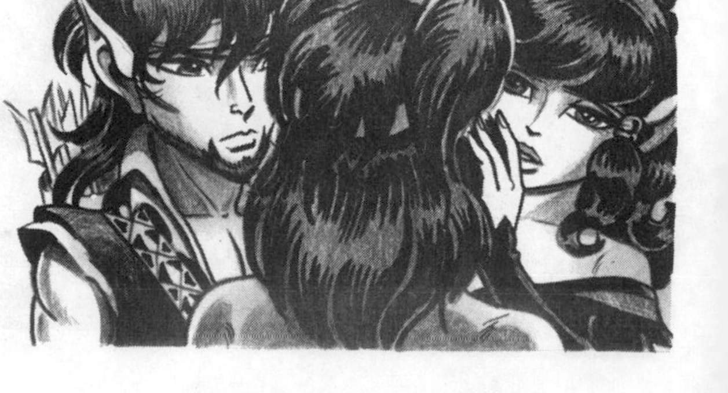

Elsewhere in the chamber, silent thoughts fly back and forth, swift as a Preserver swarm, among Cutter's family... the family royal. Heartfelt greetings are exchanged, battles recounted, losses mourned and victories celebrated.

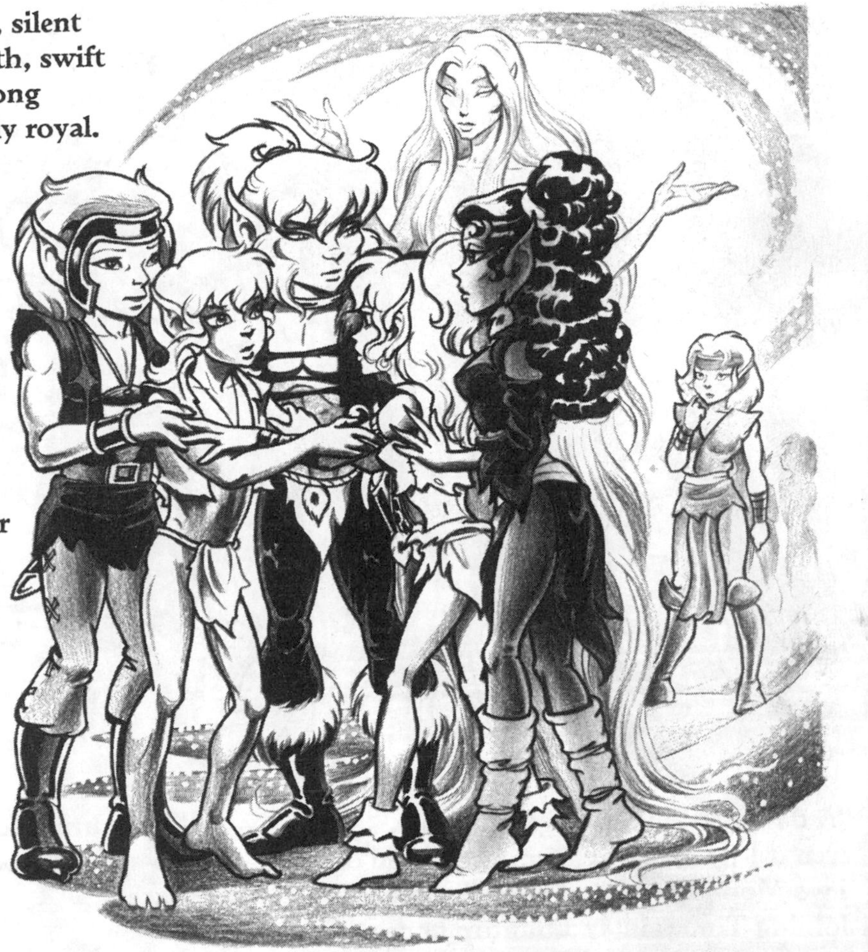

The news of Winnowill's death and her evil spirit's capture strikes like a bolt of skyfire, changing the world's face forever. Never again shall locked sendings be spied upon, soul names be stolen, nor bodies be twisted from afar.

"But my friends... Jethel and Chot!" Suntop suddenly cries aloud. "Where are they?"

"It seems they have chosen to stay put, my child," Timmain's regal voice soothes. "We take in only those who send out a call, or answer ours. Come and learn for yourself, for our minds shall all be linked, one day, through you."

The tall High One holds out her hand to young Suntop. She leads him a few paces toward the Scroll of Colors, then turns and extends her other hand to Skywise. He gulps, realizing his dream is about to come true. He has been chosen to learn the Scroll's secrets. He, too, will gain the power to make the Palace fly, guide its course, even to the stars.

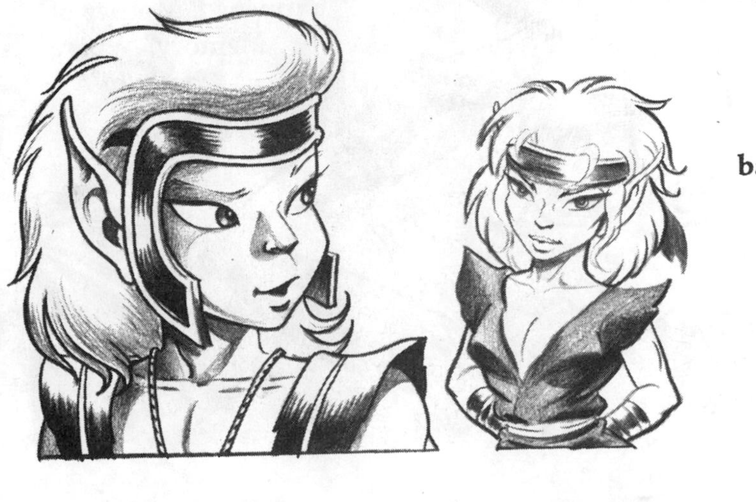

As Skywise starts toward Timmain, he senses someone staring intently at him. Over his shoulder he spots one of Dart's band, the Go-Back, Yun. The hair at the nape of his neck rises - why? Why should any maiden's ogling disturb him? "Don't worry," Yun shrugs, with a grin Skywise has often seen - in his own reflection. "I want nothing except a good look at you. I've already been weaned, you see!"

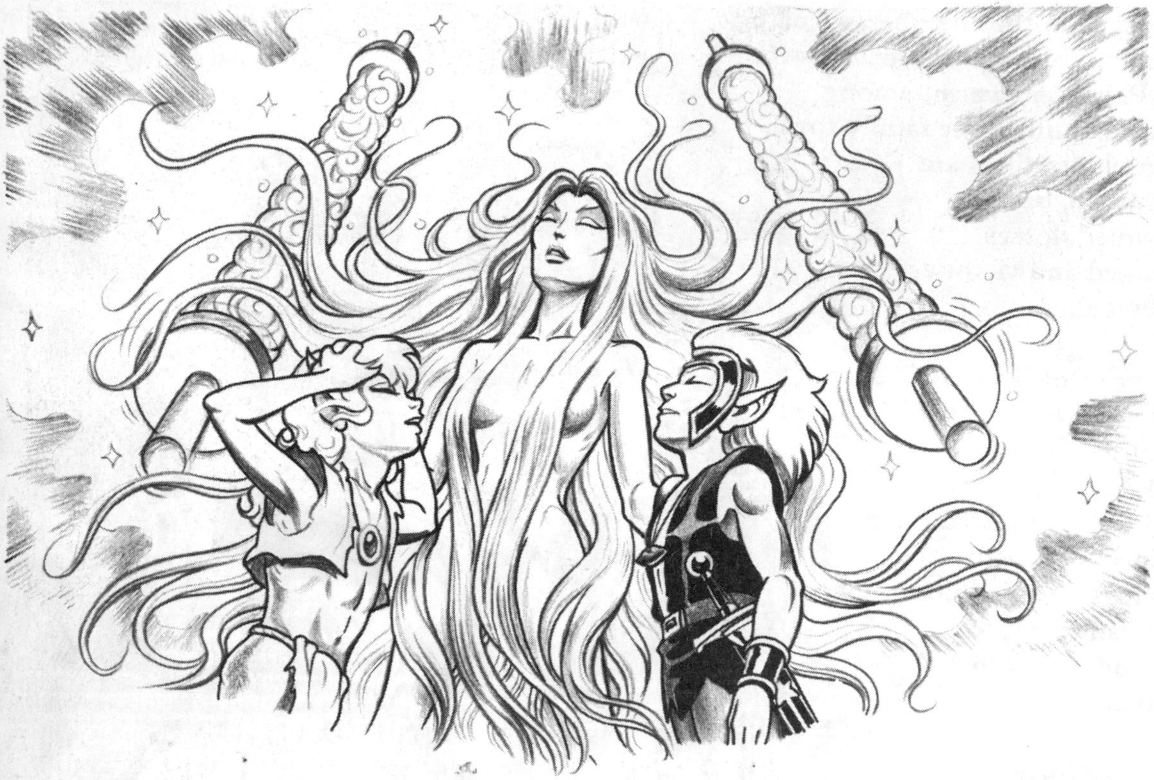

"A daughter!" the stargazer muses. "So, even if I fly far away from the World of Two Moons, a part of me will remain!" Joining Timmain and Suntop under the floating Scroll, Skywise is bathed in a pulsing aura which clears his mind and opens his heart. His two companions' thoughts become his own - no separation, nothing hidden.

Now reach, my children, the High One telepathically commands, **Send out a call and listen with all your being for a response. Let all who so desire be reunited within the Palace!**

At once Suntop thinks of his mentor, Savah, and of Windkin who flew to find the Sun Folk many days ago. Taking Timmain and Skywise with him, Suntop lets his mind travel to his birthplace, Sorrow's End, which aged ten thousand years while he spent but one night outside of time. It is deserted. **What happened, Mother of Memory? Where are you?**

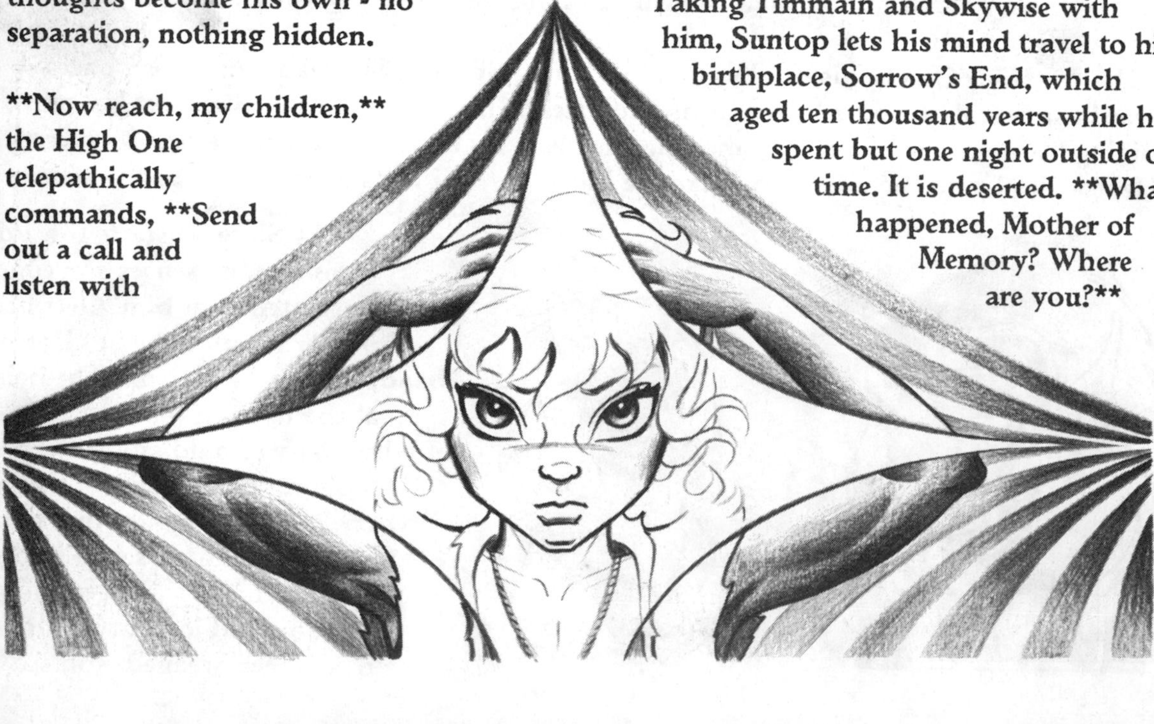

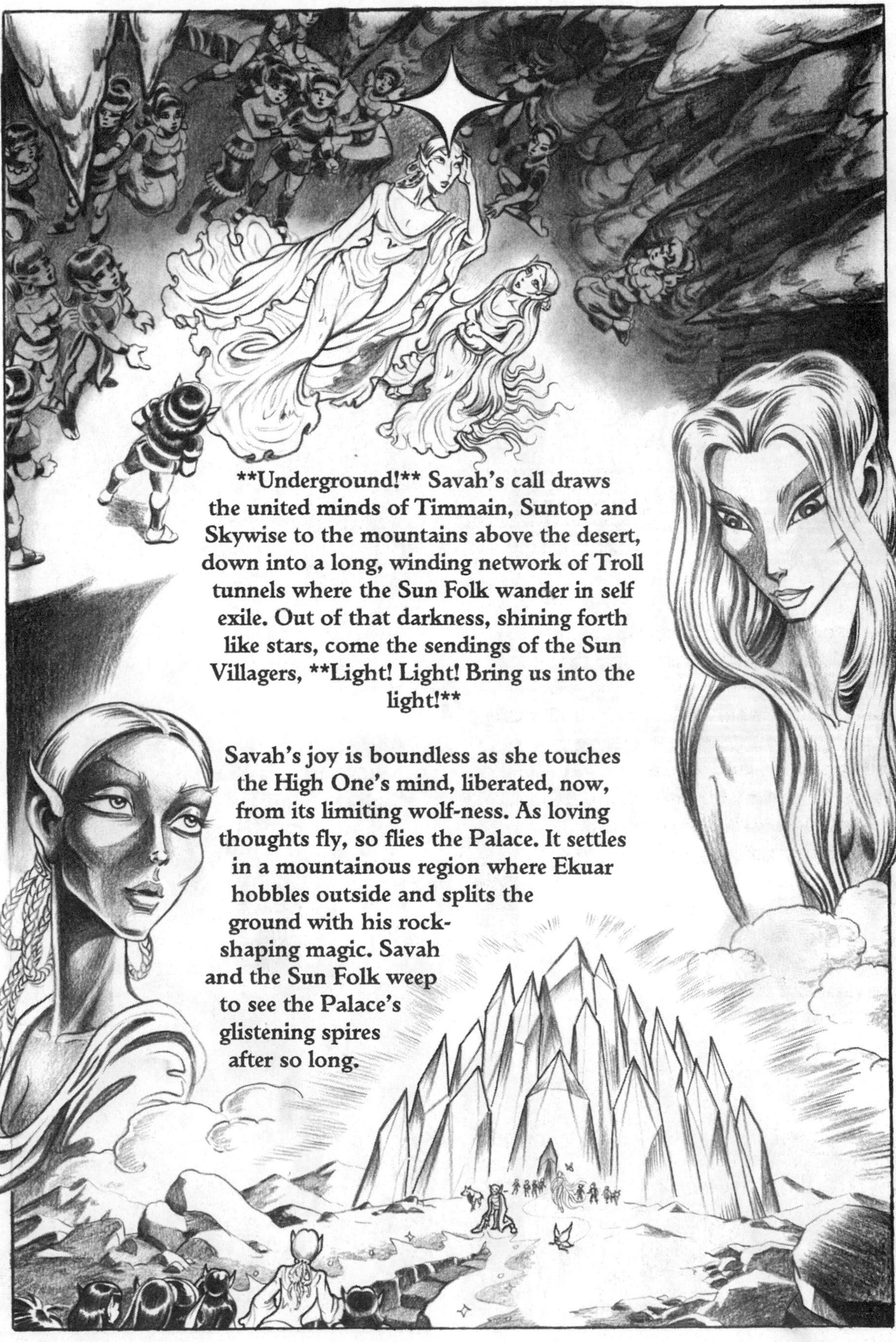
Underground! Savah's call draws the united minds of Timmain, Suntop and Skywise to the mountains above the desert, down into a long, winding network of Troll tunnels where the Sun Folk wander in self exile. Out of that darkness, shining forth like stars, come the sendings of the Sun Villagers, **Light! Light! Bring us into the light!**
Savah's joy is boundless as she touches the High One's mind, liberated, now, from its limiting wolf-ness. As loving thoughts fly, so flies the Palace. It settles in a mountainous region where Ekuar hobbles outside and splits the ground with his rock-shaping magic. Savah and the Sun Folk weep to see the Palace's glistening spires after so long.

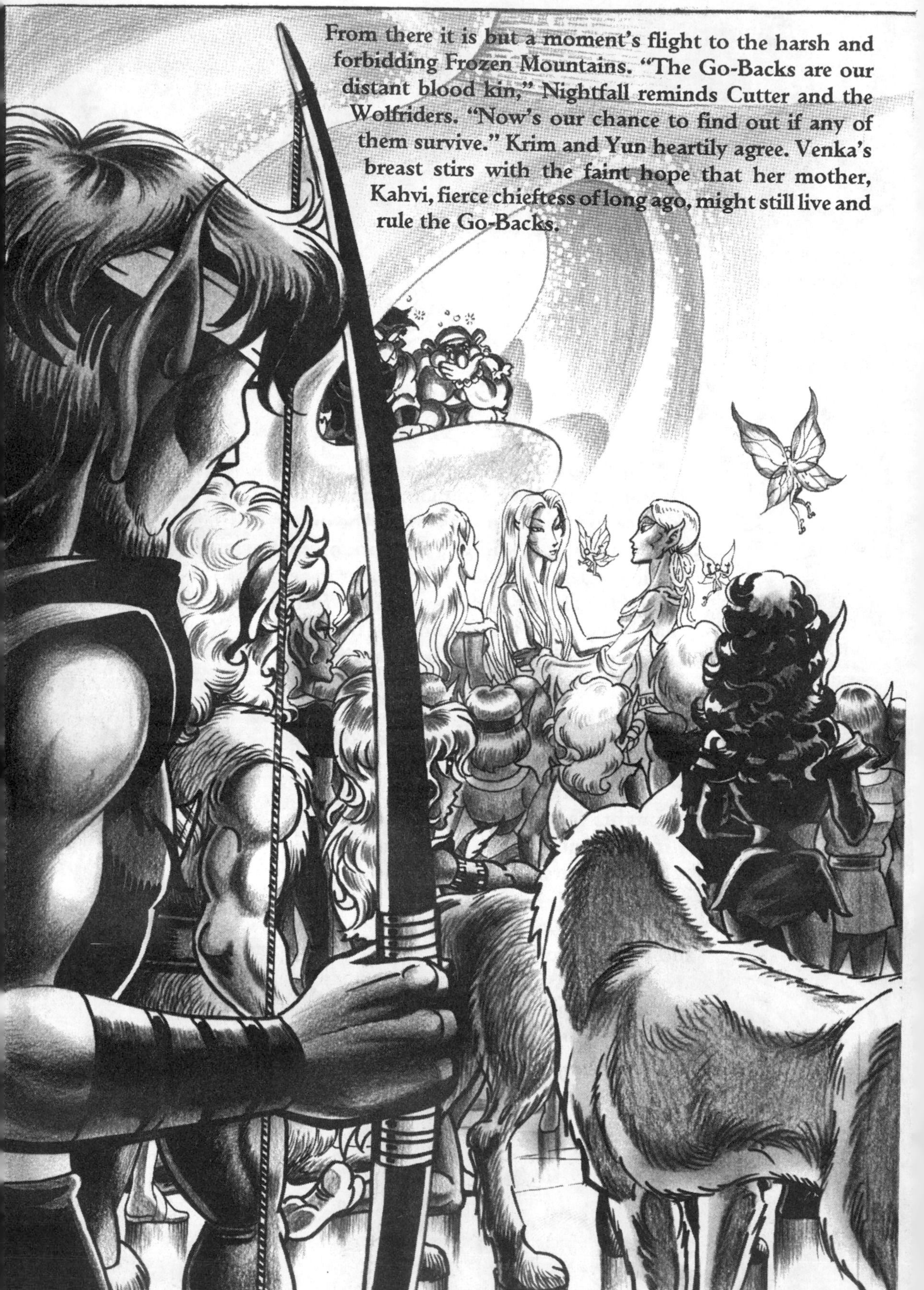
From there it is but a moment's flight to the harsh and forbidding Frozen Mountains. "The Go-Backs are our distant blood kin," Nightfall reminds Cutter and the Wolfriders. "Now's our chance to find out if any of them survive." Krim and Yun heartily agree. Venka's breast stirs with the faint hope that her mother, Kahvi, fierce chieftess of long ago, might still live and rule the Go-Backs.

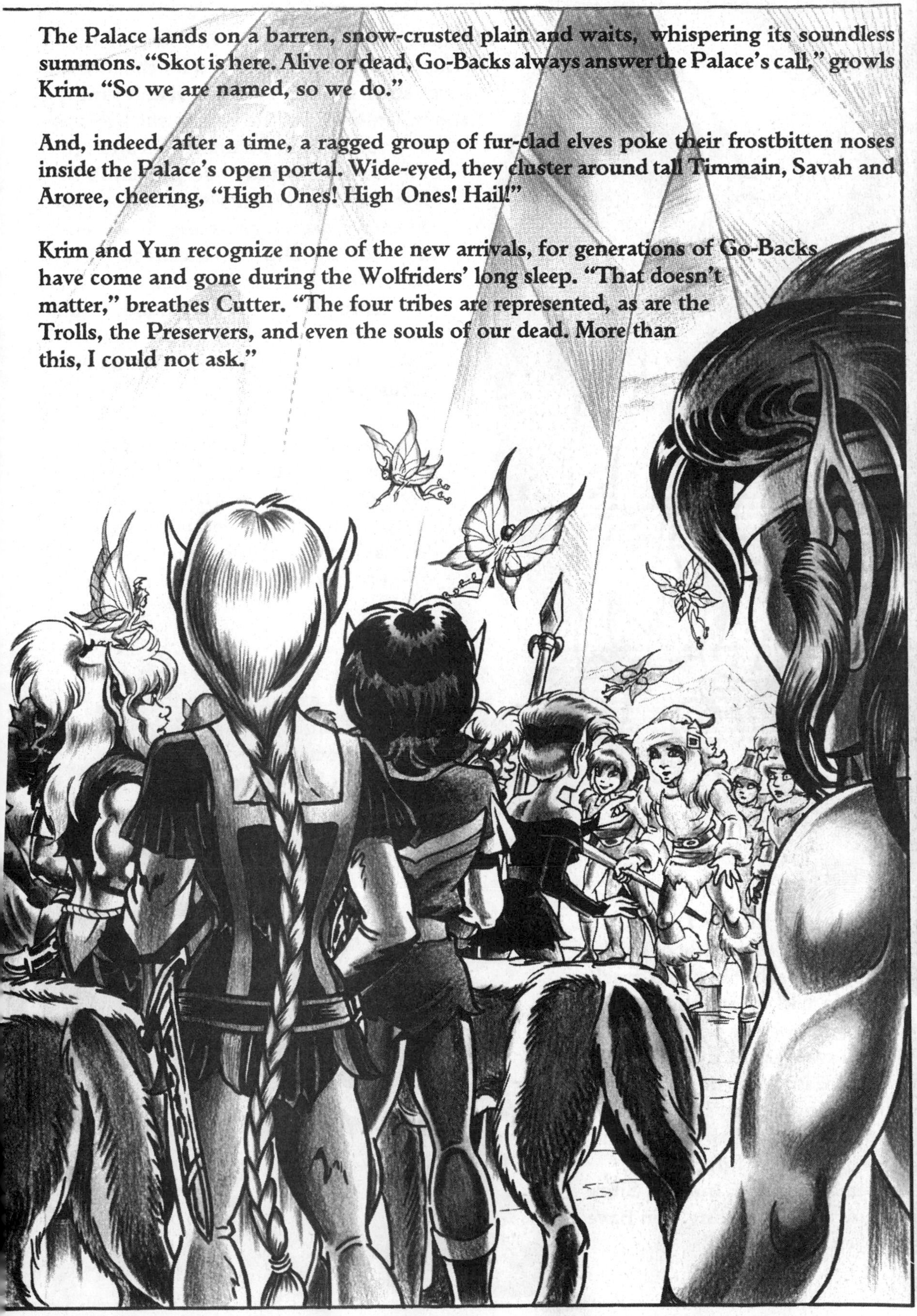
The Palace lands on a barren, snow-crusted plain and waits, whispering its soundless summons. "Skot is here. Alive or dead, Go-Backs always answer the Palace's call," growls Krim. "So we are named, so we do."
And, indeed, after a time, a ragged group of fur-clad elves poke their frostbitten noses inside the Palace's open portal. Wide-eyed, they cluster around tall Timmain, Savah and Aroree, cheering, "High Ones! High Ones! Hail!"
Krim and Yun recognize none of the new arrivals, for generations of Go-Backs have come and gone during the Wolfriders' long sleep. "That doesn't matter," breathes Cutter. "The four tribes are represented, as are the Trolls, the Preservers, and even the souls of our dead. More than this, I could not ask."

Huddled within a shell-like hollow, a lone human shivers, overwhelmed by the magical forces she has witnessed and felt. Shuna stares, dry-eyed, at the beings she believes to be good spirits. So many! So strange! And - however kindly - so powerful! Mere humans were never meant to gaze on such a sacred gathering! In the end, how can the Hidden Ones regard her as anything but an intruder? Clutching her throbbing hand, Shuna shuts her eyes, awaiting the fatal blade thrust or wolf bite that surely must come.

To her surprise, she feels instead the tenderest touch upon her brow. Her eyes open and well with tears. There before her stands Leetah, dressed in the last scraps of the velvet gown given to her by Shuna's own mother.

"It-it's you! The spirit who healed me! You're just as I remember!" the human girl exclaims. Recognizing the nearby Tyleet, she beams even more brightly. "And you! I helped you escape from my house!"

"Shhh..." hushes Leetah, understanding little of the girl's speech. "I've had much to do with death these days. Let me use my powers, now, as I was meant to." The healer undoes the bandage covering Shuna's pierced palm and begins to close the wound. "My fingers remember you, human. Since you were a cubling, you have been part of me."

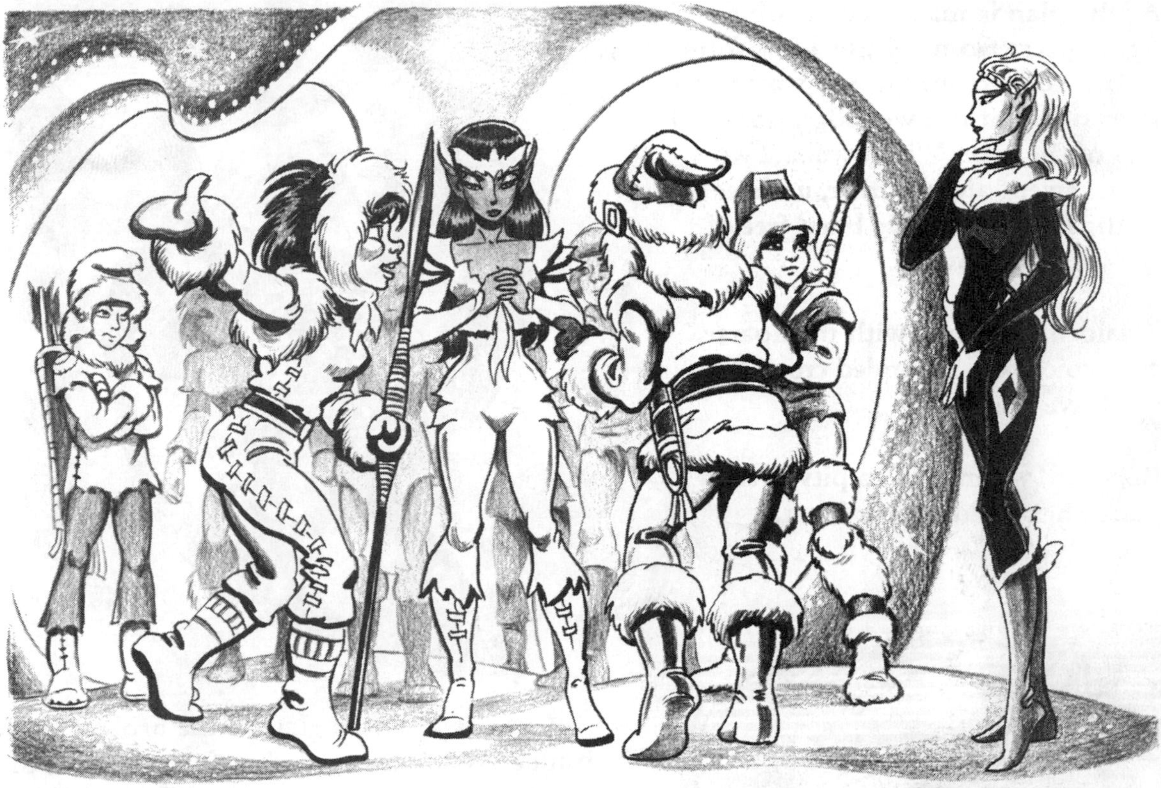

At the same time Venka asks the Go-Backs, "Do you know what became of my mother, Kahvi?" The mere mention of that legendary chieftess' name takes the snow-dwellers' attention off the High One, placing it squarely on Venka.

"You? Kahvi's daughter?!" An amazed Go-Back looks her up and down. "We still tell those ancient tales around the fire pit! Have you come to be our chief?" Venka ponders a moment, then answers, "First I would know how Kahvi died, if, indeed, she did."

The Go-Backs chew on this bold, new idea which, plainly, never entered their dull brains. "We don't know. But we'll join your search," a sooty youth grunts. "Since you found us with the Palace, it's sure you can find anything!"

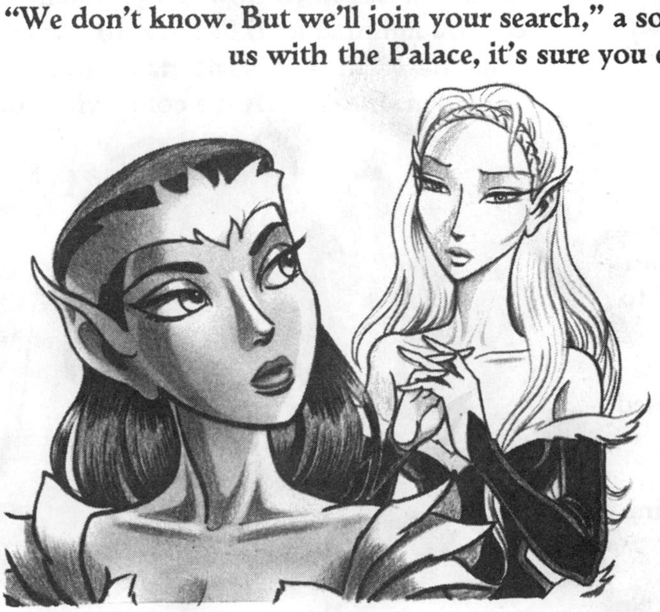

'I, too, will join you," Aroree tells Venka. "Thanks to Dart's band, I've learned I am not the last of the Gliders. Door's fate is uncertain. It could be that Tyldak lives too. If he does, then he will be with Kahvi."

"We can't tie up the Palace for this," Venka coolly decides. "Let's try on our own. We can summon it if need be."

As the plan is made, a crouching figure peers from behind a free-form pillar. The wolves growl a warning to their riders: it is Two-Edge, half-troll son of the slain Winnowill... Two-Edge, swept along earlier, undetected, as the restored Palace burst free of the Citadel's towers.

"Maiden," he calls with the hoarse, thin voice of a wounded crow, "Do not leave me!"

Repelled, yet moved to pity, Venka places her hand on her heart.

Cutter's warriors glare at the broken Master Builder. Strongbow reaches for an arrow, then pauses, remembering Two-Edge indirectly saved *his* life while defending Venka from Grohmul Djun's axe.

"She was my only means of self measure... the stone on which I kept both edges honed sharp... my mother!" The half-troll's sigh is filled with sadness, deep beyond comprehension. "I would die, if death could bind me to her. But Rayek holds her spirit now. Once touched by Leetah, I am unable to flee into the realm of madness. All that is left me is you, gentle maiden. Please... let me come with you."

Cutter's eyes narrow, studying Venka's impassive face. Rayek and Kahvi's cool-tempered child has always been hard to fathom. Rayek and Kahvi... what a heritage! Only the unusual could come of it. And so Cutter is not too surprised when Venka, after bidding her farewells, nods an invitation to the shambling Two-Edge. Supporting him, she and Aroree follow the Go-Backs out into the frozen wilderness.

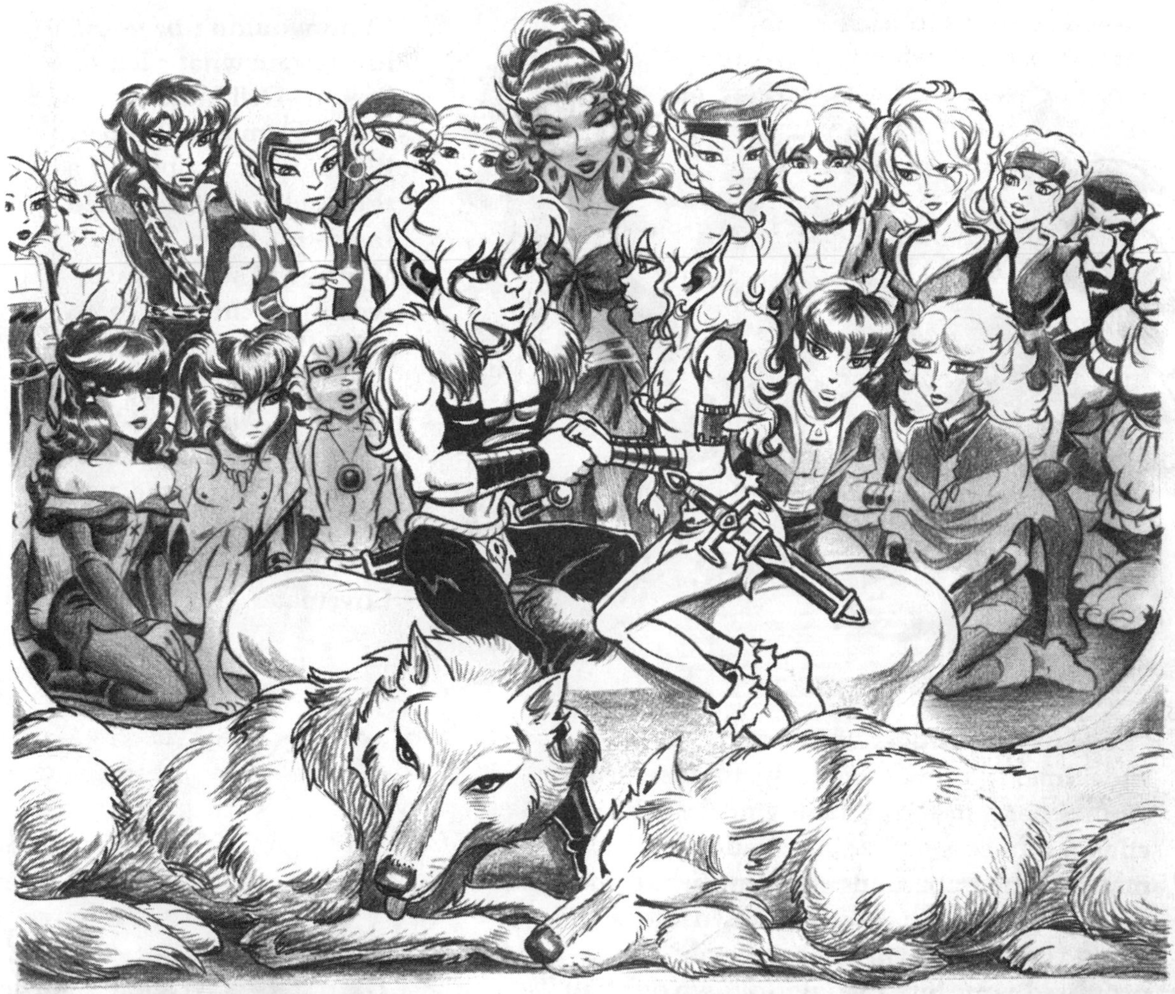

"Venka has to do this," Ember tells Cutter. "I've known she's wanted to for a while. But her first duty was to guard us all from Winnowill's black sendings. Now, because of Rayek, she's free." The young chieftess and her sire settle down for a counsel, surrounded by all their warriors and friends. Old Choplicker dozes at Ember's feet, while the yearling, Holdfast, remains alert to Cutter's slightest signal.

"And I must return to Howling Rock," Ember bravely continues, "with as many as will follow me. Winnowill may be gone, but she left things behind... terrible things... that want cleaning up."

Cutter smiles with pride at his flame-haired daughter. "You wear the chief's lock well. Never undo it." A shadow briefly crosses his features... old memories... still making it hard to let go. He shrugs them off, promising, "If you want aid, we'll always come, but only if you howl for it."

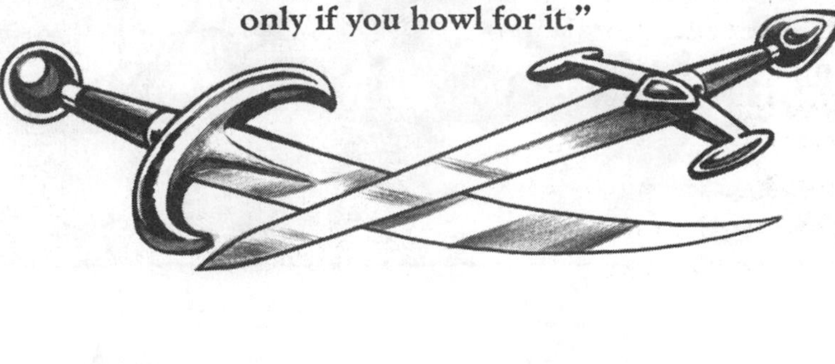

"You wouldn't be going to investigate what's left of Seet-ah-Dell Mound, would you?" Flam asks Ember, his motives as obvious as the golden spoils stuffed inside his tunic. "If Winnowill's foul beasts seek innocent prey there, of course!" Ember replies, noting Flam's sly glance at his sister. Mender steps in to vouch for his trollish chums. "Believe me, you could have worse allies than Flam and Drub, Lovemate."

"Lovemate..." Ember whispers the endearment, trying to see if it still fits. Mender studies her a moment, taking in the subtle changes. In so short a time, leadership has matured the impetuous cub, lent her an added air of mystery. What secret burdens her soul? What confidence will she not break? "I promised your Sire I would follow your lead." Mender bends close to Ember's pointed ear. "It seems you would lead me somewhere new. I'd like that," he smiles, pleased to find he can still make her blush.

"Time for mushing about later, elves!" Drub loudly announces. "I'll endure *one* more trip in this flying prongstone cluster to get home to my boodle chest!"

Not a moment too soon for the trolls, the Palace flashes around the world, returning its passengers to Howling Rock. Scouter, Dewshine and Tyleet follow Ember and Mender outside, as do Pike and Krim.

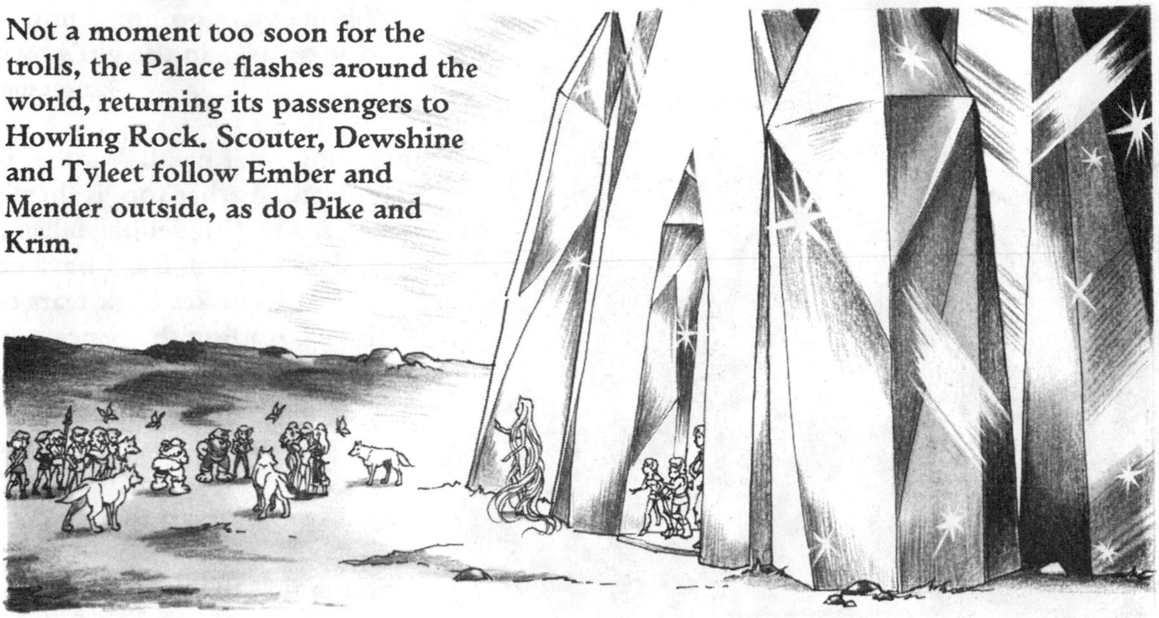

Yun sidles up to her fellow Go-Back, whispering, "Is she the kind of chief a couple of warriors like us can respect?" Cocking an eyebrow, Krim answers, "Her sire is. I'm betting wolf blood runs true. Want to test yours?" Yun nods eagerly, sizing up her new tribemates.

For Cutter there has never been an easier parting, for never has there been such assurance of ongoing connection through the Palace. Ember steps back, noticing the human waif for the first time. Shuna takes a few uncertain steps, and Leetah goes to steady her. "She held *my* hand so when I was a little cub," thinks Ember. "I bet that young human won't go motherless long." Softly smiling, the young chieftess waves farewell.

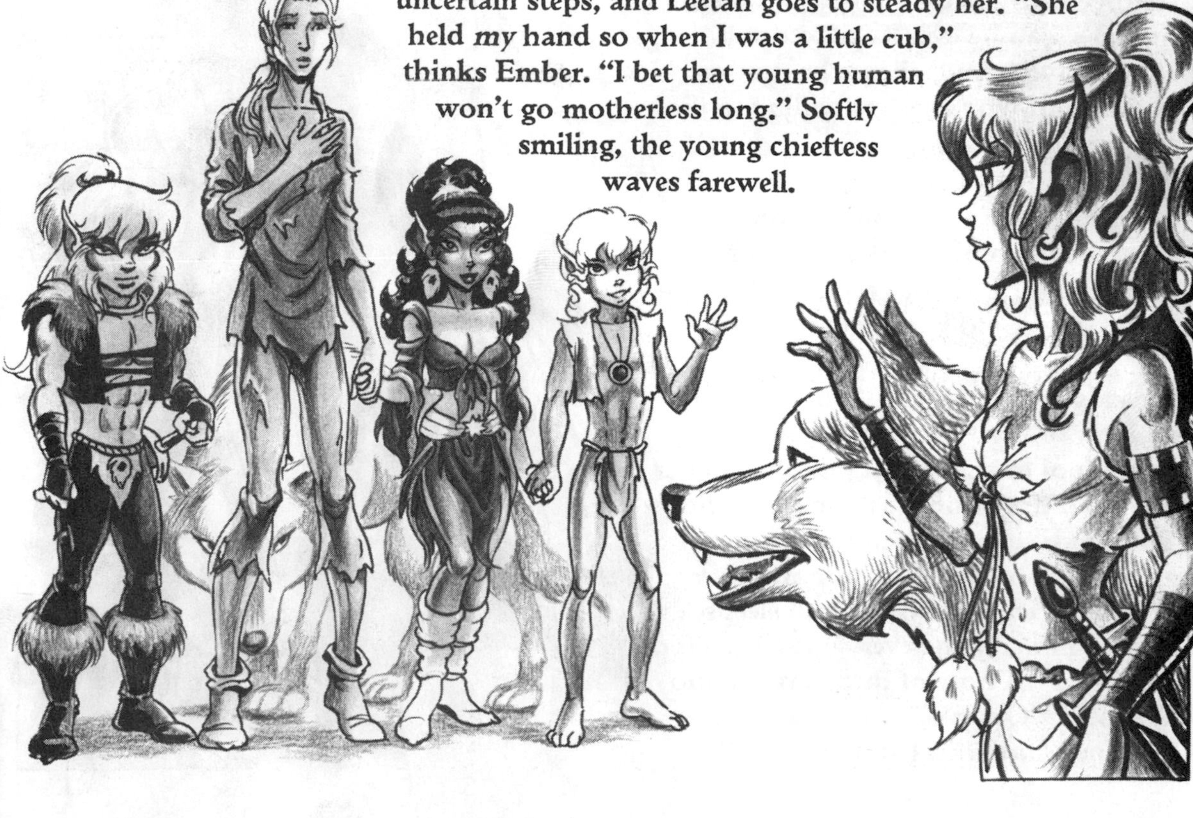

"Shuna want go home now?" Cutter asks in the girl's own language.

Shuna bows her head. "Mother is dead... Father too, if there's justice. The Citadel has fallen... just like I wanted. But I have no home." She chokes back tears of shame, reading the concern in Cutter and Leetah's eyes. "For a day I was a hero. But I failed to kill the Djun. The people of the Mound would spit on me if they knew."

"Shuna no fail," Cutter repeats. "Stay with us wolf folk 'til Shuna *knows* no fail!" His quiet words seem to lift a great weight from the young human's shoulders. "With you, good spirits," she sighs, "I could stay forever!"

From within the Palace's portal, a brooding Rayek observes the adoption. Neither with his own kind, nor among humans, can he ever hope to dwell safely. After a long silence he mutters, "I understand why she was willing to die to keep the Palace."

Standing close by, hoping to provide some small comfort, Ekuar responds, "Winnowill? But she threw her life away! She could have known love!"

Rayek's mouth twists. "Only to share mastery of the Palace with me? No. I was a fool to think that possible. In her place, I'd have done just what she did." Though Ekuar gasps in horror, Rayek goes on. "She dwells within me - my prisoner. Her malevolent soul sleeps next to mine. If she ever awakens... ever gets out..." A note of dread creeps into his voice. "Oh, Ekuar, you can't imagine! And yet... I still love her!"

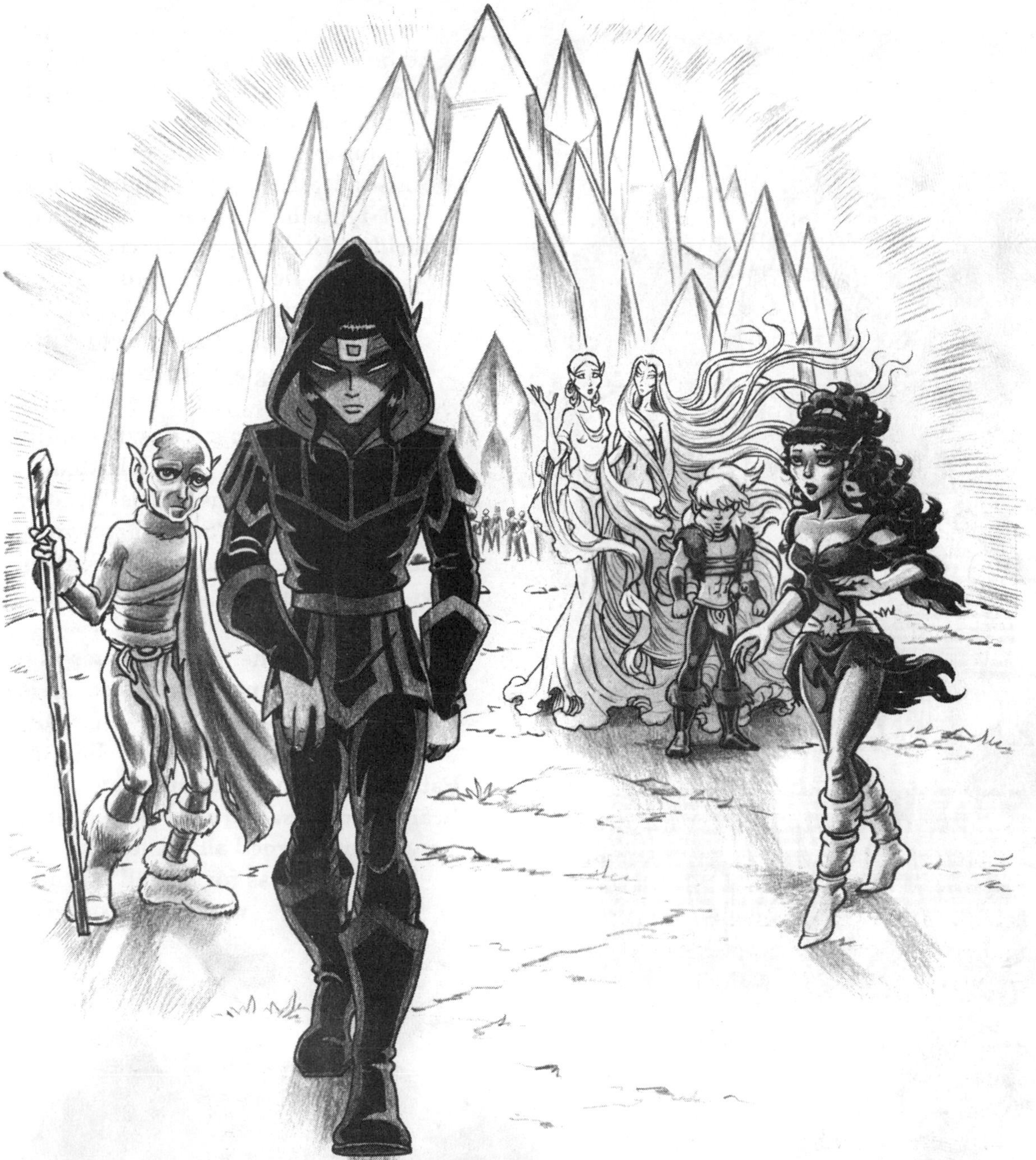

Without a word of farewell, Rayek steps from the threshold, striding out purposefully onto the grassy plain. Far more than a friend, the one source of fatherly love Rayek has ever known, Ekuar calls after him. "Brownskin! Where will you go? How will you live?"

"Live I will." Rayek doesn't look back. "I must...even if I wish it otherwise. I am the dungeon keeper, on eternal watch. And I am the dungeon."

Savah, the Mother of Memory, joins Ekuar on the threshold. Together they follow Rayek whom, deserving or not, both have mentored and loved. In full awareness of the dangers that lie ahead, Ekuar stays Savah with his staff, pursuing Rayek alone. Leetah, the High One - even Cutter - watch with deep sympathy as the pair disappear over a hill.

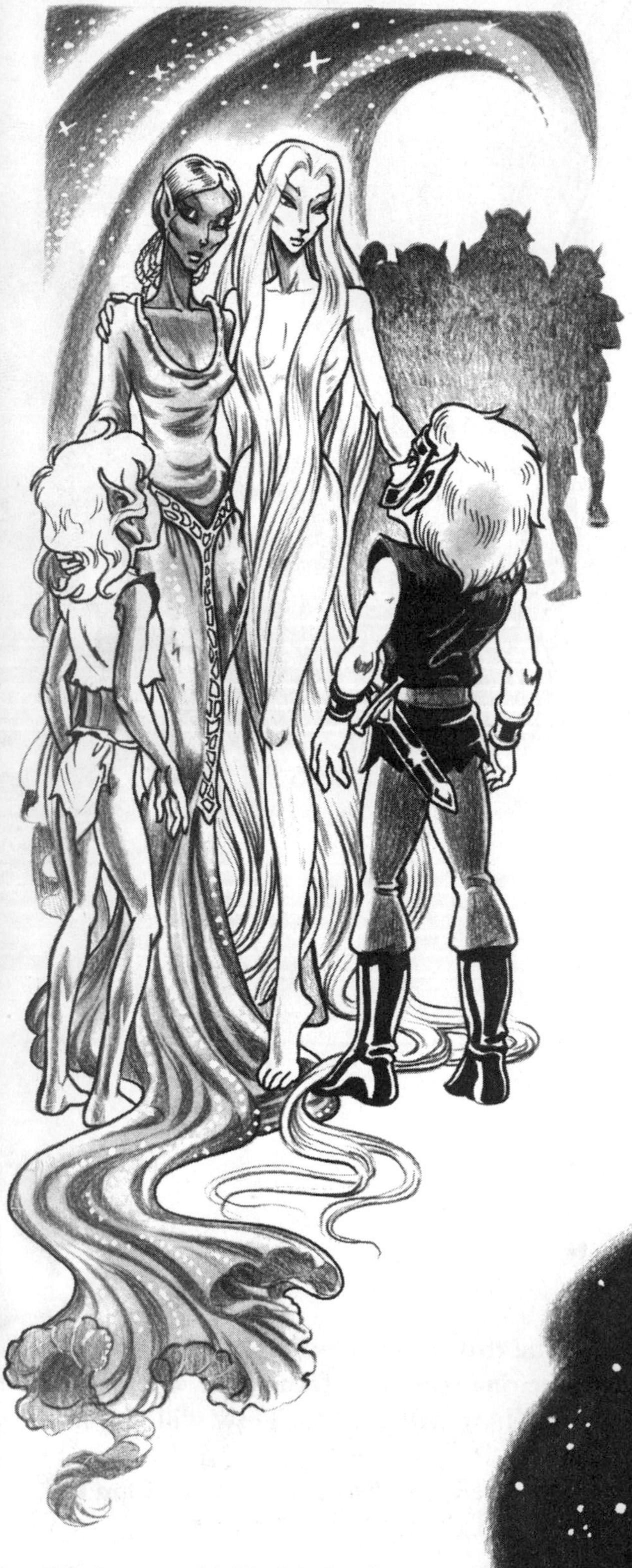

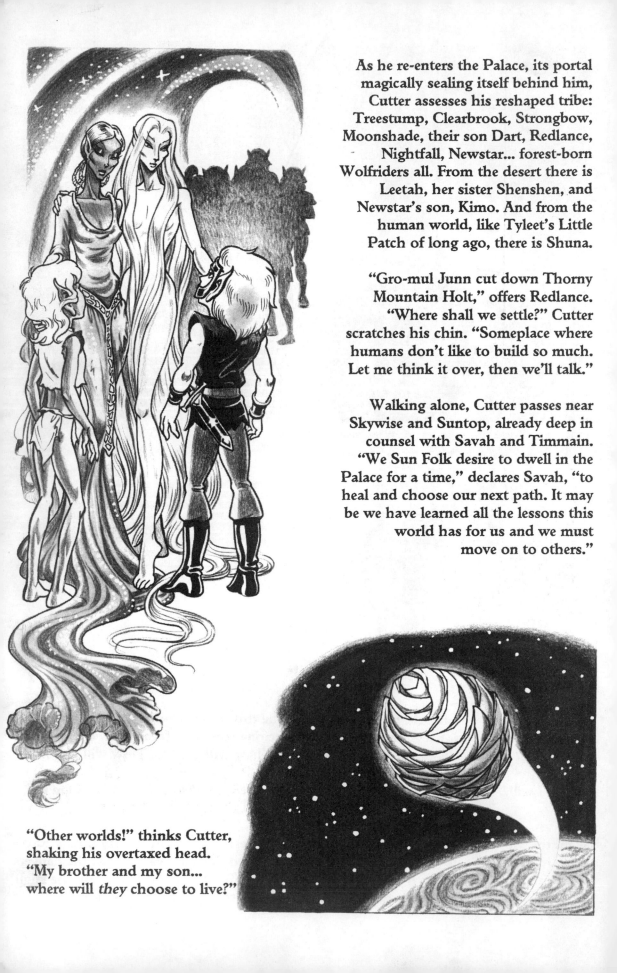

As he re-enters the Palace, its portal magically sealing itself behind him, Cutter assesses his reshaped tribe: Treestump, Clearbrook, Strongbow, Moonshade, their son Dart, Redlance, Nightfall, Newstar... forest-born Wolfriders all. From the desert there is Leetah, her sister Shenshen, and Newstar's son, Kimo. And from the human world, like Tyleet's Little Patch of long ago, there is Shuna.

"Gro-mul Junn cut down Thorny Mountain Holt," offers Redlance. "Where shall we settle?" Cutter scratches his chin. "Someplace where humans don't like to build so much. Let me think it over, then we'll talk."

Walking alone, Cutter passes near Skywise and Suntop, already deep in counsel with Savah and Timmain. "We Sun Folk desire to dwell in the Palace for a time," declares Savah, "to heal and choose our next path. It may be we have learned all the lessons this world has for us and we must move on to others."

"Other worlds!" thinks Cutter, shaking his overtaxed head. "My brother and my son... where will *they* choose to live?"

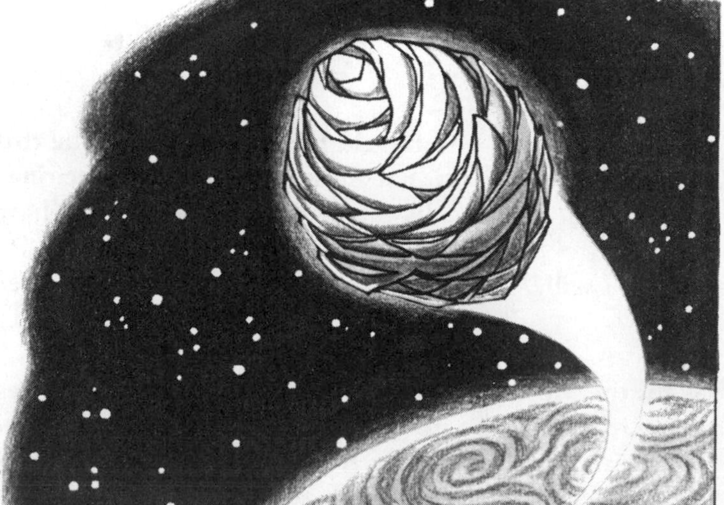

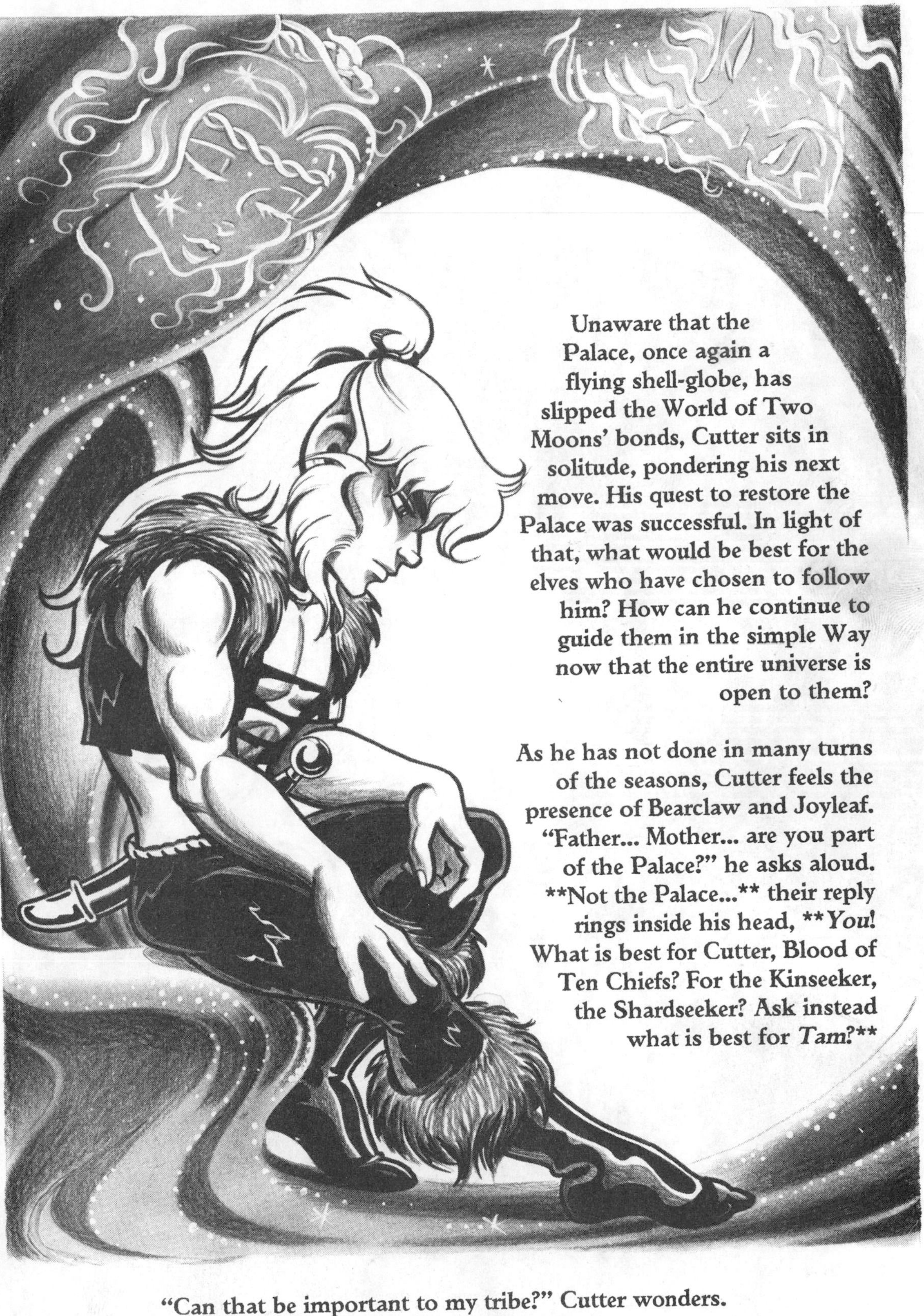
Unaware that the Palace, once again a flying shell-globe, has slipped the World of Two Moons' bonds, Cutter sits in solitude, pondering his next move. His quest to restore the Palace was successful. In light of that, what would be best for the elves who have chosen to follow him? How can he continue to guide them in the simple Way now that the entire universe is open to them?
As he has not done in many turns of the seasons, Cutter feels the presence of Bearclaw and Joyleaf. "Father... Mother... are you part of the Palace?" he asks aloud. **Not the Palace...** their reply rings inside his head, ***You*! What is best for Cutter, Blood of Ten Chiefs? For the Kinseeker, the Shardseeker? Ask instead what is best for *Tam*?**

"Can that be important to my tribe?" Cutter wonders.
"They come first... don't they?"

All at once, the floor turns transparent beneath Cutter's feet! The walls, the ceiling, even his mind-sculpted stool seem to vanish. Up, down, sideways... direction ceases to exist. Cutter falls on his face, terrified, limbs clutching like a wolf cub on thin ice. His senses betray him. Something solid supports him. Yet all around him there is nothing but an endless field of stars. Timmain and Skywise emerge from the spangled blackness, running to his aid.

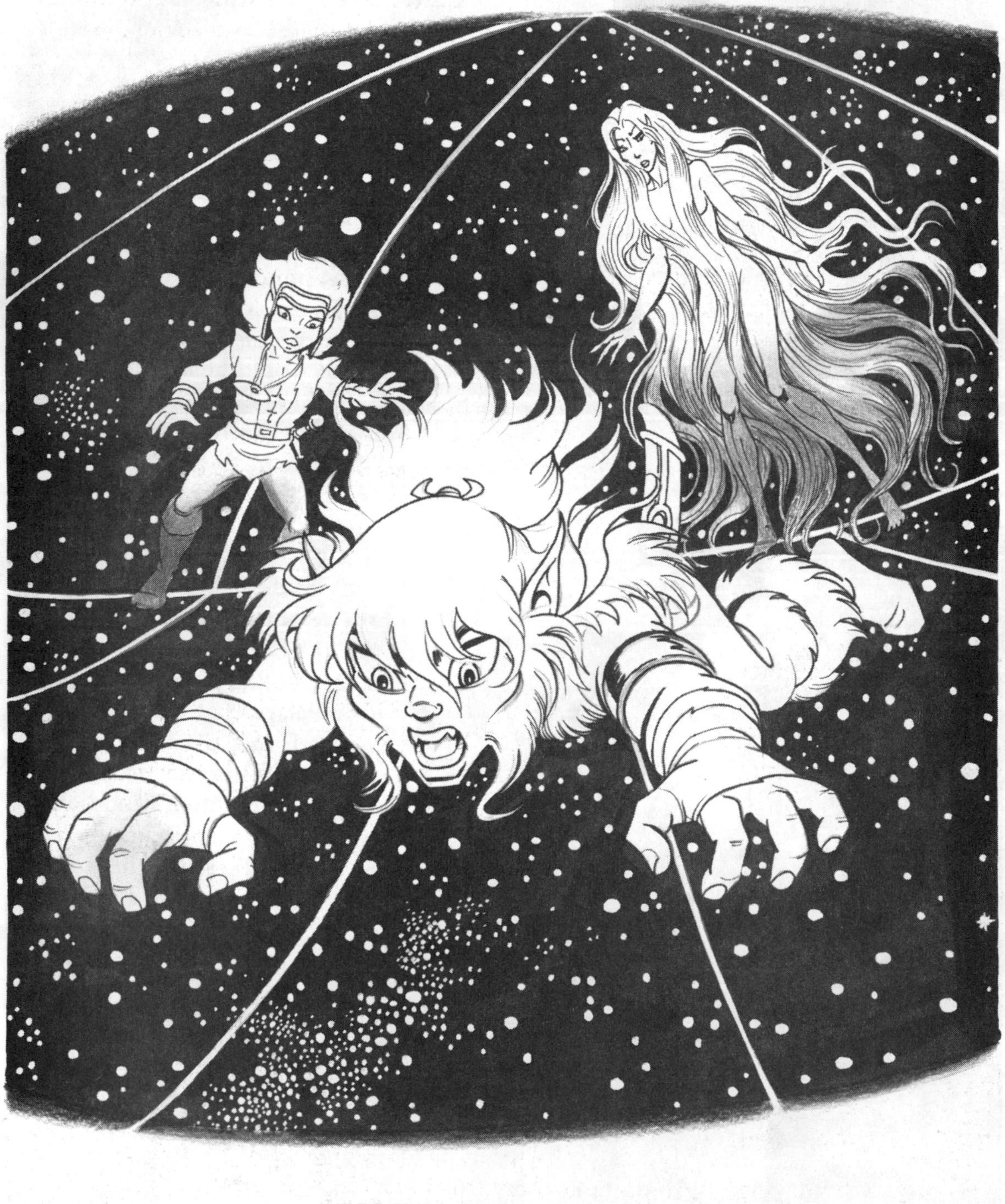

"NOOOOOOO!" Cutter screams.
"CHANGE IT BACK! CHANGE IT BACK!!"

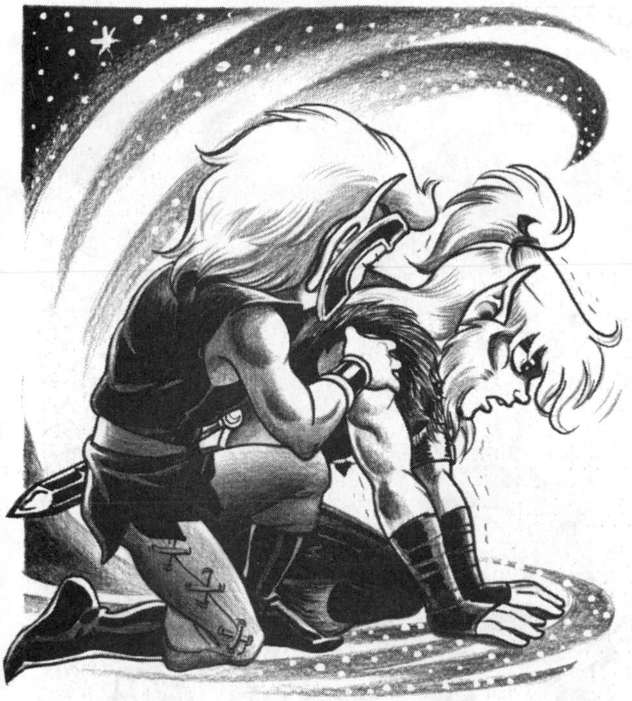

Immediately the little chamber's irridescent walls reappear. Panting and gasping, his skin glistening with cold sweat, Cutter tries to rise from the floor. Distressed, Skywise kneels to help his friend up, "I'm sorry, Cutter, so sorry! I wanted you to see how beautiful it is out there! I just wanted to share the stars with you...not scare you to death!"

"I'm not afraid to die," Cutter gasps, shuddering, "Zhantee showed me. But this...! Where were the sounds of birdsong and running water? Where were the scents of trees and flowers...of animals? Where were the *living* things?!"

Skywise's heart sinks; his dearest friend will not see the sky except in relation to the ground. Age separates them. Mortality and immortality separate them. Must all of Space separate them too? "The stars *are* alive," Skywise protests.

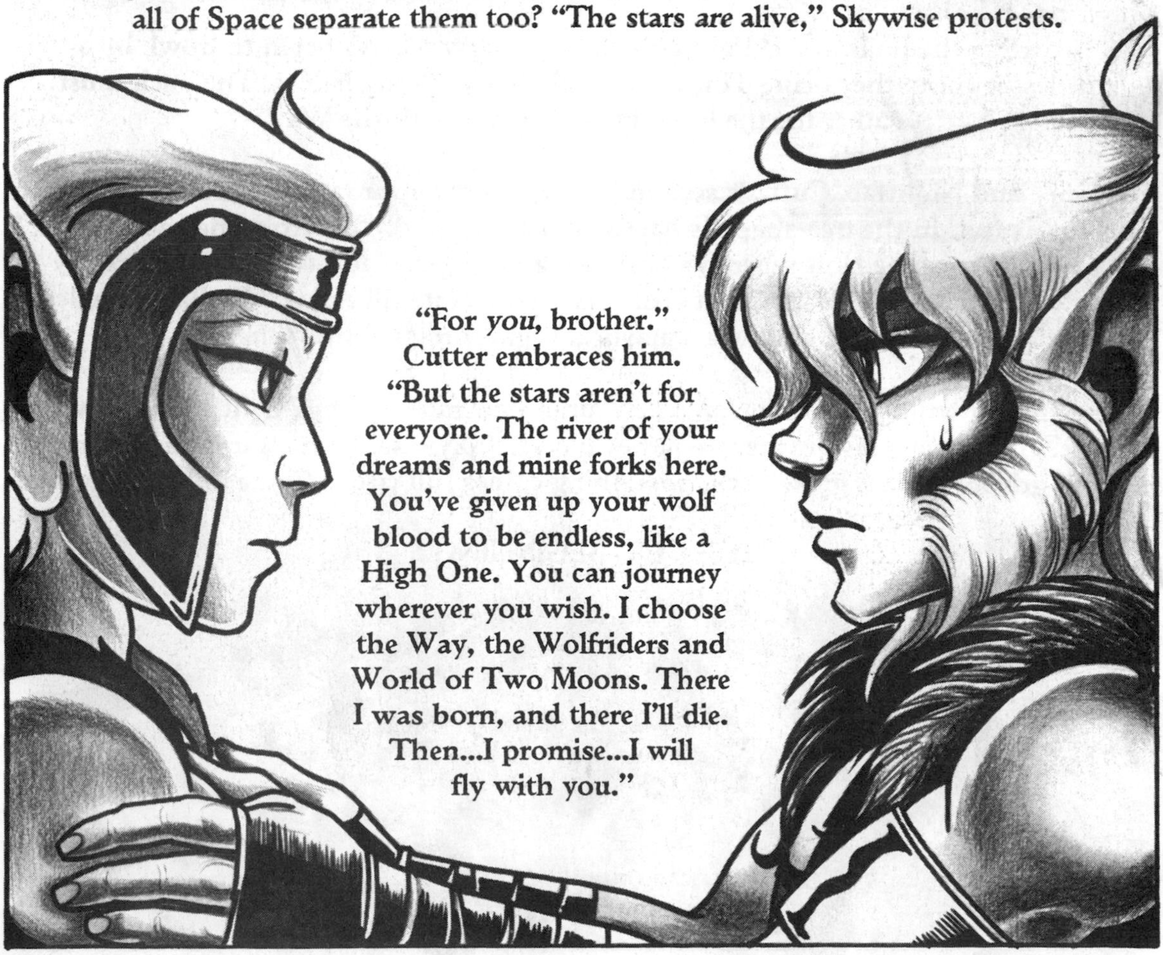

"For *you*, brother." Cutter embraces him. "But the stars aren't for everyone. The river of your dreams and mine forks here. You've given up your wolf blood to be endless, like a High One. You can journey wherever you wish. I choose the Way, the Wolfriders and World of Two Moons. There I was born, and there I'll die. Then...I promise...I will fly with you."

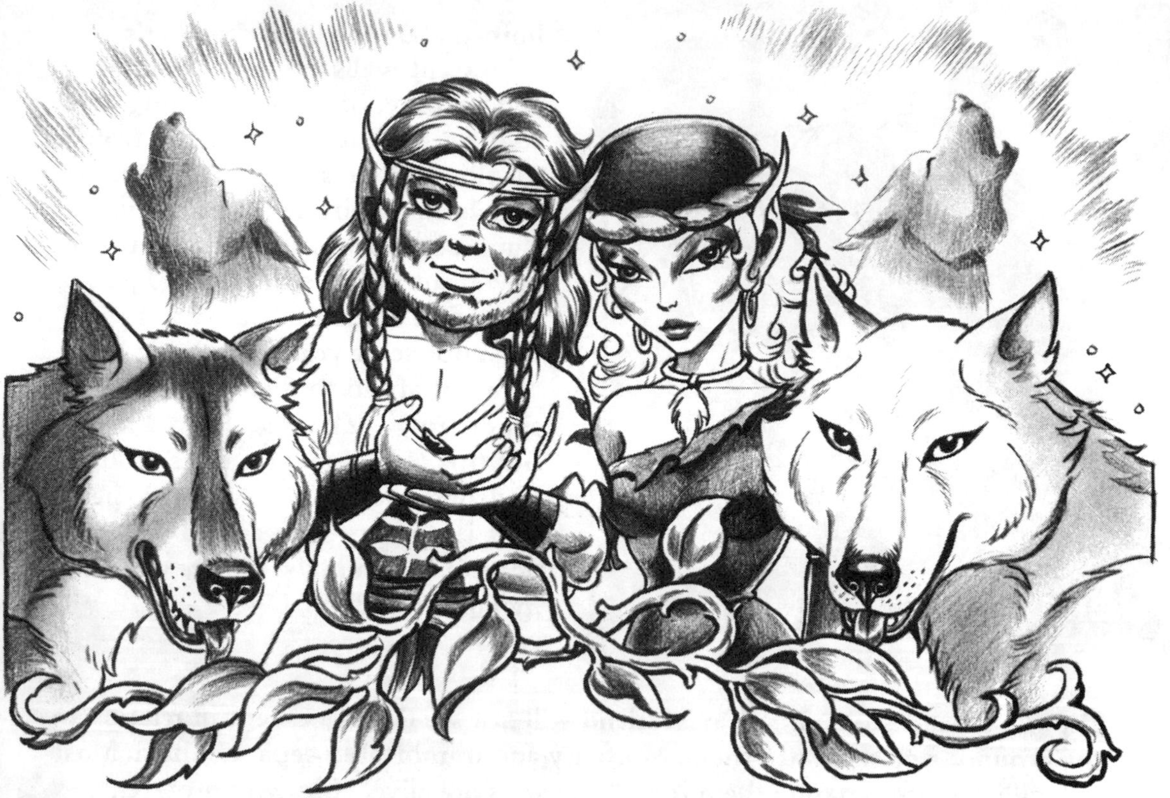

Prowling the halls of the Palace-shell, the hungry wolves begin to howl. Into timeless infinity they bring Time... inside their grumbling bellies. The pack must gather for the hunt, in accordance with the Way.

Redlance and Nightfall, Cutter's second family, quietly approach as their chosen chief rises to his feet. In the tree-shaper's hands is one tiny seed. "It's from the Father Tree," he says, "from the Holt where we three were born - the Holt that burned. It's my greatest treasure. I'd like to plant it on that spot - if it still exists." Redlance smiles impishly. "Could we... maybe... begin tonight's hunt *there*?"

"The smaller truth within the larger..." Cutter murmurs, giving Nightfall a knowing glance. He turns to his brother-in-all-but-blood. "Skywise?" The stargazer wipes his eyes and grins, "Forests grow back. Everything comes full circle. Come on! Let's go see!"

THE NEW BEGINNING...

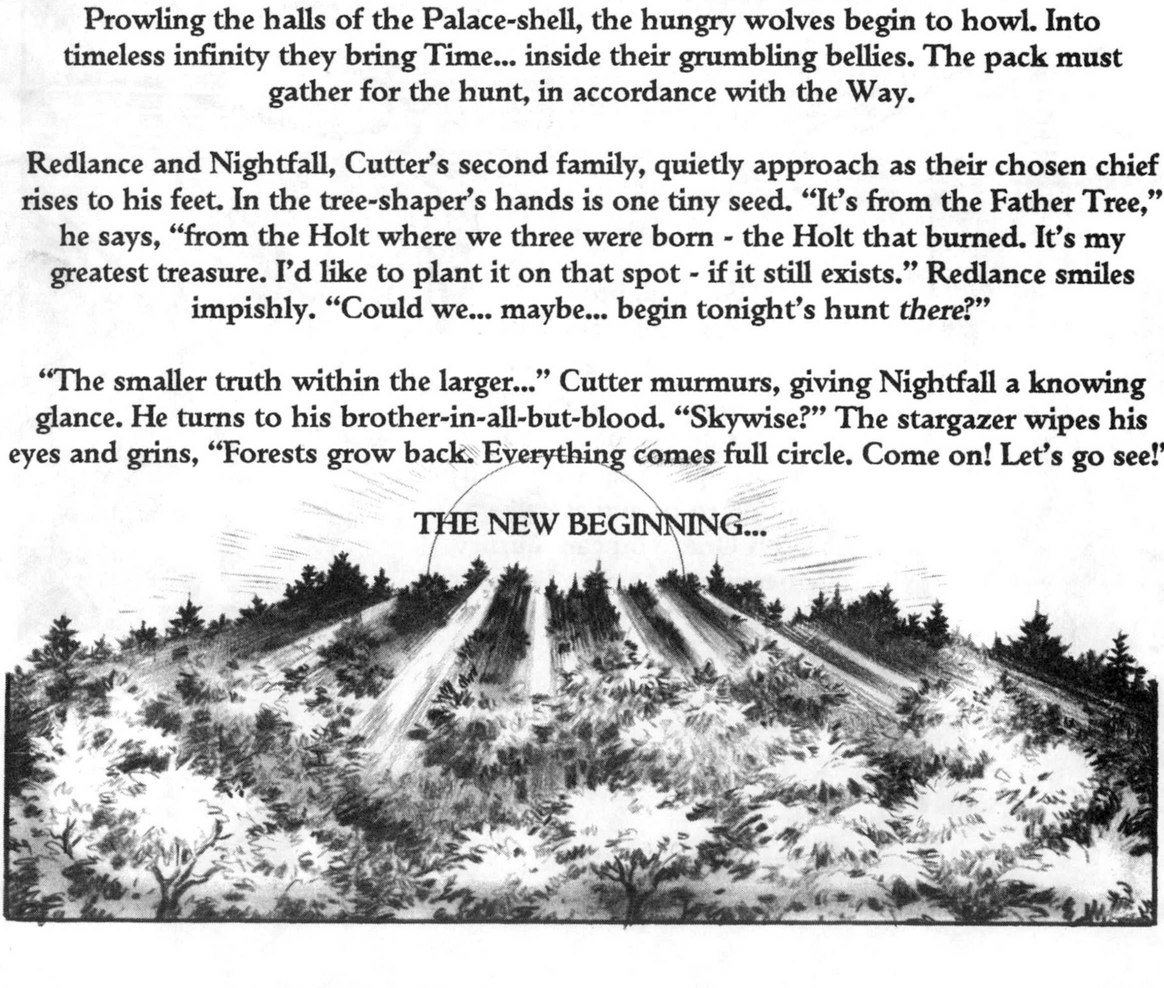

The battle for
the Palace shards is over;
the players go their different ways.

The further adventures of Cutter,
Leetah and Skywise are yet to be told.
The unfolding tales of Ember and her own
Wolfrider tribe await in volumes 11 ("Legacy"),
11a ("Huntress"), 11b ("Wild Hunt") and
beyond. Rayek, vessel of Winnowill's dark
spirit, continues his strange journey in
volume 9 ("Rogue's Curse").

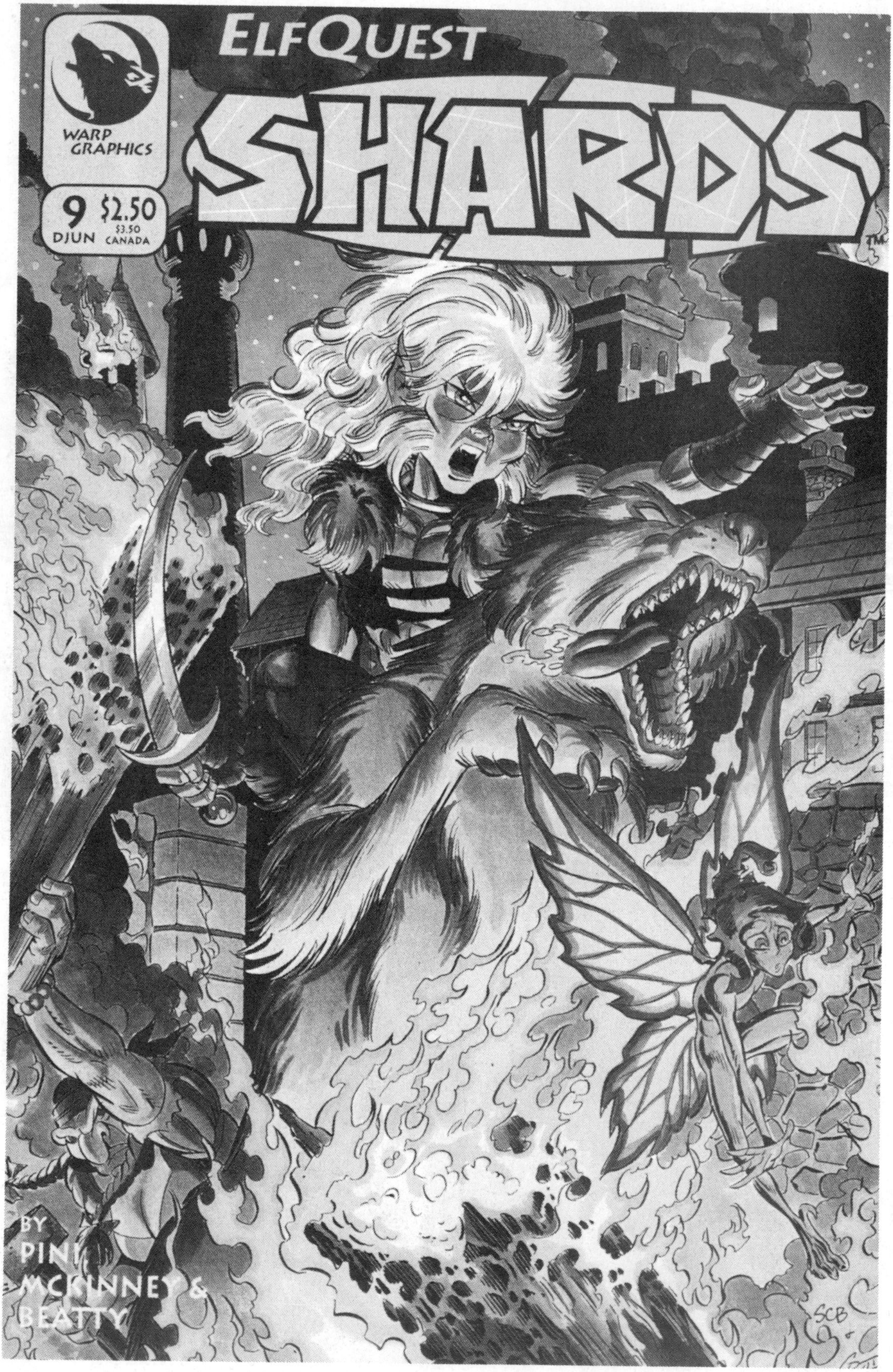

ElfQuest
SHARDS
WARP GRAPHICS
9 $2.50
DJUN
$3.50 CANADA
BY
PINI,
McKINNEY &
BEATTY
SCB

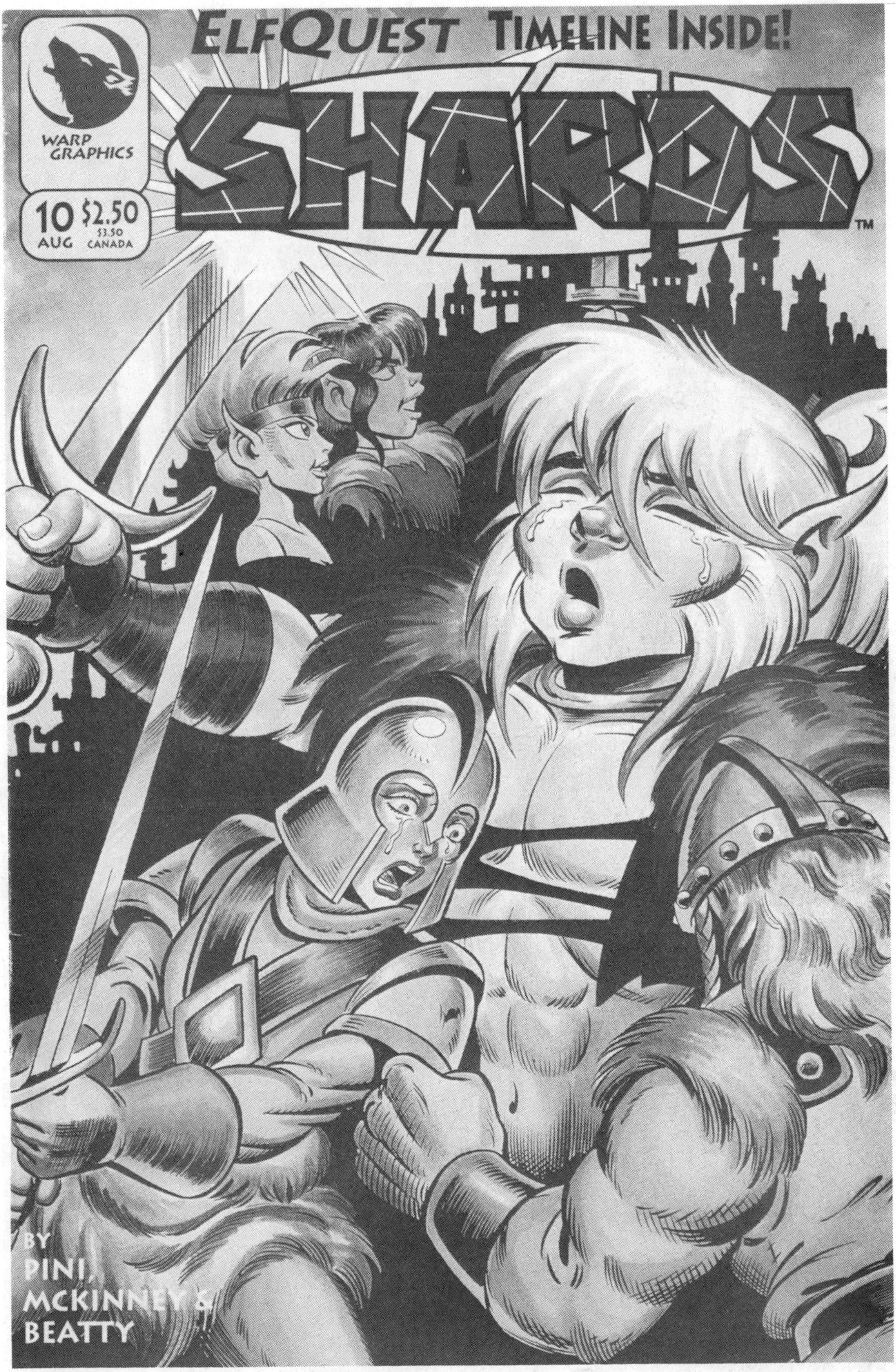
ElfQuest Timeline Inside!
WARP GRAPHICS
SHARDS™
10 $2.50
AUG $3.50 CANADA
BY
PINI,
MCKINNEY &
BEATTY

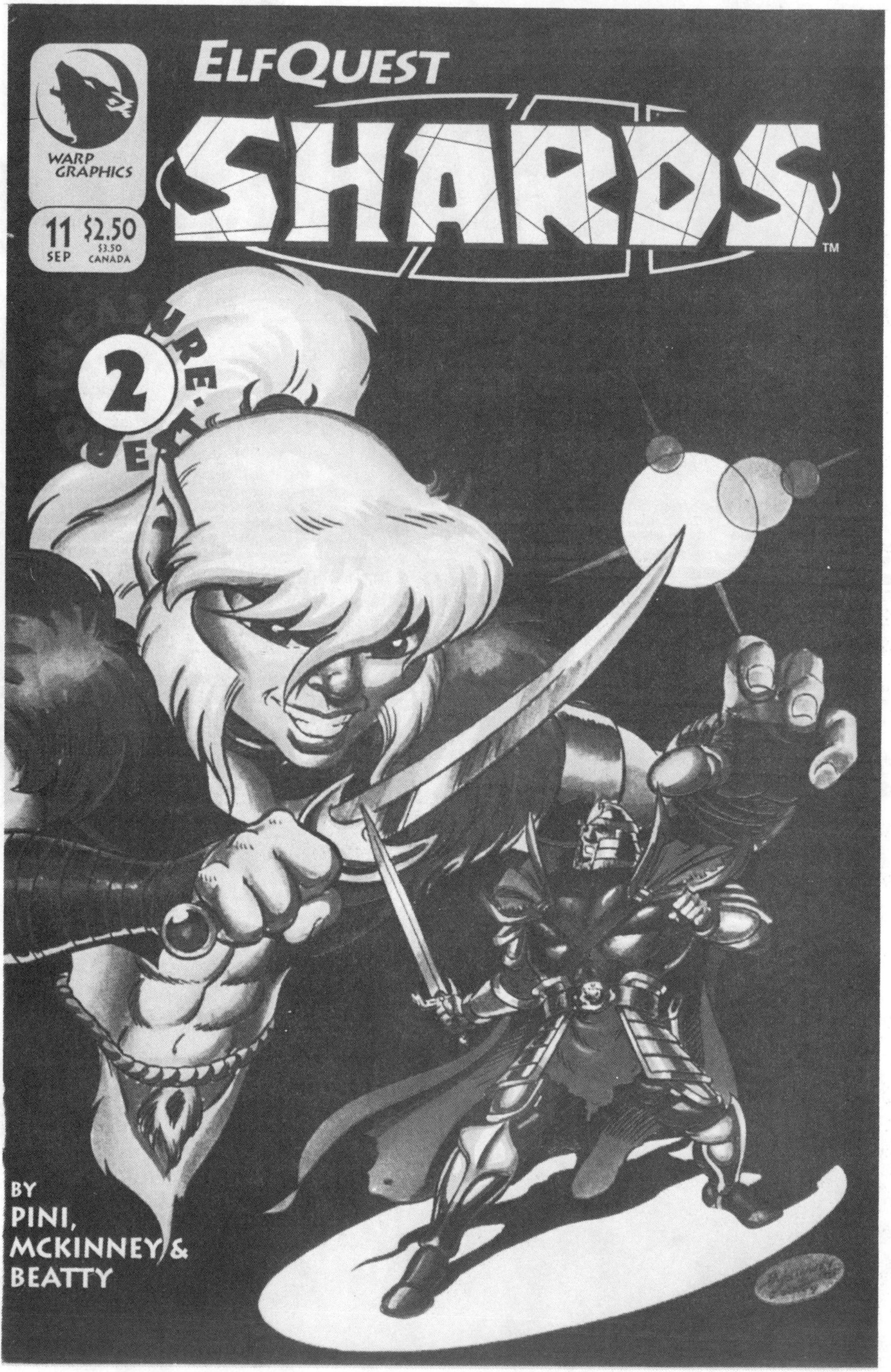
WARP GRAPHICS
ElfQuest
SHARDS™
11 SEP
$2.50
$3.50 CANADA
2
BY
PINI,
MCKINNEY &
BEATTY

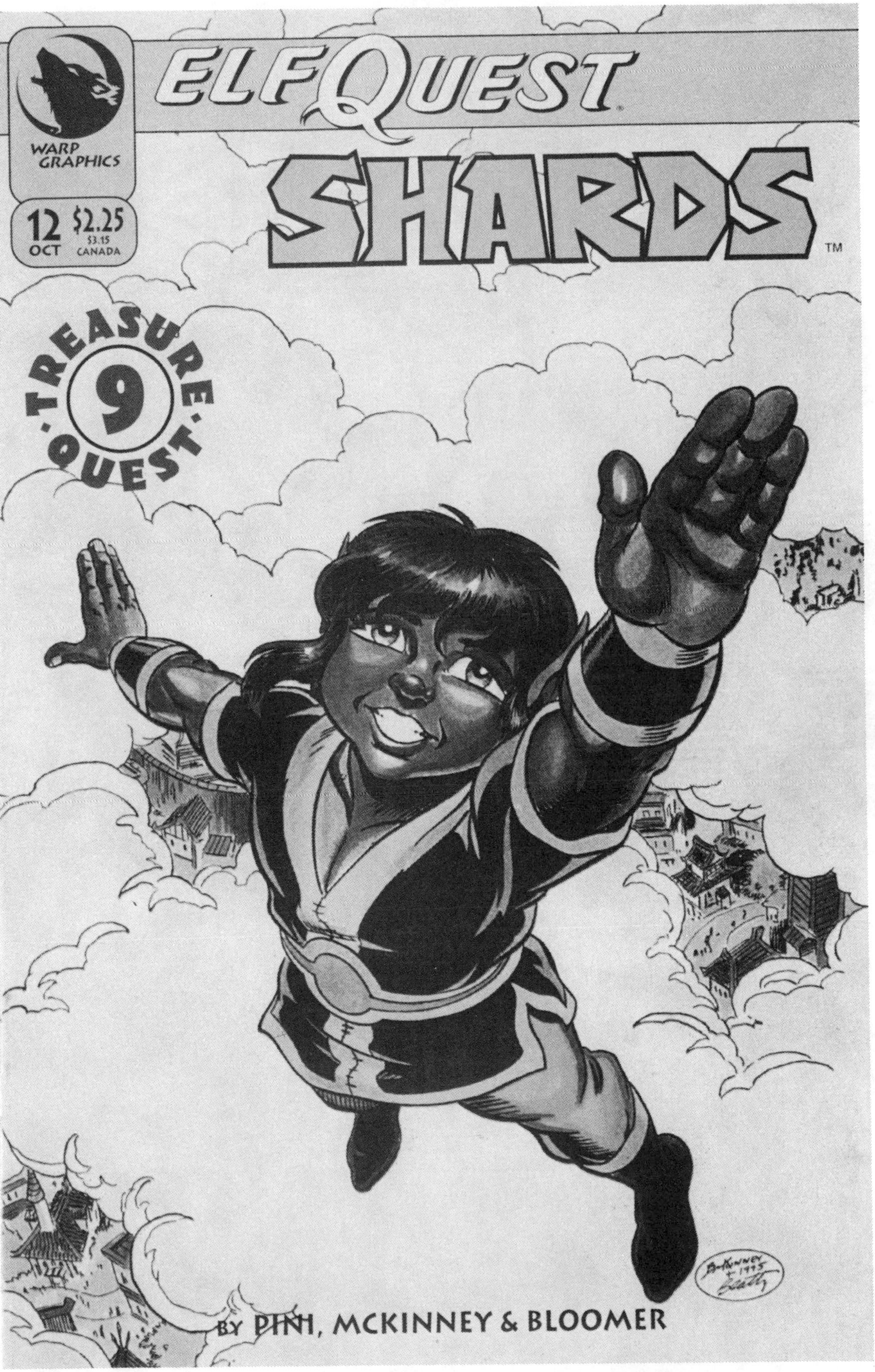
WARP GRAPHICS
ELFQUEST
SHARDS™
12 OCT $2.25 $3.15 CANADA
TREASURE 9 QUEST
BY PINI, MCKINNEY & BLOOMER

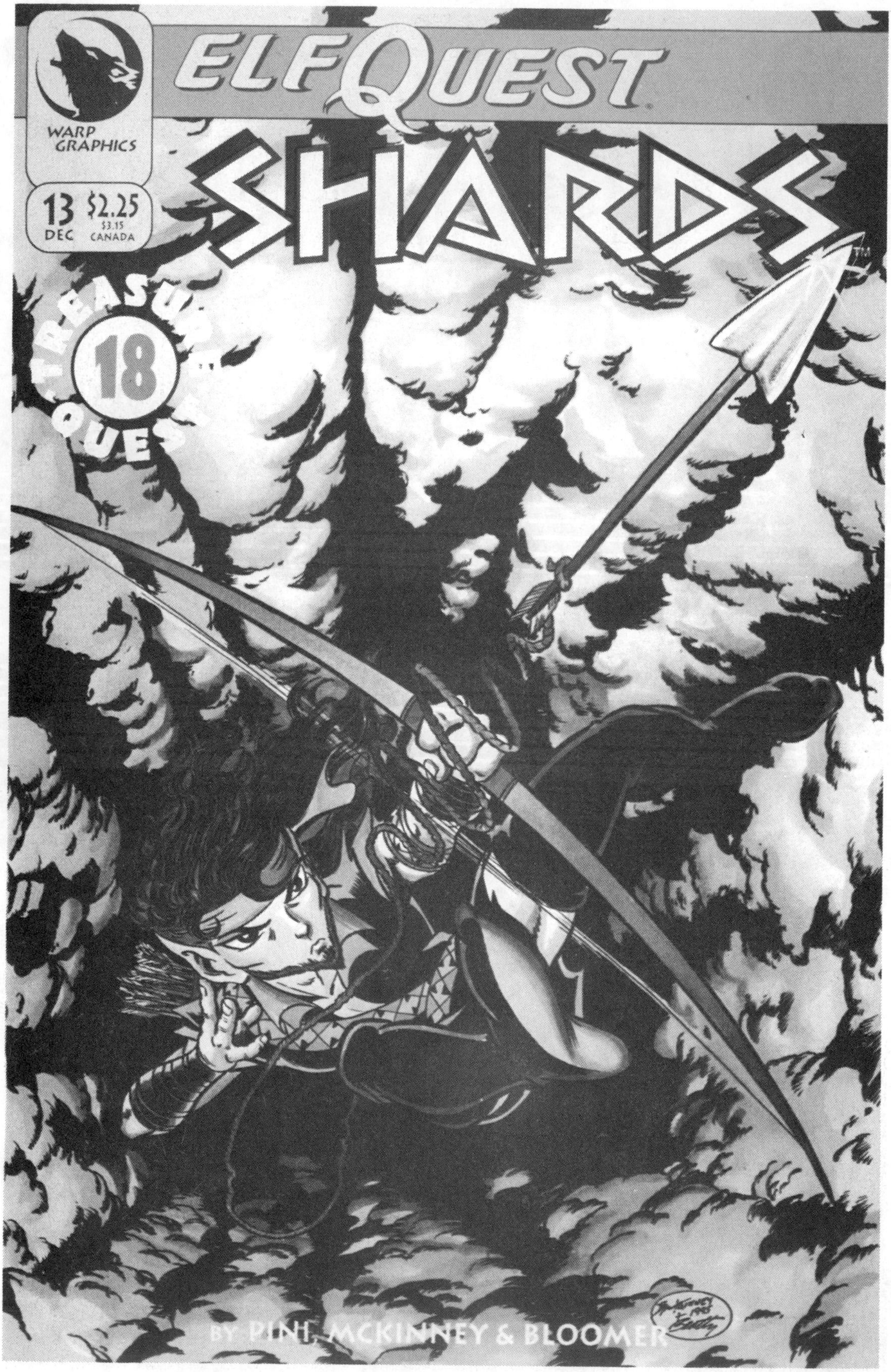
WARP GRAPHICS
ELFQUEST
SHARDS
13 DEC
$2.25
$3.15 CANADA
TREASURE QUEST
18
BY PINI, MCKINNEY & BLOOMER

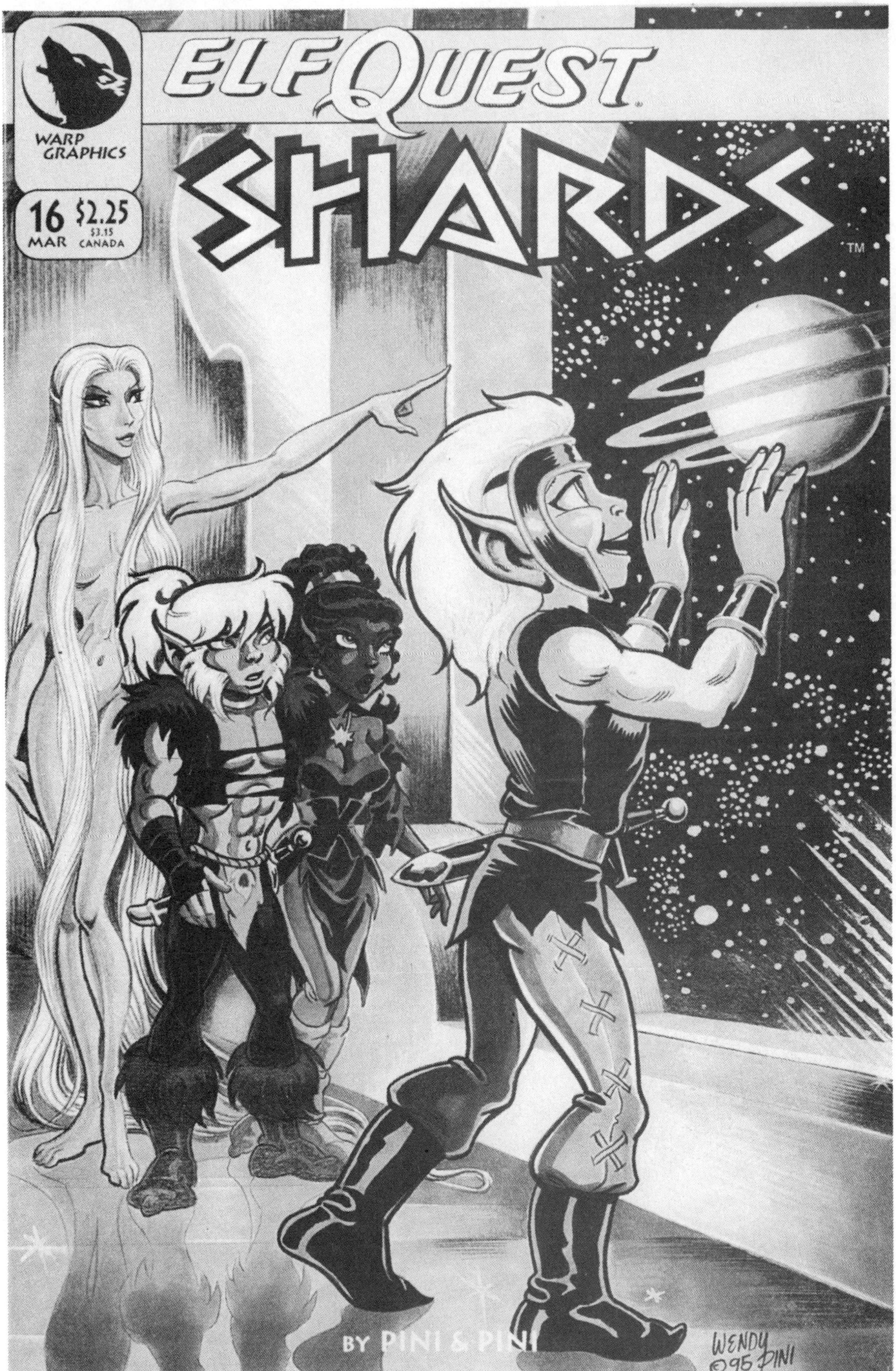
WARP GRAPHICS
ELFQUEST
SHARDS
16 MAR
$2.25
$3.15 CANADA
BY PINI & PINI
WENDY ©95 PINI